Beginning
ATL COM Programming

Dr Richard Grimes
Alex Stockton
George Reilly
Julian Templeman

Wrox Press Ltd.®

Beginning ATL COM Programming

Published by Wrox Press Ltd, 30 Lincoln Road, Olton, Birmingham B27 6PA , UK.
Printed in Canada
3 4 5 TRI 99 98

ISBN 1-861000-11-1

Trademark Acknowledgements

Wrox has endeavoured to provide trademark information about all the companies and products mentioned in this book by the appropriate use of capitals. However, Wrox cannot guarantee the accuracy of this information.

Microsoft, Visual C++, Visual Basic, Visual J++, Visual Studio, ActiveX, Win32, Windows and Windows NT are either trademarks or registered trademarks of the Microsoft Corporation.

Credits

Lead Authors
Dr Richard Grimes
Alex Stockton

Contributory Authors
George Reilly
Julian Templeman

Managing Editor
John Franklin

Editors
Jon Hill
Alex Stockton
Timothy Briggs

Technical Reviewers
Richard Grimes
Michael Hupp
Sing Li
Christian Nagel
Michael O'Keefe
M. G. "Ravi" Ravichandran
Dean Rowe
Jim Springfield
Julian Templeman

Cover/Design/Layout
Graham Butler
Andrew Guillaume

Copy Edit/Index
Wrox Team

About the Authors

Richard Grimes started programming aeons ago on 8-bit computers and hasn't looked back since. He has spent an interesting time as a research scientist (the little known "Grimes' effect" is his creation), underpaid time as a computer trainer and done time as a distributed object developer.

ATL took hold of Richard while he was part of a team developing a COM-based workflow system and its elegance and simplicity has had a lasting effect on him. Although his is not an obsessively pure COM existence, he finds that an ATL-assisted COM lifestyle gives him more time to enjoy his garden.

Richard writes and advises on COM and ATL, and can be contacted via email at **atl.dev@grimes.demon.co.uk**.

Alex Stockton is an author and editor for Wrox Press, as well as creator of the World of ATL web site (**http://www.worldofatl.com/**). Alex is barely old enough to remember the dark days before COM and has never even seen a punch card in real life. His first PC was a Pentium Pro 180.

Alex can be contacted at **alexs@wrox.com**.

George Reilly has spent ten years working with C&C++ and has developed in Windows since C7 and the SDK. He is an ActiveX expert, a member of Microsoft's IIS team and a founder member of all the IIS/ISAPI discussion forums.

Julian Templeman lives in London with his wife and three children, two cats, a dog, two PCs, a Mac and a PDP-11. He trains and consults in C++, Windows programming, Java and COM/ActiveX. In such spare time as he has, he writes articles and reviews for programming journals, and contributes as an author and technical reviewer to Wrox Press.

Author Acknowledgements

Richard Grimes
My thanks go to the guys at Wrox whose hard work and attention to detail made sure that this book reached the shelves in time. Also to Roy Bailey and Lee Spring who taught me that ATL could be applied in ways I didn't know was possible. Then there are the contributions of the technical reviewers who reined in my late-night ramblings. Finally, thanks are due to John Franklin for making sure the project stayed alive.

Alex Stockton
Thanks to the many kind people at Wrox Press who toil away behind the scenes.

Thanks also to the ATL development team for their excellent work in producing the library that is the subject of this book, as well as for the direct support they've provided.

Julian Templeman
My thanks are due to all at Richford's, for providing a stimulating and relaxed working environment. I've learnt a lot from my colleagues there, and have valued their suggestions and comments (especially the helpful ones!).

The team at Wrox has been unfailingly supportive. Special mention goes to John Franklin, for managing the project and Jon Hill, for turning my prose into something readable.

Beginning
ATL COM
Programming

Beginning
ATL COM
Programming

Introduction

Welcome to *Beginning ATL COM Programming*. With this book, you'll learn how to use Visual C++ and ATL to program COM components. You'll see how ATL wraps up the difficult and repetitive parts of COM to enable you to get the most from your coding time.

The aim of the Active Template Library development team at Microsoft is to give programmers the tools with which to produce tight, optimized COM code. Our aim with this book is to give you the best start we can down that road.

Who This Book Is For

This book is for fairly experienced C++ developers who want to get to grips with COM programming using the Active Template Library. The *Beginning* in the title of this book refers to *COM*, and it refers to *ATL*. It does not refer to *Programming*. If you're new to programming, put this book down and check out Ivor Horton's best-selling *Beginning Visual C++* instead. You'll probably be able to find it on a shelf near this book.

We don't expect you to know anything about COM. We're going to explain the essentials of COM, how to use it, and how to get the most out of it. But if you *do* already know something about COM, that's a bonus. You'll still learn a lot about the way that ATL works, and you'll be one step ahead of the COM neophytes.

We don't expect you to know anything about ATL. ATL is the prime focus of the book. If you've never touched ATL, or if you've been using it for a short while but still have many unanswered questions, this is the book for you. If you've written your own **COM_INTERFACE_ENTRY()**-style macro to handle virtual base classes, you're probably better off with *Professional ATL Programming* (available Summer 1998)!

How To Read This Book

First, particularly if you're in a bookstore, read the whole of this introduction to determine whether this book is the right one for you. The previous section described the intended audience of the book. Now you know whether you have the right skills to act as the foundation for the tutorial ahead. The next section will quickly let you know whether you have the requisite software to get any benefit from the book.

This book is designed to be read while you're at your computer. You'll get more out of the book if you have Visual C++ running as you progress through the book, giving you a chance to experiment with the examples.

This book is complementary to the existing documentation (and the source code) supplied with Visual C++. We don't try to replace Microsoft's documentation, nor do we duplicate it. We don't expect you to have read any of the Microsoft-supplied documentation before starting this book, but checking the online help for function prototypes and quick reminders will be increasingly useful as you start to use the knowledge gained from this book to strike out on your own path.

What You Need To Use This Book

To get the most out of this book, you need Visual C++ 5.0, the latest version of Microsoft's C++ compiler, and a computer on which to run it. This version of the compiler is 32-bit only, so you'll need to install it on Windows 95, Windows NT 3.51, or Windows NT 4.0, which means your computer needs a 486 CPU or better, and a minimum of 16Mb of memory.

> *If you have access to a machine with Visual C++ 5.0 installed, you have all you need to use this book.*

Optionally, you will get extra benefit by having access to a selection of other software:

Windows NT Service Pack 3

Since the initial release of Windows NT 4.0, Microsoft has made a number of service packs available, featuring bug fixes and enhancements to the operating system. However you're using Windows NT, it makes sense to take advantage of these updates, which you can freely download from Microsoft's web site. The Windows NT service packs are of particular interest to COM developers — we certainly recommend that you install service pack 3, which is the latest release at the time of writing.

Visual Studio Service Pack 3

The latest service pack released for Visual Studio (including Visual C++, Visual Basic, etc.) is service pack 3. There were no changes made to ATL in service pack 2 that weren't in service pack 1, but pack 3 does include an extra bug fix, and it always makes sense to install the latest version in any case.

DCOM for Windows 95 1.1

If you're using Windows 95, you should install the latest version of the COM library in the form of DCOM for Windows 95. DCOM for Windows 95 features bug fixes and enhancements to COM, including the ability to allow COM objects to communicate across a network (see below).

Internet Explorer

If you've installed Internet Explorer 4 (IE4), you don't need to install DCOM for Windows 95 as a separate package. IE4 relies on the latest version of the COM library, so it's installed automatically. Internet Explorer 4 is also a useful host for ActiveX controls, a fine web browser, and it's free for download from Microsoft's web site.

Microsoft Visual Basic

If you have Visual Basic, you'll be able to run the small number of Visual Basic examples contained in this book. These examples are always used as clients once we've already seen a C++ client in action, so they're a bonus for readers with Visual Basic. If you don't have Visual Basic, you won't be missing out.

Users of Visual C++ 4.x

The version of ATL covered by this book is available for free download from Microsoft's web site for users of Visual C++ 4.x. For this reason, much of the information contained in this book is useful to readers with older versions of Visual C++. However, we have not tested the contents of this book with version 4.x, and we know that many of the examples (those that use COM compiler support, for example) will not work with version 4.x. *Caveat emptor.*

Conventions and Terminology Used

We use a number of different styles of text and layout in the book to help differentiate between the different kinds of information. Here are examples of the styles we use and an explanation of what they mean:

> *These boxes hold important, not-to-be forgotten, mission-critical details that are directly relevant to the surrounding text.*

> *Background information, asides, references and extra details appear in text like this. For example,*
>
> > *'Click' or 'left-click' means click once with the primary mouse button,*
> > *'double-click' means double-click with the primary mouse button*
> > *and 'right-click' means click once with the secondary mouse button.*

- **Important Words** are in a bold type font.
- Words that appear on the screen, such as menu options, are in a similar font to the one used on screen, for example the File | New... menu. Note that the levels of a cascading menu are separated by a pipe character (|).
- Keys that you press on the keyboard, like *Ctrl* and *Enter*, are in italics.
- All filenames are in this style: **Videos.mdb**.
- Function names look like this: **sizeof()**.
- Template classes look like this: **CComObject<>**.

> ▶ Code that is new, important or relevant to the current discussion will be presented like this:

```
void main()
{
    cout << "Beginning ATL COM Programming";
}
```

> ▶ Meanwhile code you've seen before, or which has little to do with the matter at hand, looks like this:

```
void main()
{
    cout << "Beginning ATL COM Programming";
}
```

Web Support

As well as the Wrox web sites, at **http://www.wrox.com/** and **http://www.wrox.co.uk/**, you'll find a wealth of information about ATL at Alex Stockton's 'World Of ATL' site, **http://www.worldofatl.com**.

Tell Us What You Think

We have tried to make this book as accurate and enjoyable for you as possible, but what really matters is what the book actually does for you. Please let us know your views, whether positive or negative, either by returning the reply card in the back of the book or by contacting us at Wrox Press at **feedback@wrox.com**

Source Code and Keeping Up-to-date

We try to keep the prices of our books reasonable, and so to replace an accompanying disc we make the source code for the book available on our web sites:

> `http://www.wrox.com/`
> `http://www.wrox.co.uk/`

We've done everything we can to ensure your download is as fast as possible. The code is also available via FTP:

> `ftp://ftp.wrox.com`
> `ftp://ftp.wrox.co.uk`

If you don't have access to the Internet, then we can provide a disk for a nominal fee to cover postage and packing.

Errata & Updates

We've made every effort to make sure there are no errors in the text or the code. However, to err is human and as such we recognize the need to keep you, the reader, informed of any mistakes as they're spotted and corrected.

While you're visiting our web site, please make use of our *Errata* page, which is dedicated to fixing any small errors in the book, or offering new ways around a problem and its solution. Errata sheets are available for all our books — please download them, or take part in the continuous improvement of our tutorials and upload a 'fix' or pointer to the solution.

For those without access to the Net, call us on **1-800 USE WROX** and we'll gladly send errata sheets to you. Alternatively, send a letter to:

Wrox Press Inc.,
1512 N Fremont, Ste 103
Chicago,
IL 60622-2567
USA

Wrox Press Ltd,
30, Lincoln Road,
Olton,
Birmingham,
B27 6PA
UK

`http://www.wrox.com`

`http://www.wrox.co.uk`

An Introduction to COM

COM is the Component Object Model, the *raison d'être* of the Active Template Library (ATL). ATL was designed to make COM programming as simple as possible, while keeping the library extremely efficient through the use of advanced optimization techniques. We'll start to examine ATL in the next chapter, but for now we'll look at writing COM servers without the aid of ATL, so that you can separate the demands of COM from ATL's implementation.

Why COM?

The Holy Grail of computing is to put applications together quickly and cheaply from reusable, maintainable code, preferably written by someone else.

For many years now, experience and research have shown that object-oriented languages have a marked effect on the ability of software developers to write reusable, maintainable code. The ability to abstract concepts from a problem, and to turn them into classes and objects in a way that is fundamentally supported by the programming language, is a powerful draw for software engineers. The benefits from object-oriented techniques are there for all to see.

However, an object-oriented language is not sufficient for widespread reuse. As soon as we go beyond the idea of a single developer or group of developers, the real world comes crashing in. The first problem we see is that developers throughout the world are programming in *different* languages.

As much as some well-known Californian companies would like us to simplify our lives by standardizing around a single programming language, it's never going to happen. The reasons for the diversity of languages in the world today are complex, beyond one company's control, and in many cases well founded. Some languages are better suited to a particular problem domain; some programmers have a natural preference for a particular language because it more closely reflects the way they think; some languages relate well to particular hardware. New languages and tools supercede old ones, because they're based on new ideas or take advantage of processor power that wasn't previously available. The popularity of a language responds to fashion and hype, and even to the quantity of good books teaching the subject. We live, and will continue to live, in a world of many tongues.

The multitude of languages has its benefits, but the problem is that it fragments the marketplace for reusable components. A Java class is of little use to a C++ developer, and a chunk of Visual Basic code won't help a COBOL programmer. If I write a system in C++ today, will that effort be superceded five years from now by the arrival of a new programming language, as yet undreamed?

We need a system that allows developers to write code in the language of their choice, and that allows them to make use of components written in any other language. This is one of the many benefits that COM provides. COM is a language-neutral, object-oriented, binary standard.

COM is object-oriented because it allows clients to treat components as if they are objects. COM is a binary standard because it defines the way that these objects should behave in terms of the layout of an **interface** in memory — an interface is just a table of function pointers. This is the way that COM objects expose their functionality to clients. COM servers are distributed as compiled code, either DLLs or EXEs.

COM is not the first, nor is it the only, way of reusing compiled code. C-style DLLs have been used extensively in Windows programming for a very long time. The advantage of DLLs is that they allow parts of an application to be swapped out or upgraded without the need for recompilation. Code can be loaded on a just-in-time basis so that it doesn't take up any memory if it's never needed. Code can also be shared between processes, which can be more memory-efficient than linking it statically (i.e. compiling it into the application). The advantages of DLLs are clear enough, which is why COM components can be packaged as DLLs.

However, C-style DLLs have problems. Although they are callable from most languages, relatively few languages let you create them. They also expose simple functions only — they are not object-oriented. Traditionally, DLLs have been loaded by filename, which means that if the location or the name of a DLL changes, the application will not be able to load that DLL. This reliance on the client's knowledge of a DLL's filename also makes it impossible to provide different versions of a DLL on the same system, and can cause conflicts between different vendors' products.

COM tackles this problem by registering the location of a COM component in the **system registry** under an identifier (ID). The ID of a COM component is guaranteed to be unique, so conflicts with different products are avoided, and the client doesn't need to know anything about the physical location of the component.

A DLL runs in the process space of an application. If it runs in the process space of its client, the client gets good performance, but the downside is that the client's memory is not protected against any actions taken by the DLL. A badly written DLL could cause the client to crash. COM's solution is to allow components to be written as EXEs, in which case Windows gives them their own protected memory space. This trades off performance for robustness, because cross-process calls are slower than in-process calls, but it doesn't need to affect the client code. The switch from DLL server to EXE server could be made by changing a registry setting; the client wouldn't need recompiling at all.

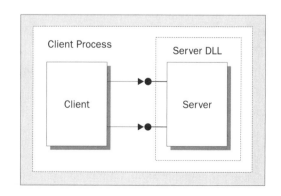

In the modern world, clients need to be able to communicate with components no matter where they are located. They could be in the same process, in a different process on the same machine, or on a different machine entirely (this location is known as the **context** of the component). COM doesn't require the client and server to behave differently depending on their relative locations. The client code can always seem as though it's acting on an in-process object. In fact, that's because it is.

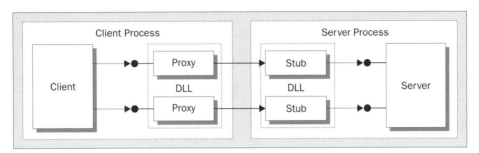

COM loads **proxy-stub DLLs** into the process space of the client and server so that they can communicate. The client can call functions directly on a proxy loaded into its address space. Each proxy looks just like an interface on the server object, so the client doesn't need to know whether it's actually talking directly to a server in its own address space, or to a proxy. Similarly, a server is always called by code in *its* own process space. It doesn't need to know whether it's being called directly by the client, or whether it's a stub that's making the call. The proxy and stub hide all the details required to make the call across the process boundary or network.

A One Sentence Description of COM

COM is a complicated topic, but we can create a simple one-sentence description, outlining its most important features:

> *COM is a specification and a set of services that allows you to create modular, object-oriented, customizable and upgradable, distributed applications using a number of languages.*

Let's look more closely at that overlong sentence and its implications to get a fuller picture of the kinds of facilities that COM offers.

▶ **COM is a specification**
   The COM specification describes the standards that you need to follow in order to create interoperable COM components. This standard describes what COM objects should look like and how they should behave.

▶ **COM is a set of services**
   The specification is backed up by a set of services or APIs. These services are provided by the **COM library**, which is part of the operating system for Win32 platforms, and available as a separate package for other operating systems.

▶ **COM allows modular programming**
COM components can be packaged as EXEs or DLLs — COM provides the communication mechanism to allow components in different modules to talk to each other.

▶ **COM is object-oriented**
COM components are true objects in the usual sense — they have identity, state and behavior. COM components that implement a common interface can be treated polymorphically.

▶ **COM enables easy customization and upgrades to your applications**
COM components link with each other dynamically, and COM defines standard ways of locating components and identifying their functionality, so individual components are swappable without having to recompile the entire application.

▶ **COM enables distributed applications**
COM provides a communication mechanism that enables components to interact across a network. More importantly, COM provides **location transparency** to applications (if desired) that enables them to be written without regard to the location of their components. The components can be moved without requiring any changes to the application.

▶ **COM components can be written in many languages**
COM is a **binary standard**. Any language that can cope with the binary standard can create or use COM objects. The number of languages and tools that support COM is increasing every day with C, C++, Java, JScript, Visual Basic, VBScript, Delphi, PowerBuilder, and MicroFocus Cobol forming just part of that growing list.

COM is not about any particular type of application. It's not about controls (that's ActiveX); it's not about compound documents (that's OLE); it's not about data access (that's OLE DB and ADO); and it's not about games and graphics (that's DirectX). But COM is the object model that underlies *all* these technologies. An understanding of COM is vital to successfully programming any of these technologies.

In the following sections, we'll look more closely at the mechanics of COM. By the end of this chapter, you'll have seen how to create a simple COM server and client using nothing more than C++ and the COM API.

The Component Object Model

The component object model itself is built around the notion of **components** (often called **coclasses**) and **interfaces**. A coclass (named from Component Object **class**) is a concrete implementation of one or more interfaces. A COM interface is a set of related functions that provide some way of manipulating **COM objects** (instantiations of a coclass).

For example, if you want to say that a coclass is both a lawyer and a philanthropist (if you don't feel that's an oxymoron), you can do that by having your component expose both **ILawyer** and **IPhilanthropist**.

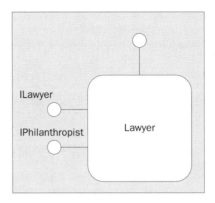

*By convention, the names of all interfaces start with '**I**'. If you want to be very silly, you can give your interfaces names like **ISpyWithMyLittleEye**, **IRobot**, **ICLAVDIVS**, or **IDo**, but you may find that the joke soon wears thin.*

From 60,000 feet, an interface is an abstraction, defining syntax (return types, parameter types and calling conventions — the signatures of the methods) and semantics (how to use the methods of the interface). The semantics of the interface are an important part of its definition. There are often requirements placed upon implementers and users of an interface that just can't be described in code (such as the need to call an **Init()** method on the interface before calling any other method). These requirements need to be clearly documented and form the semantic part of the interface definition.

Closer to the ground, an interface is a very specific memory structure — an array of pointers to the functions in that interface. This is the binary standard that we mentioned earlier. Because each of the functions in the interface is accessed by the position of its pointer in the array, the precise order of the functions in an interface is an important part of that interface's definition.

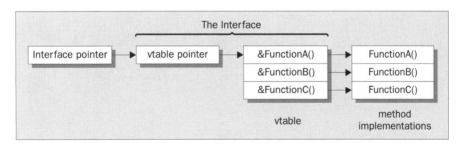

*The array of function pointers associated with an interface is usually known as a **vtable** because it has the same structure as that produced by most compilers for the virtual function table of a C++ class.*

Note that the definition of an interface does *not* include an implementation of its methods. It's up to each component to implement the methods on an interface in a way that is appropriate to that component, and which is in accordance with the semantics defined for that interface. This separation leads to more robust design — interfaces can be reused in different situations; a component that supports a particular interface can be swapped with another component supporting the same interface.

You should have a good understanding of the concepts behind the terms 'class' and 'object' from your experience of object-oriented programming with C++. These concepts are not altered by COM, but you should be careful not to assume that there is a complete one-to-one mapping that encapsulates all the secondary meanings of these terms. A coclass can be defined in C++ using a single C++ class, but it could also be defined with many C++ classes, or without any C++ classes at all (COM classes can be created in plain old C, for example). Remember that COM is a language-neutral protocol.

The abilities of a component can *only* be accessed through its interfaces. This means that COM enforces complete encapsulation of the data and implementation of a component — you can only call methods on interfaces exposed by a component; you never get direct access to data (despite appearances to the contrary when using COM objects from Visual Basic).

Getting An Interface

For the moment, we'll put aside precisely how COM objects are created, and how the client gets its first pointer to an interface. Let's assume that a client *has* an interface pointer, and that it now wants to get a pointer to another interface on the same object. As we've just discussed, the abilities of a component can *only* be accessed through its interfaces, so the only thing the client can do to get a new interface pointer is to call a method on the interface that it's already got.

> *The logical consequence of this is that all COM components must support at least one interface with a method that can return pointers to the other interfaces on that object. That interface is called **IUnknown**, and the method is called **QueryInterface()**.*

To make the life of the client programmer easier, *all* COM interfaces must support the **QueryInterface()** method. This allows clients to get a pointer to any interface supported by an object, given an initial pointer to any other interface on that object.

*Because it has a long name, because it crops up very frequently in discussions about COM, and because programmers like to make things sound more complicated than they really are, **QueryInterface()** is often abbreviated to **QI()** by the cognoscenti.*

Object Lifetime

When a client has an interface pointer, it must be able to call methods on that interface, secure in the knowledge that the code for those methods, and the underlying object, will be available for as long as the client needs it. However, we don't want immortal objects hanging around on our systems on the off chance that a client is still using them. We need a system that allows a component to be loaded when it's needed and unloaded when it isn't. This system needs to be able to cope with multiple clients using an object simultaneously, and it needs to hide as many implementation details from the client as possible.

The COM solution to this is interface-based **reference counting**. Each interface on an object keeps track of the number of clients using that interface; this number is referred to as the reference count for that interface. When its reference count reaches zero, the interface can unload itself; when the reference count for all the interfaces on an object reach zero, the object can unload itself. All the client needs to do is tell the interface when it's being used, so that it can increment its reference count, and inform the interface again when it's finished with it, so that it can decrement the reference count. In this way, the client doesn't need to know how many other clients are using the object, nor does it need to know how the memory for the object was allocated.

> *The methods to increment and decrement the reference count of an interface are called **AddRef()** and **Release()** respectively. All COM interfaces must implement these methods.*

Any function that returns an interface pointer should ensure that the interface has a reference counted on it, so that the interface doesn't suddenly die before the client gets a chance to use it — and that obviously includes **QueryInterface()**. Similarly, any time an interface pointer is copied, there should also be a call to **AddRef()**. If a function receives an interface pointer, it can use it for the lifetime of the function. If it needs it for longer than that, it should call **AddRef()**. When the interface pointer has been finished with, clients should call **Release()**.

Ultimately, the number of calls to **AddRef()** should be matched by the same number of calls to **Release()** on any particular interface, if the object is ever to unload. Clients should never dereference an interface pointer once it has been **Release()**'d as many times as it was **AddRef()**'d.

> *Note that components often use a single reference count for all the interfaces on an object. They ensure that all interfaces are available for as long as this reference count is greater than zero, then unload the whole object when it reaches zero. However, this is an implementation detail: clients cannot assume that reference counting is anything other than per-interface.*

IUnknown

These three methods — **QueryInterface()**, **AddRef()**, and **Release()** — are known collectively as the **IUnknown** methods, because they form the entire definition of the **IUnknown** interface. All COM components must implement **IUnknown**. If a component doesn't implement **IUnknown**, it's not a COM component.

> ***IUnknown** is the only interface that a component* must *implement. The intended use of the component will determine the other interfaces that it implements.*

All COM interfaces must also support the **IUnknown** methods. In fact, more than just supporting these methods, all COM interfaces must inherit or derive from **IUnknown**. If an interface doesn't derive (directly or indirectly) from **IUnknown**, it's not a COM interface.

Interface Inheritance

Interface inheritance means that the signatures and semantics for the first portion of the vtable for the derived interface are the same as the signatures and semantics in the base interface. Often, an object will implement both the base interface and a derived interface using a single implementation of the methods common to both interfaces, but this is entirely up to the implementer of the object.

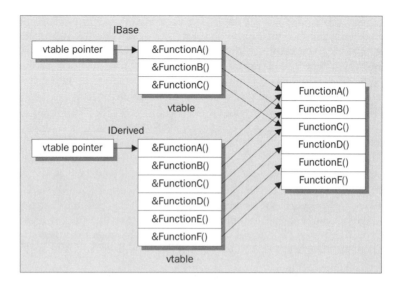

Although COM allows interface inheritance to any depth, it is always *single* inheritance. There is no multiple interface inheritance in COM. COM doesn't allow multiple interface inheritance because two sets of methods can't both be first in the vtable, and there's no standard way of choosing one set of methods over another.

> *Note that COM does not support implementation inheritance. There is no way of saying that one coclass derives from another in order to reuse the implementation of that coclass. However, COM does support other mechanisms for reusing coclass implementations, including* **aggregation**, *which is discussed in Chapter 3.*

Rules for Implementing QueryInterface

`QueryInterface()` is the method that represents the link between multiple interfaces and a single object. It is vital that `QueryInterface()` maintains the appearance and behavior of a single COM object, even if the COM object is actually implemented using many C++ objects. These rules are designed to ensure that COM works, both mechanically and conceptually, and that it does so in a way that is simple for the client programmer to use.

Identity

The first rule concerns the identity of a 'live' COM object. We have already seen that all COM objects must implement the **IUnknown** interface, and we know that clients can only ever touch an object through pointers to its interfaces. This means that the value of an **IUnknown** pointer is the only possible mechanism for comparing object identity.

The constraint that this places on the implementation of `QueryInterface()` is that it must always return the same **IUnknown** pointer for a given object, no matter when it's called (during the lifetime of that object), and no matter which interface's implementation of `QueryInterface()` is called.

> *Note that the* **IUnknown** *pointer must always be obtained by calling*
> **QueryInterface()** *directly, never by casting another interface pointer to* **IUnknown**.
> *We'll examine this point more closely when we start to look at how coclasses can be*
> *implemented in C++.*

This constraint of always returning the same interface pointer in response to a **QueryInterface()** request does *not* apply to interfaces other than **IUnknown**. This allows objects to free interfaces when they're no longer being used, and then to recreate them when they're needed again.

The remaining rules cover two main aspects of **QueryInterface()**'s behavior: how (or whether) it is allowed to change over the lifetime of an object, and how (or whether) it is allowed to change between implementations on different interfaces of the same object. The first aspect is covered by the concept of predictability, the second by the rules of reflexivity, symmetry, and transitivity.

Predictability

Once an object says that it supports an interface, it must continue to support that interface throughout its life — there are no deadbeat dads in the COM world. This does *not* mean that it has to return the same interface pointer each time (except in the case of **IUnknown** itself), only that (barring catastrophes) it returns some valid interface pointer.

In addition, if an object says that it *doesn't* support an interface at some point in its life, it can't then change its mind and start supporting that interface. If it rejects a request once, it must always reject requests for pointers to that interface.

In short, the set of interfaces for a particular object must be static over time. This rule enforces stability and simplifies client code by ensuring that an object's behavior doesn't change unpredictably over time.

> *Note that the set of interfaces supported by a particular object is not necessarily the same as*
> *that supported by other objects of the same class.*

Reflexivity

Calls to **QueryInterface()** must be **reflexive**. This just means that querying an interface for itself always succeeds.

> *Note that the new interface pointer is only guaranteed to be the same as the original pointer*
> *if the interface is* **IUnknown**.

Symmetry

Calls to **QueryInterface()** must be **symmetrical**. This means that if you can successfully query an interface **IA** for a second interface **IB**, you can also successfully query the interface **IB** for **IA**.

Transitivity

Calls to `QueryInterface()` must be **transitive**. This means that if you can successfully query **IA** for **IB**, and you can successfully query **IB** for **IC**, then you can successfully query **IA** for **IC**.

Summary

The result of all these rules is that:

- **IUnknown** is the root of a COM object's identity
- The set of interfaces supported by a particular object is consistent over time
- The set of interfaces supported by an object is the same no matter which interface's implementation of `QueryInterface()` you use

COM Diagrams

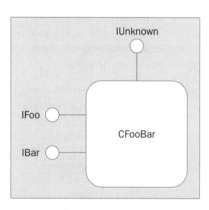

COM components are often drawn as 'plug-in jack' or 'lollipop' diagrams. By convention, the **IUnknown** interface is drawn plugged into the top of the object, while the other interfaces are plugged into the left-hand side. The **IUnknown** interface is occasionally omitted from these diagrams because it's understood that all COM components implement **IUnknown**.

Identifying Interfaces

Although we've called the interface from which all others must derive, **IUnknown**, it would be more accurate to refer to it as 00000000-0000-0000-C000-000000000046. This long number is the **interface identifier** (**IID**) of the interface known colloquially as **IUnknown**.

Interfaces are identified by IIDs because we need a unique way of referring to them with no possibility of name clashes between interfaces created by different people around the world. It's quite common to have name clashes between items identified by text strings, so COM uses **GUIDs** (**globally unique identifiers**) to avoid this possibility.

> *GUIDs are also known as* **UUIDs** (**universally unique identifiers**). *The precise reason for the two names is lost in the mists of time, but wherever you see UUID, you can think GUID, and vice versa.*

GUIDs are used to identify things uniquely, and are found all over the place in COM. Interfaces, coclasses, applications, component categories and libraries are just some of the COM-related items that need to be uniquely identified. The identifier for each of these items has its own abbreviation (IID, CLSID, APPID, CATID, and LIBID respectively), but they are all GUIDs.

Technically, a GUID is a very large, statistically unique, 128-bit number (about 10^{38}) cobbled together from the address of the Ethernet card in the machine it's generated upon (48 bits), the current time in 100-nanosecond intervals since 1582 (60 bits), and some other stuff. No two Ethernet cards anywhere have the same address. If the machine has no network card, another number is synthesized that will almost certainly be unique to the machine. It is vanishingly unlikely that duplicate GUIDs will ever be created. The GUID generation algorithm is capable of generating 10 million numbers unique to your network card every second for almost 4,000 years before it wraps around.

GUIDs are useful because they ensure that there will be no naming clashes, without requiring a central naming authority to check everything. This means that people throughout the world can independently create their own interfaces and coclasses, without worrying that someday their components will meet up with another incompatible coclass with the same ID.

A bug was present in the GUID generation algorithm in some early versions of COM. If no network card was present, but Dial-Up Networking was installed, the address of the virtual network card provided by Dial-Up Networking was used instead. Unfortunately, the address of this pseudo-card is the same on every machine, which meant that non-unique GUIDs could be — and were — generated.

Generating GUIDs

You can generate your own GUIDs using the GUID Generator supplied with Visual C++. Run the **Guidgen.exe** applet in your **DevStudio\Vc\Bin** directory or use the GUID Generator component in the Component Gallery (Project | Add to Project | Components and Controls...).

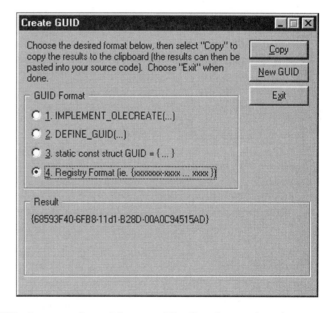

The GUID Generator lets you create GUIDs in a number of formats. The first format is only useful for MFC projects, so we won't worry about that. The second and third formats are used for defining constants to represent the GUID in C++ code. In general, these constants will be declared automatically, so you won't need to use these options very often. The final option is probably the most useful, because it generates GUIDs in the format used in the system registry and elsewhere.

Internally, the GUID Generator calls the **CoCreateGUID()** API to generate the GUIDs. If you should ever need to generate GUIDs programmatically, you can call this same function.

Versioning

An interface, once published, must not be changed. Ever. You must not add methods or remove methods. You must not change the signatures of the methods. You must not change calling conventions. If you change the IID, then you've created a new interface — interfaces are identified by their IIDs.

If you find limitations in existing interfaces, just create a new one with a new IID. It can be as similar to or different from the original interface as you require. If appropriate, you can derive the new interface from the old one.

You should also be careful how you change your coclasses. Coclasses can be upgraded by implementing new interfaces, and as long as they continue to expose the original interfaces, everything will work as expected. You should never remove interfaces from a coclass.

It's a classic COM pattern for a client to call **QueryInterface()** for the newest version of an interface that it knows about. Should that fail, it queries for the second most recent version of the interface, and so on, until it reaches the original interface. This gives a graceful degradation of functionality and allows for both forward and backward compatibility. It also allows for a 'robust evolution of functionality over time' — as you update your components to implement newer interfaces, up-to-date clients can immediately take advantage of the new interfaces, while older clients can still make use of the old, familiar interfaces.

The traditional approaches to upgrading components are either to upgrade clients and components simultaneously, or to postpone upgrading components until their clients have been upgraded. Both approaches can be horrors of logistics and administration. With immutable interfaces, and forward-only evolution of coclasses, upgrades can be much, much simpler to manage.

The Language of COM

Although COM is language-independent, it does have a language all of its own. This language, **Interface Definition Language (IDL)**, is used to provide full definitions of COM interfaces. IDL is important because it allows us to associate the methods of an interface with its IID, and it allows us to specify details of the interface in a form that can be machine-processed to produce marshaling code.

Marshaling

Marshaling is the process by which parameters are sent across apartment, process, or machine boundaries. In COM, marshaling is carried out by interface-specific proxies. A **proxy** runs in the address space of the client and looks exactly like the interface it represents. The proxy accepts function calls from the client, then packages up the parameters to transmit them to a corresponding **stub** in the receiver's address space. The stub receives the parameters from the proxy, unmarshals them, and makes the necessary calls against the server's interface in its own process. It then takes the results of the calls and passes them back to the proxy, so that it, in turn, can pass them on to the client. The proxy and stub allow the client and server code to be written without regard to their relative locations.

An **apartment** *is a conceptual unit within a process in which COM method calls can be made, and interface pointers passed about, without the intervention of proxies and stubs. For more information, see Chapter 5.*

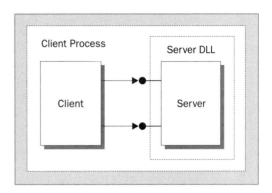

In the first diagram here, you can see the interaction between a client and server within the same process. The server has been implemented as a DLL, so the client and server can communicate directly via function calls through interface pointers.

In the next diagram, you can see how the interaction looks when the server has been implemented as an EXE. The server and client are each in separate processes and require the intervention of in-process proxies and stubs to carry out the cross-process calls transparently.

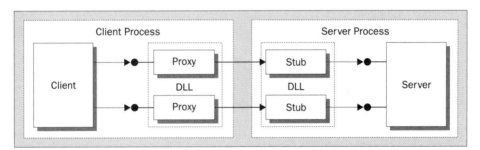

Proxy and stub code is usually created automatically by compiling an IDL interface definition with the **MIDL** compiler. The **MIDL** compiler can use the interface definition to generate marshaling code that can then be compiled into a proxy-stub DLL by a standard C or C++ compiler.

Note that the **MIDL** *compiler produces* source code, *not binary code like a C++ compiler.*

IDL

IDL is relatively simple because it's a lot like the declarative parts of C++, with the addition of **attributes**. An interface definition doesn't include an implementation, so IDL doesn't need the control structures that would be necessary for that.

Let's look at the IDL definition for **IUnknown** (you can find this definition in **DevStudio\Vc\Include\Unknwn.idl**):

The [object] attribute shows that this is a COM interface

The attributes between these brackets apply to the whole interface

The [uuid()] attribute of an interface definition contains its IID. This is the interface's true 'name'

```
[
    local,
    object,
    uuid(00000000-0000-0000-C000-000000000046),
    pointer_default(unique)
]

interface IUnknown
{
    HRESULT QueryInterface(
        [in] REFIID riid,
        [out, iid_is(riid)] void** ppvObject);
    ULONG AddRef();
    ULONG Release();
}
```

The text name given to the interface can be used by MIDL to generate the names of the class and IID constant

The braces contain the methods of the IUnknown interface

Method parameters can have attributes applied to them too

Here you can see the parameters to **QueryInterface()**. **riid** *is a reference to an IID (hence* **REFIID**), *and* **ppvObject** *is an indirect pointer to the returned interface.*

If you ignore the brackets for now, you can see that **IUnknown** has been defined using the **interface** keyword, followed by the name of the interface. The interface methods are then listed in vtable order within the interface body (which is defined by the braces). This looks a lot like the definition of a C++ class.

The brackets contain attributes that apply to the items immediately following them. The first set of brackets contains attributes pertaining to the interface. We won't look at all the possible attributes (we'll see more as we go through the book), but the most important ones here are **[object]** and **[uuid()]**.

[object] must be present in the IDL when defining COM interfaces. It's needed to distinguish COM interface definitions from RPC interface definitions, which can also be defined in IDL.

The **[uuid()]** attribute is used to identify the interface uniquely. The number in parentheses is the interface's IID. You can see that it's in registry format, as generated by the GUID Generator, minus the braces.

The IID of the interface is the most important identifier associated with it. It *is* the name of the interface. The 'name' that appears after the **interface** keyword in the IDL definition is just used to generate class names and symbolic constants when the IDL is used to create C++ code.

Memory Management

Attributes can be applied to the parameters of an interface's methods, just as they have been in the case of **IUnknown::QueryInterface()**. These attributes give important information about memory management to implementers and clients of an interface, as well as ensuring that the marshaling code knows what it should be doing.

The most important and frequently used parameter attributes are **[in]** and **[out]**. These attributes denote the direction of travel of data relative to the function. This means if you're passing data in to a function, the parameter should be specified with the **[in]** attribute; if data is being returned from a function via a parameter, it should be specified as an **[out]** parameter.

Note that attributes applying to a single item can be combined as a comma-separated list within a single pair of brackets. If a parameter is both **[in]** *and* **[out]**, *you would specify it as* **[in, out]**.

This means that if you wanted to pass a **long** into a method, you would declare it like this:

```
HRESULT MethodName([in] long lInput);
```

All **[out]** parameters must be specified as pointers to the data type being transmitted, so if you wanted to get a **long** out of a method, you would declare it like this:

```
HRESULT AnotherMethodName([out] long* plOutput);
```

When data is passed by value, as in this case, you aren't required to do any special memory allocation. However, the attributes carry with them important rules when the data isn't passed by value:

Attribute	Description
[in]	The parameter should be allocated by the caller. The called function should do nothing to free the parameter.
[out]	The parameter should be allocated by the called function.
[in, out]	The parameter should be allocated by the caller. The called function may free and reallocate the parameter.

In all cases, the parameter should ultimately be freed by the caller.

In the cases of **[out]** and **[in, out]** parameters, the memory should be allocated and freed using the standard COM memory allocator, to ensure that both sides are using the same method of memory allocation. In general, this means calling **CoTaskMemAlloc()** to allocate memory and **CoTaskMemFree()** to free it.

```
LPVOID CoTaskMemAlloc(
    ULONG cb    // Size in bytes of memory block to be allocated
);
```

```
void CoTaskMemFree(
    void* pv    // Pointer to memory block to be freed
);
```

HRESULT

When you've seen a few COM interfaces, you'll notice that 99% of them return **HRESULT**s from all of their methods. It's not a requirement of COM that *all* methods should return **HRESULT**s, but there are two good reasons for doing so. The first is that it's a consistent way of returning status information from a method. The second, and perhaps more important reason, is that it allows the COM subsystem to return errors to the caller of the method.

COM objects cannot transmit errors to their clients using standard C++ or Win32-style exceptions. These exceptions cannot cross process boundaries, and different languages handle exceptions in different ways.

The COM subsystem will intervene in a method call if it goes across an apartment, process or machine boundary. There are a number of errors that can occur during this procedure. If your methods return **HRESULT**s, COM can return information about these errors back to the caller. If your methods don't return **HRESULT**s, the caller can't find out what went wrong. In fact, **MIDL** won't be able to produce marshaling code for interfaces that contain methods that don't return **HRESULT**s.

*The net result of all COM methods returning **HRESULT**s is that any 'real' return values have to come back via the method's parameters. IDL provides a **[retval]** attribute that allows method parameters to be treated like real return values by tools that understand the attribute.*

An **HRESULT** is simply a 32-bit number containing a structured error code:

S (bit 31) is the **severity code**, indicating success or failure. The predefined severity constants are **SEVERITY_SUCCESS** (zero) and **SEVERITY_ERROR** (one). You should use the **SUCCEEDED()** or **FAILED()** macros to test an **HRESULT** for simple success or failure.

The bits labeled **R**, **C**, **N**, and **r** are reserved, while the **facility** is used to group related status codes together. The predefined facilities are given in Appendix A, along with some more detail about the specifics of **HRESULT**s.

To get text descriptions for standard **HRESULT**s, you can use the **Errlook** tool provided with Visual C++. You can find the complete list of **HRESULT**s and Win32 error codes in **<winerror.h>**, but here are a few of the more important ones.

Name	Meaning
S_OK	Success (0x0). Sometimes used in conjunction with **S_FALSE** as a Boolean **TRUE** value.
NOERROR	Old synonym for **S_OK**.
S_FALSE	Success (0x1), but function returned Boolean **FALSE**, by contrast with **S_OK**.
E_UNEXPECTED	Catastrophic failure.
E_NOTIMPL	Not implemented.
E_OUTOFMEMORY	Could not allocate needed memory.
E_INVALIDARG	One or more arguments are invalid.
E_NOINTERFACE	Returned by **QueryInterface()** if the component doesn't support the requested interface.
E_POINTER	Function has been given an invalid pointer.

Name	Meaning
E_HANDLE	Function has been given an invalid handle.
E_ABORT	Operation aborted.
E_FAIL	Unspecified failure.
E_ACCESSDENIED	General access denied error.

There are many other groups of COM-related **HRESULT**s. Prefixes include **CO_** , **OLE_** , **DV_** , **DRAGDROP_** , **CLASS_** , **REGDB_** , **MK_** , **DISP_** , and **RPC_**. Most of these **HRESULT**s are error codes, but there are dozens of success codes too.

HRESULT Tips

> When testing to see if a function failed or succeeded, never say **if (hr == S_OK)**. It is much safer to say **if (SUCCEEDED(hr))** or **if (FAILED(hr))**, and then to check for more specific **HRESULT**s as appropriate. Although you may think that you know all of the possible error codes returned from a component (especially if you wrote it yourself), COM may return additional error codes (such as network failures) when running a component on a different thread, process, or computer. Success codes, on the other hand, are part of the contract that an interface implements and, once specified, may not be augmented.

> If you want to return a Win32 error code (typically obtained from **GetLastError()**) from one of your methods, convert it to an **HRESULT** with the **HRESULT_FROM_WIN32()** macro. If you receive an **HRESULT** with a facility code of **FACILITY_WIN32**, use **HRESULT_CODE()** to extract the Win32 error code.

> Note that **S_OK** is 0 and **S_FALSE** is 1, the inverses of the usual C values for Boolean **true** and **false**, so take care when using them. Note also that many clients (particularly Visual Basic) fail to differentiate between **S_OK** and **S_FALSE**, seeing them both as successful return codes.

> Try not to return **E_FAIL** from your functions: it's frustratingly unspecific to users of the component. We'll take a look at how to return more helpful errors in Chapter 4.

> You may see **SCODE**s being used as the return value of methods and APIs in some older code and books. **SCODE**s are obsolete and you can treat **SCODE** as a synonym for **HRESULT**.

> Remember that **HRESULT**s are not just used for errors, there are various success codes too.

Creating Interfaces in C++

In C++, COM interfaces map to a special, restricted kind of abstract class. All methods are **public**, pure **virtual** (**=0**), and have no default implementation. Interfaces have no member data; hence, they have no state. These classes do not have constructors or destructors (not even virtual destructors) — they do not need them, because they have no state to construct or destroy.

The C++ definition for **IUnknown** is shown below:

```
class IUnknown
{
public:
   __stdcall virtual HRESULT QueryInterface( REFIID riid,
                                             void** ppvObject ) = 0;
   __stdcall virtual ULONG AddRef() = 0;
   __stdcall virtual ULONG Release() = 0;
};
```

You can see that all methods appear in the same order as they did in the original IDL definition. This results in a vtable being created with exactly the structure required. To hook the vtable up to some real functions and any necessary data, we can just derive a concrete class from this abstract class and implement all the functions. When we want a COM **IUnknown** pointer, we can just cast from a pointer to the concrete class to get a C++ **IUnknown*** and use that.

> *Note the use of the __**stdcall** calling convention on these methods. __**stdcall** didn't appear in the IDL definition of the interface because **MIDL** assumes __**stdcall** by default. However, the default C++ calling convention is __**cdecl**, so to ensure that the C++ and IDL definitions match, we need to use __**stdcall** explicitly in the C++ code. You can actually use any convention you like, but you'll need to specify the convention in the IDL definition of your interface if you decide not to use __**stdcall**. Most methods use __**stdcall** because it reduces code size and is the standard on Windows platforms.*

> **Because these abstract classes are so closely related to the interfaces that they represent, they are simply called 'interfaces' and are usually defined using the interface macro (which is just a #define for struct), rather than class.**

Macros

In addition to the **#define** for **interface**, the Platform SDK defines a few other macros to simplify the declarations of COM methods. These are the **STDMETHOD()**, **STDMETHOD_()** and **PURE** macros, which you can find in **<Basetyps.h>**. These macros make it possible to have a single interface definition that works for both C and C++, but we'll use them simply because it saves typing, makes the interface definitions look cleaner, and because ATL also uses these macros.

The **STDMETHOD()** macro wraps up the __**stdcall** calling convention, the **virtual** specifier, and the **HRESULT** return type. **STDMETHOD_()** does the same job, except that it allows you to specify the method's return type as the first macro argument. **PURE** simply replaces **=0**. Thus we could rewrite the C++ definition of **IUnknown** using these macros as shown below:

```
interface IUnknown
{
   STDMETHOD(QueryInterface)(REFIID riid, void** ppvObj) PURE;
   STDMETHOD_(ULONG, AddRef)() PURE;
   STDMETHOD_(ULONG, Release)() PURE;
};
```

Interface Inheritance in C++

As we've seen before, **IUnknown** is important because all other COM interfaces must derive from it, directly or indirectly. In other words, the vtables for *all* COM interfaces start with the **QueryInterface()**, **AddRef()** and **Release()** methods.

Be careful not to confuse COM inheritance with C++ inheritance. Although it turns out that we can model COM inheritance using C++ inheritance mechanisms, this isn't a requirement. For example, we could create an interface **IWroxInterface** that looks like this in IDL:

```
[
   object,
   uuid(FEB89321-6D77-11D1-B28D-00A0C94515AD)
]
interface IWroxInterface : IUnknown
{
   HRESULT Alert();
};
```

And we could describe this interface in C++ in any of the following ways (only one of which uses C++ inheritance):

```
interface IWroxInterface : public IUnknown
{
   STDMETHOD(Alert)() PURE;
};
```

```
interface IWroxInterface
{
   STDMETHOD(QueryInterface)(REFIID riid, void** ppvObj) PURE;
   STDMETHOD_(ULONG, AddRef)() PURE;
   STDMETHOD_(ULONG, Release)() PURE;

   STDMETHOD(Alert)() PURE;
};
```

```
interface IWroxInterface
{
   STDMETHOD(QueryInterface)(REFIID riid, void** ppvObj) PURE;
   STDMETHOD_(ULONG, AddRef)() PURE;
   STDMETHOD_(ULONG, Release)() PURE;

   STDMETHOD(RenamedAlert)() PURE;
};
```

The first C++ definition of the interface is the preferred one. It creates the required vtable and clearly models the relationship between the C++ classes and the COM interfaces. The second and third definitions are also fine as far as COM is concerned, as they result in the same vtable signatures, but are less useful in C++, because the relationship with the **IUnknown** interface has been lost. From the third example, you can see that the names of the methods used in the C++ definition are not important to COM — all that matters is the vtable. Changing the names of methods isn't usually a good idea as it is likely to lead to confusion, but it can be useful in some circumstances.

Creating a Basic COM DLL Server

MIDL and C++

MIDL has an important role in creating C++ interfaces from IDL definitions. By passing an IDL file through the **MIDL** compiler, we can get **MIDL** to create a header file containing the C++ definitions of the interfaces contained in that file, as well as symbolic constants for the IIDs.

Let's create an IDL file containing the definition of some interfaces that we will use in an ongoing example throughout the rest of the chapter. Create a new directory called **ComDll** to store the files for this project. Create a new text file in this directory called **ComDll_IDL.idl** and add the following text:

```
// ComDll_IDL.idl
import "oaidl.idl";

   [
       object,
       uuid(MY_GUID1)
   ]
   interface IWroxInterface : IUnknown
   {
       HRESULT Alert();
   };


   [
       object,
       uuid(MY_GUID2)
   ]
   interface IWroxSimple : IUnknown
   {
       HRESULT Display();
   };

[
   uuid(MY_GUID3),
   version(1.0)
]
library WroxComponentLib
{
   importlib("stdole32.tlb");

   [
       uuid(MY_GUID4)
   ]
   coclass WroxComponent
   {
       [default] interface IWroxInterface;
       interface IWroxSimple;
   };
};
```

Replace the symbols **MY_GUID1** to **MY_GUID4** with four GUIDs freshly generated using the GUID Generator. The GUIDs should be generated in registry format, but you should delete the braces once you've pasted them into the right place.

The **import** statement at the top of the file just brings in the standard types defined by the **oaidl.idl** file. The **import** statement in IDL is similar to C++'s **#include**, but it only lets us use the data types defined in the imported file. We import this file here simply so that we can use the **HRESULT** type.

In this code we've defined two very simple interfaces, **IWroxInterface** and **IWroxSimple**, each of which contains a single method (as well as the three **IUnknown** methods). We've also defined a **library** section in the IDL file. A **library** section is used to output a type library (which we're not interested in at the moment), but it also allows us to specify coclasses, so that **MIDL** can produce a symbolic constant for the CLSID.

Once this file has been saved, we can use **MIDL** to output some files. Open up a command prompt in the **ComDll** directory and use the following command to generate the files:

```
MIDL ComDll_IDL.idl
```

> *If necessary, run* **DevStudio\Vc\Bin\VCVars32.bat** *to set your environment variables to allow you to use* **MIDL** *from a command line.*

Once you've run this command, you'll see that a number of new files have been output in the **ComDll** directory.

The file **ComDll_IDL.h** contains the C++ interface definitions and **extern** declarations of symbolic constants for the GUIDs in the IDL file (so that the GUID constants can be used from any file that includes the header). The C++ interfaces have the same names as the simple text names given to the interfaces in the IDL file. The symbolic constants for the interfaces IDs are in the form **IID_***interfacename*, and the symbolic constant for the CLSID is in the form **CLSID_***coclassname*.

ComDll_IDL_i.c contains the *definitions* of the GUID constants declared in the header file. This file will typically be included once in a project that uses the **.h** file.

ComDll_IDL_p.c contains the marshaling code for the interfaces defined in the IDL file. **DllData.c** contains some more code that is used when building the proxy-stub DLL. **ComDll_IDL.tlb** is the type library generated from the information in the IDL file.

We'll only be using the **.h** and **_i.c** file in our project. We won't be generating the proxy-stub DLL because our simple tests won't need it, and we're not interested in the type library at this stage.

Implementing Interfaces

Now let's turn our attention to hooking up the interfaces we've just defined to some kind of functionality.

Consider a C++ class, **CWroxComponent**, which implements both interfaces. In this case, we'll see how we can implement the component using multiple inheritance. The advantage of multiple inheritance is that it's simple to implement the **IUnknown** methods just once for all the interfaces. An alternative approach would be to use different classes for each of the interfaces.

Create a new text file and save it in the **ComDll** directory as **WroxComponent.h**. We'll add the whole implementation of the component to the same file, so all the methods will be defined inline. Enter the following code:

```
// Get all the system stuff from Windows.h
#include <windows.h>

// Include the MIDL-generated header file to get interface definitions
#include "ComDll_IDL.h"

// Define a class to implement the interfaces using multiple inheritance
class CWroxComponent : public IWroxInterface,
                       public IWroxSimple
{
public:
    // Constructor
    CWroxComponent() : m_lRefCount(0)
    {...}

    // Destructor
    ~CWroxComponent() {...}

    // The IUnknown methods
    STDMETHOD(QueryInterface)(REFIID riid, void** ppv)
    {
        ...
    }

    STDMETHOD_(ULONG, AddRef)()
    {
        ...
    }

    STDMETHOD_(ULONG, Release)()
    {
        ...
    }

    // IWroxInterface method
    STDMETHOD(Alert)()
    {
        ...
    }
```

```
    // IWroxSimple method
    STDMETHOD(Display)()
    {
        ...
    }

private:
    long m_lRefCount;
};
```

Clearly, these are the very basics of the class, leaving us to fill in the method implementations as we go along.

The **#include** statements give us access to the Windows API and to the interfaces defined in the **MIDL**-generated header file. We make use of these interfaces by deriving our class from them. The methods for all the interfaces, including **IUnknown**, are laid out in the body of the class. You can see that we've declared a **private** member, **m_lRefCount**, to hold the reference count of the object, and that we've set the count to zero in the constructor's initialization list.

AddRef and Release

Implementing **AddRef()** and **Release()** is a simple matter of incrementing and decrementing the reference count:

```
STDMETHOD_(ULONG, AddRef)()
{
    return InterlockedIncrement(&m_lRefCount);
}

STDMETHOD_(ULONG, Release)()
{
    ULONG ul = InterlockedDecrement(&m_lRefCount);

    if (ul == 0)
        delete this; // The object must be created with new

    return ul;
}
```

Note that we're using a single reference count for all the interfaces on the object. Although multiple inheritance makes our lives easier by allowing us to implement the **IUnknown** methods only once for all three interfaces exposed by our object (**IUnknown**, **IWroxInterface** and **IWroxSimple**), it does mean that we can't provide a different reference count for each interface. COM allows for per-interface reference counts, but implementing per-object reference counts doesn't break the expected behavior.

Here I have used the **InterlockedIncrement()** and **InterlockedDecrement()** APIs to increase and decrease the reference count on the component, instead of the simpler **++m_lRefCount** and **--m_lRefCount**, because the APIs are thread-safe. We get the prototypes of these functions from the **Windows.h** header.

29

Note also that this implementation of **Release()** assumes that the object has been created on the heap (with **new CWroxComponent**) because it calls **delete this** to destroy the object when the reference count reaches zero. Calling **delete this** on a stack-based, static, or global object would be disastrous. In practice, COM objects are almost always created on the heap, so this is a typical implementation, but a different implementation must be used for non-heap-based COM objects.

Also, be aware that we keep the return value from **InterlockedDecrement()** (which is the value of **m_lRefCount** after being decremented) in the local variable **ul**. This is so that we can return the value from **Release()** after the object has been **delete**d. It is a bug to try and return the value of member variables (such as **m_lRefCount**) from an object that has been **delete**d.

Finally, do not rely on the return values from **AddRef()** or **Release()** being accurate (or even meaningful) in terms of the number of references held on a particular interface. COM provides various optimizations through the use of proxies that can affect the reference count of an interface, and COM objects are not required to implement true per-interface reference counting; they are simply required to provide **AddRef()** and **Release()** (and **QueryInterface()**) methods. Clients, however, must always act as if components *do* implement true per-interface reference counting, which means always calling **Release()** on the same interface that was **AddRef()**'d.

QueryInterface

The implementation of **QI()** looks like this:

```
STDMETHOD(QueryInterface)(REFIID riid, void** ppv)
{
    if ( riid == IID_IUnknown )
        *ppv = static_cast<IWroxInterface*>(this);
    else if ( riid == IID_IWroxInterface )
        *ppv = static_cast<IWroxInterface*>(this);
    else if ( riid == IID_IWroxSimple )
        *ppv = static_cast<IWroxSimple*>(this);
    else
    {
        *ppv = NULL;
        return E_NOINTERFACE;
    }

    static_cast<IUnknown*>(*ppv)->AddRef();

    return S_OK;
}
```

This implementation is straightforward — we just compare **riid** against the interface ID for each of the interfaces supported by our component. For the standard interface **IUnknown**, we use the **IID_** constant defined in the system headers. For our custom interfaces, we get the IIDs from the **MIDL**-produced header.

If the interface is not supported, we set ***ppv = NULL** and return **E_NOINTERFACE**. If **riid** matches one of the supported interfaces, we return a pointer to the appropriate interface and increment the reference count. Note that we increment the reference count by calling **AddRef()** rather than incrementing **m_1RefCount** directly. This would allow the implementation to work correctly even if per-interface reference counting was employed.

There are four casts in this implementation. The first three ensure that we are setting ***ppv** to the right pointer for the requested interface. These casts are vital, because the pointer value can change when casting to a base class from a multiply derived class.

The first cast may seem confusing because when we're asked for a pointer to **IUnknown**, we cast to **IWroxInterface*** rather than **IUnknown***. The reason we cast to **IWroxInterface*** is to disambiguate the inheritance branch for the compiler (because both **IWroxInterface** and **IWroxSimple** derive from **IUnknown**). This is really just an intermediate step — to make things clearer, we could include the cast from **IWroxInterface*** to **IUnknown*** like this:

```
*ppv = static_cast<IUnknown*>(static_cast<IWroxInterface*>(this) );
```

This would show explicitly that we are casting from **CWroxComponent***, through **IWroxInterface***, to **IUnknown***. However, this extra cast actually has no effect on the pointer we return, because casting to a base type when only single inheritance is involved (**IWroxInterface** inherits singly from **IUnknown**) has no effect on the pointer value.

The final cast just gives the **void** pointer a real type so that we can use it to call **AddRef()**.

> *As we've seen, using multiple inheritance makes it very easy to implement a COM component with multiple interfaces. ATL itself uses this technique, but it's not the only way of implementing interfaces. It's quite common, for example, to see each interface implemented by a single class. If these classes are defined as nested classes within another class that controls the lifetime of the COM object, it's possible to use offsets to delegate the nested classes'* **IUnknown** *methods to the outer class. This is the method used by MFC.*

Alert and Display

We can add extremely simple implementations for the **Alert()** and **Display()** methods:

```
// IWroxInterface method
STDMETHOD(Alert)()
{
    MessageBox(NULL, "The Alert() method was called",
               "IWroxInterface", MB_OK);
    return S_OK;
}

// IWroxSimple method
STDMETHOD(Display)()
{
    MessageBox(NULL, "The Display() method was called",
               "IWroxSimple", MB_OK);
    return S_OK;
}
```

Vtable Layout, Casting & Identity

When writing COM clients, you need to be very careful how you cast interface pointers. This can be particularly important if you're writing the server at the same time as you develop the client — don't let your knowledge of the implementation of the server cause you to write bad client code.

A **CWroxComponent** object would be laid out something like this:

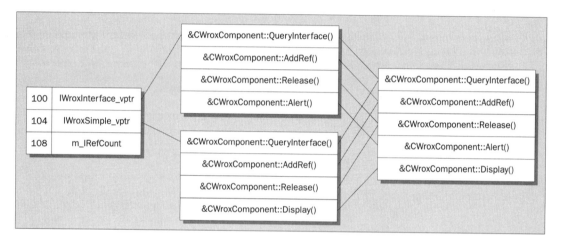

If the client was in the same apartment as the server, it could get an **IUnknown*** (**0x100**), an **IWroxInterface*** (**0x100**) or an **IWroxSimple*** (**0x104**).

To see if two interfaces really are on the same object, you need to compare **IUnknown**s. However, don't be tempted to cast interface pointers to **IUnknown** in order to compare them. You must always **QI()** for **IUnknown** making a comparison.

In other words, this is wrong:

```
//Wrong way to see if two interface pointers refer to the same COM object
if (static_cast<IUnknown*>(pIWroxInterface) ==
    static_cast<IUnknown*>(pIWroxSimple)) {...}
```

In this case, we'd be comparing **0x100** with **0x104**, which clearly aren't equal, yet we know that these two interface pointers are from the same object. This is the right way to do it:

```
//Right way to see if two interface pointers refer to the same COM object
IUnknown* punk1 = NULL;
IUnknown* punk2 = NULL;

pIWroxInterface->QueryInterface( IID_IUnknown,
                                 reinterpret_cast<void**>(&punk1) );
pIWroxSimple->QueryInterface( IID_IUnknown,
                                 reinterpret_cast<void**>(&punk2) );
```

```
if (punk1 == punk2) {...}
punk2->Release();
punk1->Release();
```

Similarly, don't be tempted to cast from **IUnknown*** to **IWroxInterface***. Although this will work if the server and client are in the same apartment, it won't work if they're not. A separate proxy is created for each interface, and the **IUnknown** proxy certainly won't implement the **IWroxInterface** methods — attempting to call non-existent methods against that pointer will almost certainly result in an access violation.

[iid_is()]

This may lead you to wonder how the marshaling code knows what proxy to create, when all the interfaces are being passed as **void****. Well, the answer is in the IDL definition of **QI()**, which looked like this:

```
HRESULT QueryInterface(
    [in] REFIID riid,
    [out, iid_is(riid)] void** ppvObject);
```

Notice the **[iid_is()]** attribute. This attribute tells the **MIDL** compiler to produce marshaling source code based on the IID of the parameter specified (in this case, **riid**). This means that when **riid** is the IID for **IUnknown**, **ppvObject** will be marshaled as if it's an indirect pointer to **IUnknown** — if a proxy is created, it will be a proxy for **IUnknown**. Similarly, when **riid** is the IID for **IWroxInterface**, **ppvObject** will be marshaled as if it's an indirect pointer to **IWroxInterface** — if a proxy is created, it will be a proxy for **IWroxInterface**; and so on.

You can pass interface pointers as parameters to COM methods without using the **[iid_is()]** attribute, and many standard interfaces have methods that do exactly that. In that case, the parameters will be marshaled as their declared types.

If you don't specify the **[iid_is()]** attribute, interface parameters will be marshaled according to their declared type. **[iid_is()]** makes the declared pointer type irrelevant from a marshaling point of view.

Summary

Now we're starting to get an idea about how to implement a coclass. The essence of the process is to get C++ interface definitions (abstract classes) for the interfaces that we're interested in, use these as base classes for the class that we're using to represent the coclass, then implement the methods on those interfaces.

We know that:

▶ All coclasses must implement **IUnknown**

▶ Every coclass is identified by a CLSID (a GUID)

▶ All interfaces must derive from **IUnknown**

▶ Every interface is identified by an IID (a GUID)

▶ We can use **MIDL** to produce C++ interface definitions from the IDL that we supply for our custom interfaces.

However, there are still a lot of questions left unanswered:

▶ How does a client create an instance of our coclass?

▶ How do you get that first interface on which to call `QI()`?

▶ How does COM locate the server (given only a CLSID)?

▶ What are the differences between DLL and EXE servers?

The Other Side

To begin to answer these questions, let's look at things from the client's point of view. A client needs to be able to create an instance of a coclass by specifying a CLSID (to identify the coclass) and an IID (to identify the initial interface it wants). Since there are performance implications, the client should also be able to specify the context of the server (whether it's in-process, local, remote, or whether it doesn't care). The client certainly *shouldn't* have to find out the physical location of the server.

COM provides a simple function that takes the information that we've outlined and returns a pointer to the desired interface. That function is called `CoCreateInstance()`.

```
STDAPI CoCreateInstance(
    REFCLSID   rclsid,        // Class identifier (CLSID) of the object
    LPUNKNOWN  pUnkOuter,      // Outer unknown pointer
    DWORD      dwClsContext,   // Context
    REFIID     riid,           // Reference to the interface identifier
    void**     ppv             // Indirect pointer to requested interface
);
```

> `STDAPI` *is a macro defined in* `<objbase.h>`*, which expands to* `extern "C" HRESULT __stdcall`*.* `WINOLEAPI` *is a synonym for* `STDAPI`*.*

The first parameter is the CLSID of the object to create. COM must use the CLSID to find out the physical location of the server and ask it to create an object of the desired type.

The second parameter is used for **aggregation**. Aggregation is a technique for reusing COM components from within other components. We'll look at aggregation in much more detail later in the book. For now, we'll assume that we'll never use aggregation, in which case this parameter must always be **NULL**.

The third parameter specifies the context for the call. The context can be one or more of the flags in the **CLSCTX** enumeration:

```
typedef enum tagCLSCTX {
    CLSCTX_INPROC_SERVER  = 1,
    CLSCTX_INPROC_HANDLER = 2,
    CLSCTX_LOCAL_SERVER   = 4,
    CLSCTX_REMOTE_SERVER  = 16 } CLSCTX;
```

Typical combinations of these values are **CLSCTX_SERVER** (which unites the
CLSCTX_xxx_SERVER values), and **CLSCTX_ALL** (which combines **CLSCTX_SERVER** with
CLSCTX_INPROC_HANDLER). You can also OR individual values together manually.

In simple terms, COM will use the server with the best performance that matches a context
specified in this parameter. That means that in-process servers take precedence over local servers
when both contexts are allowed.

The final parameters to **CoCreateInstance()** are the same as the parameters to
QueryInterface(). They identify the interface for which we want a pointer, and provide the
pointer to store the value when the function returns. **CoCreateInstance()** returns an **HRESULT**
to indicate any errors.

Clients can use **CoCreateInstance()** like this:

```
IWroxInterface* pWI = NULL;
HRESULT hr = CoCreateInstance( CLSID_WroxComponent,
                               NULL,
                               CLSCTX_INPROC_SERVER,
                               IID_IWroxInterface,
                               reinterpret_cast<void**>(&pWI) );
if (FAILED(hr))
{
    ... // Handle the error here
}
```

Initializing COM

You must initialize the COM library before you call its functions (apart from the memory
allocation functions). This applies to both clients and servers. You should initialize COM once
(and only once) on each thread from which you use it. Call **CoInitialize()** or
CoInitializeEx() to initialize the COM libraries, and **CoUninitialize()** to uninitialize
them. DLL servers should *not* initialize COM for themselves, since they will be loaded into a
thread that must already have initialized COM.

CoInitialize() and **CoUninitialize()** are extremely simple. **CoInitialize()** takes a
single reserved parameter that must always be **NULL**, and **CoUninitialize()** doesn't take any
parameters at all. **CoInitializeEx()** takes an extra parameter that specifies the threading
model (concurrency control) of objects created on that thread. We'll delay discussion of threading
models and **CoInitializeEx()** until Chapter 5, so for now, you can just use
CoInitialize().

Locating Servers

So how does COM know where to find the server containing any particular coclass? Well, it
simply looks the answer up in a database that maps CLSIDs to file locations. On Windows
systems, this database is the **registry**.

The registry is a hierarchical data store used to hold many different kinds of information. You can view and edit the registry using **RegEdit** (Windows 95 and Windows NT) or **RegEdt32** (Windows NT only). The registry consists of **hives**, **keys**, and **values**. The hives are the top-level folders shown by **RegEdit** (HKEY_CLASSES_ROOT, HKEY_CURRENT_USER, HKEY_LOCAL_MACHINE, HKEY_USERS, HKEY_CURRENT_CONFIG, and HKEY_DYN_DATA). The keys are all the other folders. Values are the list entries in the right-hand pane. Each value consists of a name and data that can be in a few different formats, such as string or binary data.

Keys in the registry are often referred to with a string made up by concatenating the names of all the keys and subkeys that lead to that key, separated by backslashes. This is just how you would refer to the location of a file in the file system. You can see that **RegEdit** shows the location of the currently selected key in this form in its status bar.

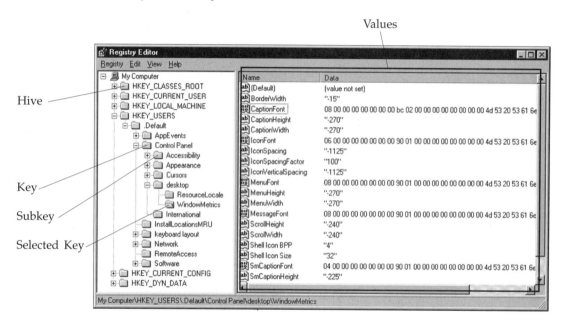

RegEdt32 *is the original Windows NT registry editor.* RegEdit *first appeared on Windows 95 and was later ported to NT 4.0.* RegEdit *has a nicer user interface and good search functionality, but it can't do everything that* RegEdt32 *can. In particular, if you need to edit the security attributes on a key, you must use* RegEdt32*.*

The most important hive, as far as COM is concerned, is HKEY_CLASSES_ROOT. This contains the information used to map CLSIDs to file locations.

You can open the key called CLSID; and you'll see hundreds of CLSIDs. Open some of CLSID's subkeys, and you'll see that almost all of the CLSIDs have an InprocServer32 or LocalServer32 key that contains information about the location of the server. Many of the components will have other keys, but those are often optional or only relevant to particular types of COM component.

Registering a Component

The server usually creates the registry entries that map the CLSID to the file of the server itself. When this is the case, the server is known as **self-registering**. A self-registering server marks itself as such by including the string **"OleSelfRegister"** in its version resource.

EXE servers are asked to add their entries to the registry when they are run with the -RegServer switch on the command line, and to unregister themselves when -UnRegServer is the command line parameter.

DLL servers export two functions for registering and unregistering themselves: **DllRegisterServer()** and **DllUnregisterServer()**. These are called by an external program, typically **RegSvr32.exe**, which is provided with the system. You can use:

    regsvr32.exe filename

to register a DLL server, and

    regsvr32.exe /u filename

to unregister it.

At a minimum, a server must add its CLSID as a key beneath HKEY_CLASSES_ROOT, and the location of its file as a value beneath an **InprocServer32** subkey (if it's a DLL) or a **LocalServer32** subkey (if it's an EXE).

The proxy-stub DLLs produced from **MIDL**-generated code are also self-registering COM DLLs. In addition to the entries under HKEY_CLASSES_ROOT\CLSID*clsid*\InprocServer32, proxy-stub DLLs make an entry under HKEY_CLASSES_ROOT\Interface*iid*\ProxyStubClsid32, which relates back to their CLSID. This allows COM to determine which proxy-stub to use for a particular interface. Note that the CLSID for a **MIDL**-produced proxy is the same as the IID of the interface that it represents.

> *ProgIDs, or Programmatic Identifiers, are sometimes a more user-friendly way of identifying COM components than CLSIDs. ProgIDs are strings of the form* company.component[.version]. *They are mostly used by clients written in scripting languages like VBScript, but are rarely necessary from languages like C++, where we tend to use symbolic constants for the CLSID.*

> *You can use the* **CLSIDFromProgID()** *or* **ProgIDFromCLSID()** *APIs to get one form of identifier from the other, based on information stored in the registry. Note that ProgIDs are a secondary form of identification — all COM components must have a CLSID, but ProgIDs are entirely optional. You can see ProgIDs in the registry directly beneath* HKEY_CLASSES_ROOT.

Creating an Object

Now we've seen how a client specifies which object it wants to create, and how COM can use that information to determine which module to load, but how does COM ask the module to create a particular object? It turns out that the COM library actually asks another COM object called a **class object** to create the requested object.

Class objects are designed simply to create objects of a particular class. Each class object is implemented in the same module as the object that it is responsible for creating. To square the circle, class objects *don't* need to be created by other COM objects.

The means by which the COM subsystem gets hold of a class object that matches the CLSID of the object that it really wants to create depends on whether the server is a DLL or an EXE.

If the server is an EXE, it must register each of its class objects with the system as it starts up using the **CoRegisterClassObject()** API. This means that the EXE server must create all the class objects when it first starts executing, then pass **IUnknown** pointers to the system. Each of the class objects is associated with the CLSID of the object it creates. When the EXE shuts down, it has to tell the system that the class objects will no longer be available by calling **CoRevokeClassObject()**.

If the server is a DLL, the system will call into a well-known entry point that all DLL servers must expose called **DllGetClassObject()**. This function takes a CLSID for the object that needs to be created, and an IID parameter for an interface on the class object that should be returned in the third parameter:

```
STDAPI DllGetClassObject( REFCLSID rclsid,
                          REFIID   riid,
                          LPVOID*  ppv );
```

Class Factories

Once the system has got a pointer to an interface on the class object, it can use it to create a new object. Class objects are often known as **class factories**, because they usually implement the **IClassFactory** interface (this interface is the only one used by **CoCreateInstance()**).

IClassFactory (stripped of some advanced features) looks like this:

```
interface IClassFactory : IUnknown
{
   HRESULT CreateInstance(
      [in, unique]          IUnknown*  pUnkOuter,
      [in]                  REFIID     riid,
      [out, iid_is(riid)]   void**     ppvObject);

   HRESULT LockServer(
      [in]                  BOOL       fLock);
};
```

For now we'll just concentrate on the **CreateInstance()** *method; we'll discuss* **IClassFactory::LockServer()** *when we look at server lifetimes later on.*

The **CreateInstance()** method creates a new, *uninitialized* component of this class factory's class, **QI()**s it for the **riid** interface, and returns the interface pointer in **ppvObject**. In fact, **riid** and **ppvObject** are the parameters for **QueryInterface()**. The **pUnkOuter** parameter is the 'outer **IUnknown**', which is used in aggregation, discussed in Chapter 3. (**pUnkOuter** will always be **NULL** when aggregation isn't involved). This new object is, of course, eventually destroyed when the caller (or some other client) **Release()**s the interface pointer.

Note that **CreateInstance()** does *not* take a CLSID parameter. By definition, a class factory only knows how to create objects of one class, so there is no need for a CLSID at this stage.

CoGetClassObject

Internally, **CoCreateInstance()** calls **CoGetClassObject()**.

```
STDAPI CoGetClassObject(
   REFCLSID       rclsid,        // CLSID associated with the class object
   DWORD          dwClsContext,  // Context
   COSERVERINFO*  pServerInfo,   // Machine info
   REFIID         riid,      // Reference to the identifier of the interface
   LPVOID*        ppv            // Indirect pointer to the interface
   );
```

CoGetClassObject() does the hard work of determining which server is responsible for the CLSID, makes sure it's loaded, and then returns a pointer to the requested interface on the class object. **CoGetClassObject()** hides the differences between EXE and DLL servers.

CoCreateInstance() always uses **CoGetClassObject()** to get the **IClassFactory** interface from the class object. However, class objects may implement interfaces other than **IClassFactory**, so you may occasionally need to call **CoGetClassObject()** directly and ask for a different interface.

You may also choose to call **CoGetClassObject()** directly if you intend to create several objects of the same class. If you call **CoCreateInstance()** several times, the class factory may be created and destroyed between each call. If you use **CoGetClassObject()**, you can keep the class factory alive while you call **IClassFactory::CreateInstance()** several times. This will give you better performance.

39

CoCreateInstance() *always sets the* pServerInfo *parameter of*
CoGetClassObject() *to* NULL, *so COM only searches for the class object on the*
current machine. You don't need to call CoGetClassObject() *directly if all you want*
is for the pServerInfo *parameter to be exposed to you, because COM also provides a*
CoCreateInstanceEx() *function. You can find more information on*
CoCreateInstanceEx() *in Chapter 5.*

Server Lifetime

So far, we've seen how components use reference counts to manage their own lifetimes, but
how is the lifetime of the module that contains the components managed? There are two
answers to that question, depending on whether the server is packaged as a DLL or an
EXE. This difference arises because while EXEs take responsibility for unloading themselves,
DLLs must be unloaded by an external force.

Unloading and Locking DLL Servers

DLLs have to rely on the client to load and unload them. The problem is that only the DLL
itself will know when it's safe to be unloaded. The DLL will not want to be unloaded while it's
serving active components, so it needs to keep a count on the number of such objects. This
count should be incremented when objects are created, and decremented when they're destroyed.

The DLL should also keep track of calls to IClassFactory::LockServer(). The client calls
IClassFactory::LockServer(TRUE) to tell the server not to let itself be unloaded (by
incrementing the lock count), and IClassFactory::LockServer(FALSE) to decrement the
lock count. A client will make a call to lock the server to ensure that any subsequent
components can be created as quickly as possible without having to reload the server.

Since both the lock count and the count of the number of active objects are simply there so that
the DLL knows when it's safe to be unloaded, it's usual to see these counts combined into a
single count for the whole DLL. The DLL knows that it shouldn't be unloaded when the count
is greater than zero, and that it can be unloaded when the count equals zero.

COM clients should never unload DLL servers directly; they should ask COM to do it by calling
CoFreeUnusedLibraries(). CoFreeUnusedLibraries() is an extremely polite API that
checks with a DLL to see if it's being used, then unloads it if it isn't.
CoFreeUnusedLibraries() discovers whether a DLL is being used by calling
DllCanUnloadNow(). If DllCanUnloadNow() returns S_OK, the DLL can be unloaded; if it
returns S_FALSE, it can't.

DllCanUnloadNow() is another standard entry point that all DLL COM servers must implement
(like DllGetClassObject(), DllRegisterServer(), and DllUnregisterServer()), so it's
also prototyped as STDAPI:

```
STDAPI DllCanUnloadNow();
```

If a client doesn't call CoFreeUnusedLibraries(), DLL COM servers loaded by that process
will remain in memory until the client uninitializes COM with a call to CoUninitialize(),
which the client should always do before shutting down.

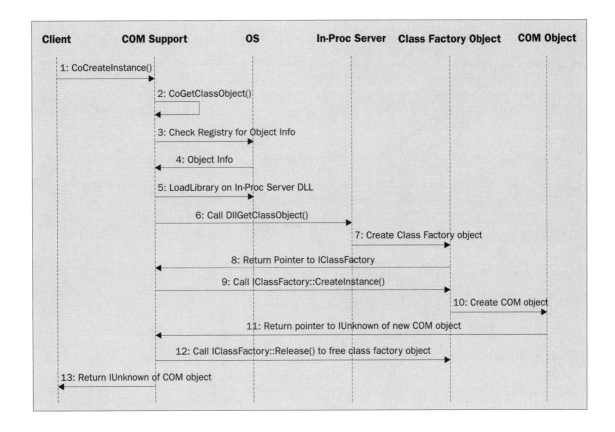

Unloading and Locking EXE Servers

Unlike passive DLLs, EXEs can be proactive and unload themselves as soon as its safe to do so. Specifically, the EXE should exit when either of two conditions occurs:

▶ If the lock count (the sum of all the **IClassFactory::LockServer()** calls) is zero, then the EXE exits when the last active object is destroyed (by its last **Release()**).

▶ If there are no active objects, then the EXE exits when the lock count goes to zero after a call to **IClassFactory::LockServer(FALSE)**.

Note that class factories are *not* included in the count of active objects. Class factories must be automatically created and registered when the EXE server starts up. COM hangs on to the class factories until the EXE revokes them while shutting down, but the EXE won't exit until its object count goes to zero. If the server included the number of active class factories in its object count, the count would never reach zero and it would never be able to shut down.

This means that having a reference count on an out-of-process server's class factory is not sufficient to keep the out-of-process server running (this runs counter to the usual rules of COM, of course), so **IClassFactory::LockServer(TRUE)** is vital to ensuring that EXE servers remain loaded if necessary.

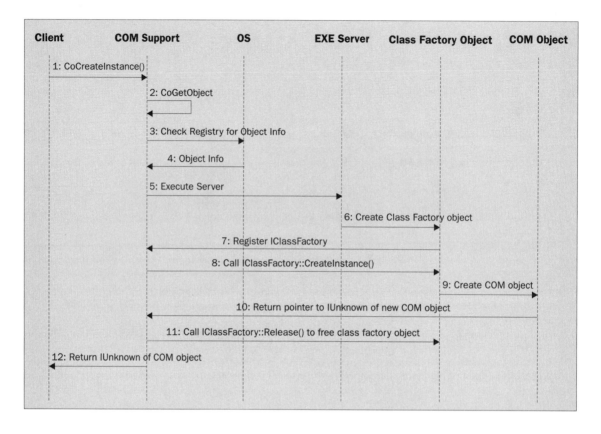

Interactive Servers

EXE COM servers can often be launched independently of COM, and may have a user interface. One example of this is Microsoft Word, which exposes a lot of its features to programmers via COM. It is important that applications like this know whether they have been launched by an interactive user or by COM, so that they can start up without the user interface when COM launches them. A local server can tell if it has been launched by COM (and not interactively by the user) by looking for /Embedding (or -embedding) on its command line.

Note also that interactive users are also clients of the server, and should be accorded a reference count. The server must not shut down until *all* clients are finished, although it can choose to hide its windows if all interactive clients are finished.

Completing the Basic COM DLL Server

Let's use the knowledge we've just gained to complete the example we began earlier in the chapter. Previously, we had a directory called **ComDll** in which we'd created an IDL definition of two simple interfaces. We passed this IDL file through the **MIDL** compiler to create C++ definitions for the interfaces and identifiers it contained. We also created a coclass implementation in the form of **CWroxComponent**. Now let's put this coclass into a DLL that we can compile, register and use.

First, run Developer Studio and use it to create a new Win32 Dynamic-Link Library project called **ComDll**. Store the project in the **ComDll** directory we created previously. Create a new source file called **ComDll.cpp**, and save it in the project directory. Add the following code to it:

```cpp
// ComDll.cpp

// The module's lock count
static long g_lLockCount = 0;

// Create class factory as global
#include "WroxClassFactory.h"
static CWroxClassFactory g_WroxClassFactory;

// MIDL-generated GUID Definitions
#include "ComDll_IDL_i.c"

extern "C"
BOOL WINAPI DllMain(HINSTANCE hInstance, DWORD dwReason,
                    LPVOID /*lpReserved*/)
{
    // No implementation needed here
    return TRUE;
}

STDAPI DllGetClassObject(REFCLSID rclsid, REFIID riid, LPVOID* ppv)
{
    if (rclsid == CLSID_WroxComponent)
        return g_WroxClassFactory.QueryInterface(riid, ppv);
    else
    {
        *ppv = NULL;
        return CLASS_E_CLASSNOTAVAILABLE;
    }
}

STDAPI DllCanUnloadNow(void)
{
    return (g_lLockCount == 0) ? S_OK : S_FALSE;
}

STDAPI DllRegisterServer(void)
{
    // Registration implementation should go here
    return S_OK;
}

STDAPI DllUnregisterServer(void)
{
    // Unregistration implementation should go here
    return S_OK;
}
```

The first thing that you can see in this file is the variable that we're using for the module's lock count, **g_lLockCount**. This will keep track of any active objects and any calls to **IClassFactory::LockServer()**. We'll see where this value gets updated shortly, but you can already see how it gets used in the implementation of **DllCanUnloadNow()**.

Next, you can see that we've included the **WroxClassFactory.h** file. We haven't actually created this file yet, but when we do, it will contain the definition of **CWroxClassFactory**, the class factory for the component we created earlier in the chapter. Beneath the **#include** statement, we've declared a global object of type **CWroxClassFactory**. This object, **g_WroxClassFactory**, is the class factory itself.

The next **#include** brings in the GUID definitions from the **_i.c** file. This file needs to be **#include**d once in any project that uses the **MIDL**-generated GUID constants.

Next up, you can see the definition of **DllMain()**. This function must be provided by all DLLs, whether they're COM servers or not. In our case, we don't need to do any special initialization in it, so we can simply return **TRUE** for success.

Following that we have **DllGetClassObject()**.This function is used to return interface pointers on the class object that creates objects of the type specified by the CLSID passed as the first parameter. You can see that we simply check the value of the CLSID against **CLSID_WroxComponent** and use **QueryInterface()** on our global class factory to return an interface pointer if appropriate. If the CLSID is for a class our server does not support, we return **CLASS_E_CLASSNOTAVAILABLE**.

The remaining functions are as simple as can be. **DllCanUnloadNow()** just returns **S_OK** if the lock count is zero, and **S_FALSE** otherwise, and we haven't provided an implementation for the registration functions at all. (We should, of course, but then we'd have to get deep into quite complicated registration manipulation. You can either implement these functions yourself, or wait until we see how ATL makes our lives much easier in the next chapter).

Next, we need to create a new module definition file to export the necessary functions from the DLL. Create a new text file containing the following text, save it in the project directory as **ComDll.def**, and add it to the project:

```
LIBRARY      "ComDll.dll"

EXPORTS
    DllCanUnloadNow      @1 PRIVATE
    DllGetClassObject    @2 PRIVATE
    DllRegisterServer    @3 PRIVATE
    DllUnregisterServer  @4 PRIVATE
```

This file just tells the linker to export the functions specified, so that they can be called from outside the DLL.

Now we'll turn our attention to the class factory. Create a new file in project directory and save it as **WroxClassFactory.h**. Add the following code to it:

```
#include "WroxComponent.h"
```

```cpp
class CWroxClassFactory : public IClassFactory
{
public:
    // Constructor
    CWroxClassFactory() : m_lRefCount(0) {}

    // The IUnknown methods
    STDMETHOD(QueryInterface)(REFIID riid, void** ppv)
    {
        if ( riid == IID_IUnknown)
            *ppv = static_cast<IUnknown*>(this);
        else if ( riid == IID_IClassFactory )
            *ppv = static_cast<IClassFactory*>(this);
        else
        {
            *ppv = NULL;
            return E_NOINTERFACE;
        }

        static_cast<IUnknown*>(*ppv)->AddRef();
        return S_OK;
    }

    STDMETHOD_(ULONG, AddRef)()
    {
        return InterlockedIncrement(&m_lRefCount);
    }

    STDMETHOD_(ULONG, Release)()
    {
        return InterlockedDecrement(&m_lRefCount);
    }

    // The IClassFactory methods
    STDMETHOD(CreateInstance)(IUnknown* punkOuter, REFIID riid, void**
ppvObject)
    {
        *ppvObject = NULL;     // Initialize

        // Disallow aggregation
        if (punkOuter != NULL)
            return CLASS_E_NOAGGREGATION;

        // Create a new CWroxComponent object
        CWroxComponent* pwc = new CWroxComponent;
        if (pwc == NULL)
            return E_OUTOFMEMORY;

        // QI for riid; destroy the object if QI fails
        HRESULT hr = pwc->QueryInterface(riid, ppvObject);
        if (FAILED(hr))
            delete pwc;
```

```
        return hr;
    }

    STDMETHOD(LockServer)(BOOL fLock)
    {
        if (fLock)
            InterlockedIncrement(&g_lLockCount);
        else
            InterlockedDecrement(&g_lLockCount);
        return S_OK;
    }

private:
    long m_lRefCount;
};
```

First we've **#include**d the **WroxComponent.h** file that contains our coclass implementation, then we've implemented the class factory. The class factory implements the **IClassFactory** interface, so we derive our class from **IClassFactory**. The C++ definition for **IClassFactory** comes from the system headers that we've got from **Windows.h** via the **WroxComponent.h** file.

Since the class factory is a COM object, it also implements **IUnknown** and the **IUnknown** methods. The implementations of these methods are very similar to the implementations that we provided for **CWroxComponent**, but note that we don't **delete** the object when the reference count gets to zero. We know that our class factory object hasn't been created on the heap, so we don't want to call **delete** on it. The class factory will live for as long as our DLL is loaded.

The implementation of **IClassFactory::CreateInstance()** is quite straightforward. We disallow aggregation (because we haven't discussed it yet), create a new instance of **CWroxComponent**, and call its **QueryInterface()** method to return the desired pointer to the caller. If **QueryInterface()** fails (which would happen if the object doesn't implement the requested interface), we make sure that the **CWroxComponent** object is **delete**d.

The implementation of **IClassFactory::LockServer()** just increments and decrements the global lock count for the module.

Now the only thing left to do is ensure that the lock count gets updated each time a **CWroxComponent** object is created or destroyed. Open up **WroxComponent.h** and add the following code to the constructor and destructor:

```
// Constructor
CWroxComponent() : m_lRefCount(0) {
                    InterlockedIncrement(&g_lLockCount); }

// Destructor
~CWroxComponent() { InterlockedDecrement(&g_lLockCount); }
```

Now we can be sure that the lock count will always be greater than zero when there are active components being served by this module.

At this stage, you can compile the **ComDll** project. We've now get a fully working COM server, the only thing that's stopping us from using it is the fact that it's not registered (remember that we didn't implement the registration functions). Since registry manipulation using the raw Win32 API can be quite convoluted, we'll add the registry entries by hand.

Open the IDL file that you created earlier in the chapter and copy the GUID for the coclass to the clipboard. (This GUID was denoted by **MY_GUID4** when we created the IDL file). Now fire up **RegEdit** and right-click the HKEY_CLASSES_ROOT\CLSID key. Choose New | Key from the context menu and paste the GUID from the clipboard into the new key. Make sure that the new key begins with an opening brace and terminates with a closing brace, like all the other keys beneath HKEY_CLASSES_ROOT\CLSID.

Select the new key and double-click on the (Default) value in the right-hand pane. This allows you to edit the default value for the new CLSID key. This default value should contain the name of the coclass for the CLSID that we just added, so type WroxComponent into the Value data box and click OK.

Now add a new key beneath the key you just created. Give this key the name InprocServer32. Edit the (Default) value of this key to give the location to the ComDll. Finally, right-click in the right-hand pane and add a new string value to the InprocServer32 key. Give the new value the name ThreadingModel and use Apartment as the data. The registry entries should look something like the ones shown below:

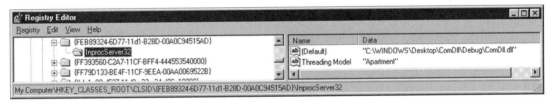

The OLE/COM Object Viewer

Now that you've compiled and registered the server, you can do a quick test to see if it's functioning by using the OLE/COM Object Viewer (**OleView.exe**). You'll find a shortcut to this program in the Microsoft Visual C++ 5.0 group in your Start | Programs menu, or you can activate it from within Developer Studio via the Tools menu. The OLE/COM Object Viewer is a useful tool for examining the COM components on your system.

Once the OLE/COM Object Viewer is running, select View | Expert Mode so that you can see all the objects on your system and expand the Object Classes folder, then All Objects. Beneath All Objects you should find an entry for WroxComponent; this represents the coclass that we just registered.

If you click on the text of this item to select it, the right hand pane will show the registry entries for this component on the Registry page. If you click on the + icon, the Object Viewer will create an instance of your component.

A list will appear beneath the name of the component showing all the interfaces that the Object Viewer knows are supported by the component. It determines this by calling

QueryInterface() for every interface listed in the registry. In our case, we only see **IUnknown**, because we haven't registered either of our custom interfaces. If we had built and registered the proxy-stub for our component, the other interfaces would also appear.

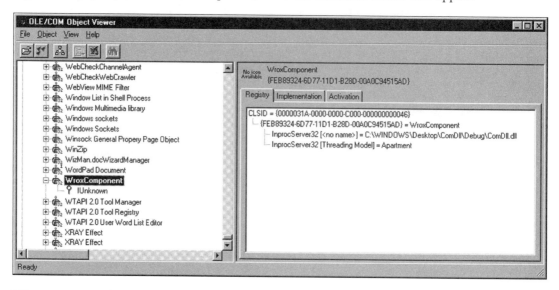

When you've got bored of seeing that your server can be instantiated with the Object Viewer, you can release it by right-clicking on WroxComponent and selecting Release Instance from the context menu. Note that clicking on the - sign will not release the component. The Object Viewer lets you know when a component is active by making its name bold.

Creating a Basic Client

Now we need to create a custom client to test this server. Create a new Win32 Console Application called Client in a subdirectory of the **ComDll** directory. Create a new text file, save it in the **Client** project directory as **Client.cpp**, and add the file to the project. Add the following code to the file:

```
// Client.cpp
#include <windows.h>

#include <iostream>
```

Here we've just added the headers that we'll need for the code to come. The **Windows.h** file gives us access to all the COM APIs and data types that we'll need, and **iostream** will enable us to use the standard library's stream classes so we can output text to the console.

Next, we need to **#include** the **MIDL**-generated header file and **_i.c** file from the **ComDll** project.

```
#include "..\comdll_idl.h"
#include "..\comdll_idl_i.c"
```

Here we've used the relative path to **#include** these files. These files give us access to the interface and GUID definitions that we need to be able to create and manipulate instances of the **WroxComponent** coclass.

Next, we can create the **main()** function for our project:

```
int main()
{
   CoInitialize(NULL);

   IWroxInterface* pWI = NULL;
   HRESULT hr = CoCreateInstance( CLSID_WroxComponent,
                                  NULL,
                                  CLSCTX_INPROC_SERVER,
                                  IID_IWroxInterface,
                                  reinterpret_cast<void**>(&pWI) );
   if (FAILED(hr))
   {
      std::cout << "CoCreateInstance() failed : 0x"
                << std::hex << hr << "\n";
      CoUninitialize();
      return 0;
   }

   pWI->Alert();
```

The first step here is to initialize the COM library, as all EXE clients and servers must do before making use of its functions. Then we declare a pointer to the **IWroxInterface** interface and call **CoCreateInstance** to create an instance of the **WroxComponent** coclass and get a pointer to **IWroxInterface**. We check the **HRESULT** returned by **CoCreateInstance()** for failure, and output a message, uninitialize COM, and leave the function if it did fail. If everything worked, we call the interface's **Alert()** method.

Since the **WroxComponent** implements two interfaces, we can add some code to call **QueryInterface()** to retrieve a pointer to the other interface:

```
   IWroxSimple* pWS = NULL;
   hr = pWI->QueryInterface(IID_IWroxSimple,
                            reinterpret_cast<void**>(&pWS));

   if (FAILED(hr))
   {
      std::cout << "QueryInterface() failed : 0x"
                << std::hex << hr << "\n";
      pWI->Release();
      CoUninitialize();
      return 0;
   }

   pWS->Display();
```

Once again, we check for failure before attempting to use the **pWS** interface pointer. This time if there's a failure, we have to remember to **Release()** the **pWI** interface pointer before returning. If the call to **QueryInterface()** succeeds, we can call the **IWroxSimple::Display()** method.

Finally, we can **Release()** both the interface pointers, call **CoUninitialize()**, and return from the function:

```
    pWS->Release();
    pWI->Release();
    CoUninitialize();
    return 0;
};
```

Now you can run and test the code. If all goes well, you will see two message boxes appear telling you when the **Alert()** and **Display()** methods have been called. If anything goes wrong, the error code will be output to the console window. You can use this error code to find out what the problem is by using the Error Lookup utility provided with Visual C++ (Tools | Error Lookup). Just enter the code into the Value box provided and hit the Look Up button.

Summary

We've seen a lot of theory in this chapter, and in the example you've learned just how hard it can be to set up even the simplest of COM classes. Imagine that we wanted to create a new module that contained more objects — we'd have to:

- Create class factories for every coclass in the module
- Implement the **IUnknown** functions on every one of the objects
- Keep track of reference counts for each object and for the module itself
- Implement slightly different code depending on whether the module was an EXE or a DLL
- Write registration code

This is without even considering some of the subtleties and more advanced features of COM that we haven't met yet. There's a lot of housekeeping to do when implementing COM servers!

Fortunately, as you'll see in the next chapter, ATL comes to our rescue. A combination of ATL itself and Developer Studio's Wizards make it incredibly easy to write high quality COM servers. ATL makes it possible for you to concentrate on the code that's specific to your component by providing the implementations for the class factories, the **IUnknown** methods, reference counting and registration. You'll see just how easy it is starting from the next chapter.

2

Building and Calling a COM Object Using ATL

In the last chapter, you saw a lot of the theory behind COM. In this chapter, we're going to start our practical exploration of what ATL can do by building a simple COM server DLL, and a couple of client applications to test it. ATL programming is mainly about writing COM servers, but just to show it can be done, we'll also use ATL to write a client. While we're doing this, we'll be covering the following topics:

- The ATL COM AppWizard
- Examining the generated code
- The ATL Object Wizard
- Registry Scripts
- Adding methods and properties to a server
- Creating a client using ATL
- Using the `#import` directive
- Creating a client in Visual Basic

You'll see how easy it is to create fully functional COM servers without having to write all the code we considered in the last chapter, thanks to the combination of Wizard-generated code, and library code provided by ATL. As we progress, we'll compare the stages we go through in this example with the work that we had to do in the last chapter. You'll see how the two approaches compare, and some of the facilities that ATL provides to make COM programming easier.

Using the ATL COM AppWizard

First, we're going to create the skeleton of a new DLL server project using the ATL COM AppWizard. Fire up Developer Studio and create a new project. Give your project the name Simple, and choose ATL COM AppWizard as the project type.

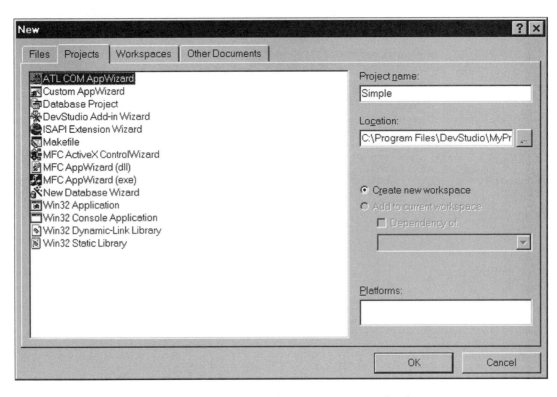

When you press OK, the Wizard will run and show you its one-and-only screen:

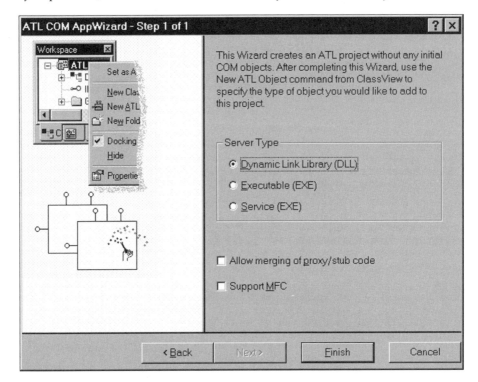

Like the other AppWizards supplied with Visual C++, the ATL COM AppWizard presents you with a number of options related to the creation of a new project. In this case, all the options fit on to a single step of the Wizard.

Server Type

The ATL COM AppWizard lets you package your COM server in one of three ways:

- As a DLL
- As an executable (an EXE file)
- As an NT service

We saw in the last chapter that the code necessary for creating a COM server differs depending on whether it's packaged as a DLL or an EXE. By picking one of the first two options, the AppWizard will generate the code appropriate to the module type. If you pick the final option, the AppWizard will create a project suitable for an EXE COM server, but will also add extra code to allow the executable to act as an **NT service**. A service is a special type of application that can be started automatically at boot-up, and can be run under the **SYSTEM** account. We won't be looking at services in this book — for more information about them, see *Professional DCOM Programming*. We'll use the default option to create a DLL server for this example.

> *In most cases, choosing a DLL server will be a good choice. Full controls are almost always created as in-process servers, because they require access to things like device contexts that can't easily be shared between processes. Creating a DLL server doesn't mean that you have to live without the benefits of process isolation or remoting. It is possible to isolate DLL servers from the client process, or to allow them to be accessed remotely, by using* **surrogates**, *which are explained in Chapter 5.*

Allow Merging of Proxy-Stub Code

This option lets you choose to merge the proxy-stub code into your server DLL so that you can get just one file to redistribute. The proxy-stub code won't *actually* be compiled into your DLL unless you also manually define the symbol **_MERGE_PROXYSTUB**, but the option adds code to your project to make everything work if you do. For this simple example, we'll leave the proxy-stub generation as it is.

> *Note that this checkbox is disabled for either of the EXE server types. Proxy-stub code needs to be in a DLL so that it can run in the process of the client. Also be aware that proxy-stub code is often required even when the server itself is implemented in a DLL; we'll see why in Chapter 5.*

Support MFC

Checking the Support MFC checkbox gives you access to MFC classes, which may make writing your code easier. This is especially useful when you're writing ATL COM servers that wrap existing C++ objects that use MFC. Be aware, though, that including MFC support will increase the size of your server, and will make it necessary for clients to have the correct MFC libraries on their machines. You can choose to link to MFC statically, in which case you'll just get a much larger control!

Note that Microsoft does not provide MFC support for EXE-based servers. It is possible to add MFC to ATL EXE servers yourself, and if you have a need to do this, you can consult the Microsoft Knowledge Base article Q173974. We won't go into this topic in any more detail in this book, as we won't be including MFC support in the servers we write.

Now press <u>F</u>inish to exit from the Wizard. As usual, you'll get a summary screen, telling you what the Wizard is intending to create for you:

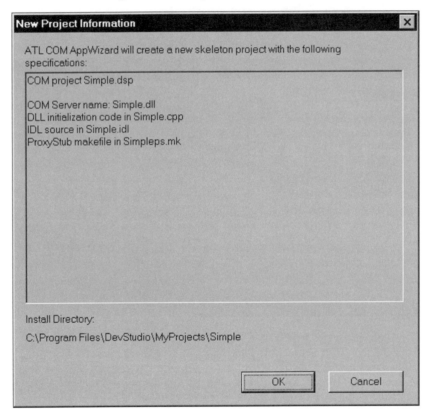

Examining the Generated Code

Now that we have the skeleton for our container application, let's take a look at what's been produced.

The Files

The list of files produced by the Wizard is shown in the following picture. You'll see that there are far fewer than for a typical MFC project — we have:

▶ Precompiled header files, **StdAfx.h** and **StdAfx.cpp**

▶ An IDL file, **Simple.idl**

▶ Resource files, **Resource.h** and **Simple.rc**

▶ A module definition file, **Simple.def**

▶ A C++ source file, **Simple.cpp**

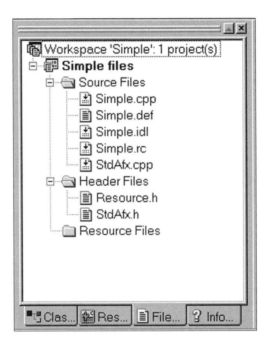

If you look at the project directory, you will also see three more files: **Simple.h**, **Simpleps.mk** *and* **Simpleps.def**. *The first is simply an empty header file, but the other two are the makefile and module definition file for the proxy-stub DLL. We'll look at creating the proxy-stub DLL in Chapter 5.*

The Precompiled Header Files

Let's take a brief look at **Stdafx.h**, as it contains some interesting information, as well as including the ATL headers:

```
// stdafx.h : include file for standard system include files,
//      or project specific include files that are used frequently,
//      but are changed infrequently

#if
!defined(AFX_STDAFX_H__CD5356E5_6C8B_11D1_A607_00A0C94BC9C3__INCLUDED_)
#define AFX_STDAFX_H__CD5356E5_6C8B_11D1_A607_00A0C94BC9C3__INCLUDED_
```

```
#if _MSC_VER >= 1000
#pragma once
#endif // _MSC_VER >= 1000

#define STRICT


#define _WIN32_WINNT 0x0400
#define _ATL_APARTMENT_THREADED


#include <atlbase.h>
//You may derive a class from CComModule and use it if you want to
//override something, but do not change the name of _Module
extern CComModule _Module;
#include <atlcom.h>

//{{AFX_INSERT_LOCATION}}
// Microsoft Developer Studio will insert additional declarations
// immediately before the previous line.

#endif //
!defined(AFX_STDAFX_H__CD5356E5_6C8B_11D1_A607_00A0C94BC9C3__INCLUDED)
```

_WIN32_WINNT

This symbol is used by ATL and the Windows system headers to protect code that is only available for a particular version of Windows NT. If this symbol is defined to be greater than or equal to **0x400**, then code specific to Windows NT 4.0 can be compiled into your project. If this symbol is not defined, or it is defined to be a value less than **0x400**, then that code will not be compiled into your project.

In most cases the code protected by this symbol is related to DCOM (DCOM first became available with Windows NT 4.0), and will now work on Windows 95 with DCOM installed. To get access to just this code, you can define the **_WIN32_DCOM** symbol instead.

The implications of this are summarized below:

▶ If your code is destined to run only on version 4.0 or later of Windows NT, you can leave the **_WIN32_WINNT** symbol in **StdAfx.h**.

▶ If your code is intended to run on any system with DCOM installed (Windows NT 4.0 or Windows 95 with DCOM), you should remove the **#define** for **_WIN32_WINNT** and replace it with **#define _WIN32_DCOM**.

▶ If your code is intended to run on older versions of Windows 95 or Windows NT without DCOM installed, just remove the **#define** for **_WIN32_WINNT**.

_ATL_APARTMENT_THREADED

The next definition in this file is for the symbol **_ATL_APARTMENT_THREADED**. The definition of this symbol defines the default threading model of the DLL to be the apartment model. We'll be looking at threading in Chapter 5.

_Module

The other item of interest in **StdAfx.h** is the declaration of a **CComModule** object called **_Module**. **CComModule** implements the basic functionality of a COM server (whether in a DLL or EXE), and provides basic services such as registering and instantiating the objects supported by the server, and managing their lifetimes by means of an object map. We'll look at **CComModule** in more detail later in the chapter, and object maps are covered in Chapter 3.

> *Note that the* **CComModule** *object must be global and it must be called* **_Module**, *since it's referenced throughout the ATL header files.*

The IDL File

The IDL file is used by **MIDL** to produce several things: the C++ headers for our interfaces, the type library for our server, and the marshaling source code. At this stage, the IDL only contains the bare minimum needed for it to compile, such as the name of the library and its GUID. Once we start adding coclasses, interfaces, and their methods and properties, the Wizards will insert the appropriate code into the IDL for us.

```
// Simple.idl : IDL source for Simple.dll
//

// This file will be processed by the MIDL tool to
// produce the type library (Simple.tlb) and marshaling code.

import "oaidl.idl";
import "ocidl.idl";

[
    uuid(CD5356E1-6C8B-11D1-A607-00A0C94BC9C3),
    version(1.0),
    helpstring("Simple 1.0 Type Library")
]
library SIMPLELib
{
    importlib("stdole32.tlb");
    importlib("stdole2.tlb");

};
```

You saw some IDL in Chapter 1, but here you can see some more elements of the language. First, there's the **import** statement. This is similar to **#include** in C++. **import** provides access to all the typedefs, declarations and interface definitions in the file being **import**ed. The IDL files being imported here are system IDL files containing definitions of all the standard interfaces and types.

The next new element is the **library** statement. Items declared or referenced in the **library** block will be compiled into the type library file. Type libraries can also have IDL attributes associated with them, such as the **[uuid()]**, **[version()]** and **[helpstring()]** attributes used here.

Within the type library block, you can see that the **importlib()** statement has been used to bring in the standard COM (OLE) type libraries. It's worth making the distinction between this and the quite similar **import**. The latter is used to include actual definitions from another IDL file, in the same way that **#include** is used to include structure and class definitions in C++. **importlib()** is used where you don't have the original IDL, but only the type library; it inserts a reference to the type library into the IDL. This means that at runtime, clients accessing **simple.tlb** will be able to use the information in **stdole32.tlb** and **stdole2.tlb** via these references. A consequence of this is that any libraries referenced in **importlib()** statements must be distributed with the application (or be already present on the target machine).

Custom Build Step

The **MIDL** compilation step occurs automatically when the project is built, because the AppWizard created a custom build step. We can see that step by examining the settings for our IDL file — right-click on the IDL file's icon in FileView and select the Settings... menu item from the context menu.

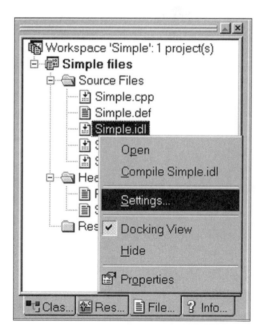

Now you can see the command line used to get **MIDL** to generate output based on the IDL file:

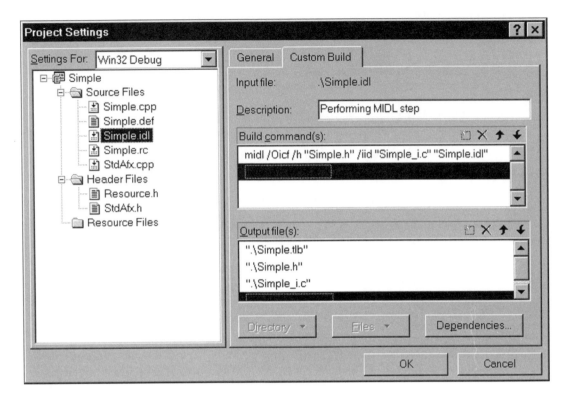

The flags used by the **MIDL** command are as follows:

▶ **/Oicf** specifies the marshaling method to be used.

▶ **/h** gives the name for the header file. This isn't absolutely necessary in this case, as the default action is to add '**.h**' onto the IDL filename.

▶ **/iid** gives the name for the file that will hold the interface identifier code. Again, this isn't absolutely necessary, as the default action is to add '**_i.c**' onto the IDL filename.

We'll be seeing the IDL file and the significance of **MIDL**'s output again as we progress through the chapter.

The Module Definition File

Simple.def just lists the functions that need to be exported from the DLL:

```
; Simple.def : Declares the module parameters.

LIBRARY      "Simple.DLL"
```

```
EXPORTS
    DllCanUnloadNow       @1 PRIVATE
    DllGetClassObject     @2 PRIVATE
    DllRegisterServer     @3 PRIVATE
    DllUnregisterServer   @4 PRIVATE
```

You can see that all the functions you'd expect to see exported by a COM DLL server are listed. We looked at these functions in Chapter 1, and we'll see exactly how ATL implements them in the next section.

The Source File

At the top of **Simple.cpp** you can see a number of header files included:

```
#include "stdafx.h"
#include "resource.h"
#include "initguid.h"
#include "Simple.h"

#include "Simple_i.c"
```

Simple.h is a **MIDL**-maintained header file that will contain the C++ definitions for all the interfaces defined in the project's IDL file (once we've added some), as well as **extern** declarations of constants for the GUIDs. **Simple_i.c** is generated entirely by **MIDL**, and contains the non-**extern** definitions of the GUIDs. The fact that it is generated by **MIDL** explains why you won't be able to find it until you've built the whole project, and why you'll get a compiler error if you try to compile **Simple.cpp** in isolation.

> The non-**extern** definition of a GUID actually defines the GUID. Obviously, this must be done only once, and all other references to this GUID must be **extern**.

MIDL-generated GUID constants have the name of the interface, coclass, or library prefixed with **IID_**, **CLSID_** or **LIBID_** respectively, and must be included exactly once in a file in your project.

Confusingly, **initguid.h** is a system header file, despite the fact that it's enclosed in quotes, rather than the more usual angled brackets. It just allows you to use the **DEFINE_GUID()** macro to initialize GUIDs. Neither the **.h** nor the **_i.c** file produced by **MIDL** make use of the **DEFINE_GUID()** macro, so its usefulness is questionable.

Further down **Simple.cpp**, you can see the definition of **_Module** and the server's object map, which is used to list the coclasses that this server implements. The object map is currently empty because we don't have any coclasses in our project yet. We'll look at the object map again when there's more to see.

```
CComModule _Module;

BEGIN_OBJECT_MAP(ObjectMap)
END_OBJECT_MAP()
```

The remainder of **Simple.cpp** is taken up with the implementations of the DLL's exposed functions. The first function is **DllMain()**, the standard Windows entry point to a DLL.

```
extern "C"
BOOL WINAPI DllMain(HINSTANCE hInstance, DWORD dwReason,
   LPVOID /*lpReserved*/)
{
   if (dwReason == DLL_PROCESS_ATTACH)
   {
      _Module.Init(ObjectMap, hInstance);
      DisableThreadLibraryCalls(hInstance);
   }
   else if (dwReason == DLL_PROCESS_DETACH)
      _Module.Term();
   return TRUE;    // ok
}
```

Its main purpose is to initialize and free the data members used by the **CComModule** object, by calling its **Init()** and **Term()** functions. Note that the module is passed the object map as the first parameter to the **Init()** method.

The call to **DisableThreadLibraryCalls()** disables the calls that the operating system would normally make to **DllMain()** when threads attach to or detach from the DLL. This can reduce the amount of server code that will have to be kept in memory, and is entirely in keeping with the ATL team's constant quest for extreme efficiency. As you will see time and again during the book, ATL was designed to be as small and fast as possible.

The rest of the functions in **Simple.cpp** call the corresponding methods on the server's **CComModule** object:

```
STDAPI DllCanUnloadNow(void)
{
    return (_Module.GetLockCount()==0) ? S_OK : S_FALSE;
}
```

```
STDAPI DllGetClassObject(REFCLSID rclsid, REFIID riid, LPVOID* ppv)
{
    return _Module.GetClassObject(rclsid, riid, ppv);
}
```

```
STDAPI DllRegisterServer(void)
{
    // registers object, typelib and all interfaces in typelib
    return _Module.RegisterServer(TRUE);
}
```

```
STDAPI DllUnregisterServer(void)
{
    _Module.UnregisterServer();
    return S_OK;
}
```

It's worth saying a few words about each of these functions, which need to be implemented by all DLLs that support COM. In our case, the implementation is pretty simple, since all the hard work is done by **CComModule**:

➤ **DllCanUnloadNow()** is a function that's called to determine whether a DLL is still in use. If it's OK for the DLL to be unloaded, it will return **true**. In the case of our ATL server, the **CComModule** object maintains a lock count, and it is safe to unload when that reaches zero.

➤ **DllGetClassObject()** retrieves the class object (class factory) for a coclass. Given a **CLSID** and an interface ID, the function will attempt to create a class object and return a pointer to the interface.

➤ **DllRegisterServer()** is used to tell the DLL to create registry entries for all the classes supported by this server.

➤ **DllUnregisterServer()** tells the DLL to remove those entries which were created using **DllRegisterServer()**.

Building the Server

Although our server doesn't do anything at all at this stage, it's still worth building it, in order to see the files that **MIDL** creates for us. When you build, you'll find that five new files are produced, and three of these (**Simple.h**, **Simple.tlb** and **Simple_i.c**) are listed under the External Dependencies folder in FileView. The other two (**Simple_p.c** and **dlldata.c**) are created to help with the marshaling for this DLL.

We discussed the **.h** and **.c** files when we looked at the **#include**s in **Simple.cpp**. You shouldn't ever need to touch these, as they're maintained by **MIDL** from the information in the IDL file. The file **Simple.tlb** is the (currently empty) type library for the server. Once again, it is **MIDL**'s task to maintain it.

Using the ATL Object Wizard

In order to make our server do anything useful, we need to add a coclass to it, which is done using the ATL Object Wizard. You can start up the Object Wizard using the Insert | New ATL Object... menu item. The dialog that is displayed shows all the different types of COM object that can be added to a server:

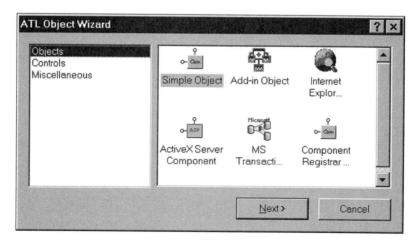

Here's a quick summary of the different types of component available:

Group	Object
Objects	Simple Object adds a minimal COM object
	Add-in Object creates a COM object that can be used to extend Developer Studio
	Internet Explorer Object creates an object that contains all the interfaces necessary for it to work with Internet Explorer, but has no user interface
	ActiveX Server Component creates an object that can be used as part of an Active Server Page (ASP) with Internet Information Server
	MS Transaction Server Component includes the header files needed by MTS, and makes the object non-aggregatable
	Component Registrar Object adds an object that implements the **IComponentRegistrar** interface, which is used to register the objects in a server individually
Controls	Full Control adds an object that implements all the interfaces needed by a full ActiveX control (OCX), such that it should work with any ActiveX control container
	Internet Explorer Control adds a control that has all the interfaces (and UI functionality) needed by Internet Explorer and other compatible browsers
	Property Page adds a property page object
Miscellaneous	Dialog adds a class that implements a dialog

Many of these (such as the Microsoft Transaction Server components or the Add-ins) are pretty specialized, and we'll meet the Controls group later. For the present, we just want to add a basic, simple object to the project.

Click on the Simple Object icon, and then on the Next button to bring up the Properties dialog. The Properties dialog consists of two pages: Names and Attributes.

Names

As you might expect, the Names page allows you to specify the names of various aspects of the component. The Short Name acts as the root for all the other names on the dialog. If you fill in the Short Name with CalcEaster (we're going to be writing a simple component to calculate the date of Easter for any year), you'll see how the remaining boxes are populated automatically.

If you want to change any of the names from their default values, you can just alter the text in the appropriate edit box. In this case, we'd like to ensure that our component has a unique Prog ID, so we'll change it to Wrox.CalcEaster. You should end up with something like this:

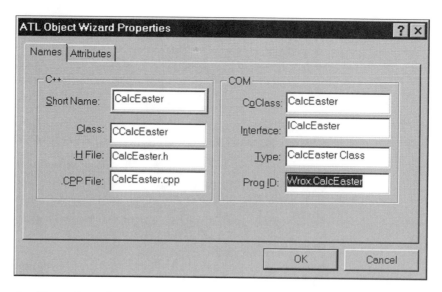

The Wizard will use the information you provide to create a C++ class with the name specified in the **Class** field, in a header and source file named after the values in the **.H** File and **.CPP** File boxes. The C++ class will represent a coclass with the name specified in the **CoClass** field (this value will be used as the name of the coclass in the IDL file). The coclass will expose a single interface with the name specified in the **Interface** box. The values of the **Type** and **Prog ID** fields will ultimately end up in the registry:

▶ **Type** will be used to provide a readable description of the coclass

▶ **Prog ID** will be used to allow the coclass to be created via its ProgID.

Attributes

Once you've entered the names as shown, click on the **Attributes** tab. This tab displays a page showing several options that affect the functioning of our control:

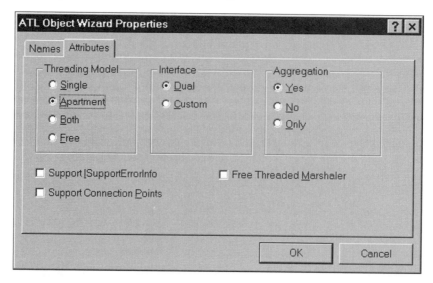

We don't need to change any of these options for our simple example — that's what default settings are for, after all — but rest assured that we'll be looking at all these settings and what they mean as we progress through the book. For the determinedly curious, however, we'll just give you a quick description, and tell you when we'll be looking at them in more detail.

The Threading Model determines how this component will implement threading. The various COM threading models (and how to choose the one you need) are covered in more detail in Chapter 5. For most simple components, you're quite safe sticking with the apartment threading model.

The Interface determines whether this component will support the **IDispatch** interface required by Automation. Leaving our selection as Dual ensures that it will. Automation, **IDispatch** and dual interfaces are covered in Chapter 4.

The Aggregation setting determines whether this object can be part of a composite COM object; the default value says that it can. Aggregation is covered in Chapter 3.

The three checkboxes at the bottom of the window provide some advanced options. The Free Threaded Marshaler option has to do with marshaling interface pointers between threads in the same process. We won't be looking at this option in the book. Checking the Support ISupportErrorInfo box adds support for the **ISupportErrorInfo** interface, which will enable your object to return rich error and status information to callers. Finally, Support Connection Points makes the object capable of originating events. We'll look at connection points in Chapter 6, and rich error-reporting in Chapter 4.

For this example, you can leave all these options as they are, and simply press the OK button to generate the code.

Examining the Generated Code

Let's look at what has been generated for us by the Wizard. We have three new files, and a few changes to existing ones. The new files are:

> **CalcEaster.h**
>
> **CalcEaster.cpp**
>
> **CalcEaster.rgs**

The **CalcEaster.h** and **.cpp** files implement the simple COM object itself. The **.cpp** file is essentially empty apart from a **#include** for the header file, **CalcEaster.h**, which looks like this:

```
// CalcEaster.h : Declaration of the CCalcEaster

#ifndef __CALCEASTER_H_
#define __CALCEASTER_H_

#include "resource.h"        // main symbols
```

```
////////////////////////////////////////////////////////////////////////////
// CCalcEaster
class ATL_NO_VTABLE CCalcEaster :
   public CComObjectRootEx<CComSingleThreadModel>,
   public CComCoClass<CCalcEaster, &CLSID_CalcEaster>,
   public IDispatchImpl<ICalcEaster, &IID_ICalcEaster, &LIBID_SIMPLELib>
{
public:
   CCalcEaster()
   {
   }

DECLARE_REGISTRY_RESOURCEID(IDR_CALCEASTER)

BEGIN_COM_MAP(CCalcEaster)
   COM_INTERFACE_ENTRY(ICalcEaster)
   COM_INTERFACE_ENTRY(IDispatch)
END_COM_MAP()

// ICalcEaster
public:
};

#endif //__CALCEASTER_H_
```

There are several important points to note from this file. Firstly, notice that our class definition uses multiple inheritance to inherit from three ATL classes. As you might expect, given the name of the library, all the classes are templates. **CComObjectRootEx<>** handles object reference count management, **CComCoClass<>** defines the class factory and aggregation model for the component, and **IDispatchImpl<>** provides the implementation of the **IDispatch** portion of the dual interface.

The **ATL_NO_VTABLE** macro wraps **__declspec(novtable)**, a special compiler optimization introduced for Visual C++ 5.0, which tells the compiler to create a class without initializing the vtable in the constructor. This means that the linker can eliminate both the vtable, and all the functions it points to, reducing the size of your code. It also means that you can't call any virtual functions in the constructor of such a class.

> *Not having a vtable is useful for classes that are only ever used as base classes, but any class that can be independently instantiated must not use **ATL_NO_VTABLE**. Such classes need a properly initialized vtable pointer. As you'll see, the class we've just created with the Object Wizard is only ever used as a base class.*

DECLARE_REGISTRY_RESOURCEID() implements script-based registry support (described in the following section), and provides the resource ID for the registry script information.

The **BEGIN_COM_MAP** and **END_COM_MAP** macros define the COM interface map, which is the way in which the COM interfaces in your object can be exposed to clients using **QueryInterface()**. This means that if an interface isn't in the map, a client can't get a pointer to it. The way in which COM maps work is covered in the next chapter.

Registry Scripts

The RGS file contains a script for adding entries to the registry for our component. This script is compiled into the server as a custom **"REGISTRY"** resource, and is used when the server is told to register itself.

The registry script is understood by the ATL Registrar, which is ultimately responsible for adding the entries to the registry. Your code has to have access to the Registrar in order for this to work, and there are two ways in which this can be achieved.

The first method relies on the fact that the Registrar lives in a DLL called **Atl.dll**, so you'd normally make sure that **Atl.dll** is present and registered on any machine that wants to register this component. This may require you to distribute **Atl.dll** with your component.

> *Note that there are two versions of **Atl.dll** on the VC++ 5 CD: one ANSI (for Windows 95 systems), the other Unicode (for Windows NT). Make sure that you install the correct one!*

The second method uses static linking. If you choose the Win32 MinDependency target when building the component, the Registrar code will be linked into the component, so that it doesn't rely on **Atl.dll**. In this case, of course, your component will be larger in size.

Here's the **CalcEaster.rgs** file for our project:

```
HKCR
{
    Wrox.CalcEaster.1 = s 'CalcEaster Class'
    {
        CLSID = s '{2D15E122-6CA4-11D1-A607-00A0C94BC9C3}'
    }
    Wrox.CalcEaster = s 'CalcEaster Class'
    {
        CurVer = s 'Wrox.CalcEaster.1'
    }
    NoRemove CLSID
    {
        ForceRemove {2D15E122-6CA4-11D1-A607-00A0C94BC9C3}
                                            = s 'CalcEaster Class'
        {
            ProgID = s 'Wrox.CalcEaster.1'
            VersionIndependentProgID = s 'Wrox.CalcEaster'
            ForceRemove 'Programmable'
            InprocServer32 = s '%MODULE%'
```

```
            {
                val ThreadingModel = s 'Apartment'
            }
        }
    }
}
```

Although it may look slightly unfamiliar, the syntax is relatively straightforward. Registry scripts use the following keywords:

Keyword	Description
ForceRemove	When creating the following key, ensures that any existing key has been completely removed first before adding the key back. This is useful if the key already exists, but subkeys or values beneath it need changing
NoRemove	Doesn't remove the following key during unregistration. (With the exception of root keys, all keys specified in the script will be removed during unregistration unless this keyword is present)
val	The following is a named value
Delete	Deletes the following key during registration
s	The following value is a string
d	The following value is a DWORD

Any text that isn't one of these keywords is either a key or a named value, or the data for that item. Anything to the right of an equals sign is data to be placed in the registry. If the item to the left of the equals sign has the word **val** in front of it, then the data will be added to a named value; otherwise, it will be added as the default data for that key. The nested braces represent the levels of the keys in the registry. The **%MODULE%** keyword represents a replaceable parameter, rather like those you can use in DOS batch files. In this case, it represents the full pathname of our DLL.

There are a few important things to note:

- HKCR is **HKEY_CLASSES_ROOT**, so all the registry entries will be within that hive, as you would expect.

- The **CLSID** subkey has the **NoRemove** keyword applied. This is very important because the information in the RGS file is used to unregister the component, as well as to register it. When instructed to unregister the server, the Registrar can use the information in this file to find all the entries to remove. You can now see why **NoRemove** is important — if it weren't there, the entire **CLSID** key (and all its subkeys) would be wiped out when the server unregistered itself. RGS files can be very dangerous — be careful with them!

- The registry script as generated won't allow anyone to use the version-independent ProgID (**Wrox.CalcEaster**) to activate our component, because it doesn't have a **CLSID** subkey. We can fix that by copying the **CLSID** line from the versioned prog ID (**Wrox.CalcEaster.1**) like this:

```
Wrox.CalcEaster = s 'CalcEaster Class'
{
    CLSID = s '{2D15E122-6CA4-11D1-A607-00A0C94BC9C3}'
    CurVer = s 'Wrox.CalcEaster.1'
}
```

Changed Files

The IDL file shows the biggest change now that we've added our coclass. Now it looks like this, with the new lines shown highlighted:

```
import "oaidl.idl";
import "ocidl.idl";

    [
        object,
        uuid(2D15E121-6CA4-11D1-A607-00A0C94BC9C3),
        dual,
        helpstring("ICalcEaster Interface"),
        pointer_default(unique)
    ]
    interface ICalcEaster : IDispatch
    {
    };
[
    uuid(CD5356E1-6C8B-11D1-A607-00A0C94BC9C3),
    version(1.0),
    helpstring("Simple 1.0 Type Library")
]
library SIMPLELib
{
    importlib("stdole32.tlb");
    importlib("stdole2.tlb");

    [
        uuid(2D15E122-6CA4-11D1-A607-00A0C94BC9C3),
        helpstring("CalcEaster Class")
    ]
    coclass CalcEaster
    {
        [default] interface ICalcEaster;
    };
};
```

The IDL now contains entries for the **CalcEaster** coclass, and its interface **ICalcEaster**, derived from **IDispatch**. You can see that GUIDs have been automatically generated for the coclass and its interface, and that the CLSID in the IDL file matches the CLSID in the RGS file, as it should.

The only other significant change at this stage is to **Simple.cpp**, where we find a new header and an addition to the object map:

```
#include "stdafx.h"
#include "resource.h"
#include "initguid.h"
#include "Simple.h"

#include "Simple_i.c"
#include "CalcEaster.h"


CComModule _Module;

BEGIN_OBJECT_MAP(ObjectMap)
    OBJECT_ENTRY(CLSID_CalcEaster, CCalcEaster)
END_OBJECT_MAP()
```

The object map is essentially a list of the objects in this server. When the **CComModule** object is initialized by calling its **Init()** function, it updates the registry for each object in the object map. We'll talk more about these in the next chapter.

Adding Methods and Properties

We now have a server that we can build, but it doesn't do much except register itself, because we haven't added any methods that clients can call, or properties that they can manipulate. We need a simple task for the server to perform, and for this example, we'll get it to calculate the date of Easter Day in any year.

Methods and Properties

A word is required about terminology at this point. **Methods** are the functions that clients call, and that map straight onto functions in an interface. It is also convenient for clients to think of servers as having **properties** (i.e. data items) that they can manipulate, so that instead of having to say something like:

```
myObj.SetYear(n)
```

one can write:

```
myObj.Year = n
```

However, we know that interfaces only expose functions, and that it isn't actually possible to access data within a COM object. This deception is managed through the IDL file, where properties are implemented in terms of 'get' and 'put' methods, as we'll see shortly. A language such as Visual Basic is then at liberty to let users write code in terms of variable-like properties, which it maps onto the appropriate get and put functions.

Since the main aim of this exercise is to demonstrate how to add methods and properties to an ATL component, we'll go about doing this in a fairly roundabout way, as follows:

▶ Add a property to set the desired year

▶ Add a method to do the calculation

▶ Add properties to return the day and month for Easter

In a real server, you probably wouldn't drag things out like this — you could merge the entire operation into one call. However, we want to see both properties and methods in use, so we'll split it up.

Adding Properties

To add a property, right-click on the entry for the **ICalcEaster** interface in ClassView.

> **ICalcEaster** *appears twice in ClassView, once in its own right, and once as a member of the* **CCalcEaster** *wrapper class. You can click on either one.*

This will bring up a context menu that contains entries allowing you to add methods and properties. Select Add Property... to bring up the Add Property to Interface dialog, and enter a property called Year, of type short.

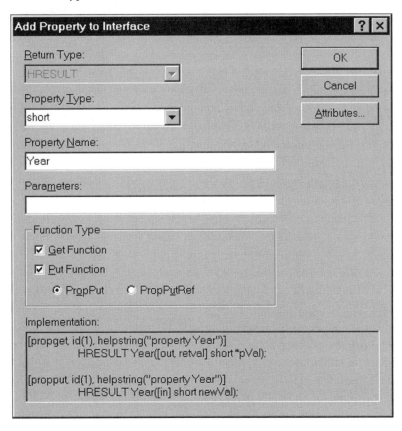

We can add a Get Function, a Put Function or both, depending on whether we want to be able to read or write the property. For the 'put' function, we can choose to make the function accept a copy of the property (PropPut), or a reference to it (PropPutRef). PropPut is the default, and you'd use this for most simple types.

The bottom pane in the dialog shows the entries that will be added to the IDL file. If you want to edit the attributes, such as the **id()** or the **helpstring()**, press the Attributes... button:

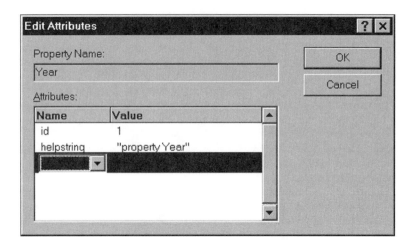

Once you're happy with the property name, type and attributes, press the OK button to generate the code.

Back in the project, several alterations have been made to the project files. First, look at the IDL file, where you'll see additions for the property:

```
[
    object,
    uuid(2D15E121-6CA4-11D1-A607-00A0C94BC9C3),
    dual,
    helpstring("ICalcEaster Interface"),
    pointer_default(unique)
]
interface ICalcEaster : IDispatch
{
    [propget, id(1), helpstring("property Year")]
    HRESULT Year([out, retval] short *pVal);
    [propput, id(1), helpstring("property Year")]
    HRESULT Year([in] short newVal);
};
```

We've defined two new methods, which are used to implement the **Year** property. Both are called **Year** and have the same help string and ID, but they're distinguished by their attributes. The method that returns a value has the **[propget]** attribute. Since its parameter is used to return a value, the parameter has to have the **[out]** attribute, and as this is also the conceptual return value of the method, it has the **[retval]** attribute too. (Remember that the real return value of a COM method is always an **HRESULT**). As you might expect, a method can have several parameters with **[out]** attributes, but only one with **[out, retval]**.

The method to set the value has the **[propput]** attribute, and its parameter is marked as an input parameter by the use of the **[in]** attribute.

Similar changes have been made to **CalcEaster.h**, adding the property **get_** and **put_** functions to the class:

```
// CalcEaster.h : Declaration of the CCalcEaster

...

// ICalcEaster
public:
    STDMETHOD(get_Year)(/*[out, retval]*/ short *pVal);
    STDMETHOD(put_Year)(/*[in]*/ short newVal);
};
```

In **CalcEaster.cpp**, we have skeleton code for the two methods:

```
// CalcEaster.cpp : Implementation of CCalcEaster
#include "stdafx.h"
#include "Simple.h"
#include "CalcEaster.h"

/////////////////////////////////////////////////////////////////////////////
// CCalcEaster


STDMETHODIMP CCalcEaster::get_Year(short * pVal)
{
    // TODO: Add your implementation code here

    return S_OK;
}

STDMETHODIMP CCalcEaster::put_Year(short newVal)
{
    // TODO: Add your implementation code here

    return S_OK;
}
```

You can see that both functions use the **STDMETHOD**xxx**()** macros that we discussed back in Chapter 1.

More Properties

You should add two other **short** properties to the interface, representing the month and the day. Since these are read-only, you can uncheck the Put Function when defining them. You should end up with an interface in your IDL file looking something like this:

```
[
    object,
    uuid(2D15E121-6CA4-11D1-A607-00A0C94BC9C3),
    dual,
    helpstring("ICalcEaster Interface"),
    pointer_default(unique)
]
interface ICalcEaster : IDispatch
{
    [propget, id(1), helpstring("property Year")]
     HRESULT Year([out, retval] short *pVal);
    [propput, id(1), helpstring("property Year")]
     HRESULT Year([in] short newVal);
    [propget, id(2), helpstring("property Month")]
     HRESULT Month([out, retval] short *pVal);
    [propget, id(3), helpstring("property Day")]
     HRESULT Day([out, retval] short *pVal);
};
```

Implementing the Properties

Notice that there are no data members in the **CCalcEaster** class to represent these properties
yet — we've only dealt with the COM interface aspects, and not the C++ implementation details.
We therefore need to add three variables of type **short** to the **CCalcEaster** class, and initialize
them appropriately in the constructor:

```
class ATL_NO_VTABLE CCalcEaster :
    public CComObjectRootEx<CComSingleThreadModel>,
    public CComCoClass<CCalcEaster, &CLSID_CalcEaster>,
    public IDispatchImpl<ICalcEaster, &IID_ICalcEaster, &LIBID_SIMPLELib>
{
public:
    CCalcEaster() : m_Year(-1), m_Month(-1), m_Day(-1)
    {
    }

DECLARE_REGISTRY_RESOURCEID(IDR_CALCEASTER)

BEGIN_COM_MAP(CCalcEaster)
    COM_INTERFACE_ENTRY(ICalcEaster)
    COM_INTERFACE_ENTRY(IDispatch)
END_COM_MAP()

private:
    short m_Year;
    short m_Month;
    short m_Day;

// ICalcEaster
public:
    STDMETHOD(get_Day)(/*[out, retval]*/ short *pVal);
```

```
        STDMETHOD(get_Month)(/*[out, retval]*/ short *pVal);
        STDMETHOD(get_Year)(/*[out, retval]*/ short *pVal);
        STDMETHOD(put_Year)(/*[in]*/ short newVal);
    };
```

We can now edit the property **put_** and **get_** method skeletons to connect with these variables:

```
    STDMETHODIMP CCalcEaster::get_Year(short* pVal)
    {
        // Retrieve the year value
        *pVal = m_Year;
        return S_OK;
    }

    STDMETHODIMP CCalcEaster::put_Year(short newVal)
    {
        // Store the year value
        m_Year = newVal;
        return S_OK;
    }

    STDMETHODIMP CCalcEaster::get_Month(short* pVal)
    {
        // Retrieve the month value
        *pVal = m_Month;
        return S_OK;
    }

    STDMETHODIMP CCalcEaster::get_Day(short* pVal)
    {
        // Retrieve the day value
        *pVal = m_Day;
        return S_OK;
    }
```

Adding Methods

Having added a way to get data in and out of the server, we now need to add the calculation method. Right-click on the **ICalcEaster** interface in ClassView, but this time select Add Method... to bring up the Add Method to Interface dialog. Add a method called **CalculateEaster()**, which takes no parameters, like this:

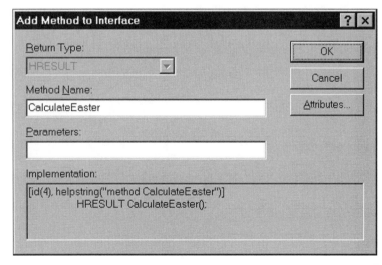

When you press OK and let the Wizard generate the code, you'll find another entry in the IDL file, and a skeleton function in the **CCalcEaster** class:

```
STDMETHODIMP CCalcEaster::CalculateEaster()
{
    // TODO: Add your implementation code here

    return S_OK;
}
```

All we now need to do is to add the code to perform the calculation, and we're ready to test the server. In a real server we'd probably pass the year as a parameter to this function and not split it up as we have, but that wouldn't have given us as much to demonstrate!

Calculating when Easter Sunday will fall is not trivial. There are several algorithms available, and the one you use will depend on factors such as what year you want, which part of the world you live in, and whether you're using the Julian or Gregorian calendar. We'll keep things simple, and use an algorithm suitable for calculating the Easter date for Europe and the US, for any date between 326AD and 4099AD. As you'll see, the algorithm is fairly complicated, and makes a lot of use of magic numbers! However, it does come up with the correct date.

```
STDMETHODIMP CCalcEaster::CalculateEaster()
{
    // First, check we have a year set, and that it is within the
    // range for the calculation
    if (m_Year < 326 || m_Year > 4099)
        return E_FAIL;

    short first = m_Year / 100;    // first two digits
    short div19 = m_Year % 19;     // remainder when divided by 19

    // Find the date of the PFM (Paschal Full Moon)
    short temp = (first - 15) / 2 + ((first > 26) ? -1 : 0) +
                 ((first > 38) ? -1 : 0) + 202 - 11 * div19;

    if (first == 21 | first == 24 | first == 25 |
                    first == 33 | first == 36 | first == 37)
        temp += -1;

    temp %= 30;

    short ta = temp + ((temp == 29) ? -1 : 0) +
                ((temp == 28 && div19 > 10) ? -1 : 0) + 21;

    // Find the next Sunday
    short tb = (ta - 19) % 7;
    temp = (40 - first) % 4;
    short tc = temp - ((temp > 1) ? -1 : 0) - ((temp == 3) ? -1 : 0);

    temp = m_Year % 100;
    short td = (temp + temp / 4) % 7;
    short te = ((20 - tb - tc - td) % 7) + 1;
```

```
    m_Day = ta + te;

    // Find the month
    if (m_Day > 61)
    {
        m_Day -= 61;
        m_Month = 5;
    }
    else if (m_Day > 31)
    {
        m_Day -= 31;
        m_Month = 4;
    }
    else
        m_Month = 3;

    return S_OK;
}
```

Once you've entered this code (or downloaded it from the Wrox Press web site), you'll be able to build the server, ready for testing. Notice that the server is automatically registered when you build the project.

Creating an ATL Test Client

Although ATL is primarily concerned with writing COM servers, it's possible to use it to write COM clients as well, so that's what we'll do next. As we build the client, you'll see:

▶ What an ATL executable looks like

▶ ATL's window classes

▶ More of the Wizards

Creating the Skeleton

Close your Simple project, and use the ATL COM AppWizard to create a new ATL project called ATLClient. All the Wizards will talk about servers, but ignore them — we're using ATL slightly out of context here to write a client!

Put the project in a subdirectory of the Simple server's directory, so that we can use relative paths to the server's files. This time, make the project an executable, rather than a DLL or a service. As we said before, when you select the executable server type, you'll notice that executables don't have the option for supporting MFC, or merging the proxy-stub code.

Once you've generated the project, a brief look will show that the list of files generated is the same as for the DLL project. However, there are some important differences in content.

CExeModule

To start with, **Stdafx.h** defines **_Module** as being of type **CExeModule** — a class derived from **CComModule**:

```
class CExeModule : public CComModule
{
public:
   LONG Unlock();
   DWORD dwThreadID;
};
extern CExeModule _Module;
```

CExeModule overrides the **Unlock()** method of **CComModule**. The implementation of **CExeModule::Unlock()** is in **ATLClient.cpp**:

```
LONG CExeModule::Unlock()
{
   LONG l = CComModule::Unlock();
   if (l == 0)
   {
#if _WIN32_WINNT >= 0x0400
      if (CoSuspendClassObjects() == S_OK)
         PostThreadMessage(dwThreadID, WM_QUIT, 0, 0);
#else
      PostThreadMessage(dwThreadID, WM_QUIT, 0, 0);
#endif
   }
   return l;
}
```

Essentially, all this method does is post a message to the module's main thread telling the application to quit. If the **_WIN32_WINNT** symbol is defined, **CoSuspendClassObjects()** tells COM not to allow any more requests to activate the object, so that it can shut down in an orderly fashion.

_tWinMain()

Most of **ATLClient.cpp** is taken up with the implementation of the **WinMain()** function, the standard entry point for Windows executables. This is actually specified as **_tWinMain()** so that it can be conditionally compiled for ANSI or for Unicode.

```
extern "C" int WINAPI _tWinMain(HINSTANCE hInstance,
   HINSTANCE /*hPrevInstance*/, LPTSTR lpCmdLine, int /*nShowCmd*/)
{
   lpCmdLine = GetCommandLine(); //this line necessary for _ATL_MIN_CRT
   HRESULT hRes = CoInitialize(NULL);
// If you are running on NT 4.0 or higher you can use the following call
// instead to make the EXE free threaded.
// This means that calls come in on a random RPC thread
// HRESULT hRes = CoInitializeEx(NULL, COINIT_MULTITHREADED);
   _ASSERTE(SUCCEEDED(hRes));
```

```
    _Module.Init(ObjectMap, hInstance);
    _Module.dwThreadID = GetCurrentThreadId();
    TCHAR szTokens[] = _T("-/");

    int nRet = 0;
    BOOL bRun = TRUE;
    LPCTSTR lpszToken = FindOneOf(lpCmdLine, szTokens);
    while (lpszToken != NULL)
    {
        if (lstrcmpi(lpszToken, _T("UnregServer"))==0)
        {
            _Module.UpdateRegistryFromResource(IDR_ATLClient, FALSE);
            nRet = _Module.UnregisterServer();
            bRun = FALSE;
            break;
        }
        if (lstrcmpi(lpszToken, _T("RegServer"))==0)
        {
            _Module.UpdateRegistryFromResource(IDR_ATLClient, TRUE);
            nRet = _Module.RegisterServer(TRUE);
            bRun = FALSE;
            break;
        }
        lpszToken = FindOneOf(lpszToken, szTokens);
    }

    if (bRun)
    {
        hRes = _Module.RegisterClassObjects(CLSCTX_LOCAL_SERVER,
            REGCLS_MULTIPLEUSE);
        _ASSERTE(SUCCEEDED(hRes));

        MSG msg;
        while (GetMessage(&msg, 0, 0, 0))
            DispatchMessage(&msg);

        _Module.RevokeClassObjects();
    }

    CoUninitialize();
    return nRet;
}
```

If you've come to Windows programming through MFC or a similar class library that hides many of the details, it is possible that you may never have seen a **WinMain()** function before. In the same way that a C or C++ program has to have a **main()** function, which is where execution commences, a Windows program must have a function called **WinMain()**. In many class libraries, it is buried deep in the library code.

Let's take a look at what **_tWinMain()** does.

```
extern "C" int WINAPI _tWinMain(HINSTANCE hInstance,
  HINSTANCE /*hPrevInstance*/, LPTSTR lpCmdLine, int /*nShowCmd*/)
{
  lpCmdLine = GetCommandLine(); //this line necessary for _ATL_MIN_CRT
```

The standard set of arguments will be familiar to anyone who has written a bare-bones Windows program:

▶ **hInstance** gives the instance handle of this task.

▶ **hPrevInstance** is a legacy from 16-bit days and is always **NULL** under Win32.

▶ **lpCmdLine** is used to pass in the command line string (but see below).

▶ **nShowCmd** says how the executable ought to display on startup — full-screen, as an icon, hidden or normal. This parameter isn't used here.

_ATL_MIN_CRT

In the first line of code, we get the command line via a call to **GetCommandLine()**. You may be used to getting the command line from the **lpCmdLine** parameter, but that is not possible if you have the **_ATL_MIN_CRT** macro defined. This macro is defined for you automatically in Release builds of ATL projects.

Again, we can see evidence of the care taken to ensure the efficiency of ATL-generated code. By default, the Visual C++ compiler links to the C RunTime library (CRT), giving you access to the functions contained within that library. However, linking to the CRT means that startup code is automatically compiled into your project, increasing the size of the executable image. This occurs even if you don't make any use of the CRT functions in your own code, due to the need to define static buffers for things like ANSI to Unicode conversion, **gmtime()**, and so on.

When **_ATL_MIN_CRT** is defined, ATL comes to the rescue by defining its own entry points for EXEs and DLLs, independent of the CRT's. This avoids incurring the overhead of the CRT startup code. However, if you *need* to make use of the CRT functions, you'll need to remove the **_ATL_MIN_CRT** macro from the settings of your project. There are a few CRT functions that you can use without requiring the startup code (such as the memory functions), but if you hit one that does require it, you will be able to tell because you'll receive a link error complaining about **_main** being missing:

```
error LNK2001:'unresolved external symbol _main
```

The error will appear when you build using one of the Release configurations, not under a Debug build. You can remove the **_ATL_MIN_CRT** macro by deleting it from the preprocessor definitions listed on the C/C++ tab of the Project Settings for each of the Release configurations.

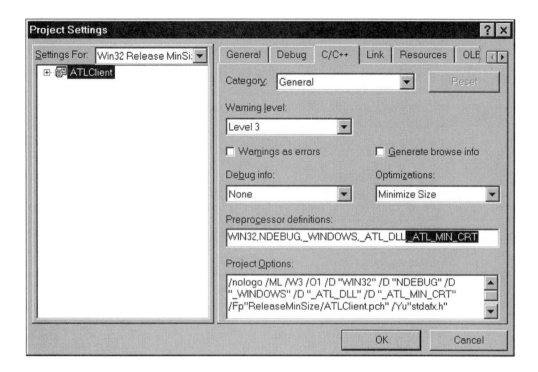

CoInitialize()

The second line of code makes sure that the COM libraries are loaded and ready to go, by calling **CoInitialize()**.

```
        HRESULT hRes = CoInitialize(NULL);
//    If you are running on NT 4.0 or higher you can use the following
//    call instead to make the EXE free threaded.
//    This means that calls come in on a random RPC thread
//    HRESULT hRes = CoInitializeEx(NULL, COINIT_MULTITHREADED);
        _ASSERTE(SUCCEEDED(hRes));
```

If our code is to run under NT 4.0 (or Windows 95 with DCOM installed), we have the option of making the main thread of the executable run in a multi-threaded apartment by replacing the call to **CoInitialize()** with one to **CoInitializeEx()**. The default call to **CoInitialize()** simply calls **CoInitializeEx()** with the **COINIT_APARTMENTTHREADED** option, to create an apartment-threaded executable. COM threading models are discussed in detail in Chapter 5.

Init()

If the COM initialization worked, the code then initializes the module object, and stores the current thread ID in its **dwThreadID** member. This thread will be the one implementing the message pump for the server, and storing its ID is necessary so that **_Module** knows where to send the **WM_QUIT** message when it is time for the server to shut down.

```
        _Module.Init(ObjectMap, hInstance);
        _Module.dwThreadID = GetCurrentThreadId();
```

Checking the Command Line

In the next section, the code parses the command line to determine whether the server should register or unregister itself:

```
TCHAR szTokens[] = _T("-/");

int nRet = 0;
BOOL bRun = TRUE;
LPCTSTR lpszToken = FindOneOf(lpCmdLine, szTokens);
while (lpszToken != NULL)
{
   if (lstrcmpi(lpszToken, _T("UnregServer"))==0)
   {
      _Module.UpdateRegistryFromResource(IDR_ATLClient, FALSE);
      nRet = _Module.UnregisterServer();
      bRun = FALSE;
      break;
   }
   if (lstrcmpi(lpszToken, _T("RegServer"))==0)
   {
      _Module.UpdateRegistryFromResource(IDR_ATLClient, TRUE);
      nRet = _Module.RegisterServer(TRUE);
      bRun = FALSE;
      break;
   }
   lpszToken = FindOneOf(lpszToken, szTokens);
}
```

The code uses the helper function **FindOneOf()** to find the start of a command line parameter, and then compares it with **"UnregServer"** and **"RegServer"** to determine what action to take. If we're registering the server, the call to **UpdateRegistryFromResource()** adds the entries from the server's RGS file to the registry, which usually just means adding an AppID key. After this, **RegisterServer()** calls each of the classes listed in the object map, telling them to register themselves, and also registers the type library. If we're unregistering, the call to **UpdateRegistryFromResource()** *removes* the entries from the RGS file (and doesn't register the type library), and then the server tells each of the classes to unregister itself.

The Running Server

Registration is a standalone process, so if either of the registration flags was found, **bRun** is set to **FALSE** and the application exits. If the server wasn't started in order to register or unregister itself, it needs to register its class objects and go into a message loop:

```
if (bRun)
{
   hRes = _Module.RegisterClassObjects(CLSCTX_LOCAL_SERVER,
      REGCLS_MULTIPLEUSE);
   _ASSERTE(SUCCEEDED(hRes));

   MSG msg;
```

```
    while (GetMessage(&msg, 0, 0, 0))
        DispatchMessage(&msg);

    _Module.RevokeClassObjects();
}
```

When the message loop receives a **WM_QUIT** message, **GetMessage()** will return **0**, the message loop will end and the class objects will be revoked ready for shutdown. We have seen that the application will be sent a **WM_QUIT** message when the lock count of the module goes to zero, so clearly the message loop is necessary for this mechanism to work. It is also necessary to provide a message loop in any apartment-threaded server, because COM uses the message queue to sequence calls to the server.

The loop is preceded by a call to **RegisterClassObjects()**, which registers the server's class factory. In this case, our server is a local server — an EXE file that runs in its own address space — and it can be used by multiple clients.

CoUninitialize()

The final step is to call **CoUninitialize()**, to tell COM that the application is exiting so that it can adjust its reference counts accordingly. This means that every time we use **CoInitialize()** or **CoInitializeEx()** to initialize COM, we must also call **CoUninitialize()** on the same thread when we have finished using COM:

```
    CoUninitialize();
    return nRet;
}
```

> **CoInitialize()** *and* **CoInitializeEx()** *are both used to initialize COM for use by a thread.* **CoInitializeEx()** *can be used to specify various flags that control how COM is initialized, in particular which threading model to use.* **CoInitialize()** *is an older function, which now simply calls* **CoInitializeEx()** *with the* **COINIT_APARTMENTTHREADED** *flag, to specify apartment-model threading.*

Adding a Dialog

Well, we have an application, but it doesn't do anything. The next step, then, is to add a dialog, which we'll use to start up the server and test it. Use the Insert | New ATL Object... menu item to bring up the ATL dialog, and select the Miscellaneous tab:

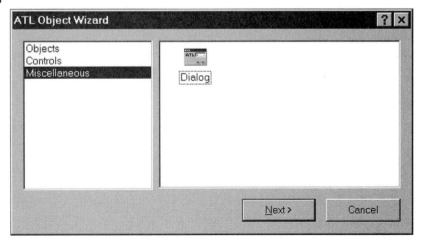

Since Dialog is the only choice, click on Next >, to bring up the Properties dialog:

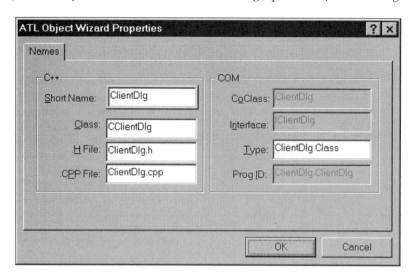

Give the dialog a suitable Short Name, such as ClientDlg, and press OK. The Wizard will add two files to the project, representing the dialog header and implementation. The header file (**ClientDlg.h**) shows that we have a dialog class derived from **CDialogImpl<>**:

```
// ClientDlg.h : Declaration of the CClientDlg

#ifndef __CLIENTDLG_H_
#define __CLIENTDLG_H_

#include "resource.h"        // main symbols

/////////////////////////////////////////////////////////////////////////////
// CClientDlg
class CClientDlg :
   public CDialogImpl<CClientDlg>
{
public:
   CClientDlg();
   ~CClientDlg();

   enum { IDD = IDD_CLIENTDLG };

BEGIN_MSG_MAP(CClientDlg)
   MESSAGE_HANDLER(WM_INITDIALOG, OnInitDialog)
   COMMAND_ID_HANDLER(IDOK, OnOK)
   COMMAND_ID_HANDLER(IDCANCEL, OnCancel)
END_MSG_MAP()

   LRESULT OnInitDialog(UINT uMsg, WPARAM wParam, LPARAM lParam,
      BOOL& bHandled);
```

```
    LRESULT OnOK(WORD wNotifyCode, WORD wID, HWND hWndCtl,
        BOOL& bHandled);
    LRESULT OnCancel(WORD wNotifyCode, WORD wID, HWND hWndCtl,
        BOOL& bHandled);
};


#endif //__CLIENTDLG_H_
```

Notice that **CDialogImpl<>**, the class that implements the dialog box creation for us, takes our class as a template parameter. In effect, we're using the template to customize the base class to work with our derived dialog class. The ATL dialog implementation class knows how to create and use dialogs, but it knows nothing about what our particular dialog wants to do. The use of a template provides a useful way to add our custom dialog behavior to the standard template class. This is a common idiom in ATL; we'll see precisely how it's used when we take a closer look at some of the classes that ATL provides, in the next chapter.

Although this code doesn't use MFC, we can see some similarities with the way MFC handles dialogs. Just like MFC dialogs, the ATL dialog is linked to a dialog resource (**IDD_CLIENTDLG**), and it uses a message map to implement message handlers. We'll see more about *exactly* how it does this in Chapter 8, but it's fairly clear from the code that by default we get message handlers for **WM_INITDIALOG**, and the OK and Cancel buttons. These handlers don't currently do very much, as you can see from the implementation file:

```
// ClientDlg.cpp : Implementation of CClientDlg
#include "stdafx.h"
#include "ClientDlg.h"


/////////////////////////////////////////////////////////////////////////////
// CClientDlg

CClientDlg::CClientDlg()
{
}


CClientDlg::~CClientDlg()
{
}


LRESULT CClientDlg::OnInitDialog(UINT uMsg, WPARAM wParam,
                                            LPARAM lParam, BOOL& bHandled)
{
    return 1;  // Let the system set the focus
}


LRESULT CClientDlg::OnOK(WORD wNotifyCode, WORD wID, HWND hWndCtl,
                                            BOOL& bHandled)
{
    EndDialog(wID);
    return 0;
}
```

```
LRESULT CClientDlg::OnCancel(WORD wNotifyCode, WORD wID, HWND hWndCtl,
                                                     BOOL& bHandled)
{
    EndDialog(wID);
    return 0;
}
```

Displaying the Dialog

We want to structure our application so that it displays the dialog automatically on startup, and so that dismissing the dialog will terminate the application. We'll start by adding code to the **_tWinMain()** function to display the dialog, but first, make sure you **#include "ClientDlg.h"** near the top of **ATLClient.cpp**.

Before we start, though, we can do a little weeding on the code skeleton. We've generated ourselves an ATL server executable, and have been looking at what is in the skeleton code. You know that we're actually implementing a client program here, so we aren't acting as a server for any COM objects. Some of the source code in the **ATLClient.cpp** file is therefore surplus to requirements, and we can remove it.

Since we have no COM objects, we don't need the object map, and since we aren't going to check the command line for registration options, all that code (and the **FindOneOf()** function) can also disappear. Tidying out everything we don't need, you should end up with a **_tWinMain()** function that looks like this:

```
extern "C" int WINAPI _tWinMain(HINSTANCE hInstance,
    HINSTANCE, LPTSTR lpCmdLine, int)
{
    HRESULT hRes = CoInitialize(NULL);
    _Module.Init(NULL, hInstance);
    _Module.dwThreadID = GetCurrentThreadId();

    int nRet = 0;

    MSG msg;
    while (GetMessage(&msg, 0, 0, 0))
        DispatchMessage(&msg);

    CoUninitialize();
    return nRet;
}
```

Now we can add the code to create and display the dialog, just before the message loop:

```
    int nRet = 0;

    // Create and show a dialog
    CClientDlg dlg;
    dlg.Create(NULL);
    dlg.ShowWindow(SW_SHOWNORMAL);
```

```
MSG msg;
while (GetMessage(&msg, 0, 0, 0))
{
    TranslateMessage(&msg);
    DispatchMessage(&msg);
}
```

You can see that we have declared an object (**dlg**) of class **CClientDlg**, called its **Create()** member, to create the window for the class (the parameter is for the handle to the dialog's parent — it doesn't have one), and then called **ShowWindow()** to make the window show itself. ATL's dialog class is derived from a generic window class, **CWindow**, which provides thin wrappers for the Win32 APIs related to windows, much as MFC's **CWnd** class does.

Note also that we have changed the message loop itself. The addition of the call to **TranslateMessage()**, ensures that virtual key messages are translated into character messages (**WM_KEYDOWN** and **WM_KEYUP** combinations produce a **WM_CHAR**, for example).

OnCancel()

Now we need to change the code in **CClientDlg::OnCancel()** to close the dialog and dismiss the server by sending a **WM_QUIT** message to the application. The Wizard-generated dialog class code assumes that it will run as a modal dialog, so we need to replace the call to **EndDialog()** with one to **DestroyWindow()**:

```
LRESULT CClientDlg::OnCancel(WORD wNotifyCode, WORD wID, HWND hWndCtl,
                                                    BOOL& bHandled)
{
    DestroyWindow();
    PostQuitMessage(0);
    return 0;
}
```

At this stage, you could run the application and dismiss the dialog by pressing the close icon or the Cancel button.

> *Don't try to close the dialog with the OK button — we haven't added a call to*
> **PostQuitMessage()** *to the handler for that button, so you'll end up with running,*
> *but invisible tasks. We'll add code to the handler for this button shortly.*

Editing the Dialog Resource

The next step is to edit the dialog resource so that it allows us to enter the year for which we want to calculate the date of Easter. Go to ResourceView and double-click the **IDD_CLIENTDLG** icon to open the dialog resource in Developer Studio's resource editor.

Change the caption of the OK button to read Calculate. We'll add code that will respond to this button to calculate Easter for any year.

Now add an edit box to the dialog, and change its ID to **IDC_YEAR**. On the Styles page, check the <u>N</u>umber check box, so users of the dialog can only enter numbers into the edit box.

Add a static text control just to the left of the dialog, bring up its properties window, and set its caption to Enter Year:.

Finally, bring up the properties window for the dialog itself. On the More Styles page, check the Center box. This will make the dialog appear in the center of the screen automatically when it's displayed. Your dialog resource should now look something like this:

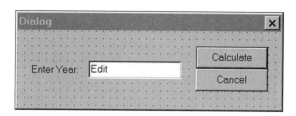

Now we're ready to change the code in **CClientDlg::OnOK()** to test our server. First, we need to get information about the server into our client. We'll do this in two ways, so that you can compare the methods. First, we'll use the **MIDL**-generated header and **_i.c** files; then we'll use the type library and the Visual C++ compiler's new preprocessor directive, **#import**.

Using MIDL-Generated Files

Add the following lines just below the **#include**s at the top of **ClientDlg.cpp**:

```
#include "stdafx.h"
#include "ClientDlg.h"
#include "..\Simple.h"
#include "..\Simple_i.c"
```

This brings the header file (containing the server's interface definitions) and the **_i.c** file (containing the GUID definitions) into the project, so that we can use them from code in the client dialog. Next, replace the code in **CClientDlg::OnOK()** with that shown below:

```
LRESULT CClientDlg::OnOK(WORD wNotifyCode, WORD wID, HWND hWndCtl,
                                            BOOL& bHandled)
{
    ICalcEaster* p = NULL;
    HRESULT hr = CoCreateInstance(CLSID_CalcEaster, NULL, CLSCTX_ALL,
        IID_ICalcEaster, (void**)&p);

    if (SUCCEEDED(hr))
    {
        p->put_Year(GetDlgItemInt(IDC_YEAR));
        p->CalculateEaster();

        short Day = -1;
        short Month = -1;
```

```
        // We should really check the return values of the next two method
        // calls but the logic would get quite messy
        hr = p->get_Day(&Day);
        hr = p->get_Month(&Month);

        TCHAR buff[255] = {0};
        wsprintf(buff, _T("Easter: %d/%d in %d"), Day, Month,
                GetDlgItemInt(IDC_YEAR));
        MessageBox(buff, _T("Calculation"));

        p->Release();
    }
    else
    {
        // Don't Release() the pointer if CoCreateInstance() failed
        TCHAR buff[255] = {0};
        wsprintf(buff, _T("Error: 0x%x "), hr);
        MessageBox(buff, _T("Error") );
    }
    return 0;
}
```

The first part of the code declares an **ICalcEaster** pointer, then calls **CoCreateInstance()** to create an instance of our **CalcEaster** coclass, asking for a pointer to that interface:

```
ICalcEaster* p = NULL;
HRESULT hr = CoCreateInstance(CLSID_CalcEaster, NULL, CLSCTX_ALL,
    IID_ICalcEaster, (void**)&p);
```

Next, we check the return value of **CoCreateInstance()** to determine whether we successfully created the object. If not, we display a simple message and leave the function. Note that we don't call **Release()** on the pointer unless **CoCreateInstance()** succeeded.

If **CoCreateInstance()** did succeed, we can set the year, call the **CalculateEaster()** method, and get back the day and month.

The year that we pass to the **put_Year()** method is obtained by calling the **CWindow::GetDlgItemInt()** function. This function is a thin wrapper around the Win32 **GetDlgItemInt()** function, which returns an integer version of the text in a control. In this case, we're getting the value of the year entered by the user in our **IDC_YEAR** edit box.

> *You can see that the requirement for COM methods to return* **HRESULT***s can lead to some ugly code. We have to declare some storage (the* **short***s* **Month** *and* **Day***) and pass pointers to the* **get_()** *methods, and we should be checking the return values of each of the method calls to check whether they succeeded.*

Finally, we display a message box with the results of the calculation, then **Release()** the interface pointer. Once again, we are using a thin wrapper to the Win32 API provided by ATL's **CWindow** class to display the message box.

When you build and run the project, you should see something like this:

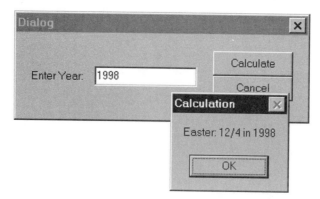

Using the Type Library: the #import Statement

The second way that we're going to test the server is by importing the type library using Visual C++ compiler COM support. Remove the **#include**s for **Simple.h** and **Simple_i.c** from the top of **ClientDlg.cpp** and replace them with the single line shown highlighted below:

```
#include "stdafx.h"
#include "ClientDlg.h"
#import "..\Simple.tlb"
```

#import is a new preprocessor directive that instructs VC++ to use the information in the specified type library to generate wrapper classes for the interfaces in that type library. These wrapper classes have a number of advantages over the header files that **MIDL** generates:

▶ The wrapper class functions can return values specified as **[retval]** directly

▶ The wrappers can throw errors instead of returning **HRESULT**s

▶ The wrappers hide the details of reference counting

▶ The wrappers replace certain types (**VARIANT**s and **BSTR**s) with classes (**_variant_t**, **_bstr_t**)

▶ The wrappers allow property methods to be accessed like data members

There are a number of ways of customizing the output of the **#import** *directive that we won't look at here. However, you can find further examples and a fuller description of* **#import** *at* http://www.worldofatl.com.

When processed, the **#import** directive produces the header for the wrapper classes in a file called **Simple.tlh**, and the implementation for these classes in a file called **Simple.tli**. These files will appear in the output directory for the current configuration. If you compile **ClientDlg.cpp** now, you can see these files being produced, but you'll get several compiler errors. This is because **#import** generates some C++ classes to wrap our server, and you'll need to change the implementation to use them. We'll come to those changes in good time; for now, let's look at the files that were generated.

If you examine them closely, you'll find that there's a big difference between the **MIDL**-generated interface classes and those generated by **#import**. The **MIDL**-generated classes have no implementation at all — they're abstract classes designed purely to translate a vtable layout into C++ terms. The **#import**-generated classes, on the other hand, have an implementation for the wrapper methods that will be compiled into your application.

Let's open the files generated by **#import** to see what they contain. First, **Simple.tlh** (slightly edited for length):

```
#include <comdef.h>

namespace SIMPLELib {

// Forward references and typedefs
struct /* coclass */ CalcEaster;
struct __declspec(uuid("2d15e121-6ca4-11d1-a607-00a0c94bc9c3"))
/* dual interface */ ICalcEaster;

// Smart pointer typedef declarations
_COM_SMARTPTR_TYPEDEF(ICalcEaster, __uuidof(ICalcEaster));

// Type library items
struct __declspec(uuid("2d15e122-6ca4-11d1-a607-00a0c94bc9c3"))
CalcEaster;
    // [ default ] interface ICalcEaster

struct __declspec(uuid("2d15e121-6ca4-11d1-a607-00a0c94bc9c3"))
ICalcEaster : IDispatch
{
    // Property data
    __declspec(property(get=GetYear,put=PutYear))
    short Year;
    __declspec(property(get=GetMonth))
    short Month;
    __declspec(property(get=GetDay))
    short Day;

    // Wrapper methods for error-handling
    short GetYear ( );
    void PutYear (
        short pVal );
    short GetMonth ( );
    short GetDay ( );
    HRESULT CalculateEaster ( );

    // Raw methods provided by interface
    virtual HRESULT __stdcall get_Year (
        short* pVal ) = 0;
    virtual HRESULT __stdcall put_Year (
        short pVal ) = 0;
    virtual HRESULT __stdcall get_Month (
        short* pVal ) = 0;
```

```
      virtual HRESULT __stdcall get_Day (
          short* pVal ) = 0;
      virtual HRESULT __stdcall raw_CalculateEaster ( ) = 0;
   };


   // Wrapper method implementations
   #include "Debug/Simple.tli"


   } // namespace SIMPLELib
```

The first thing that you can see is the **#include** for **comdef.h**. This header file contains the definitions for the classes that are used in the generated wrappers (**_com_ptr_t<>**, **_bstr_t**, **_variant_t** and **_com_error**). If you ever want to use any of these classes in your own code without **#import**ing a type library, you can just **#include <comdef.h>** directly.

Next, you can see the start of the namespace **SIMPLELib**. By default, all the code produced by **#import** will be wrapped in a namespace with the same name as the type library (its internal name, as specified in IDL, *not* its filename). This not only helps to avoid naming collisions, but can also help the readability of our code. If you find that the namespace is not to your liking, you could change the directive in **ClientDlg.cpp** and rename it, using the **rename_namespace** attribute, or remove it completely, using **no_namespace**:

```
// This line would rename the namespace to 'Wrox'
#import "..\Simple.tlb" rename_namespace("Wrox")
```

```
// This line would generate the wrappers without a namespace
#import "..\Simple.tlb" no_namespace
```

Smart Pointers

Within the namespace block, you can see several items of interest. The first item (ignoring the forward references) is the 'smart pointer typedef declaration' for the **ICalcEaster** interface:

```
// Smart pointer typedef declarations
_COM_SMARTPTR_TYPEDEF(ICalcEaster, __uuidof(ICalcEaster));
```

This uses the **_COM_SMARTPTR_TYPEDEF()** macro to declare a template specialization of a class called **_com_ptr_t<>**. This class takes two template parameters: the interface name and its IID. The **_COM_SMARTPTR_TYPEDEF()** macro takes the same parameters as **_com_ptr_t<>**, and declares a **typedef**'d specialization of that class with the name of the interface plus a suffix of **Ptr**. Thus, the line shown above declares **ICalcEasterPtr** to be a smart pointer class for our server's **ICalcEaster** interface. The IID is obtained from the **ICalcEaster** interface using the **__uuidof()** operator. This operator is specific to Microsoft's Visual C++ compiler..

_com_ptr_t<> specializations are called smart pointers because they are used like pointers (we use the indirect member selection operator **->** to access most of their functionality), but they take responsibility for allocating and freeing the memory that the pointer represents when it's no longer in use. The COM smart pointers that we're discussing here take responsibility for freeing interface pointers (they call **Release()** on them). You may come across other classes that are also referred to as smart pointers, but which have different capabilities and uses.

Type Library Items

Following the smart pointer **typedef**s, we have the type library items. The first item is a **struct** for the coclass, **CalcEaster**. All that the **struct** does here is associate the CLSID with **CalcEaster** so that we can use the expression **__uuidof(CalcEaster)** in our code:

```
struct __declspec(uuid("5dc86882-58f2-11d1-a159-04dcf8c00000"))
CalcEaster;
    // [ default ] interface ICalcEaster
```

The only other item in the type library section is the **ICalcEaster** interface itself. You can see the use of **__declspec(uuid())** to associate the IID with the interface, so that it can be retrieved with **__uuidof()**. You can also see a selection of methods in the body of the **struct**, which is split into three main sections.

Property Data

The first section is entitled **Property data**. This section uses another extension to the Microsoft C++ compiler to allow COM properties to be called as if they were public data members:

```
// Property data
__declspec(property(get=GetYear,put=PutYear))
short Year;
__declspec(property(get=GetMonth))
short Month;
__declspec(property(get=GetDay))
short Day;
```

The **property()** attribute creates what Microsoft terms a **virtual data member** of a class. That is, although it looks like the class should contain a **Year** data member of type **short**, and you can write code that manipulates **Year** as if it were a data member of the class, it doesn't actually exist as a data member!

Instead, the compiler converts code that manipulates **Year** into the appropriate function calls using the information provided in the **get** and **put** statements, depending on whether **Year** is being used as an rvalue or an lvalue. The same is true of the **Month** and **Day** properties, except they are read-only, since there's no **put** in the property specification. This means that **Month** and **Day** can only be used as rvalues — you'll get compiler errors if you try to use either of them on the left side of an assignment:

```
// These two statements are equivalent
p->Year = 1984;
p->PutYear(1984);

// This will cause the compiler to emit an error
// Day is a read-only property
p->Day = 21;
```

Note that the functions specified in the **get** and **put** statements need to be independently defined elsewhere in the class. We'll see that they are in the next section.

Wrapper Methods

The second section holds the wrapper methods. There is a wrapper method for each method in the original interface:

```
// Wrapper methods for error-handling
short GetYear ( );
void PutYear (
    short pVal );
short GetMonth ( );
short GetDay ( );
HRESULT CalculateEaster ( );
```

These wrapper methods do three things:

- They return **[retval]** parameters directly
- They throw errors if there is a failure in the method call
- They use **_bstr_t** and **_variant_t** types in place of standard **VARIANT**s and **BSTR**s (not shown here, because our example doesn't use these types)

These wrappers need implementations, which can be found in **Simple.tli**:

```
inline short ICalcEaster::GetYear ( ) {
    short _result;
    HRESULT _hr = get_Year(&_result);
    if (FAILED(_hr)) _com_issue_errorex(_hr, this, __uuidof(this));
    return _result;
}

inline void ICalcEaster::PutYear ( short pVal ) {
    HRESULT _hr = put_Year(pVal);
    if (FAILED(_hr)) _com_issue_errorex(_hr, this, __uuidof(this));
}

inline short ICalcEaster::GetMonth ( ) {
    short _result;
    HRESULT _hr = get_Month(&_result);
    if (FAILED(_hr)) _com_issue_errorex(_hr, this, __uuidof(this));
    return _result;
}

inline short ICalcEaster::GetDay ( ) {
    short _result;
    HRESULT _hr = get_Day(&_result);
    if (FAILED(_hr)) _com_issue_errorex(_hr, this, __uuidof(this));
    return _result;
}

inline HRESULT ICalcEaster::CalculateEaster ( ) {
    HRESULT _hr = raw_CalculateEaster();
```

```
        if (FAILED(_hr)) _com_issue_errorex(_hr, this, __uuidof(this));
        return _hr;
    }
```

These simple **inline** functions simply call the raw versions of the methods, check the **HRESULT**s for failure, and throw a C++ error via the **_com_issue_errorex()** function if the method call failed.

Raw Interface Methods

The raw interface methods are declared in the third section of the **struct**. You can see that the properties are prefixed with **get_** or **put_**, as appropriate, and the methods are prefixed with **raw_**:

```
// Raw methods provided by interface
virtual HRESULT __stdcall get_Year (
    short * pVal ) = 0;
virtual HRESULT __stdcall put_Year (
    short pVal ) = 0;
virtual HRESULT __stdcall get_Month (
    short * pVal ) = 0;
virtual HRESULT __stdcall get_Day (
    short * pVal ) = 0;
virtual HRESULT __stdcall raw_CalculateEaster ( ) = 0;
```

These method declarations are here to match the vtable of this **struct** to the vtable of the **ICalcEaster** interface, which is pretty important since the use of vtables depends on their layout, and not on method or property names. These method declarations are entirely equivalent to the ones generated by **MIDL** that we used earlier. Remember how we saw in Chapter 1 that the names of the methods don't affect the layout of the vtable.

Using the Wrappers

Now that we've seen the format that the wrappers take, it's time to put them to use. Replace the code in **CClientDlg::OnOK()** with the code shown below:

```
LRESULT CClientDlg::OnOK(WORD wNotifyCode, WORD wID, HWND hWndCtl,
                                                    BOOL& bHandled)

{
    try
    {
        SIMPLELib::ICalcEasterPtr p( __uuidof(SIMPLELib::CalcEaster) );

        p->Year = GetDlgItemInt(IDC_YEAR);
        p->CalculateEaster();

        TCHAR buff[255] = {0};
        wsprintf(buff, _T("Easter: %d/%d in %d"), p->Day, p->Month,
                                                            p->Year);

        MessageBox(buff, _T("Calculation"));
    }
    catch (const _com_error& Err)
```

```
    {
      TCHAR buff[255] = {0};
      wsprintf(buff, _T("Error: 0x%x "), Err.Error());
      MessageBox(buff, _T("Error") );
    }
  return 0;
}
```

I hope you can see that the essential structure of the code is the same as the previous example:

- Create an instance of the **CalcEaster** coclass
- Set the year
- Tell the component to calculate Easter
- Display a message box with the results

The differences are important, however:

- We don't call **CoCreateInstance()** because we make use of one of the **_com_ptr_t<>** constructors:

```
      SIMPLELib::ICalcEasterPtr  p( __uuidof(SIMPLELib::CalcEaster) );
```

- This constructor takes the CLSID of a component, creates an instance of it, and queries for the appropriate interface (in this case, **ICalcEaster**), storing this in the smart pointer. If the underlying call to **CoCreateInstance()** fails, the constructor throws an error.
- We have complete error handling on *all* method calls thanks to the **try/catch** blocks, and the logic is cleaner because of it.
- We set and get the properties directly, as if they were data members.
- We don't call **Release()** because the smart pointer will handle that for us. This also has the benefit of simplifying the error-handling logic.

Enabling Exception Handling

When you compile this code, you will get a warning that exception handling hasn't been enabled:

warning C4530: C++ exception handler used, but unwind semantics are not enabled. Specify -GX

What does this mean in practice? If you don't have exception handling enabled and an exception occurs, then any objects with automatic storage (i.e. local objects) in the stack frame between the function doing the **throw** and the function **catch**ing the exception won't be properly destroyed.

You will need to enable exception handling for all the configurations in the project to ensure that everything works as it should in all circumstances. You can enable exception handling by using the Project | Settings... menu item to display the Project Settings dialog. Change the Settings For at the top-left of the dialog to say All Configurations, go to the C/C++ tab and select C++ Language from the Category list, then check the box labeled Enable exception handling.

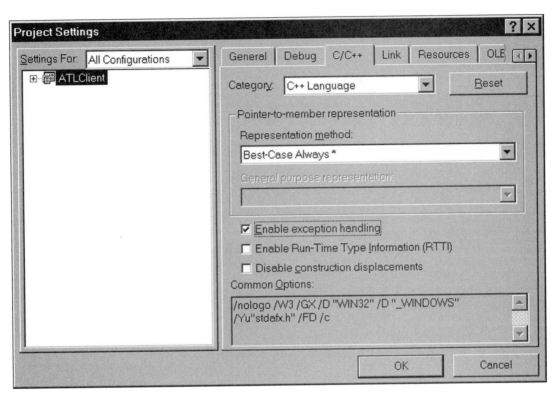

The reason you have to change the settings is that by default, all ATL projects have no facility for exception handling. This is another optimization measure designed to keep the size of the code down. If you want to make use of exception handling within an ATL project, you'll need to make sure that you have explicitly enabled it.

> *In most cases, you can avoid using code that will throw exceptions in your ATL project. ATL code itself doesn't throw exceptions, for example, and neither does any raw Win32 or COM code that you use. If you do need to use code that will throw or handle exceptions, you may still be able to get away without enabling exception handling in your project, but you should only do this after carefully analyzing the code you're using and if module size is an issue. In general, if you see the warning, enable exception handling. If you don't, don't.*

Now you can run the project and see that it still works.

Testing the Server from Visual Basic

If you have access to Visual Basic, it is very easy to write the equivalent test application for our server:

- Create a Standard EXE project
- Add a reference to the server's type library (Simple 1.0 Type Library) using Project | References...

> ▶ Add a command button and text box to the form
>
> ▶ Add the following code to the button's **Click** handler:

```
Private Sub cmdCalculate_Click()
On Error GoTo err_Generic
    Dim itf As SIMPLELib.ICalcEaster
    Set itf = New SIMPLELib.CalcEaster

    itf.Year = CInt(txtYear)
    itf.CalculateEaster

    MsgBox "Easter: " & itf.Day & "/" & itf.Month & " in " & itf.Year
    Exit Sub

err_Generic:
    MsgBox "Error: " & Err.Number & vbCrLf & Err.Description
End Sub
```

The code just serves to show that the server can be controlled from Visual Basic as well as from a Visual C++ client.

> *Perhaps the most interesting thing about this code is that it shows how to declare interface references in Visual Basic. The variable* **itf** *is declared as being of type* **SIMPLELib.ICalcEaster** — *in other words,* **itf** *is a reference to an* **ICalcEaster** *interface. The following line of code creates an instance of the* **CalcEaster** *coclass and* **QueryInterface()**s *for the* **ICalcEaster** *interface:*
>
> ```
> Set itf = New SIMPLELib.CalcEaster
> ```
>
> *You may be more used to seeing object references used in Visual Basic, such as the following line of code:*
>
> ```
> Dim obj As SIMPLELib.CalcEaster
> ```
>
> *For COM objects, an object reference is equivalent to an interface reference to the* **[default]** *interface on a coclass.*

Summary

We've covered a lot of ground in our first look at ATL. You've seen how to:

- Create a simple DLL server
- Add a coclass with a single interface
- Add properties and methods to that coclass

We also looked at:

- The structure of an ATL executable
- Using an ATL dialog
- How to create clients for our server in three ways — using raw interface pointers, compiler COM support smart pointers, and Visual Basic.

In the next chapter, we'll take a deeper look at the structure of ATL, we'll move beyond the wizards, and we'll see how ATL provides the COM foundation of class factories and reference counting that we had to build for ourselves in the last chapter.

ATL Architecture

In the first chapter, you saw how COM works and what COM requires from the coclasses that you write and the modules that serve them.

In Chapter 2, you saw how to use the ATL COM AppWizard to create an ATL project, how to use the ATL Object Wizard to add coclasses to your project, and how to use the dialogs provided by ClassView to add methods and properties to your coclass. We also started to take a look at how ATL provides the infrastructure necessary for your COM servers.

In this chapter, we'll take a closer look at ATL and particularly at the way that it provides class factories and the **IUnknown** methods for your coclasses. As we progress through the chapter, you'll build up an understanding of the relationship between the classes you create, their base classes, and their derived classes.

We'll start by taking a high-level look at the structure of ATL before getting a little deeper into the macros that make it all work.

The Structure of an ATL Class

All COM classes generated with ATL follow a similar pattern:

```
class ATL_NO_VTABLE CYourClass :
    public CComObjectRootEx<CComxxxThreadModel>,
    public CComCoClass< CYourClass, &CLSID_YourClass >,
    public ISomeInterface1,
    public ISomeInterface2,
    ... // List of interfaces
{
    ... // Construction

DECLARE_REGISTRY_RESOURCEID(IDR_YOURCLASS)

BEGIN_COM_MAP(CYourClass)
    COM_INTERFACE_ENTRY(ISomeInterface1)
    COM_INTERFACE_ENTRY(ISomeInterface2)
```

```
    ... // List of interface entry macros
  END_COM_MAP()

    ... // Method implementations
  };
```

CComObjectRootEx<> and its base class **CComObjectRootBase** are responsible for handling the implementation of the **IUnknown** methods for your class. Although they don't provide the **IUnknown** methods themselves, these classes provide much of the code used in their implementation.

CComCoClass<> defines how COM objects should be created from your class, so it's used as a base class for all externally creatable classes. **CComCoClass<>** provides a couple of **typedef**s that determine what sort of class factory is responsible for creating your objects, and how (or whether) your class supports aggregation. By default, objects will be created by ATL's class factory implementation (**CComClassFactory**), and the objects will support aggregation.

> *All ATL COM classes derive from* **CComObjectRootEx<>**. *Externally creatable classes also derive from* **CComCoClass<>**.

Your class also derives from the interfaces that it implements. In general, these interface classes just provide the vtable layout. However, ATL does provide some classes that provide default implementations of various interfaces, which you may also use as base classes. We'll meet some of these implementation classes later in the book.

All the interfaces (except **IUnknown**) exposed by the coclass have entries in the COM map. The COM map provides the information used by ATL's **QueryInterface()** implementation.

> *Your class derives from the interfaces that it implements. Each interface has an entry in the COM map.*

The **DECLARE_REGISTRY_RESOURCEID()** macro links the registry script identified by the resource ID to your class so that it can be automatically registered. This macro is present in all the Wizard-generated ATL COM classes. Registration is only necessary for externally creatable classes.

The Object Map

Each externally creatable coclass in the project has an entry in the object map (which lives in the project's main source file). The object map has the following layout:

```
  BEGIN_OBJECT_MAP(ObjectMap)
    OBJECT_ENTRY(CLSID_YourClass, CYourClass)
    OBJECT_ENTRY(CLSID_YourClass2, CYourClass2)
    ...
  END_OBJECT_MAP()
```

Each **OBJECT_ENTRY** hooks your class up to a class factory. If your class doesn't have an entry in the map, clients won't be able to create objects of that type, and your class won't even register itself. Classes that do appear in the object map should derive from **CComCoClass<>**, as mentioned previously.

CComObject<>

The important thing to realize is that your class is never instantiated directly; it always acts as a base class. There's at least one important clue to this in the definition of the class itself — the **ATL_NO_VTABLE** macro. In the last chapter, we explained how this macro provides an optimization that eliminates the initialization of the vtable from your class's constructor. We also explained that it couldn't be used in classes at the end of the inheritance chain. Clearly, there is a class beneath the class that we define.

In simple terms, that class is **CComObject<>**, or more accurately **CComObject<CYourClass>**. **CComObject<>** provides the actual implementation of the **IUnknown** functions (which ultimately delegate to methods in **CComObjectRootEx<>**). It also provides the code for locking the module while the object is alive.

Here you can see the class hierarchy of COM objects based on your class:

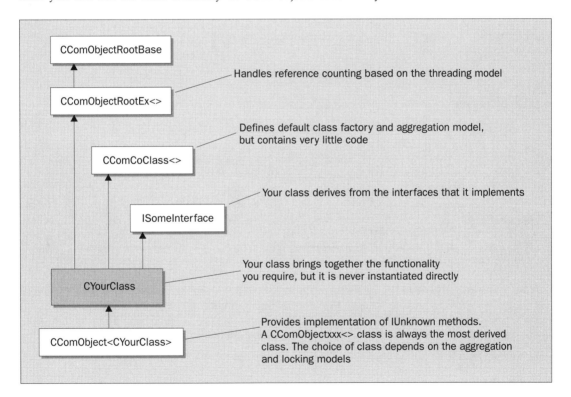

CComObjectxxx<> classes

Why *does* ATL use your class as a base class, rather than instantiating it directly? The simple reason is that the behavior provided by the class at the bottom of the hierarchy can be changed depending on circumstances. This change can be accomplished without changing the class that you create, which wouldn't be possible if all the behavior was provided by base classes of your class.

ATL provides a number of classes (which I shall refer to as the **CComObject***xxx*<> classes) to fulfil the role of most-derived class in this hierarchy. The **CComObject***xxx*<> classes are responsible for three key areas:

- Aggregation
- Locking
- Destruction

We'll discuss 'aggregation' later in the chapter; 'locking' refers to the way in which the COM object interacts with the lock count of the module; and 'destruction' refers to the mechanism used (if any) to destroy the object when the final reference count is released on it. None of these issues is part of the functionality of a specific coclass, they are generic features that can be switched around as the need arises. Some classes may support aggregation, others may not; some objects may need to keep the module locked while they're active and others may not; some objects may need to be created on the heap and others on the stack.

All of these requirements can be accommodated without the need for any changes to the classes that you create.

The Maps

In the sections that follow, we'll explore the macros that provide a good deal of ATL's COM support. Specifically, we'll take a close look at the COM map and object map macros. Although you can do quite a lot with the knowledge you've gained up to now, the following sections will form a solid foundation that can inform all your future use of ATL.

We're going to examine the COM map and object map *in detail*. If you find that you're getting bogged-down, skip through the text until you get to the summary at the end of each section. Use the examples (starting with *Adding COM Support to a Dialog*) to get a better feeling for ATL, then come back to this part of the chapter as your comfort level and experience with ATL grows.

You can use the knowledge that you glean from the following sections to give you a starting point for debugging any problems that you might encounter. By the end, you'll be in a position where you understand what's possible and what's not, you won't start writing code that ATL already provides for you, and you'll be able to decide whether to use the code provided by the Wizards or some alternatives provided by ATL.

The COM Map

We'll start by examining the **COM map**, the macro-wrapped structure that ATL uses to keep track of the interfaces exposed by your classes. In the last chapter, we had a class called **CCalcEaster**, with a COM map (in **CalcEaster.h**) that looked like this:

```
BEGIN_COM_MAP(CCalcEaster)
    COM_INTERFACE_ENTRY(ICalcEaster)
    COM_INTERFACE_ENTRY(IDispatch)
END_COM_MAP()
```

Each interface exposed by **QueryInterface()** for the **CCalcEaster** class has an entry in the COM map.

BEGIN_COM_MAP()

BEGIN_COM_MAP() is a macro defined in the file **Atlcom.h**.

```
#define BEGIN_COM_MAP(x) public: \
    typedef x _ComMapClass; \
    static HRESULT WINAPI _Cache(void* pv, REFIID iid, void** ppvObject,
        DWORD dw)\
    {\
        _ComMapClass* p = (_ComMapClass*)pv;\
        p->Lock();\
        HRESULT hRes = CComObjectRootBase::_Cache(pv, iid, ppvObject, dw);\
        p->Unlock();\
        return hRes;\
    }\
    IUnknown* GetUnknown() \
    { _ASSERTE(_GetEntries()[0].pFunc == _ATL_SIMPLEMAPENTRY); \
      return (IUnknown*)((int)this+_GetEntries()->dw); } \
    HRESULT _InternalQueryInterface(REFIID iid, void** ppvObject) \
    { return InternalQueryInterface(this, _GetEntries(), iid, ppvObject); \
    } \
        const static _ATL_INTMAP_ENTRY* WINAPI _GetEntries() { \
        static const _ATL_INTMAP_ENTRY _entries[] = { DEBUG_QI_ENTRY(x)
```

Although it looks pretty confusing at first glance, we can soon see the important elements of the macro.

> *If you're not used to looking at complicated macros, remember that each line of a multi-line macro must end with a backslash, which acts as a line continuation character.*

typedef

First, we have a **typedef** for **_ComMapClass** that evaluates to the class used as the macro argument. In other words, **_ComMapClass** is *our* class — the one that we have control over, and the one that contains the COM map itself. In this example, that's **CCalcEaster**.

```
#define BEGIN_COM_MAP(x) public: \
    typedef x _ComMapClass; \
```

This **typedef** is used in the definition of the **_Cache()** method and in many of the ATL macros associated with the COM map, including **COM_INTERFACE_ENTRY()**. You'll get to see these other macros shortly. The **typedef** is a great way of simplifying the code associated with the COM map macros.

_Cache()

_Cache() is a **static** function used for returning cached interface pointers. It is typically used for advanced features like autoaggregation and tear-off interfaces. If you're interested in these features, take a look at the documentation supplied with Visual C++ they are beyond the scope of this book.

107

GetUnknown()

`GetUnknown()` is a function that simply returns a pointer to **IUnknown** for the object.

```
IUnknown* GetUnknown() \
{ _ASSERTE(_GetEntries()[0].pFunc == _ATL_SIMPLEMAPENTRY); \
  return (IUnknown*)((int)this+_GetEntries()->dw); } \
```

If you ever need to get an **IUnknown*** for your object from within one of its methods, **GetUnknown()** is a convenient way of getting it. You'll see an example of when you might want to do this later in the chapter.

GetUnknown() uses the **_GetEntries()** function, partially defined at the end of the **BEGIN_COM_MAP()** macro, to get the pointer offset to **IUnknown**. It adds this value to the **this** pointer for the object, then casts to **IUnknown*** to get the appropriate pointer. We'll discuss the **_GetEntries()** function and pointer offsets shortly.

_InternalQueryInterface()

_InternalQueryInterface() is the function responsible for returning the interface pointers supported by this object, but it's not the **QueryInterface()** function itself (note that it's not **virtual**, for example).

```
HRESULT _InternalQueryInterface(REFIID iid, void** ppvObject) \
{ return InternalQueryInterface(this, _GetEntries(), iid, ppvObject);
} \
```

_InternalQueryInterface() delegates to **ComObjectRootBase::InternalQueryInterface()**, which in turn delegates to **AtlInternalQueryInterface()**. This latter is the function that actually contains the code to handle the **QI()** functionality.

This rather convoluted sequence of function calls is actually incredibly efficient. The code in **CComObjectRootBase::InternalQueryInterface()** provides some useful asserts and debugging aids, but in release builds it disappears, leaving only the call to **AtlInternalQueryInterface()**. Keeping all the code in this global function, rather than duplicating it among all the different classes that you might define in a project, keeps the size of the compiled code as tight as possible.

_GetEntries()

_GetEntries() returns an array of **_ATL_INTMAP_ENTRY** structures.

```
const static _ATL_INTMAP_ENTRY* WINAPI _GetEntries() { \
    static const _ATL_INTMAP_ENTRY _entries[] = { DEBUG_QI_ENTRY(x)
```

The array that it returns is a **static** constant called **_entries**, defined within the function.

Each **_ATL_INTMAP_ENTRY** structure relates an interface identifier with a way of getting the interface pointer related to that IID. You can see the definition of this structure in **Atlbase.h**.

```
struct _ATL_INTMAP_ENTRY
{
  const IID* piid;                    // The interface id (IID)
```

```
    DWORD dw;
    _ATL_CREATORARGFUNC* pFunc;          // NULL:end, 1:offset, n:ptr
};
```

A pointer to the IID is held in the **piid** member. The meaning of the **DWORD** value, **dw**, depends on the contents of **pFunc**:

▶ If **pFunc** is **NULL**, **dw** has no meaning and both **dw** and **piid** should also be **NULL**. A NULL **_ATL_INTMAP_ENTRY** is used to signify the end of the array.

▶ If **pFunc** is **1** (or **_ATL_SIMPLEMAPENTRY**, which is defined as **1**), **dw** is the offset to use to get from a pointer to the **_ComMapClass** to a pointer to the desired interface. As you'll see, this is the most common type of entry.

▶ If **pFunc** is anything other than **NULL** or **1**, **pFunc** is a pointer to a function to call to get the desired interface pointer, and **dw** is passed as an argument to the function. ATL uses **pFunc** in this form to deal with autoaggregation and tear-off interfaces. Since these are advanced topics, we won't concern ourselves with them.

COM_INTERFACE_ENTRY()

The elements of the **_entries** array are defined using the **COM_INTERFACE_***xxx***()** macros, of which there are a number defined in **Atlcom.h**. The most important of them is the **COM_INTERFACE_ENTRY()** macro, which we used to expose the **IDispatch** and **ICalcEaster** interfaces in our example in the previous chapter:

```
#define COM_INTERFACE_ENTRY(x)\
    {&IID_##x, \
    offsetofclass(x, _ComMapClass), \
    _ATL_SIMPLEMAPENTRY},
```

Whenever we use **COM_INTERFACE_ENTRY()**, we're just adding another **_ATL_INTMAP_ENTRY** structure to the **_entries** array. The interface ID pointer is generated using the token-pasting operator (**##**), so in the case of **ICalcEaster**, we'd be taking the address of **IID_ICalcEaster**. This works well when we're using system or **MIDL**-generated headers because that's exactly the form the IID constants have.

offsetofclass() is defined in **Atlbase.h**. This macro just determines the offset of a derived class from its base class. In the context of **COM_INTERFACE_ENTRY()**, the **offsetofclass()** macro is used to determine the offset of the interface class from the class that derives from it.

```
#define offsetofclass(base, derived)
((DWORD)(static_cast<base*>((derived*)8))-8)
```

The **offsetofclass()** *macro works like this:*

Take a value (in this case 8)

Tell the compiler that it's a pointer to the derived class (by using a C-style cast)

Cast the value to a pointer to the base class (using **static_cast<>***)*

Subtract the original value from the value returned by the cast (to determine the offset)

Cast the result to a **DWORD***.*

> *The number **8** is not significant in this macro. All that really matters is that it's a non-zero value — zero is the same as **NULL**, and the C++ language says that casting a null pointer will always result in a null pointer.*

Other important **COM_INTERFACE_ENTRY_***xxx***()** macros are:

▶ **COM_INTERFACE_ENTRY_IID()**, which allows you to pass the name of the IID directly. You might want to use this macro if the interface identifier isn't in the form **IID_***interfacename*.

```
#define COM_INTERFACE_ENTRY_IID(iid, x)\
   {&iid,\
   offsetofclass(x, _ComMapClass),\
   _ATL_SIMPLEMAPENTRY},
```

▶ **COM_INTERFACE_ENTRY_IMPL()**, which is designed to simplify the entry for an interface implemented by one of ATL's classes when it doesn't derive from the interface it implements, but instead redeclares the vtable directly. In this situation, it's not possible to determine an offset to the original interface (because it's not actually in the inheritance hierarchy), so the macro determines the offset to the implementation class. You'll see this macro in use later in the book.

```
#define COM_INTERFACE_ENTRY_IMPL(x)\
   COM_INTERFACE_ENTRY_IID(IID_##x, x##Impl<_ComMapClass>)
```

▶ **COM_INTERFACE_ENTRY2()**, which is used when you want to expose an interface that is a base class to two or more of your class's base classes. Once again, you'll see this macro in use later in the book.

```
#define COM_INTERFACE_ENTRY2(x, x2)\
   {&IID_##x,\
   (DWORD)((x*)(x2*)((_ComMapClass*)8))-8,\
   _ATL_SIMPLEMAPENTRY},
```

END_COM_MAP()

Finally, the COM map is closed with the **END_COM_MAP()** macro, the definition of which you can find in **Atlcom.h**:

```
#ifdef _ATL_DEBUG_QI
#define END_COM_MAP()    {NULL, 0, 0}};\
   return &_entries[1];}
#else
#define END_COM_MAP()    {NULL, 0, 0}};\
   return _entries;}
#endif // _ATL_DEBUG_QI
```

Ignoring the **#ifdef _ATL_DEBUG_QI**, you can see that **END_COM_MAP()** just terminates the array with a null entry, and returns the array.

If you **#define _ATL_DEBUG_QI** *for your project, the Debug tab of Developer Studio's Output window will display the name of each interface that is queried for on your object. You might be surprised by some of the interfaces that your object gets asked for in different circumstances.*

COM Map Summary

The COM map defines a few important functions in your class. The most important of these is **_GetEntries()**, which returns an array of **_ATL_INTMAP_ENTRY** structures. This array is vital to the correct operation of ATL's mechanism for handling **QueryInterface()**. You can add to the array by adding **COM_INTERFACE_ENTRY_***xxx***()** entries within the COM map.

Note that you don't need an entry for **IUnknown** — **IUnknown** is handled by the first entry in the COM map. Also be aware that the order in which the entries appear is the order in which the entries are searched. For maximum performance, place the interfaces that are queried for most frequently at the top of the map.

The COM map also defines an **_InternalQueryInterface()** function which delegates to **CComObjectRootBase::InternalQueryInterface()**, and ultimately to **AtlInternalQueryInterface()**.

The Object Map

Another important map in the world of ATL is the **object map**. The object map is present in all ATL projects, and lives in a project's main CPP file. The object map controls the class factories and registration for the coclasses in your project. Each class that you want to be independently creatable — in other words, creatable by a call to **CoCreateInstance()** or a similar function — must have an entry in the object map.

In the example from the previous chapter, the object map looked like this:

```
BEGIN_OBJECT_MAP(ObjectMap)
    OBJECT_ENTRY(CLSID_CalcEaster, CCalcEaster)
END_OBJECT_MAP()
```

Let's crack open these macros to see how it all works.

BEGIN_OBJECT_MAP() and END_OBJECT_MAP()

The **BEGIN_OBJECT_MAP()** and **END_OBJECT_MAP()** macros are extremely simple. You can find them defined in **Atlcom.h**:

```
#define BEGIN_OBJECT_MAP(x) static _ATL_OBJMAP_ENTRY x[] = {
#define END_OBJECT_MAP()    {NULL, NULL, NULL, NULL}};
```

You can see that the object map is a straightforward, null-terminated array of **_ATL_OBJMAP_ENTRY** structures. The **BEGIN_OBJECT_MAP()** and **END_OBJECT_MAP()** macros define the start and end of the array, and each **OBJECT_ENTRY()** is a new element in the array.

111

_ATL_OBJMAP_ENTRY

Unfortunately, the **_ATL_OBJMAP_ENTRY** structure isn't quite as straightforward. You can see this for yourself by examining its definition, taken from **Atlbase.h**:

```
struct _ATL_OBJMAP_ENTRY
{
    const CLSID* pclsid;
    HRESULT (WINAPI *pfnUpdateRegistry)(BOOL bRegister);
    _ATL_CREATORFUNC* pfnGetClassObject;
    _ATL_CREATORFUNC* pfnCreateInstance;
    IUnknown* pCF;
    DWORD dwRegister;
    _ATL_DESCRIPTIONFUNC* pfnGetObjectDescription;
    HRESULT WINAPI RevokeClassObject()
    {
        return CoRevokeClassObject(dwRegister);
    }
    HRESULT WINAPI RegisterClassObject(DWORD dwClsContext, DWORD dwFlags)
    {
        IUnknown* p = NULL;
        HRESULT hRes = pfnGetClassObject(pfnCreateInstance, IID_IUnknown,
                (LPVOID*) &p);
        if (SUCCEEDED(hRes))
            hRes = CoRegisterClassObject(*pclsid, p, dwClsContext, dwFlags,
                &dwRegister);
        if (p != NULL)
            p->Release();
        return hRes;
    }
};
```

The structure holds a number of pointers and defines a couple of methods, all of which are related to the creation or registration of a particular class. The methods **RegisterClassObject()** and **RevokeClassObject()** just register and unregister the class object with the class table (as described in Chapter 1). The data members are more interesting:

Data Member	Description
`pclsid`	Pointer to the CLSID
`pfnUpdateRegistry`	Pointer to the function used to update the registry with information about the class
`pfnGetClassObject`	Pointer to the function used to create a class object and return a pointer to one of its interfaces
`pfnCreateInstance`	Pointer to the function used to create an instance of the class specified by `pclsid`
`pCF`	Pointer to the class factory's **IUnknown** interface

Data Member	Description
`dwRegister`	A **DWORD** used to store the cookie returned from `CoRegisterClassObject()`. (`CoRegisterClassObject()` returns a cookie to the caller that it can pass back via `CoRevokeClassObject()` when the class object needs to be unregistered)
`pfnGetObjectDescription`	Pointer to the function used to return a text description for the class. Used for registration purposes by the component registrar.

OBJECT_ENTRY()

The **OBJECT_ENTRY()** macro provides values for all the structure's data members based on two pieces of information: the CLSID, and your class. **OBJECT_ENTRY()** is defined like this:

```
#define OBJECT_ENTRY(clsid, class) {&clsid, &class::UpdateRegistry,\
    &class::_ClassFactoryCreatorClass::CreateInstance,\
    &class::_CreatorClass::CreateInstance, NULL, 0,
&class::GetObjectDescription },
```

We'll look at where each of these entries comes from in turn.

pclsid = &clsid

pclsid is just set to the address of the CLSID passed as the first parameter to the macro. In the case of our simple example from the previous chapter, this CLSID constant is automatically generated by **MIDL** when it compiles the IDL file.

pfnUpdateRegistry = &class::UpdateRegistry

pfnUpdateRegistry is the address of our class's **UpdateRegistry()** function. The **UpdateRegistry()** function is actually hidden behind a macro of its own in the definition of our class:

```
class ATL_NO_VTABLE CCalcEaster :
    public CComObjectRootEx<CComSingleThreadModel>,
    public CComCoClass<CCalcEaster, &CLSID_CalcEaster>,
    public IDispatchImpl<ICalcEaster, &IID_ICalcEaster, &LIBID_SIMPLELib>
{
public:
    CCalcEaster() : m_Year(-1), m_Month(-1), m_Day(-1)
    {
    }
```

```
    DECLARE_REGISTRY_RESOURCEID(IDR_CALCEASTER)
```

The **DECLARE_REGISTRY_RESOURCEID()** macro is defined in **Atlcom.h**, along with a number of other **DECLARE_REGISTRY_***xxx***()** macros that each define **UpdateRegistry()** in slightly different ways. All of them get their functionality from the **_Module** object:

```
#define DECLARE_NO_REGISTRY()\
    static HRESULT WINAPI UpdateRegistry(BOOL /*bRegister*/)\
    {return S_OK;}

#define DECLARE_REGISTRY(class, pid, vpid, nid, flags)\
    static HRESULT WINAPI UpdateRegistry(BOOL bRegister)\
    {\
        return _Module.UpdateRegistryClass(GetObjectCLSID(), pid, vpid,
nid,\
            flags, bRegister);\
    }

#define DECLARE_REGISTRY_RESOURCE(x)\
    static HRESULT WINAPI UpdateRegistry(BOOL bRegister)\
    {\
    return _Module.UpdateRegistryFromResource(_T(#x), bRegister);\
    }

#define DECLARE_REGISTRY_RESOURCEID(x)\
    static HRESULT WINAPI UpdateRegistry(BOOL bRegister)\
    {\
    return _Module.UpdateRegistryFromResource(x, bRegister);\
    }
```

If you don't want to make any registry entries for your class, you can add the
DECLARE_NO_REGISTRY() macro to your class definition. If you want to add registry entries
based on a CLSID, ProgID, version-independent ProgID and a description string resource, you
can use **DECLARE_REGISTRY()**. If you want to update the registry based on a resource created
from an RGS file, use **DECLARE_REGISTRY_RESOURCE()** or
DECLARE_REGISTRY_RESOURCEID().

You don't have to use any of these macros if you don't want to, but if you want to make use
of the **OBJECT_ENTRY()** macro, you will need to provide an **UpdateRegistry()** method in
your class.

pfnGetClassObject = &class::_ClassFactoryCreatorClass::CreateInstance

OBJECT_ENTRY() sets the **pfnGetClassObject** member to be
&class::_ClassFactoryCreatorClass::CreateInstance(). This **CreateInstance()**
function is used to create class factories. The **_ClassFactoryCreatorClass** is just a **typedef**
scoped within your class. This **typedef** is usually defined by one of the
DECLARE_CLASSFACTORYxxx**()** macros defined in **Atlcom.h**.

By default, your class uses the **typedef** defined by the **DECLARE_CLASSFACTORY()** macro,
because this macro is used in **CComCoClass<>**, from which your class derives.

```
#define DECLARE_CLASSFACTORY() DECLARE_CLASSFACTORY_EX(CComClassFactory)

#if defined(_WINDLL) | defined(_USRDLL)
#define DECLARE_CLASSFACTORY_EX(cf)
    typedef CComCreator< CComObjectCached< cf > >
_ClassFactoryCreatorClass;
```

```
#else
// don't let class factory refcount influence lock count
#define DECLARE_CLASSFACTORY_EX(cf)
      typedef CComCreator< CComObjectNoLock< cf > >
_ClassFactoryCreatorClass;
#endif
```

CComCreator<> is the class that exposes the **CreateInstance()** method to which we store a pointer in **pfnGetClassObject**. It creates instances of the class specified by its template parameter. When the project is a DLL, **CreateInstance()** will create objects of class **CComObjectCached<CComClassFactory>**; when the project is an EXE, **CreateInstance()** will create objects of class **CComObjectNoLock<CComClassFactory>**.

ATL's **CComObject**xxx**<>** classes provide the implementation of the **IUnknown** methods. These classes not only handle the basics of reference counting for the object itself, but also interact appropriately with the module's (i.e. the EXE's or the DLL's) lock count. There are a number of **CComObject**xxx**<>** classes, each of which has slightly different behavior, but all the **CComObject**xxx**<>** classes derive from the class specified as their template parameter, and delegate most of the functionality of **QueryInterface()** through the base class's **_InternalQueryInterface()** method.

> *Remember from Chapter 1 that a class object is a COM object, so it must expose* **IUnknown** *at a minimum.*

CComObjectCached<> is used when you want to cache COM objects. In other words, if you want to keep a COM object around even when there are no external clients with references to it, you should create it from **CComObjectCached<>**. **CComObjectCached<>** is aware that the first reference count on the object shouldn't also be used to hold the module in memory (or else it will never unload), so **AddRef()** and **Release()** are coded such that the module is only locked when the reference count rises to 2, and the module is unlocked when the reference count falls to 1. That means that you can create a **CComObjectCached<>** object as your module loads so that it can be accessed swiftly. This is sensible behavior for class objects, and may also make sense if you decide to expose an **Application** object, for example.

CComObjectNoLock<> is used when you don't want the reference count of the object to affect the lock count of the module at all. We discussed the reason why the reference count on the class objects of an executable can't also be used to keep that module in memory way back in Chapter 1 (COM hangs on to the class factories). It should make sense to see the class objects for an ATL executable using **CComObjectNoLock<>** to provide the implementation of the **IUnknown** methods.

CComClassFactory is the class that implements the **IClassFactory** interface. The implementations of that interface's methods are extremely simple (as you can see if you take a look in **Atlimpl.cpp**). The **LockServer()** method just calls **_Module.Lock()** or **_Module.Unlock()** depending on the value of the method's parameter. The **CreateInstance()** method doesn't do much more than call the **CreateInstance()** function that is passed to it as a pointer when the object is created by **CComCreator<>**. It turns out that this function pointer is the same pointer as specified in the **pfnCreateInstance** member of the **_ATL_OBJMAP_ENTRY** structure.

Here you can see the class hierarchy for the class factory used to generate ATL objects by default.

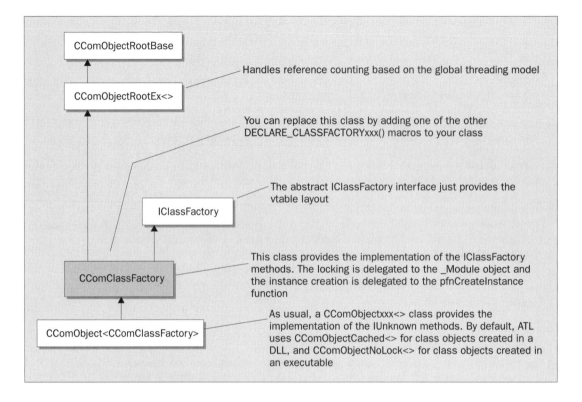

You can override the **typedef** defined in **CComCoClass<>** for the class factory by setting up your own. The easiest way to do that is just add one of the other **DECLARE_CLASSFACTORY***xxx***()** macros to the definition of your class. Typical alternatives are **DECLARE_CLASSFACTORY2()** if you want to support licensing, or **DECLARE_CLASSFACTORY_SINGLETON()** if you want all clients to connect to the same instance of an object. We'll look at an example using **DECLARE_CLASSFACTORY_SINGLETON()** later in the chapter.

```
#define DECLARE_CLASSFACTORY2(lic)
   DECLARE_CLASSFACTORY_EX(CComClassFactory2<lic>)
#define DECLARE_CLASSFACTORY_SINGLETON(obj) \
   DECLARE_CLASSFACTORY_EX(CComClassFactorySingleton<obj>)
```

pfnCreateInstance =&class::_CreatorClass::CreateInstance

OBJECT_ENTRY() sets the **pfnCreateInstance** member to be **&class::_CreatorClass::CreateInstance**. This **CreateInstance()** function is used to create COM objects. Once again, **_CreatorClass** is just a **typedef** scoped within your class. This **typedef** is provided, by default, by the **DECLARE_AGGREGATABLE()** macro in the definition of **CComCoClass<>**.You can override this in your own class using one of the other **DECLARE_***xxx***AGGREGATABLE()** macros.

We'll look at the **DECLARE_***xxx***AGGREGATABLE()** macros later in the chapter, when we examine aggregation in detail and look at an example. For now, we'll just take a closer look at the macro used by default:

```
#define DECLARE_AGGREGATABLE(x) public:\
   typedef CComCreator2< CComCreator< CComObject< x > >, \
                       CComCreator< CComAggObject< x > > >
_CreatorClass;
```

CComCreator2<> is just a simple class that exposes a single **CreateInstance()** function. The implementation of that function checks whether an object is being aggregated. If it isn't being aggregated, the function delegates to the **CreateInstance()** method of the first template parameter (in this case, **CComCreator< CComObject< x > >**). If it is being aggregated, **CComCreator2<>::CreateInstance()** calls the **CreateInstance()** method of the second template parameter (**CComCreator< CComAggObject< x > >**).

> *Note that the* **CreateInstance()** *functions in both the*
> **_ClassFactoryCreatorClass** *and* **_CreatorClass** *must be* **static** *because*
> *they're not called through an object.*

Here, you can see that the COM object that actually gets created by the class factory is *not* an instance of the class that we defined (represented by **x** in the macro, and evaluating to **CCalcEaster** in our example). It is actually an instance of **CComObject< x >** (when it's not being aggregated). Remember that our class, **CCalcEaster**, is abstract — it doesn't implement the **IUnknown** methods, and it doesn't have an independently instantiable vtable, thanks to the **ATL_NO_VTABLE** optimization applied to it. The COM classes that we create are only ever used as base classes for objects created from one of the **CComObject***xxx***<>** classes, which provide the implementation of the **IUnknown** methods.

pCF = NULL and dwRegister = 0

The **OBJECT_ENTRY()** macro sets the **pCF** and **dwRegister** members of the **_ATL_OBJMAP_ENTRY** structure to **NULL** and **0** respectively. These members are set with useful values once a class factory has been created (in which case a pointer to its **IUnknown** interface is stored in the **pCF** member) and registered (the cookie returned by a call to **CoRegisterClassObject()** is stored in the **dwRegister** member).

pfnGetObjectDescription = &class::GetObjectDescription

The **pfnGetObjectDescription** member is set to the address of the **static** **GetObjectDescription()** function provided by your class, or, more accurately, provided by **CComCoClass<>** from which your class derives. The implementation of this function in **CComCoClass<>** just returns a **NULL** pointer.

You can override (mask) this function in your own class to return something other than **NULL**, but you should be aware that if you return a non-**NULL** result from **GetObjectDescription()**, ATL's standard registration code will *not* register your coclass. This is because **GetObjectDescription()** is designed for use with a component registrar object, which is one of the object types that you can add to your project using the ATL Object Wizard. It is designed to help you register your coclasses. We won't examine how to use the component registrar in this book. Just be aware that returning anything other than **NULL** from **GetObjectDescription()** will cause problems unless you understand how to register your coclasses using the component registrar.

Object Map Summary

The object map is a null-terminated array of **_ATL_OBJMAP_ENTRY** structures. Each element controls the registration and creation of one type of object.

Each element of the array is defined by using an **OBJECT_ENTRY()** macro. Object entries are usually added to the map automatically by the Object Wizard.

The class specified in the second macro parameter must implement the **UpdateRegistry()** and **GetObjectDescription()** functions, as well as provide **typedef**s for **_ClassFactoryCreatorClass** and **_CreatorClass**, each of which must implement a **CreateInstance()** function.

The **UpdateRegistry()** function is usually provided by one of the **DECLARE_REGISTRY_***xxx***()** macros. Typically, the **DECLARE_REGISTRY_RESOURCEID()** macro is added to your class when it's generated by the Object Wizard.

The **typedef** for **_ClassFactoryCreatorClass** is usually provided by one of the **DECLARE_CLASSFACTORY***xxx***()** macros. **CComCoClass<>** uses the **DECLARE_CLASSFACTORY()** macro by default. You can override this by adding a different macro to your class.

The **typedef** for **_CreatorClass** is usually provided by one of the **DECLARE_***xxx***AGGREGATABLE()** macros. **CComCoClass<>** uses the **DECLARE_AGGREGATABLE()** macro by default. You can override this by adding a different macro to your class.

ATL COM objects are instances of a template specialization of one of the **CComObject***xxx***<>** classes. The **CComObject***xxx***<>** class usually derives from the class that implements the COM methods. By default, objects are instances of a **CComObject<>** class when not being aggregated, or instances of a **CComAggObject<>** class when they are. The **CComObject***xxx***<>** classes provide the implementation of the **IUnknown** methods and the code for locking the module if appropriate.

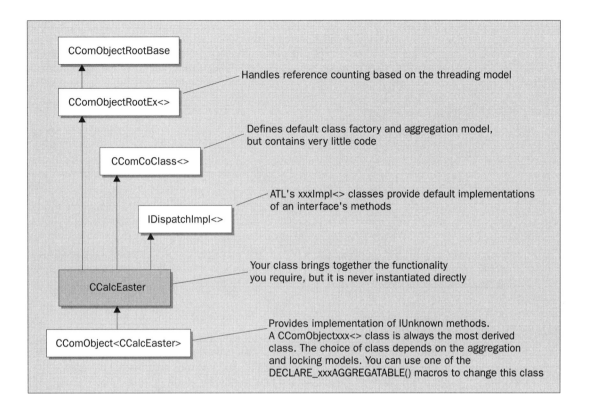

Here's the class hierarchy for the **CCalcEaster** class from the last chapter.

Object Creation

Now that we've got a good understanding of the structure of ATL's COM map and object map, let's set that knowledge in stone by tracing through the creation of a COM object. We'll look at a typical example from the points of view of an EXE server and a DLL server. The differences arise in the creation of the class objects. Once the client has a pointer to an interface on a class object (usually **IClassFactory**), the code is identical for DLL and EXE.

If you want to see the code in action as we discuss it, you can put a breakpoint in the **DllGetClassObject()** function of the simple object and step through the code in the debugger.

Class Factory Creation in a DLL

We'll start by looking at **DllGetClassObject()**, the global function called by COM when a client is requesting an interface on one of the class objects, and a prelude to creating the object that the client's really after. At this stage, the DLL has been loaded and the **_Module** object has got hold of the object map.

```
STDAPI DllGetClassObject(REFCLSID rclsid, REFIID riid, LPVOID* ppv)
{
   return _Module.GetClassObject(rclsid, riid, ppv);
}
```

DllGetClassObject() just calls **CComModule::GetClassObject()**, which in turn calls the global function **AtlModuleGetClassObject()**. Once again, we can see an inline class method delegate to a global function to ensure that the compiled code is as tight as possible.

```
// Obtain a Class Factory (DLL only)
HRESULT GetClassObject(REFCLSID rclsid, REFIID riid, LPVOID* ppv)
{
   return AtlModuleGetClassObject(this, rclsid, riid, ppv);
}
```

AtlModuleGetClassObject()

AtlModuleGetClassObject() loops through the object map, comparing the **pclsid** member of each element of the array with the CLSID passed to **DllGetClassObject()**. When it finds a match, it checks the **pCF** member of the **_ATL_OBJMAP_ENTRY** against **NULL**.

If **pCF** is **NULL**, **AtlModuleGetClassObject()** knows that it needs to create the class object. It does this by calling the class object **CreateInstance()** function pointed to by **pfnGetClassObject**. It passes the COM object **CreateInstance()** function pointed to by **pfnCreateInstance** to initialize the class object as the first parameter. It also passes **IID_IUnknown** so that the function knows that we want a pointer to the class object's **IUnknown** interface, and the address of the entry's **pCF** member so that the **IUnknown** pointer can be stored there.

If **pCF** isn't **NULL**, it must be a pointer to the **IUnknown** interface of a valid class object, so the code just calls **QueryInterface()** against it, using the IID and the indirect pointer passed to **DllGetClassObject()**, and its work is complete.

```
ATLAPI AtlModuleGetClassObject(_ATL_MODULE* pM, REFCLSID rclsid,
                                            REFIID riid, LPVOID* ppv)
{
   _ASSERTE(pM != NULL);
   if (pM == NULL)
      return E_INVALIDARG;
   _ASSERTE(pM->m_pObjMap != NULL);
   _ATL_OBJMAP_ENTRY* pEntry = pM->m_pObjMap;
   HRESULT hRes = S_OK;
   if (ppv == NULL)
      return E_POINTER;
   while (pEntry->pclsid != NULL)
```

```
    {
        if (InlineIsEqualGUID(rclsid, *pEntry->pclsid))
        {
            if (pEntry->pCF == NULL)
            {
                EnterCriticalSection(&pM->m_csObjMap);
                if (pEntry->pCF == NULL)
                    hRes = pEntry->pfnGetClassObject(
                    pEntry->pfnCreateInstance, IID_IUnknown, (LPVOID*)&pEntry-
                        >pCF);
                LeaveCriticalSection(&pM->m_csObjMap);
            }
            if (pEntry->pCF != NULL)
                hRes = pEntry->pCF->QueryInterface(riid, ppv);
            break;
        }
        pEntry++;
    }
    if (*ppv == NULL && hRes == S_OK)
        hRes = CLASS_E_CLASSNOTAVAILABLE;
    return hRes;
}
```

Class Factory Creation in an EXE

An executable doesn't wait for a client to request its class factories before creating them;
instead, it creates them as it starts up and registers them with the class table. This process
begins with a call to **CComModule::RegisterClassObjects()**, which you can find in the
Wizard-generated **_tWinMain()** function of an ATL executable:

```
if (bRun)
{
    hRes = _Module.RegisterClassObjects(CLSCTX_LOCAL_SERVER,
        REGCLS_MULTIPLEUSE);
```

Just as **CComModule::GetClassObject()** calls **AtlModuleGetClassObject()**, so
CComModule::RegisterClassObjects() calls **AtlModuleRegisterClassObjects()**.

```
HRESULT RegisterClassObjects(DWORD dwClsContext, DWORD dwFlags)
{
    return AtlModuleRegisterClassObjects(this, dwClsContext, dwFlags);
}
```

AtlModuleRegisterClassObjects()

AtlModuleRegisterClassObjects() just loops through the object map calling
RegisterClassObject() on each entry.

```
ATLAPI AtlModuleRegisterClassObjects(_ATL_MODULE* pM,
                            DWORD dwClsContext, DWORD dwFlags)
{
```

121

```
      _ASSERTE(pM != NULL);
      if (pM == NULL)
         return E_INVALIDARG;
      _ASSERTE(pM->m_pObjMap != NULL);
      _ATL_OBJMAP_ENTRY* pEntry = pM->m_pObjMap;
      HRESULT hRes = S_OK;
      while (pEntry->pclsid != NULL && hRes == S_OK)
      {
         hRes = pEntry->RegisterClassObject(dwClsContext, dwFlags);
         pEntry++;
      }
      return hRes;
   }
```

We saw **RegisterClassObject()** earlier in the chapter when we looked at the
_ATL_OBJMAP_ENTRY structure; it calls **pfnGetClassObject()** followed by
CoRegisterClassObject(). Note that unlike **AtlModuleGetClassObject()**,
_ATL_OBJMAP_ENTRY::RegisterClassObject() doesn't store the class factory pointer in the
pCF member of the structure — once the class factories are registered, clients retrieve the class
factory directly from the class table without intervention from the executable. COM knows that
the server's an EXE, so it *has* to look in the class table. EXE servers don't expose any entry
points.

Object Creation in DLLs and EXEs

Once the client has a pointer to the requested interface on the class factory, whether it's been
created by a DLL or an EXE, it can use it to create an instance of the required object. In our
example from the previous chapter, that means that the client has a pointer to the
IClassFactory interface. Calling **CreateInstance()** through this interface pointer results in a
call to **CComClassFactory::CreateInstance()**, which uses the **pfnCreateInstance**
member of the **_ATL_OBJMAP_ENTRY** to create the object. In our example, **pfnCreateInstance**
is the address of the **CComCreator2< T1, T2 >::CreateInstance()** function, where **T1**
is **CComCreator< CComObject< CCalcEaster > >** and **T2** is **CComCreator<
CComAggObject< CCalcEaster > >**.

```
template <class T1, class T2>
class CComCreator2
{
public:
   static HRESULT WINAPI CreateInstance(void* pv, REFIID riid, LPVOID*
ppv)
   {
      _ASSERTE(*ppv == NULL);
      HRESULT hRes = E_OUTOFMEMORY;
      if (pv == NULL)
         hRes = T1::CreateInstance(NULL, riid, ppv);
      else
         hRes = T2::CreateInstance(pv, riid, ppv);
      return hRes;
   }
};
```

This means that ultimately **CComCreator<>::CreateInstance()** is called to construct either a **CComObject<>** or a **CComAggObject<>** object.

```
template <class T1>
class CComCreator
{
public:
   static HRESULT WINAPI CreateInstance(void* pv, REFIID riid, LPVOID*
ppv)
   {
      _ASSERTE(*ppv == NULL);
      HRESULT hRes = E_OUTOFMEMORY;
      T1* p = NULL;
      ATLTRY(p = new T1(pv))
      if (p != NULL)
      {
         p->SetVoid(pv);
         p->InternalFinalConstructAddRef();
         hRes = p->FinalConstruct();
         p->InternalFinalConstructRelease();
         if (hRes == S_OK)
            hRes = p->QueryInterface(riid, ppv);
         if (hRes != S_OK)
            delete p;
      }
      return hRes;
   }
};
```

ATLTRY() *is a macro used to prevent exceptions from propagating. If exception handling isn't enabled, the macro just resolves to its argument (that is, it does nothing). If exception handling is enabled, it wraps its argument in a **try** block and provides an empty 'catch all' block (**catch(...)**) to stop the exception propagating out of the current function.*

Although the essence of the function is to create a new object on the heap (using **new**) and call **QueryInterface()** on it to return the pointer requested by the **riid** argument, there's a bit more going on here.

First, note that the function's first argument, **pv**, is passed to the constructor of the object, *and* to the object itself, via the call to the **SetVoid()** method. When objects are being created, **pv** is **NULL** unless the object is being aggregated. In this situation, the value is of interest to the **CComObject***xxx***<>** class (because it affects the implementation of the **IUnknown** methods), which receives it via the constructor argument. The call to **SetVoid()** isn't used in that case (**SetVoid()** has an empty implementation).

When a class factory is being created, **pv** represents the **pfnCreateInstance** member of the **_ATL_OBJMAP_ENTRY** structure. In other words, **pv** is the pointer to the function used by the class factory to create its objects. In this case, the constructor ignores the argument (because the **CComObject***xxx***<>** classes used for class factories don't care about aggregation), and it's the call to **SetVoid()** that is used to pass the pointer to the **CComClassFactory** class.

The reason that there are two ways of passing the **pv** pointer to the object is that the constructor is always defined by the most-derived class. The most-derived class is usually a **CComObject***xxx***<>** class that won't pass on the pointer to its base classes. **SetVoid()** gives the base class a chance to get hold of the pointer. **CComObjectRootBase** defines an implementation of **SetVoid()** that does absolutely nothing, just to ensure that this function is always defined.

Also note the call to **FinalConstruct()**. This call is present to allow you to have code that will be executed as the final step of constructing your object. **FinalConstruct()** is defined in **CComObjectRootBase** to simply return **S_OK**, but you can add a **FinalConstruct()** member to your own class to provide a different implementation. If you return *any* code other than **S_OK** from **FinalConstruct()**, your object will be destroyed and that code returned to the client. That includes other success codes, so only ever return **S_OK** if you want to indicate success and continue with the creation of your object.

> *You should use* **FinalConstruct()** *in preference to adding code to your class's constructor for two reasons. First,* **FinalConstruct()** *gives you the opportunity to return errors and abort creation if something goes wrong. Second, the* **ATL_NO_VTABLE** *optimization limits the calls that you can make from the constructor — you can't make calls to virtual functions, because the vtable isn't properly initialized at that point.*

The call to **FinalConstruct()** is wrapped in a pair of strange-looking **InternalFinalConstructAddRef()** and **InternalFinalConstructRelease()** calls. By default, these functions are implemented by **CComObjectRootBase** to do nothing in the release build. (There's an **ASSERT** in the debug build). These functions only need to be replaced with some real code to increment and decrement the reference count if the code that you add to your **FinalConstruct()** functions results in a pair of **AddRef()** and **Release()** calls on your object. This can cause your object to delete itself prematurely, and might happen if you pass out a pointer to your object for some reason. The **ASSERT** in the debug build is designed to let you know when you need this code.

You can see how the object might delete itself in these circumstances when you realize that **FinalConstruct()** is called as an object is being created, but *before* the reference count has been incremented for the first time. Any code from within **FinalConstruct()** that results in a pair of **AddRef()** (or **QueryInterface()**) and **Release()** calls on your object can cause your object's reference count to reach zero. At this point the object will delete itself, even though code in the object still needs to be executed to satisfy the creation of the object.

The easiest way to add the code to combat this problem is to add the **DECLARE_PROTECT_FINAL_CONSTRUCT()** macro to your class definition. This macro provides code to bump up the reference count for long enough to avoid premature deletion.

```
#define DECLARE_PROTECT_FINAL_CONSTRUCT()\
    void InternalFinalConstructAddRef()   {InternalAddRef();}\
    void InternalFinalConstructRelease()  {InternalRelease();}
```

InternalAddRef() and **InternalRelease()** are inherited from **CComObjectRootEx<>**.

CComObjectRootBase also defines a **FinalRelease()** *function, which can be overridden (masked) in your class to provide code that should be executed when the last reference to your object has been released.*

Creation Summary

Class factories are created in different ways, depending on whether the module is an EXE or a DLL.

In a DLL, class objects are created by the first request made for that object to **DllGetClassObject()**. The **IUnknown** pointer for a class object is stored in the **pCF** member of the corresponding **_ATL_OBJMAP_ENTRY** structure, ready for subsequent requests.

In an EXE, all class objects are created as soon as the application loads. The **IUnknown** pointer for each class object is stored in the class table by a call to **CoRegisterClassObject()**.

Once a client has a pointer to an interface on a class object, DLL or EXE packaging makes no difference to the ATL code.

During creation, ATL calls the **FinalConstruct()** member of your class to give you a chance to initialize your class once the vtable is fully initialized, and a way of returning errors if something goes wrong. Add code to **FinalConstruct()** in preference to your class's constructor.

Adding COM Support to a Dialog

We've seen quite a lot of theory so far in this chapter. Now let's get our hands dirty with a simple example to demonstrate the concepts that we've discussed so far. We've seen the important elements that make an ATL class into a creatable COM object, so we'll start with a class without any COM features, and add all the elements necessary to turn it into a COM class. Along the way, you'll see how you can take advantage of the **FinalConstruct()** and **FinalRelease()** functions, we'll look at ways of avoiding some subtle (but common) reference counting pitfalls, and finally we'll see how to change the class factory to get different behavior.

Create a New Project

First, we need to create a new project, so fire up Developer Studio, and generate a new ATL COM AppWizard project called ComDialogProject. This project needs to be an Executable (EXE), so choose that option on Step 1 of the AppWizard, and press Finish.

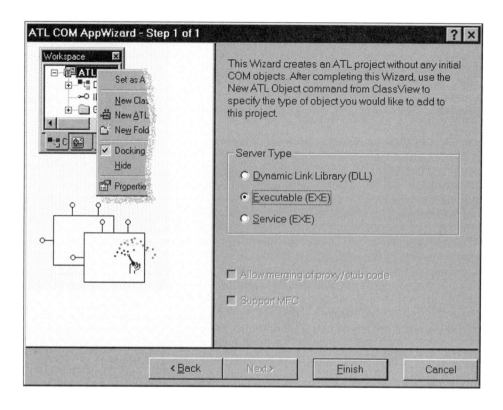

Insert a Dialog Class

Now we need to add a new class to our project. We'll start with an ATL dialog class, which has no COM functionality built in, and then we'll add all the necessary elements to turn it into an independently creatable COM class.

Choose the Insert | New ATL Object... menu item, select the Miscellaneous category, then Dialog, and then click the Next > button. Give the dialog a Short Name of ComDialog, and leave the automatic fields with their default values.

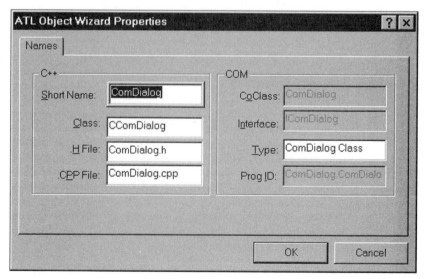

Define the Interface

Now we have to decide what functionality we're going to expose via COM. In this case, we'll just define a simple interface that allows a COM client to show or hide our dialog. We'll do this by means of a read/write property called **Visible**. The logical place to define an interface is in the IDL file, which **MIDL** will use to generate a header file, a type library, and marshaling code.

Add the interface definition shown below to **ComDialogProject.idl**, just below the **import** statements.

```
import "oaidl.idl";
import "ocidl.idl";
```

```
[
    uuid(624235B3-64CB-11D1-A159-64D6F8C00000),
    oleautomation,
    pointer_default(unique),
    helpstring("IComDialog interface")
]
interface IComDialog : IUnknown
{
    [propget, helpstring("property Visible")]
     HRESULT Visible([out, retval] VARIANT_BOOL* pbVisible);
    [propput, helpstring("property Visible")]
     HRESULT Visible([in] VARIANT_BOOL bVisible);
};
```

The square brackets contain attributes that apply to the interface.

The **[uuid()]** attribute contains the IID for the interface. When you create your own interfaces, you should generate your IIDs in registry format using the GUID Generator, which you can find in the Components and Controls Gallery of Visual C++ (Project | Add To Project | Components and Controls...). Don't forget to remove the braces from GUIDs generated in this way!

The **[oleautomation]** attribute is used to tell **MIDL** that your interface uses a limited set of data types known as **Automation-compatible data types**. If you apply this attribute to your interfaces, **MIDL** will warn you when you try to use an incompatible data type. The advantage of these types is that they are widely understood by many different languages, and can be marshaled by the **Universal Marshaler**. We'll describe the universal marshaler in the coming chapters; for now, all you need to know is that we don't need to build and register a proxy-stub DLL for this interface, as long as the type library is registered. You may remember from our examination of the registration code in the previous chapter that the **BOOL** parameter to **CComModule::RegisterServer()** determines whether the type library is registered when **RegisterServer()** is called. This parameter is set to **TRUE** by default in the Wizard-generated code.

The **[pointer_default()]** attribute has some quite subtle effects that are beyond the scope of this book. If you're interested in learning more, take a look at the online documentation supplied with Visual C++.

The **[helpstring()]** attribute just associates a text string with whatever it's applied to. Object browsers can display these strings to the user where appropriate.

The interface itself is called **IComDialog** and derives directly from **IUnknown**. The interface just adds two methods (or one property) to the standard **IUnknown** methods. The **[propget]** method is the one used to retrieve the value of the **Visible** property, so the parameter has the **[out]** attribute applied (and is therefore specified as a pointer). **[retval]** ensures that the value seems to be returned directly in languages such as Visual Basic that understand this attribute. The **[propput]** method is used when the client wishes to set the value of the **Visible** property, so the parameter has the **[in]** attribute and is passed directly.

> *Remember that the **[in]** and **[out]** attributes are used to specify the direction of travel of the data for a parameter; **[retval]** indicates that an **[out]** parameter can be used as a return value by languages and tools that understand the attribute. **[propput]** is used to specify a method used to set the value of a property, and **[propget]** is used to specify that a method is used to retrieve the value of a property.*

> *Once you get the hang of it, it's quite straightforward to specify the right IDL attributes on your interfaces, methods, and parameters. If you're not sure, however, you can use the OLE/ COM Object Viewer to examine the IDL of components on your system and see how other people do it.*

The parameter itself is specified as **VARIANT_BOOL**. This is the IDL equivalent of Visual Basic's native **Boolean** type, and is Automation-compatible (unlike **MIDL**'s **boolean** type). The Win32 **BOOL** data type is also Automation-compatible, but Visual Basic sees it as a **Long**, so if you want a Visual Basic-compatible Boolean data type, use **VARIANT_BOOL**.

Define the Coclass

Within the **library** block, we need to define the coclass for our COM dialog component. A **coclass** definition is always extremely simple — at a minimum, all you need to supply is a new UUID (for the CLSID), a name, and a list of the interfaces supported by that coclass. Add the code shown shaded below to the library block in **ComDialogProject.idl**.

```
[
    uuid(4C061FE3-64D0-11D1-A159-64D6F8C00000),
    version(1.0),
    helpstring("ComDialogProject 1.0 Type Library")
]
library COMDIALOGPROJECTLib
{
    importlib("stdole32.tlb");
    importlib("stdole2.tlb");

    [
        uuid(D55039F0-61B3-11D1-B28D-00A0C94515AD),
        helpstring("ComDialog class")
    ]
    coclass ComDialog
    {
        [default] interface IComDialog;
    };
};
```

We've decided to really go to town here and provide a **[helpstring()]** attribute too!

Add the Base Classes

Now we need to put some work into our **CComDialog** class to turn it into an honest and upstanding COM citizen. The dialog class generated by the Wizard doesn't have any COM capabilities; it's up to us to provide them. The first part of this is to add some new **public** base classes to the dialog:

```
class CComDialog :
    public CDialogImpl<CComDialog>,
    public CComObjectRootEx<CComSingleThreadModel>,
    public CComCoClass<CComDialog, &CLSID_ComDialog>,
    public IComDialog
```

You can see that we need three new base classes. The first two, **CComObjectRootEx<>** and **CComCoClass<>**, are required as base classes for all creatable ATL COM objects (all the creatable COM objects in this book, anyway).

CComObjectRootEx<> provides reference counting and **QueryInterface()** functionality. Its template parameter provides the threading model class used to ensure that the reference counting is as efficient and robust as the threading model will allow. In this case, we can use **CComSingleThreadModel** because the object will only ever be called from a single thread.

CComCoClass<> defines the default class factory and aggregation model for our class, as well as a default implementation of **GetObjectDescription()**. **CComCoClass<>** takes our class and its CLSID as template parameters. Remember that the CLSID constant for our class will be generated by **MIDL** from the **coclass** definition in the IDL file by prefixing the **coclass** name with **CLSID_**.

The third base class is the **IComDialog** interface that we defined in the IDL file. If we wanted our COM object to expose further interfaces, we would add them as base classes also.

To get the **MIDL**-generated C++ definition of the **IComDialog** class, we need to **#include** the header file that contains it at the top of **ComDialog.h**:

```
#include "resource.h"        // main symbols
#include "ComDialogProject.h"
```

ATL AppWizard-generated projects always have a *projectname*.**idl** file that **MIDL** uses to generate a *projectname*.**h** file containing the corresponding C++ definitions.

Add the COM Map

Once the base classes have been added, it's time to ensure that our interface is exposed via **QueryInterface()** by adding a COM map and the appropriate interface entry. You can add the code shown to the class definition in **ComDialog.h**, just below the message map:

```
BEGIN_MSG_MAP(CComDialog)
    MESSAGE_HANDLER(WM_INITDIALOG, OnInitDialog)
    COMMAND_ID_HANDLER(IDOK, OnOK)
```

```
        COMMAND_ID_HANDLER(IDCANCEL, OnCancel)
    END_MSG_MAP()
```

```
    BEGIN_COM_MAP(CComDialog)
        COM_INTERFACE_ENTRY(IComDialog)
    END_COM_MAP()
```

Remember that the COM map is an important structure and needs an entry for every interface (except **IUnknown**) in a COM class. In this case, the requirement is easy to fulfil — our dialog class needs to expose only a single interface.

Add Method Implementations

Now that we've inherited from the abstract **IComDialog** class, we need to provide implementations for its methods. Add prototypes to the end of the **CComDialog** class, as shown:

```
    // IComDialog
    public:
        STDMETHOD(get_Visible)(/*[out, retval]*/ VARIANT_BOOL* pbVisible);
        STDMETHOD(put_Visible)(/*[in]*/ VARIANT_BOOL bVisible);
    };
```

You can see that we're using the **STDMETHOD()** macro, as described in Chapter 1. The function names **get_Visible()** and **put_Visible()** match the names provided by **MIDL** for the **IComDialog** class. **MIDL** prefixes **get_** to the names of any **[propget]** methods, and **put_** to the names of **[propput]** methods.

> Note that I've included the IDL attributes of the parameters as inline comments, just as the Wizard-generated code does. It's important to be fully aware of the status of COM parameters, so it's often useful to have a reminder of these attributes in the header.

The implementations for the **IComDialog** methods need to go in **ComDialog.cpp**. This time we specify the signatures using the **STDMETHODIMP** macro. We'll just stub out the implementations by returning **S_OK** for now, but we'll come back to fix them up later.

```
    STDMETHODIMP CComDialog::get_Visible(VARIANT_BOOL* pbVisible)
    {
        return S_OK;
    }


    STDMETHODIMP CComDialog::put_Visible(VARIANT_BOOL bVisible)
    {
        return S_OK;
    }
```

Create the Registry Script

From this point, we need to start thinking about registering our class. Without registration entries, clients won't be able to create instances of our class using the CLSID. In this case, we'll create a registry script (RGS file) and use the **DECLARE_REGISTRY_RESOURCEID()** macro to execute the script when our class needs to be registered.

Create a new text file called **ComDialog.rgs** and save it in the project directory. You can add it to the project if you choose. This script needs to register, at the very least, the CLSID of the component, and map it to the physical location of the module. If you want your component to be widely used, it should also create entries for the ProgID and version-independent ProgID.

Add the following text to the RGS file:

```
HKCR
{
    Wrox.ComDialog.1 = s 'ComDialog Class'
    {
        CLSID = s '{D55039F0-61B3-11D1-B28D-00A0C94515AD}'
    }
    Wrox.ComDialog = s 'ComDialog Class'
    {
        CurVer = s 'Wrox.ComDialog.1'
        CLSID = s '{D55039F0-61B3-11D1-B28D-00A0C94515AD}'
    }
    NoRemove CLSID
    {
        ForceRemove {D55039F0-61B3-11D1-B28D-00A0C94515AD} = s 'ComDialog
              Class'
        {
            ProgID = s 'Wrox.ComDialog.1'
            VersionIndependentProgID = s 'Wrox.ComDialog'
            LocalServer32 = s '%MODULE%'
            val AppID = s '{4C061FE4-64D0-11D1-A159-64D6F8C00000}'
        }
    }
}
```

This RGS file will give our component a ProgID of **Wrox.ComDialog.1**, and a version-independent ProgID of **Wrox.ComDialog**, as well as registering the component under its CLSID. Note that the GUID beginning 'D55039F0' is the CLSID of our component and must match the CLSID specified for the coclass in the IDL file. The GUID beginning '4C061FE4' is the AppID for the application. This must match the GUID specified in the project's RGS file (in this case, **ComDialogProject.rgs**, shown below).

```
HKCR
{
    NoRemove AppID
    {
        {4C061FE4-64D0-11D1-A159-64D6F8C00000} = s 'ComDialogProject'
        'ComDialogProject.EXE'
        {
            val AppID = s {4C061FE4-64D0-11D1-A159-64D6F8C00000}
        }
    }
}
```

The AppID groups together registry entries related to a single executable. We'll see how the AppID registry entries are used in Chapter 5, when we discuss DCOM.

131

Since we're going to be using the **DECLARE_REGISTRY_RESOURCEID()** macro, we need to import the RGS file as a **"REGISTRY"** resource. By storing the RGS file as a resource within our executable, we have one less file to distribute with our component.

Right-click on the "REGISTRY" folder in ResourceView and select the Import... menu item from the pop-up menu. This will bring up the Import Resource dialog. Set the Files of type box to display all files and set Open as to Custom, then select the **ComDialog.rgs** file and hit Import.

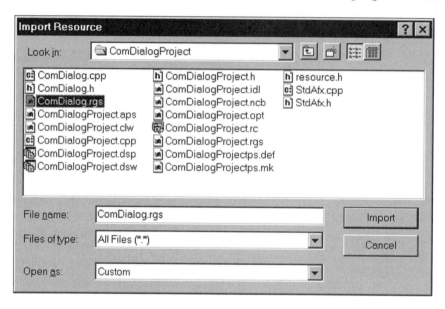

On the next dialog, you will be asked what type you'd like to assign to the RGS file. Select **"REGISTRY"** as the custom resource type, and click OK to import the RGS file.

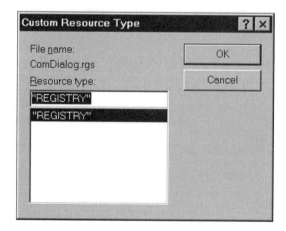

Finally, the resource has been imported and it's just a matter of setting its ID to something appropriate. Right-click the newly added resource in ResourceView, and click Properties to bring up the Custom Resource Properties dialog. Set the resource's ID to IDR_ComDialog.

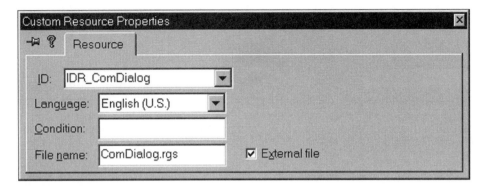

As the last step to ensuring that our class will register itself, we need to hook it up to the new resource by adding the **DECLARE_REGISTRY_RESOURCEID()** macro to the class definition. Add it just below the destructor for the dialog class:

```
~CComDialog();
DECLARE_REGISTRY_RESOURCEID(IDR_ComDialog)
```

Add an Entry to the Object Map

Finally, we need to add an entry for our class to the object map in **ComDialogProject.cpp**, so that it can be externally created.

```
BEGIN_OBJECT_MAP(ObjectMap)
    OBJECT_ENTRY(CLSID_ComDialog, CComDialog)
END_OBJECT_MAP()
```

This also requires a **#include** for **ComDialog.h** to be added to the same file, so that the compiler knows about the definition for **CComDialog**:

```
#include "ComDialogProject_i.c"
#include "ComDialog.h"
```

Compile And Test

At this stage, it's possible to compile and test the component. You could see for yourself that the **CComDialog** class is now a genuine component, exposing a single interface with a single property. The component would be usable right after building it, without having to build or register anything else. Remember that a custom build step automatically registers the component, the component registration automatically registers the type library, and the registration of the type library automatically associates any **[oleautomation]** interfaces in that library with the Universal Marshaler, so we don't need to build a separate proxy-stub DLL in this case.

However, the component doesn't do anything yet, because we haven't added any functional code to the property methods, so we'll delay testing the component until we can see it in action. Let's add some functionality to the class.

Adding the Code

FinalConstruct()

First, we want to create the dialog window when the component is first created. Any code that needs to be executed when a component is first created should live in the **FinalConstruct()** method, as we discussed earlier in the chapter. **FinalConstruct()** is happy as a simple inline function, so add the following code directly to the **CComDialog** class definition, just below the COM map.

```
HRESULT FinalConstruct()
{
    // Create the window for the dialog as soon as
    // the object is constructed
    if (Create(NULL))
        return S_OK;
    else
        return HRESULT_FROM_WIN32(GetLastError());
}
```

The code to create a dialog window is extremely simple, consisting of a single call to **CDialogImpl<>::Create()**. **Create()** returns a **HWND** if successful, or **NULL** if it fails. We just check the result and return a simple success or failure code. The failure code is an **HRESULT** built from a Win32 error code using the **HRESULT_FROM_WIN32()** macro. **GetLastError()** is the standard Win32 function that returns the error code.

FinalRelease()

We also want to ensure that the window is destroyed as the last step in the destruction of our component — we don't want the window procedure running once our object has been deleted. To that end, we also need to add a **FinalRelease()** implementation to our class. This is another inline function, so you can add this just below the code for **FinalConstruct()**.

```
// Called as the last step before deleting your object
void FinalRelease()
{
    DestroyWindow();
}
```

The code for this function couldn't be simpler. The call to **CWindow::DestroyWindow()** does exactly what we need it to (**CWindow** is a base class of **CDialogImpl<>**). There is nothing to return from **FinalRelease()**, because once our object is being destroyed, there are no clients left to return error results to, and nothing we can reasonably do to prevent destruction.

IsWindowVisible()

Now we need to start thinking about the **Visible** property. We want this property to match the state of the dialog window precisely, so we need to use the Win32 function **IsWindowVisible()** (or rather its ATL wrapper provided by **CWindow**) to determine whether the window is visible.

CWindow::IsWindowVisible() returns a **BOOL**, while our **Visible** property returns a **VARIANT_BOOL**, so we need to be a bit careful how we handle this. Although **FALSE** (for **BOOL**) and **VARIANT_FALSE** (for **VARIANT_BOOL**) both evaluate to zero, **TRUE** is **1** and **VARIANT_TRUE** is **-1**. This introduces the possibility of errors creeping into the code. To try to avoid these errors, we'll introduce a new inline helper function called **IsVisible()** that will return the visible state of the window as a **VARIANT_BOOL**.

Add the code shown to the **CComDialog** class definition, just below **FinalRelease()**.

```
VARIANT_BOOL IsVisible()
{
   return IsWindowVisible() ? VARIANT_TRUE : VARIANT_FALSE;
}
```

get_Visible()

The implementation of **get_Visible()** is now extremely easy. Add the following code to **ComDialog.cpp**:

```
STDMETHODIMP CComDialog::get_Visible(VARIANT_BOOL* pbVisible)
{
   *pbVisible = IsVisible();
   return S_OK;
}
```

OnOK() and OnCancel()

Pressing the OK, Cancel or close buttons on the dialog should result in it disappearing. However, we don't want to destroy the window, nor do we want to quit the application completely, in case there are clients still using the component. The solution is to add code to the **OnOK()** and **OnCancel()** message handlers to simply hide the dialog.

```
LRESULT CComDialog::OnOK(WORD wNotifyCode, WORD wID, HWND hWndCtl, BOOL&
bHandled)
{
   put_Visible(VARIANT_FALSE);
   return 0;
}

LRESULT CComDialog::OnCancel(WORD wNotifyCode, WORD wID, HWND hWndCtl,
BOOL& bHandled)
{
   // OnCancel() handles the Close button too
   put_Visible(VARIANT_FALSE);
   return 0;
}
```

put_Visible()

put_Visible() is the most complicated method to implement because it brings a few subtleties with it. In essence, **put_Visible()** is extremely simple — we just need to show and hide the dialog window, which we can do with a call to **CWindow::ShowWindow()**.

However, we also need to think about reference counting. We need to increment the reference count for the component whenever the dialog is made visible, and decrement the reference count whenever the dialog is hidden. This reference count is the one for the interactive user, and ensures that the dialog won't suddenly disappear if all the programmatic clients release their references on the object.

Add the code shown below to the implementation of **put_Visible()**:

```
STDMETHODIMP CComDialog::put_Visible(VARIANT_BOOL bVisible)
{
    // Do nothing if the visible state doesn't change
    // This ensures that we always have matched AddRef()s and Release()s
    if (bVisible == IsVisible())
       return S_OK;

    // Show or hide the window
    ShowWindow( bVisible ? SW_SHOW : SW_HIDE );

    // Now AddRef() or Release() the object.
    // This is the reference count for the interactive user
    bVisible ? GetUnknown()->AddRef() : GetUnknown()->Release();

    // Don't use any methods or members in this class from this point on,
    // because we may have called Release() in the previous statement.
    // The final call to Release() results in the object deleting itself,
    // and we don't want to access any members of a deleted object!
    return S_OK;
}
```

The comments in the code are extremely important. If the visible state of the component wouldn't be changed by the call to **put_Visible()**, we don't do anything except return **S_OK**. Without this check, we could have unmatched calls to **AddRef()** and **Release()**, which could result in premature termination or eternal life for the component.

To see how immortality could arise, for example, consider how the object would behave with the check removed. Look at the following sequence of events:

Action	Reference Count	Visibility
A client creates the dialog object	1	False
The client sets the **Visible** property to True	2	True
The client sets the **Visible** property to True again. (Note that the client should *not* have to check whether the dialog is already visible before setting this property).	3	True
The client releases the dialog	2	True
A user clicks the OK button	1	False

At this stage, the dialog is invisible to the user and has no programmatic clients connected to it. The server will hang around on the system until a user spots it in the task list and terminates it or until the system itself shuts down. This is not what we want, and the simple check eliminates this possibility.

The next line of code simply shows or hides the window. Note that it comes *before* the code that calls either **AddRef()** or **Release()** on the component. The line of code that affects the reference count could result in the object being deleted if **Release()** is called. We do *not* want to attempt to call methods or manipulate members on a deleted object.

The calls to **GetUnknown()** return a pointer to the **IUnknown** interface for our component — remember that the implementation of this function is provided by the **BEGIN_COM_MAP()** macro. We then call **AddRef()** or **Release()** to provide a reference count for the interactive user. This prevents the component from being unloaded while it's still in use.

If the component were being aggregated, **AddRef()**'ing and **Release()**'ing the pointer returned by **GetUnknown()** wouldn't be sufficient. We'll leave the discussion of why this is until later in the chapter. However, because executables cannot be aggregated, we don't have a problem in this case.

If you want to ensure that your component is *never* aggregated, you can add the **DECLARE_NOT_AGGREGATABLE()** macro to your class definition, whether your component is in an EXE or a DLL. I think it is always useful to add this macro to components that reside in executables. EXE servers can not be aggregated whether this macro is there or not, but the macro acts as a reminder to anyone that sees the source code that this component cannot be aggregated, and ensures that aggregation fails unequivocally if a client should attempt to aggregate an EXE-based component. It also has the benefit of reducing the size of your compiled code.

We'll add the **DECLARE_NOT_AGGREGATABLE()** macro to our class definition, just below the registry macro in **CComDialog**:

```
DECLARE_REGISTRY_RESOURCEID(IDR_ComDialog)
DECLARE_NOT_AGGREGATABLE(CComDialog)
```

Once again, the component is fit to be compiled, and now it's ready for testing. You should compile the project now so that the client can use an up-to-date type library.

Creating a Client

For this client, we're going to create a simple console application. First, create a new project workspace for a Win32 Console Application called ConsoleClient in a subdirectory of the **ComDialogProject** directory. Create a new text file, save it as **Main.cpp**, and add the file to the project. Now add the following code to the file.

```
// Main.cpp
#import "..\ComDialogProject.tlb"
#include <iostream>

int main(int argc, char* argv[], char* envp[ ])
{
    HRESULT hr = CoInitialize(NULL);
    if (FAILED(hr))
        return hr;
```

```
    try
    {
        COMDIALOGPROJECTLib::IComDialogPtr
p(__uuidof(COMDIALOGPROJECTLib::ComDialog));
        p->Visible = VARIANT_TRUE;
    }
    catch (const _com_error& Err)
    {
        std::cout << Err.ErrorMessage()
                  << "0x" << std::hex << Err.Error() << '\n';
        hr = Err.Error();
    }

    CoUninitialize();
    return hr;
}
```

This simple client uses **#import** to generate a wrapper class for the **IComDialog** interface. The **main()** function just initializes the COM libraries, creates an instance of the **ComDialog** coclass using the smart pointer's constructor, and makes the dialog visible. Finally, the call to **CoUninitialize()** frees the COM libraries.

If you compile and run this code, you can see that the dialog survives even when the console application has terminated. Dismissing the dialog with the OK, Cancel, or close buttons causes the component to shut down as the final reference is released. When all instances of the dialog are gone, the **ComDialogProject.exe** process unloads itself. You can check that everything is working as expected by using Process Viewer to check the running processes.

Process Viewer is an applet provided with Visual C++. There's a shortcut for it in the *Microsoft Visual C++ 5.0* folder in the *Programs* group on your *Start* menu.

If you try running the console client many times without shutting down the dialog, you'll see that you get multiple dialogs on the screen, each one corresponding to an instance of the **CComDialog** class, but you only ever get one instance of the **ComDialogProject.exe** process loaded.

If you have any trouble running the example (which you shouldn't!), you can see the error code and its description in the console window. Alternatively, you can look at the return value of the console application in the Debug tab of the Output window, and put this value into the Error Lookup applet to get a reasonable description of the error. You can run Error Lookup from within Developer Studio, by choosing the *Tools | Error Lookup* menu item.

> *Don't run the EXE server directly and expect to see a dialog. The dialog is the visible representation of the* **ComDialog** *object, which can only be created by a COM client. If you wanted a dialog project that could be used as a stand-alone executable, you could create a very simple COM client for the user to run. The code in the console client that we've just created would be ideal for this job, but you'd want to move it into a standard Win32 Application so that the unsightly console window wouldn't appear.*

Singletons

We can change the behavior of the component we've written with just a single macro. This macro doesn't even change the component; instead, it affects the class factory used to create the component. By adding the **DECLARE_CLASSFACTORY_SINGLETON()** macro to the definition of **CComDialog**, we can ensure that only a single instance of our coclass gets created, and all clients get connected to the same instance.

> *You might want to use a singleton if you have a resource intensive component and you only want to allow a single instance of it to run, or more generally, you might want to use a singleton as a single point of contact for multiple clients.*

To see this in action, add the macro to the class definition, just below the 'not aggregatable' macro:

```
DECLARE_NOT_AGGREGATABLE(CComDialog)
DECLARE_CLASSFACTORY_SINGLETON(CComDialog)
```

Now build the project and run the client again. No matter how many clients you run, you'll only ever get one dialog on the screen, representing the single instance of the coclass.

If you have Visual Basic, you may be able to see more clearly that all the clients are connecting to the same instance of the coclass by creating the following simple project to show and hide the dialog.

> *You could create an equivalent application in MFC or ATL, or you could alter the console application to take command line arguments to show and hide the dialog. We'll leave that as an exercise. (Or you can download the source code from the Wrox or World of ATL web sites).*

Create a new Standard EXE application and add two command buttons — **cmdShow** and **cmdHide** — to the form, and add a reference to the ComDialogProject 1.0 Type Library. Add the following code to the form:

```
Private itf As COMDIALOGPROJECTLib.IComDialog

Private Sub cmdHide_Click()
   itf.Visible = False
End Sub

Private Sub cmdShow_Click()
   itf.Visible = True
End Sub

Private Sub Form_Load()
   Set itf = New COMDIALOGPROJECTLib.ComDialog
End Sub
```

When you run multiple instances of this client and click the buttons to show and hide the COM dialog, you'll quickly see that all of the clients are connected to the same instance of the coclass.

Limitations

Singletons have a couple of limitations that you should be aware of. First, singletons within a DLL are only per-process. If there are many client creation requests from a single process, then only one instance will be created, but if a number of processes request an object declared as a singleton, then an object will be created for each process. This is a result of the fact that a DLL must be loaded into each client process.

> *You can download an example showing the difference between DLL and EXE singletons from The World of ATL web site (*http://www.worldofatl.com/*) or from the Wrox Press web site (*http://www.wrox.com/*).*

On NT, the success of singletons is also limited by security. COM servers run in the context of a user account, and each account has its own WinStation (a virtual Windows NT machine, running on the same physical hardware). A COM object in one WinStation does not know anything about the objects in another WinStation, so for the singleton to apply to the whole machine, the server must be set to run under a particular user account (*not* the launching user). This can be done using the OLE/COM Object Viewer. Since our server displays a dialog, we would need to set it to run under the interactive user's account, so that the dialog can be seen.

Example Summary

Knowledge of the structure of ATL allows us to add COM abilities to non-COM classes without the aid of a Wizard. The steps for doing this break down as follows:

▶ Define the interface(s) and the coclass in IDL. If necessary, use the OLE/COM Object Viewer to examine the IDL for other components on your system.

▶ Add the base classes to your class. All creatable COM classes need to derive from **CComObjectRootEx<>** and **CComCoClass<>**. In addition, you should derive your class from the interfaces it supports.

▶ Add the COM map. This provides all the necessary functions and data for ATL's **QueryInterface()** mechanism to do its thing. Make sure that each interface has an entry in the COM map.

▶ Add the method implementations. These make your COM objects useful!

▶ Create the registry script. The registry script is the easiest way to add information about your class to the system registry.

▶ Add the script to your project as a custom resource and use **DECLARE_REGISTRY_RESOURCEID()** to hook it up to your class.

▶ Add an entry to the object map. This ensures that a class factory will be created for your class when necessary.

You've also seen a few useful tips put into action. They're summarized here:

▶ Use **VARIANT_BOOL** for compatibility with Visual Basic, but remember that **VARIANT_TRUE** is **-1** while **TRUE** (and **true**) is **1**.

▶ If you've got an object with a user interface, remember to include a reference count for the interactive user, where appropriate, so that the server doesn't suddenly disappear while someone's using it.

- Don't manipulate member functions or data after calling **Release()** on an object. A call to **Release()** may release the last reference on an object and cause it to **delete** itself. However, you can continue to use local or static data (or static functions) after a call to **Release()**.

- Use the **DECLARE_NOT_AGGREGATABLE()** macro on all components packaged as EXEs to disallow aggregation unambiguously.

- Use the **DECLARE_CLASSFACTORY_SINGLETON()** macro to turn your COM class into a singleton. If you only ever want a single instance of your component, and all clients should connect to that instance, this is the macro to use.

- Be aware of the limitations of singletons. A DLL is always loaded into the process space of its client, so a DLL singleton means a single instance per client process. Security considerations also limit the singularity of singletons.

- Use the Error Lookup applet to convert **HRESULT**s into text descriptions.

Creating Objects

Now that we've seen how ATL provides class factories and the **IUnknown** methods for us, and how we can use that knowledge to add COM functionality to a non-COM-enabled class, let's look at another quick example. This time, we're going to create a project that contains *two* coclasses. We want only one of these classes to be externally creatable — clients will only be able to create instances of the second class by calling methods on the first. If you look at any reasonably complex COM server (like Microsoft Word, for example), you will see that it is built up of a hierarchy of objects, with many of the objects in the hierarchy only accessible through methods of the classes higher up.

First, create a new **ATL COM AppWizard** project called ReturningAnObject. Make this project a DLL server. Now use the **ATL Object Wizard** to create a new simple object. Give it the short name MainObject, and leave the rest of the dialog with its default settings. The class generated will act as the main (externally creatable) class for the server.

Start the **ATL Object Wizard** again. This time, generate a class with the short name SeparateObject, and once again leave the rest of the dialog with its default settings. This class will only be creatable via a call to one of the methods on the main object's interface.

To prevent clients from being able to create SeparateObjects, we simply need to remove the appropriate entry from the object map. Open **ReturningAnObject.cpp** and delete the entry for the separate object. The map should now look like this:

```
BEGIN_OBJECT_MAP(ObjectMap)
    OBJECT_ENTRY(CLSID_MainObject, CMainObject)
END_OBJECT_MAP()
```

Once the **OBJECT_ENTRY()** macro has been removed, the class factory that creates separate objects will no longer be compiled into our DLL, and clients can't create objects of that type. We can further slim down the size of our module by removing **CComCoClass<>** from the list of base classes and the registry resource associated with the separate object, since they are only used for externally creatable objects. Once you've deleted **CComCoClass<>** from the list of base classes, go to ResourceView, expand the "REGISTRY" folder, select IDR_SEPARATEOBJECT, and hit the *Delete* key. You should also delete the **DECLARE_REGISTRY_RESOURCEID()** macro from the class definition in **SeparateObject.h**. Finally, you can delete the **SeparateObject** coclass definition from the IDL file.

Now we can add one simple method to the **ISeparateObject** and **IMainObject** interfaces. We'll just use these methods to display a dialog box, so that we know everything's working as it should. Right-click on the ISeparateObject interface name in ClassView and select Add Method... from the context menu. Call the method Display and click OK. Repeat the process for the IMainObject interface.

Now add the following code to **CMainObject::Display()**:

```
STDMETHODIMP CMainObject::Display()
{
    MessageBox(NULL, _T("IMainObject::Display()"),
                     _T("IMainObject::Display()"), MB_OK);
    return S_OK;
}
```

And add this code to **CSeparateObject::Display()**:

```
STDMETHODIMP CSeparateObject::Display()
{
    MessageBox(NULL, _T("ISeparateObject::Display()"),
                     _T("ISeparateObject::Display()"), MB_OK);
    return S_OK;
}
```

Next up, we can add a method to **IMainObject** to return an interface pointer to a newly created **SeparateObject**. Use ClassView's Add Method to Interface dialog to add a new method called **CreateSeparateObject()**, as shown:

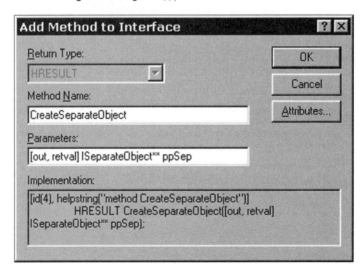

Implement the method as shown below, and add a **#include** for **SeparateObject.h** to the top of the file:

```
STDMETHODIMP CMainObject::CreateSeparateObject(ISeparateObject * * ppSep)
{
    *ppSep = NULL;
    return CComCreator< CComObject<CSeparateObject> >::CreateInstance(
        NULL, IID_ISeparateObject, reinterpret_cast<void**>(ppSep) );
}
```

The first line of the method simply ensures that the pointer returned to the client is **NULL** in case of failure (and avoids an assert from the ATL code). The **return** statement is the line that does all the hard work.

In this case, we're not interested in doing anything except creating the object and returning an interface to the client, so we can use the same mechanism that the ATL class factory would use to create an object of this type. We've called the **static** function **CComCreator<>::CreateInstance()**, passing in **NULL** for the first parameter (which is usually used for aggregation), **IID_ISeparateObject** as the second parameter (the interface that we wish to receive a pointer to), and **ppSep** as the third parameter (the storage for the returned interface pointer).

CComCreator<> takes the type of object to create as its template parameter. In this case, we're creating objects of type **CComObject<CSeparateObject>**. Remember that **CComObject<>** is usually used to provide the **IUnknown** method implementations for your class, and that you can't instantiate your class directly.

You can have a look back to our discussion of **CComCreator<>::CreateInstance()** earlier in the chapter to see precisely what it's doing for you, but you can be assured that it constructs your objects fully, calling **FinalConstruct()** and handling errors as necessary. **CComCreator<>::CreateInstance()** is a nice bit of code; it makes sense to reuse it.

Be aware that the **CreateSeparateObject()** function has introduced an order dependency into your IDL file, since the parameter requires **MIDL** to know about the **ISeparateObject** interface in order to compile it. The solution for this kind of problem in IDL is the same as the one you'd use in C++: you can forward declare the interface at the top of the file. In fact, by adding partial definitions for *all* the interfaces defined in the file, you can rid yourself completely of the blight of order dependency:

```
import "oaidl.idl";
import "ocidl.idl";

interface IMainObject;
interface ISeparateObject;
```

At this stage, build the project so that it's ready to be tested.

Client

Now we can create a simple client to test the server. Create a new Win32 Console Application and give it the name ConsoleClient. Save this project in a subdirectory of **ReturningAnObject** so that we can use a relative path to get to the server's type library.

143

Add a new source file to the project and add the following code to it:

```
#import "..\ReturningAnObject.tlb"
using namespace RETURNINGANOBJECTLib;
#include <iostream>
using namespace std;

int main()
{
    CoInitialize(NULL);
    try
    {
        IMainObjectPtr pMain(__uuidof(MainObject));
        pMain->Display();

        // Uncomment the following line to trigger a compile-time error
        // ISeparateObjectPtr pCantCreateSep(__uuidof(SeparateObject));
        ISeparateObjectPtr pSep = pMain->CreateSeparateObject();
        pSep->Display();
    }
    catch (const _com_error& Err)
    {
        cout << Err.ErrorMessage()
             << hex << "0x" << Err.Error() << '\n';
    }
    CoUninitialize();
    return 0;
}
```

The code simply initializes COM, creates an instance of the main object class, calls **Display()** to show that the main object's working, calls **CreateSeparateObject()** to create a new separate object, then calls **Display()** on the separate object to show that's working too. When you build the project and run this code, you'll see two message boxes in succession, telling you when each of the **Display()** methods is called.

If you uncomment the line indicated, you'll get a *compile-time* error because we removed the **coclass** definition for **SeparateObject** from the IDL file. If we had left the **coclass** definition in that file, uncommenting the line would cause a *run-time* error. The code would happily compile because it would have the CLSID it's expecting, but we'd get a run-time error complaining that the object isn't registered.

Initializing Objects

One reason that you might want to allow the creation of objects only through a method call on another object's interface is so that you can perform some initialization of the object before returning it to the client (you may not be able to add all your initialization code to **FinalConstruct()**). Our existing method for creating separate objects doesn't provide any initialization of the object, so we'll add a new method to the **IMainObject** interface to return initialized objects to the client.

Before we do that, we need to add a little bit of code to **CSeparateObject** to demonstrate whether it's been initialized or not. For this simple example, we'll just add a **public** member to the class to act as an initialization flag, and we'll change the **Display()** code to show whether this flag has been set or not.

First, add a **public** Boolean member called **m_bInitialized** to **CSeparateObject**:

```
public:
    STDMETHOD(Display)();
    bool m_bInitialized;
```

Initialize this member to **false** in the constructor:

```
public:
    CSeparateObject() : m_bInitialized(false)
    {
    }
```

Alter the code in **CSeparateObject::Display()**, so that we can tell whether the object has been initialized or not:

```
STDMETHODIMP CSeparateObject::Display()
{
    if (!m_bInitialized)
        MessageBox(NULL, _T("ISeparateObject::Display()"),
                         _T("ISeparateObject::Display()"), MB_OK);
    else
        MessageBox(NULL, _T("ISeparateObject::Display() - Initialized"),
                         _T("ISeparateObject::Display() - Initialized"),
           MB_OK);
    return S_OK;
}
```

Now add a new method to the **IMainObject** interface to return an initialized separate object. Use the ClassView dialog as usual and call the method **CreateAndInitializeSeparateObject()**:

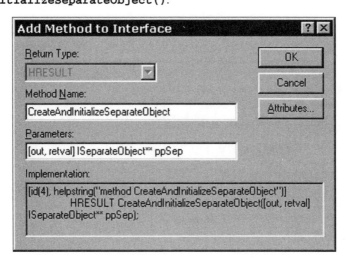

The code to implement this new method is shown below:

```
STDMETHODIMP
CMainObject::CreateAndInitializeSeparateObject(ISeparateObject * * ppSep)
{
    *ppSep = NULL;

    // Declare a CComObject<> pointer using your class as the
    // template parameter
    CComObject<CSeparateObject>* pSub;

    // Call the static CComObject<>::CreateInstance() member,
    // passing a pointer to your pointer. This creates an instance of your
    // CComObject<> class, without any references counted on it.
    HRESULT hr = CComObject<CSeparateObject>::CreateInstance(&pSub);

    // Check the return result, and pass it back to the client on failure
    if (FAILED(hr))
        return hr;

    // Initialize the object according to your own rules
    pSub->m_bInitialized = true;

    // Call QueryInterface() to get the interface pointer to pass
    // back to the client
    hr = pSub->QueryInterface(IID_ISeparateObject,
        reinterpret_cast<void**>(ppSep));

    // If the QueryInterface() failed, delete the object
    if (FAILED(hr))
        delete pSub;

    // Return the HRESULT
    return hr;
}
```

Once again, we set ***ppSep** to **NULL** right at the start, but this time the rest of the code is more involved because we can't let **CComCreator<>** do all the work.

First, we declare a **CComObject<CSeparateObject>*** which will hold the pointer to our newly created object, once it's been created. Next, we pass the address of this pointer to **CComObject<>::CreateInstance()**. This method creates an instance of its own class and stores a pointer to it in the parameter passed to the function. **CreateInstance()** ensures that our object is fully created (it calls **FinalConstruct()** for example) before returning the pointer. It creates an object without any references counted on it (since references are counted on interfaces, and we haven't actually got a pointer to an interface on the object yet).

Assuming that the object is successfully created, we initialize it. In our case, it's a simple matter of setting a Boolean member to **true**, but in a real server, this code would be much more complicated and would depend on your particular circumstances.

Once initialized, we query for the **ISeparateObject** interface, using the **ppSep** parameter that was passed to our method to store the interface pointer. If successful, the client will receive the interface pointer and can **Release()** it when it's done. The only thing to watch out for is that if the call to **QueryInterface()** is *not* successful, we need to make sure that the object gets deleted ourselves.

Now you can build the server project again, ready to be tested with a client.

Updating the Client

The changes that need to be made to the client are extremely simple, and they're shown below:

```
#import "..\ReturningAnObject.tlb"
using namespace RETURNINGANOBJECTLib;
#include <iostream>
using namespace std;

int main()
{
   CoInitialize(NULL);
   try
   {
      IMainObjectPtr pMain(__uuidof(MainObject));
      pMain->Display();

      // Uncomment the following line to trigger a run-time error
      // ISeparateObjectPtr pCantCreateSep(__uuidof(SeparateObject));
      ISeparateObjectPtr pSep = pMain->CreateSeparateObject();
      pSep->Display();

      ISeparateObjectPtr pSepInit = pMain->CreateAndInitializeSeparateObject();
         pSepInit->Display();
   }
   catch (const _com_error& Err)
   {
      cout << "Error : " << Err.ErrorMessage()
         << hex << "0x" << Err.Error() << '\n';
   }
   CoUninitialize();
   return 0;
}
```

We just create a new smart pointer called **pSepInit** and fill it with the interface pointer returned from **CreateAndInitializeSeparateObject()**. The call to **pSepInit->Display()** just results in a new message box that proves that the object was initialized.

Example Summary

Here's a quick summary of the lessons learned from this example:

▶ You can prevent Wizard-generated coclasses from being externally creatable by removing their entries from the object map.

▶ You can remove the following items from classes that aren't externally creatable:

> The registry script resource
> The **DECLARE_REGISTRY_RESOURCEID()** macro
> The **CComCoClass<>** base class
> The **coclass** definition in the IDL file

▶ If you want to create an instance of a coclass and pass an interface pointer directly to a client, the easiest way is to use **CComCreator<CComObject<CYourClass>>::CreateInstance()**.

▶ If you want to do some initialization of an object before returning an interface pointer to the client, use **CComObject<CYourClass>::CreateInstance()** to create the object.

▶ If you use **CComObject<CYourClass>::CreateInstance()**, don't forget to **delete** the object if the call to **QueryInterface()** fails.

Reusability

COM is a great way of reusing code by packaging it as programmable objects, but so far we've only looked at clients using COM objects. What happens when we want to reuse a component from within another component? How can we take advantage of the features of a commercial component, and how can we add to the functionality of a component once it's been compiled?

In COM, there are two primary mechanisms for reusing one component within another: **containment** and **aggregation**.

Containment

Containment is the equivalent of having one component as a member variable of another. The outer (controlling, containing) component makes use of the inner (contained) component, but does not directly expose the contained component to its clients.

The outer component can choose to use the inner component to implement some of its functionality. If the outer component decides to implement one or more of the interfaces of the inner component, as shown in the following figure, it must provide a wrapper for every method on the exposed interfaces. The method wrappers can simply call the inner component's methods directly, or they can perform additional tasks such as validating parameters, recording usage, or otherwise extending the inner component's interface.

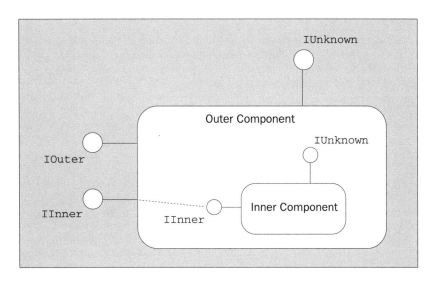

The outer component manages the lifetime of the inner component. It typically creates the inner component with **CoCreateInstance()** when it initializes itself (**FinalConstruct()**), and releases the inner component's interface pointer when it uninitializes itself (**FinalRelease()**). In containment, the outer component isn't doing anything very different from what a standard client would do.

Aggregation

Sometimes it's more convenient to expose the interfaces of the inner object directly, without writing a collection of wrappers. This is aggregation. A client creates the outer object, and when it asks **QueryInterface()** for an interface supported by the inner object, it gets passed a pointer to the inner object's interface.

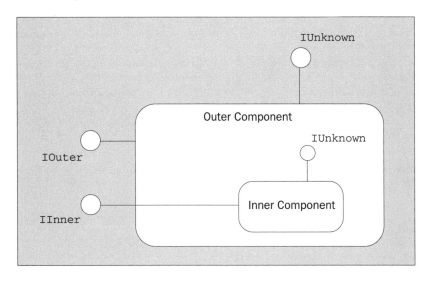

To a client, an aggregation (like containment) looks like one seamless object; the client does not know that there are actually two separate components acting in unison. (In fact, there could be more than two. There's no reason why the outer component cannot aggregate several different components, or why the inner component cannot aggregate another component into itself, like one of those Russian dolls that opens up to reveal another, smaller doll inside.)

One advantage of aggregation over containment is that it requires much less knowledge of the inner component on the part of the person implementing the outer component. Another is that bypassing the wrapper layer makes the component that bit more efficient.

The disadvantages of aggregation are that the inner (aggregated) object must be specially written so that it can be aggregated, and that the inner object can only be implemented in a DLL that is loaded directly into the same process space as the outer object. There is no cross-process or cross-machine aggregation.

To see why aggregation requires the knowledge and cooperation of the inner component, consider the diagram above. Suppose the client creates the aggregated object and asks for an **IOuter** interface pointer. Later, the client **QI()**s for and receives an **IInner** pointer. What happens when the client does a **pIInner->QueryInterface(IID_IOuter)**? If the inner component doesn't know that it has been aggregated, it's not going to be able to return an **IOuter** pointer. In Chapter 1, you saw that **QueryInterface()** must be both symmetric and transitive, so the inner component has somehow to return an **IOuter** interface pointer.

Identity and lifetime also force the inner object to know that it is being aggregated. Clients know nothing of the aggregation, and see a single object. They expect **AddRef()** and **Release()** to control the lifetime of this object, no matter which interface pointer is being used. Thus, an **AddRef()** on the **IInner** interface should be sufficient to keep both the outer and inner objects alive, just as an **AddRef()** on the **IOuter** interface should.

An object knows when it's being aggregated because the aggregator calls **IClassFactory::CreateInstance()** (or **CoCreateInstance()**) with the **punkOuter** parameter set to the **outer unknown** of the aggregating component, and it asks for a pointer to the **IUnknown** interface. The outer unknown of a component is its own **IUnknown** interface if it's not being aggregated, or the outer unknown that was passed to it through **IClassFactory::CreateInstance()** if it is. Thus, if there are many levels of aggregation, all the aggregated objects have a pointer to the same outer unknown that controls the lifetime and **QueryInterface()** functionality for the whole object.

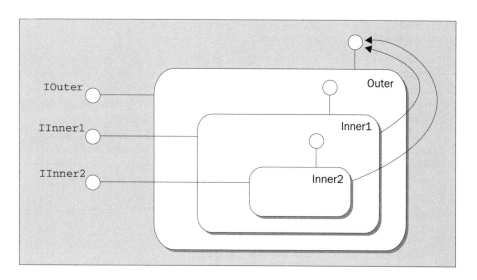

To be aggregatable, the inner component must have *two* distinct implementations of the three **IUnknown** methods, **QueryInterface()**, **AddRef()** and **Release()**. One of these is for all the interfaces except **IUnknown** itself. For this implementation, the three methods must delegate all calls to the outer unknown, because a client can get a pointer to any of these interfaces, and so call these methods directly.

The other implementation of these methods is used for **IUnknown** only. This implementation is known as the **explicit IUnknown implementation**. These methods do not delegate; they provide a traditional implementation of **IUnknown** and manage the lifetime and **QueryInterface()** of the inner object. These methods do not delegate because the inner component still needs some way of managing its own lifetime and exposing its own interfaces, even when aggregated. A *client* can never get a pointer to this **IUnknown** when a component is being aggregated; only the outer object has a pointer to this interface. The outer component must ask for a pointer to **IUnknown** when creating the inner object so that it can call **QueryInterface()**, **AddRef()** and **Release()** on the non-delegating implementation.

The outer component is required to follow a handful of rules when dealing with the inner component:

> When creating the inner component, it must ask for **IUnknown** (the inner component should fail if any other interface is asked for when it's created as part of an aggregate).

> After obtaining any interface pointer on the inner object other than **IUnknown**, the outer object must **Release()** its own outer unknown pointer (which resolves to either its explicit unknown or the outermost outer unknown). This counteracts the implicit **AddRef()** delegated to the outer unknown by the inner object in its implementation of **QueryInterface()**.

▶ Conversely, before releasing an interface pointer on the inner object, the outer object must **AddRef()** its outer unknown.

▶ When the outer object shuts down, it must release the inner object. This means that it must **AddRef()** its outer unknown, then call **Release()** on the inner object. The call to **Release()** may, in turn, cause the inner object to call **Release()** on the outer object's interface. Without artificially bumping the reference count, we'd end up with problems. You can see this by looking at the sequence of events below:

Event	Outer Object's Reference Count
1. Client has reference to object	1
2. Client calls **Release()**	0
3. Outer object calls **AddRef()** on itself	1
4. Outer object Releases inner object	1
5. Inner object releases outer object (back to Step 3)	0

▶ Generally, the outer object should not blindly delegate **QI()**s for unrecognized interfaces to the inner object. An inner object could support more interfaces than the outer object knows about.

The Inner Object in ATL

Thankfully, ATL handles the hard parts of aggregation for you. The **DECLARE_AGGREGATABLE()** macro, which is provided by default for your COM classes, means that when an object is being aggregated, it's created as a **CComAggObject<>**; when an object is being created independently, it's created as a **CComObject<>**.

CComAggObject<> provides the implementations of the explicit unknown methods, so it implements **AddRef()**, **Release()** and **QueryInterface()**. **QueryInterface()** returns a pointer to the **CComAggObject<>**'s **IUnknown** interface if there is a request for **IID_IUnknown**; otherwise, it delegates to the **_InternalQueryInterface()** function of its **m_contained** member.

Unlike **CComObject<>**, **CComAggObject<>** doesn't derive from your class (for example, **CYourClass**). Instead, its **m_contained** member is an object of type **CComContainedObject<CYourClass>**, which *does* derive from **CYourClass**. This means that **m_contained**'s **_InternalQueryInterface()** function is the one provided by the **BEGIN_COM_MAP()** macro in your class.

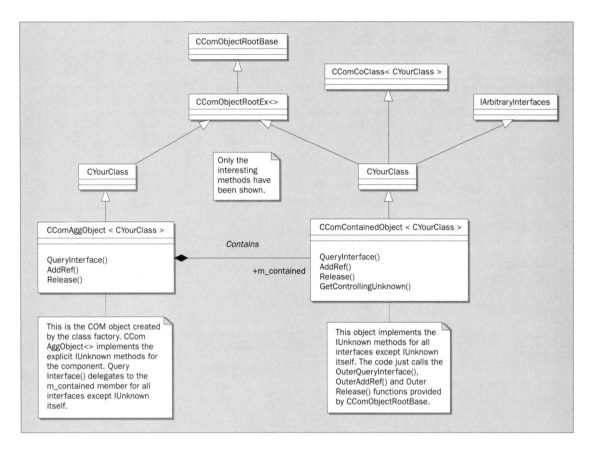

CComContainedObject<> therefore provides the other implementation of the **AddRef()**, **Release()** and **QueryInterface()** methods. This implementation delegates to the **OuterAddRef()**, **OuterRelease()** and **OuterQueryInterface()** functions provided by **CComObjectRootBase**. These implementations are just simple inline functions that call **AddRef()**, **Release()**, and **QueryInterface()** through the outer unknown pointer. They don't require any information about the interfaces provided by your class.

GetControllingUnknown()

CComContainedObject<> also provides a function called **GetControllingUnknown()**, which returns a pointer to the controlling unknown. If there's a chance that your object might be aggregated, and you need to get a pointer to the **IUnknown** interface for your object (as we did back in the **ComDialog** example), have a think about whether you really want the explicit **IUnknown** of the component, or the controlling unknown.

In the **ComDialog** example, we wanted to get an **IUnknown** pointer so that we could call **AddRef()** and **Release()** on it to keep the component alive. That means we wanted the **IUnknown** responsible for the lifetime of the component *as it appears to the client*. When there's no aggregation involved, we don't have a choice to make — we can call **GetUnknown()** and all will be well. But if our component could be aggregated, we would need to get the outer **IUnknown** by calling **GetControllingUnknown()**.

There's just one problem with calling `GetControllingUnknown()` from our class: it's defined by a class lower down the inheritance tree. We can't call a function in our class if it's not defined!

The solution is simply to add the `DECLARE_GET_CONTROLLING_UNKNOWN()` macro to the definition of your class. This defines `GetControllingUnknown()` as a **virtual** function in your class. It's always safe to use this macro and call the function (even if the object is never aggregated) because it's implemented as a call to `GetUnknown()`. If the function isn't overridden by `CComContainedObject<>::GetControllingUnknown()`, then things will still work as expected.

```
#define DECLARE_GET_CONTROLLING_UNKNOWN() public:\
    virtual IUnknown* GetControllingUnknown() {return GetUnknown();}
```

Changing the Aggregation Model

It's possible to change the aggregation model for your class by using one of the other `DECLARE_`*xxx*`AGGREGATABLE()` macros. These macros can be added to your class definition by the ATL Object Wizard when you generate a Simple Object, by choosing the appropriate option in the **Aggregation** frame on the **Attributes** tab. Alternatively, you can add these macros by hand after your class has been generated.

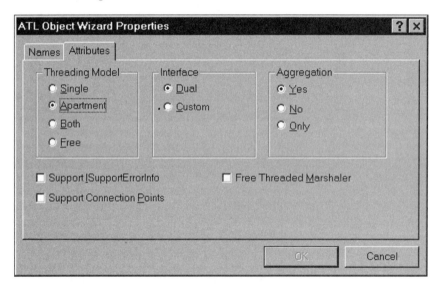

If you want to disallow aggregation, you can use the `DECLARE_NOT_AGGREGATABLE()` macro, as we did earlier in the chapter. As we discussed, for efficiency reasons, you should add this macro to EXE-packaged classes when you generate them.

If, for some strange reason, you want objects of your class to be created *only* as part of an aggregation, add the `DECLARE_ONLY_AGGREGATABLE()` macro to your class definition.

If you want to have your objects created from the same class whether they are being aggregated or not, add the `DECLARE_POLY_AGGREGATABLE()` macro to your class definition. The `DECLARE_POLY_AGGREGATABLE()` macro means that your COM objects will always be created as objects of type `CComPolyObject<CYourClass>`.

If you look at the documentation for **CComPolyObject<>**, you might be forgiven for thinking that **CComPolyObject<>** is a wildly different class from **CComAggObject<>**, but a look at the source code soon reveals that the difference is tiny. You can see it below:

```
// Constructor for CComAggObject<>
CComAggObject(void* pv) : m_contained(pv)
{
    _Module.Lock();
}

// Constructor for CComPolyObject<>
CComPolyObject(void* pv) : m_contained(pv ? pv : this)
{
    _Module.Lock();
}
```

The only difference between these two classes is in the initializer list for their constructor. The **pv** parameter represents the outer unknown. In the case of **CComAggObject<>**, **pv** is passed untouched to the **CComContainedObject<>** constructor. In the case of **CComPolyObject<>**, **pv** is passed if it's not **NULL**, otherwise the **CComPolyObject<>**'s **this** pointer is passed as the outer unknown.

If you want your objects to be created both as part of an aggregation *and* independently, then switching over to **CComPolyObject<>** will almost certainly reduce the size of your compiled code, since you will no longer get the vtable and functions of **CComObject<CYourClass>** compiled into it. However, the **CComObject<>** class will be smaller at runtime than the **CComPolyObject<>** equivalent, so you may take a hit in your module's working set. ATL is designed to allow you maximum flexibility in optimizing your code for different circumstances.

The Outer Object in ATL

From the other side of things, how does ATL help us when we want to aggregate a component into one that we've written? We'll see just how easy it is to aggregate a component by aggregating the simple example from the previous chapter into the COM dialog example from this one. Sure, it's a completely arbitrary example, but the principles are sound! We'll start with the COM dialog project, as it was when we last left it, and we'll aggregate the **ICalcEaster** interface into the **CComDialog** class.

The steps you need to follow for aggregating an object are extremely simple:

▶ Add a member in the outer class to store an **IUnknown** pointer

▶ Create an instance of the object that we're aggregating (the inner object). Pass in a pointer to the outer class's outer unknown, and ask for the inner object's **IUnknown** interface when you do this. Store the resulting pointer in the member you added to the outer class.

▶ Add **COM_INTERFACE_ENTRY_AGGREGATE()** macros to the COM map for each interface on the inner object that you want to expose from your object. You do *not* have to add an entry for *every* interface exposed by the inner object, only those that you want clients to get hold of.

155

> Make sure that the inner object's **IUnknown** pointer is released when the outer object shuts down.

> Add the new interfaces to the **coclass** definition in the outer object's IDL file if appropriate.

First, we need to get the CLSID and IID definitions from the **Simple** project into the **ComDialogProject**, so open **ComDialogProject** in Developer Studio and add a **#include** for **Simple.h** to the top of **ComDialog.h**. You should use the relative path from the **ComDialogProject** directory to the **Simple** directory:

```
#include "ComDialogProject.h"
#include "..\Simple\Simple.h"
```

Remember that **Simple.h** is the **MIDL**-generated header containing the **extern** declarations of the **Simple** project's GUIDs.

We also need to add the non-**extern** definitions of the IDs into our project. The easiest way to do this is to add a **#include** for **Simple_i.c** to **ComDialogProject.cpp**.

```
#include "ComDialog.h"
#include "..\Simple\Simple_i.c"
```

It's a good idea to add this **#include** in the same file as the existing **#include** for **ComDialogProject_i.c**, if only for consistency's sake.

Now we need to add a member to the **CComDialog** class to hold the **IUnknown** pointer that we're going to get back from the aggregate when we create it. In this example, we're going to add a **CComPtr<>** member. Add the code shown to the **CComDialog** class definition, just below the enumeration for the dialog resource:

```
enum { IDD = IDD_COMDIALOG };
CComPtr<IUnknown> m_pAgg;
```

CComPtr<> is a smart pointer class that handles reference counting automatically. It is similar to the **_com_ptr_t<>** class, but is an intrinsic part of ATL, so we don't need to add any extra headers when we use this class, and we don't need to worry about it dragging in huge amounts of code into our project. We'll use **CComPtr<>** simply so that we can forget about releasing the inner object's interface pointer when the outer component is released for the last time — **CComPtr<>** will do that for us without any intervention.

The next step is actually to create an instance of the inner object when the outer object (**CComDialog**) first gets initialized. The place to do this is in **FinalConstruct()**, so add the code shown highlighted below:

```
HRESULT FinalConstruct()
{
    if (Create(NULL))
    {
        // Create the inner object
        return CoCreateInstance( CLSID_CalcEaster,
                                 GetUnknown(),
```

```
                            CLSCTX_INPROC_SERVER,
                            IID_IUnknown,
                            (void**)&m_pAgg );
      }
   else
      return HRESULT_FROM_WIN32(GetLastError());
}
```

You can see that we're using **CoCreateInstance()** to create an instance of the **CalcEaster** coclass. The second parameter to **CoCreateInstance()** is the outer unknown of the **CComDialog** object. Remember that we know that our **CComDialog** class will never be aggregated (because it is part of an EXE), and also because we applied the **DECLARE_NOT_AGGREGATABLE()** macro, so it's safe to use **GetUnknown()** here.

> *If your class might be used as the inner object of an aggregation, you must use* **GetControllingUnknown()** *and add the* **DECLARE_GET_CONTROLLING_UNKNOWN()** *macro to your class.*

The third parameter specifies the context for the server we're creating. We know that aggregation only works with in-process objects, so we're quite happy to be as specific as possible and request an inproc server.

The fourth parameter is the interface we're asking for, which must be **IUnknown** when we're creating an object as part of an aggregate.

The final parameter is the address of the pointer that will store the **IUnknown** pointer for which we're asking. The **CComPtr<>** class implements an **operator&()** function that returns the address of the member that it uses to store its interface pointer — we're not actually taking the address of the **CComPtr<>** object itself.

Now we need to add a **COM_INTERFACE_ENTRY_AGGREGATE()** macro to the COM map for the **ICalcEaster** interface.

```
BEGIN_COM_MAP(CComDialog)
   COM_INTERFACE_ENTRY(IComDialog)
   COM_INTERFACE_ENTRY_AGGREGATE(IID_ICalcEaster, m_pAgg.p)
END_COM_MAP()
```

The **COM_INTERFACE_ENTRY_AGGREGATE()** macro takes an interface identifier for the interface that we're exposing, and an **IUnknown*** for the inner object that implements the interface. The macro itself hides the details that handle the implementation of **QueryInterface()**.

At this stage, we could compile and test the project and everything would work, but we'll just make the finishing touches by adding the new interface to the **coclass** definition in the type library. Add the code shown highlighted below to the **library** section of **ComDialogProject.idl**:

```
library COMDIALOGPROJECTLib
{
   importlib("stdole32.tlb");
   importlib("stdole2.tlb");
```

```
importlib("..\simple\simple.tlb");


    [
        uuid(D55039F0-61B3-11D1-B28D-00A0C94515AD),
        helpstring("ComDialog class")
    ]
    coclass ComDialog
    {
        [default] interface IComDialog;
        interface ICalcEaster;
    };
};
```

You can see that we've used the **importlib** statement to introduce the types from the **Simple** type library into the **ComDialogProject** type library. This means that we can use the types and interfaces from **Simple.tlb** in the current library, without the types actually being duplicated in the library.

The **coclass** block just includes an extra line for the new interface exposed by **ComDialog**.

Clients

Now we can compile the project and adapt the existing clients to test the new interface exposed by the server. Before we do that, you can run the existing clients for the COM dialog to see that they still work unchanged.

Console Client

The first client is based on the console client that we developed to test the COM dialog. The new client should look like this:

```
// Main.cpp
#include "Tchar.h"
#import "..\ComDialogProject.tlb"
#import "..\..\Simple\Simple.tlb"
#include <iostream>

int main(int argc, char* argv[], char* envp[ ])
{
    HRESULT hr = CoInitialize(NULL);
    if (FAILED(hr))
        return hr;

    try
    {
        COMDIALOGPROJECTLib::IComDialogPtr
p(__uuidof(COMDIALOGPROJECTLib::ComDialog));
        p->Visible = VARIANT_TRUE;

        SIMPLELib::ICalcEasterPtr pCalcEaster( p );
```

```
        pCalcEaster->Year = 1984;
        pCalcEaster->CalculateEaster();

        TCHAR buff[255] = {0};
        wsprintf(buff, _T("Easter was %d/%d in %d"),
                pCalcEaster->Day, pCalcEaster->Month, pCalcEaster->Year);
        MessageBox(NULL, buff, _T("Calculation"), MB_OK);
    }
    catch (const _com_error& Err)
    {
        std::cout << Err.ErrorMessage()
                << "0x" << std::hex << Err.Error() << '\n';
        hr = Err.Error();
    }

    CoUninitialize();
    return hr;
}
```

The code is nothing particularly new. We just use the **#import**-generated wrappers to manipulate the newly exposed interface, just as we did in the original simple object's client. The only difference is that we use the smart pointer's constructor to automatically call **QueryInterface()** on the original pointer, rather than creating an instance of the **CalcEaster** coclass.

Visual Basic Client

We can also adapt the Visual Basic client to demonstrate the new interface exposed by the **ComDialog** coclass. Open the client project, and add a new command button called **cmdCalculate** to the form. Also, add a reference to the Simple 1.0 Type Library. Now add the code shown below:

```
Private itf As COMDIALOGPROJECTLib.IComDialog
Private itfCalcEaster As ICalcEaster

Private Sub cmdHide_Click()
    itf.Visible = False
End Sub

Private Sub cmdShow_Click()
    itf.Visible = True
End Sub

Private Sub Form_Load()
    Set itf = New COMDIALOGPROJECTLib.ComDialog
    Set itfCalcEaster = itf
End Sub


Private Sub cmdCalculate_Click()
On Error GoTo err_Generic
```

```
        itfCalcEaster.Year = 1984
        itfCalcEaster.CalculateEaster

        MsgBox "Easter was " & itfCalcEaster.Day & _
                "/" & itfCalcEaster.Month & " in " & itfCalcEaster.Year
        Exit Sub

    err_Generic:
        MsgBox "Error: " & Err.Number & vbCrLf & Err.Description
    End Sub
```

The new code in **Form_Load()** is the Visual Basic equivalent of calling **QueryInterface()** on the original interface pointer for the new interface. The code in response to the button click is almost identical to the code from the Visual Basic client we used to test the Simple example in the last chapter.

Aggregation Summary

▶ Aggregation is a technique for reusing COM objects.

▶ Aggregation requires the inner object to be implemented in a DLL.

▶ Aggregation requires the inner object to be written with the possibility of aggregation in mind.

▶ When the outer object creates the inner object as part of an aggregation, it *must* pass in its outer unknown pointer, and it *must* ask for the inner object's **IUnknown** interface.

▶ ATL provides macro support for creating aggregatable objects and for exposing interfaces from objects that have been aggregated.

Summary

In this chapter, we've taken a close look at the way ATL provides core COM functionality to your classes. We've seen how the object map and COM map hide a lot of code that we can use in our ATL projects, and we've seen how to customize our objects using the various macros that ATL provides.

With this essential knowledge under our belts, we can turn our attention to the next chapter, where we look at creating objects suitable for use from scripting clients.

Automation and Error Handling

COM has two broad types of interface, categorized according to how the methods in the interfaces are accessed — static or dynamic invocation. **Static invocation** is the mechanism used by custom interfaces. **Dynamic invocation**, on the other hand, is the means by which Automation interfaces go about their business.

Static invocation is a contract between the client and a server object. The client knows *exactly* the number of methods in an interface, and the signatures of those methods. The object, for its side of the contract, *must* implement the methods described by the interface; if it does not, the two will not be able to communicate.

With custom interfaces, the only negotiation involved is the client querying for an interface with **QueryInterface()**, and therefore the client can only ask a server whether it supports a particular interface that it already knows about. There is no other negotiation possible — the client cannot ask the object to list the interfaces it supports, nor can it ask the object to tell it about the methods on its interfaces. Further, if the object only supports interfaces that the client does not know about, the client cannot access the object.

Automation interfaces use dynamic invocation. We'll see exactly how this works later on, but basically, Automation allows the client to ask an object to return information about the interfaces that it supports. Through **type information**, the object can list all the interfaces it supports and, when queried, it can return information about the methods on a specified interface. Using this information, the client can invoke a method *dynamically* — in other words, the client can package the parameters in a generic way, and then tell the object to call a particular method with those parameters. This invocation is done on the fly, and can be performed with no prior knowledge of the object.

Terminology

During this chapter, you'll see a number of different terms to describe the interfaces supported by an Automation object. This is largely for historical reasons. The term 'Automation' was first coined in the phrase 'OLE Automation' when COM was first developed. The philosophy then was that a programmer could write several Automation objects — some with user interfaces and others without — and then 'glue' them together to create an application with a scripting language like VB3. Visual Basic would 'automate' these objects, that is, it would create them and then tell them what to do.

Over time, Automation (the 'OLE' has been dropped) has become a wider-ranging technology. Visual Basic is still important, of course, but now there is VBA (present as a macro language in many applications), Microsoft Java and VBScript. All of these languages will talk to Automation objects.

Automation objects use an interface called **IDispatch**, so you can tell if an object can be 'automated' by querying for this interface. However, unlike those early OLE Automation objects that typically *only* exposed **IDispatch**, these days the interface is often just one way to get access to an object.

Server objects implement Automation by allowing clients to use a method on the **IDispatch** interface to call other methods. The collection of methods it makes available in this way is called a **dispinterface** (short for 'dispatch interface'). **IDispatch** allows an object to indicate what dispinterface methods it supports in two different ways. It can be done at runtime, through other **IDispatch** methods; or else the object can be a little more expressive and maintain information about its dispinterfaces that a client can use at compile time. The client can still ask the object for information about its dispinterfaces, and can call those interface methods dynamically.

As you can imagine, the information an object provides must include details of all the dispinterfaces it supports, all the methods on those dispinterfaces, and all the parameters of those methods. This information is called **type information**. For an object to be an Automation object, it means that a client should be able to get access to its type information. The object can supply this directly, or more typically it can be supplied by the **type library** files that we have seen generated by our projects in earlier chapters. A type library is effectively a tokenized version of the IDL file, and so it describes all the interfaces supported by the object, all the methods, and the parameters of those methods. Since a type library describes *exactly* what an interface can do, it can be used to marshal data between processes.

All Automation methods must use the Automation-compatible data types we mentioned in the last chapter. This means that the Universal Marshaler can be used to marshal Automation method calls, although to do so it must read the type library whenever it wants to marshal a method request. This is slower than the case with a proxy-stub DLL, where the proxy object 'knows' about the data that needs to be marshaled. Furthermore, when you access a method in a dispinterface, the call always has to go through **IDispatch**, even if the object is inproc. There is obviously a performance issue here. To get round this, you can describe an interface as being both a dispinterface *and* a custom interface. This way, you have the convenience of being able to call the interface methods using **IDispatch** or the custom part of the interface. Such an interface is called a **dual** interface, and the Object Wizard allows you to write Automation interfaces through its Dual interface option.

The Need for Automation

There are several reasons why you would want to use Automation over custom interfaces; the most important of which is when you're programming for clients that *only* support Automation interfaces. Such clients include those that use VBA and VBScript, but *not* clients programmed in VB5, which can use both Automation and custom interfaces.

Automation is useful for VBScript because the interpreter does type checking at runtime. When a web developer writes VBScript, the code is not compiled and so there is no checking on the methods that are called or on the data types of the parameters that are passed. Since a VBScript client passes parameters without knowing beforehand what the types of those parameters are, this check must be done at runtime using type information. If the object does not support a particular method, then the call will fail. If, however, the data passed from the client is of the wrong type, the object is free to **coerce** the data to the required type.

How would the object know that the data is of the wrong type? All data passed through Automation interfaces is self-describing, using a data type called a **VARIANT**. The Universal Marshaler knows about **VARIANT**s and the types of data it can be used to pass, and thus the only criteria for marshaling an interface with the Universal Marshaler is that the interface parameters must be compatible with **VARIANT**. Incidentally, VBScript only has a **Variant** data type anyway, and the interpreter uses type information to coerce data before it is transmitted.

Another situation where you may want to use Automation interfaces is when you want to add functionality dynamically at runtime. Imagine you have an object that represents the business rules of some kind of transaction. The object could be changed at runtime to support extra business rules, perhaps through a scripting mechanism. If this new business rule is described by type information, the client can simply query for the type information and then use the rule.

As you can see, Automation offers a great deal, and COM carries out much of the functionality. Before looking at some of these features of Automation, however, let's take a proper look at how it actually works.

Automation Interfaces

IDispatch is the COM interface behind Automation. Every machine that supports COM has the proxies and stubs for **IDispatch**. Once a client obtains this interface on an object, it can use the interface's methods to do three things:

- ▶ Query for type information — that is, ask the object about the Automation interfaces it supports, and the methods and properties implemented in those interfaces
- ▶ Ask the object to translate from locale-dependant method and property names to locale-independent **dispatch IDs** (also called DISPIDs)
- ▶ Invoke a method, or access a property via a dispatch ID

Combined, these abilities allow a client to have no prior knowledge about an object, and yet still be able to access it. In the following sections, I will outline what the **IDispatch** methods do. Even at this early stage, though, I should point out that my aim is to familiarize you with Automation. You won't have to implement these methods yourself, and in most cases you won't even need to access them, because ATL does all this work for you.

Methods and Properties

COM interfaces follow the accepted OO principles of encapsulation and data hiding, and therefore they only export functions. A client does not have direct access to internal data members of the object. From a purely practical point of view, an interface can *only* export functions, because ultimately it is just an array of function pointers. However, this does not prevent an object from providing functions as accessors for data members. The client's calling mechanism can be arranged to make the calling of these accessors look like an object's data members *are* being accessed directly.

165

It follows that Automation objects can have both methods and properties (public functions and data members) that are available through Automation methods. For example, the Word 8.0 Object Library ('object library' is just another name for a type library) defines methods and properties on the Automation objects exported by Word 97. The following Visual Basic code starts Word, loads a document and makes it visible:

```
Dim wordapp As New word.Application
wordapp.Documents.Open "c:\my documents\test.doc"
wordapp.Visible = True
```

Here, the first line creates the **Application** Automation object, and the second line invokes the **Open()** method on the **word.Application.Documents** sub-object. The syntax of VB is that the parentheses are missed out when a method returns no result. **Open()** is used to load a document, and it takes *ten* arguments. In this VB code only *one* argument is passed: the name of the file that holds the document. The object must be able to handle this situation, determining which argument has been passed, and using default values for the rest. The last line sets the **Visible** property to **True** and makes Word 97 visible, displaying the document.

Accessing methods and properties like this is an artifact of using VB. If you used C++ to access the **word.Application** object, then both calls would be made through the methods on a dispinterface.

Notice that here the property is called **Visible**: it is in English. If VB had to pass this name to the object, it would make the Automation interface useful only to English speakers. In fact, VB does not pass this string. Instead, it passes a unique ID called a **DISPID** (or dispatch ID), which identifies the property. Methods and their parameters have DISPIDs, too.

Since a VB programmer will use textual names for properties and methods, VB must have some mechanism to get hold of the appropriate DISPIDs. In fact, VB uses one of two mechanisms, depending on how the code is written. In the above code, the type checking is actually done at compile time through the type library of the object. The VB compiler looks at the code, sees that the **Open()** method and **Visible** property will be used, and then uses the type library to find the DISPIDs. These are then placed in the compiled code so that when the object is accessed at runtime, the application can call the method (and access the property) directly. Notice that since DISPIDs are locale-independent, this compiled code will work in all locales.

If VB does not have access to the type library at compile time, the code can be written to perform the type checking at runtime:

```
Dim wordapp As Object
Set wordapp = CreateObject("Word.Application")
wordapp.Documents.Open "c:\my documents\test.doc"
wordapp.Visible = True
```

This code and the earlier code do the same thing, but whereas the latter accessed the Automation object through a typed variable (of type **word.Application**), this code uses an untyped variable (**Object**). You can think of this as being a bit like accessing a C++ object through a **void*** pointer. The **CreateObject()** line checks the local system to see if there is a **Word.Application** object type, and if so the object is created. In the following line, VB asks the object whether it has a method with the name **Open**, and if so the object will return the DISPID for this method. VB then uses the DISPID to invoke the method with the string parameter. This is in contrast to the previous code where VB *knew* that the object supported **Open()** because the variable was typed.

For this second example to work, the Automation interface must implement a method to return the DISPIDs for named methods, parameters and properties for locale, so that the VB application can ask the object what the DISPIDs for **Open** and **Visible** are. When this code is compiled, the strings "Open" and "Visible" are put into the compiled code. If this code is run on a machine in a non-English locale the machine *must* still have the English type library to be able to get the right DISPIDs. This is clearly an administrative nightmare, and means that scripting languages that can only access Automation interfaces in this way are extremely locale-specific.

IDispatch

Now the scene has been set, let's look at the **IDispatch** interface itself. Automation interfaces use dynamic invocation, but since the client must use *some* interface to call the object, the invocation cannot be completely dynamic. In particular, Automation objects must implement **IUnknown** (as required by the COM specification) to define their identity and to manage their lifetime. In addition to this, Automation objects must provide a generic interface through which a client can talk to the object and ask the object what it can do. This is the **IDispatch** interface.

Here is the definition of **IDispatch**, as given in **Oaidl.idl** (and edited a bit for clarity):

```
[
    object,
    uuid(00020400-0000-0000-C000-000000000046),
    pointer_default(unique)
]
interface IDispatch : IUnknown
{
    HRESULT GetTypeInfoCount(
        [out] UINT* pctinfo);

    HRESULT GetTypeInfo(
        [in] UINT iTInfo,
        [in] LCID lcid,
        [out] ITypeInfo** ppTInfo);

    HRESULT GetIDsOfNames(
        [in] REFIID riid,
        [in, size_is(cNames)] LPOLESTR* rgszNames,
        [in] UINT cNames,
        [in] LCID lcid,
        [out, size_is(cNames)] DISPID* rgDispId);

    HRESULT Invoke(
        [in] DISPID dispIdMember,
        [in] REFIID riid,
        [in] LCID lcid,
        [in] WORD wFlags,
        [in, out] DISPPARAMS* pDispParams,
        [out] VARIANT* pVarResult,
        [out] EXCEPINFO* pExcepInfo,
        [out] UINT* puArgErr);
}
```

All Automation objects must implement **IDispatch**, and through it servers can implement methods and properties. The methods of **IDispatch** allow a client to ask an object about the methods and properties it supports, and also to invoke those methods and access those properties.

IDispatch looks wonderfully flexible. A client can ask the object, "Do you support a method called *MethodX*?" and the object can reply, "Yes, and it has a DISPID of *x*". The client can then ask the object, "So, what are the parameters of the method with DISPID *x*?" and the object can respond, "The parameters have DISPIDs of *0*, *1*, *2* and *3*. Oh, and by the way, they have names and types, and some of them have default values so they're optional." The client can now ask... well, you get the idea.

This is indeed wonderfully flexible, but terribly anarchic. If this conversation had to take place every time a client wanted to access an object, it would require a great many calls to the object. Since the object could quite easily be on another machine, the client could be in for a long wait. To ease the situation, an object can say that it supports only particular DISPIDs, and these are collected together in Automation interfaces called dispinterfaces.

Dispinterfaces

A **dispinterface** is not a new type of interface. Basically, it is an interface that supports a collection of methods and properties that can be called through **IDispatch::Invoke()**. The description of this interface is passed back to the client through the **IDispatch** type information methods, or through the object's type library.

Remember that a COM interface can inherit from another, single, interface — and that interface could perfectly well be **IDispatch**. This does not mean that the methods of the interface *must* be called through **IDispatch::Invoke()**, but if they will be, then each must have a DISPID. These methods and properties are then part of a dispinterface.

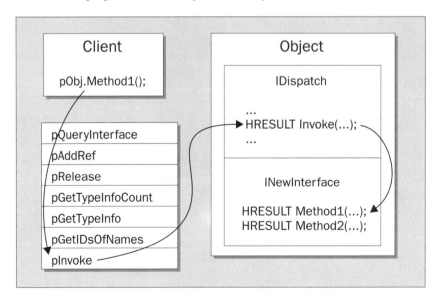

In the above diagram, a client obtains an interface pointer on an object that implements **INewInterface**; this interface is a dispinterface, and so derives from **IDispatch**. The interface pointer the client obtains is to **IDispatch** (shown on the left); notice that the **INewInterface** methods do no appear in the vtable. The client calls **Method1()** by calling **Invoke()** with the DISPID for **Method1()**. **Invoke()** then calls (or *dispatches* the request to) **Method1()**. Contrast this with calling a method on a derived non-dispinterface (custom interface), where the client calls the derived interface method directly:

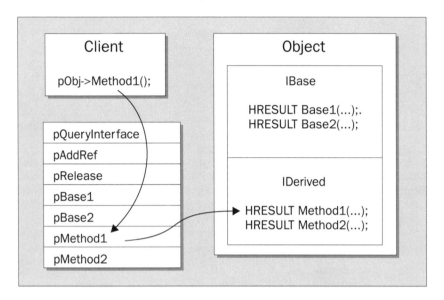

This time, the client obtains the **IDerived** interface, which derives from **IBase** and therefore implements the methods of **IBase** *and* the additional methods of the new interface. Since the interface is not a dispinterface, the methods *are* available through the vtable, and the client can call **Method1()** through its function pointer.

The term 'dispinterface' was originally used when describing interfaces with ODL (Object Description Language), but IDL has been extended to use the **dispinterface** statement, so that ODL is now regarded as largely obsolete. The only place where you would see ODL is if you were to create Automation objects with MFC — but then we're not using MFC, we're using ATL!

When you develop objects using the ATL Wizards, you will not have to worry about writing IDL, because the Wizard will do it for you. When you create an ATL object, you specify through the Object Wizard whether the methods of the object's interfaces are accessed directly through a vtable, or both directly *and* using DISPIDs. This is done by choosing either Custom or Dual interface on the Attributes tab in the Object Wizard. Dual interfaces will be explained a little later on; at this point you should be aware that this is the only way that you can use the Object Wizard to create an Automation interface.

IDispatch Methods

Let's take a look at the methods in **IDispatch**. Remember that when you implement a dual interface with the ATL Wizards, these methods will be provided for you by ATL. When a client application accesses your object, it will not normally need to access these methods directly (although the example will show you how to do this if necessary).

Invoke

Let's start with the last method, **Invoke()**. This is the workhorse of **IDispatch**, and as its name suggests, it passes to the server an identifier indicating the method it wants invoked, and an array with the parameters it wants to pass to that method. The object can then take these parameters and *dispatch* the call to the appropriate method. Here's the definition of **Invoke()**, along with an explanation of its parameters:

```
HRESULT Invoke(
    [in] DISPID dispIdMember,
    [in] REFIID riid,
    [in] LCID lcid,
    [in] WORD wFlags,
    [in, out] DISPPARAMS* pDispParams,
    [out] VARIANT* pVarResult,
    [out] EXCEPINFO* pExcepInfo,
    [out] UINT* puArgErr);
```

Parameter	Type	Description
dispIdMember	DISPID	A unique number identifying the method to invoke
riid	REFIID	Reserved
lcid	LCID	A locale ID
wFlags	WORD	A flag indicating the context of the method to invoke
pDispParams	DISPPARAMS*	A structure with the parameters to pass to the method
pVarResult	VARIANT*	The result from calling the method
pExcepInfo	EXCEPINFO*	Returned exception information
puArgErr	UINT*	An index indicating the first argument that is in error

Once a client knows about the methods and properties that an object supports (and you'll see how it does that in a moment), it uses **Invoke()** to tell the object to invoke a method. The first parameter is the DISPID of the method to invoke. Scripting languages will use a locale-dependent name for the method, but ultimately this must be converted to the unique ID of that method. The translation of name to DISPID is carried out by **GetIDsOfNames()**, which is called by the VBScript interpreter, for example. The **riid** parameter is not used and should always have a value of **IID_NULL**.

An Automation method may process some text or return a text value. If an error occurs in the method, information should be passed back to the client. This text will be locale-dependent — if the locale is France, for example, then French will be used. Locales can be more specific than language; they can be dialect-based too: a locale could be French-speaking Canada, which is distinct from French-speaking France. The client must tell the object what locale it is in, so that the object can handle text (as well as other things like date format and decimal separators) accordingly. This is the reason for the **lcid** parameter.

The **wFlags** parameter takes one of the following values that define to what action the **DISPID** refers:

Value	Description
DISPATCH_METHOD	An object method
DISPATCH_PROPERTYGET	Retrieving the value of a property
DISPATCH_PROPERTYPUT	Setting the value of a property
DISPATCH_PROPERTYPUTREF	The property is set by reference

These give the implementation of **Invoke()** in the object a hint as to what the client wants to be done. Retrieving a property value is the same as invoking a method that takes no parameters but returns a value, and so some objects do not distinguish between **DISPATCH_METHOD** and **DISPATCH_PROPERTYGET**. The oddball here is **DISPATCH_PROPERTYPUTREF**, which means that the parameter being passed in **pDispParams** is a reference to an object that is used to initialize the property referred to by the **dispIDMember**. Since a reference is used, this is equivalent to the C++ code:

```
pObj1 = pObj2;
```

where **pObj1** and **pObj2** are pointers to objects of the same class (and it is assumed that there is no overloaded **operator=()**). Any changes to the object's property will affect the referenced object; conversely, if the object passed to **Invoke()** through **pDispParams** changes, then so does the property in the Automation object. Compare this to **DISPATCH_PROPERTYPUT**, which means that the property's *value* should be set to the *value* of the object passed. This is equivalent to the C++:

```
*pObj1 = *pObj2;
```

The parameters of a method call (or the data used in a property put) are passed in the **pDispParams** parameter, which points to a structure that contains an array of IDs for the parameters, and an array of the values that those parameters should take. It also contains the number of arguments that are passed. If a method parameter is optional, and the client does not want to send a value, an empty value must be sent. The client may decide to pass the method parameters in the order that they are declared in the type library, or it may decide to pass them in a different order. In the latter case, the client must pass the parameters as **named parameters**, so that the object knows which parameter is which. You'll see how this works later in the chapter.

The implementation of **Invoke()** can then parse through the passed parameters and check the types of the data passed. If the type of a parameter is different from the type expected, the server object can try to coerce the data to the required type. If this is not possible, or the parameter is invalid, the object can return an error and indicate in **puArgErr** the parameter in the **pDispParams** that caused the problem.

If the client is asking for a method invocation, the object can then find the method (it may be as simple as implementing a **switch** using the DISPID, or it may involve some other, more complicated mechanism). If that method fails for some reason, it can pass back an **HRESULT**, but for a more detailed explanation of the problem it can pass back information in the **pExcepInfo** parameter.

The **EXCEPINFO** structure is quite interesting. It passes back to the client an error code and strings giving information about the source, a description of the error, a help context and a help file to find more information about the error. In addition to this, it can also pass back a function pointer that allows the server to ignore the other members, and only to return the values when the client calls this callback function. This deferment saves the object from incurring the cost of filling the other values when the client may well ignore them.

Finally, a method (or a property get) will return a value, and this is returned in the **pVarResult** parameter. The **VARIANT** type you can see being returned is a discriminated union that's used for passing data to and from the **Invoke()** function. **VARIANT**s and other Automation types will be covered later in the chapter.

DISPIDs

As I have already mentioned, the methods, properties and parameters of a method all have identifiers called DISPIDs. Scripting languages do not work with DISPIDs; instead they use textual names that are locale-specific. The interpreter of the scripting language must convert the textual name into a DISPID, and to do this it can call **GetIDsOfNames()** on the object's Automation interface. The caller passes in an array containing the name of a function and any named parameters, an array to accept the DISPIDs, and the locale identifier. The method should return the DISPIDs corresponding to the names. If the object does not recognize a name, then it will return **DISPID_UNKNOWN** in the appropriate element.

When you write the IDL for an Automation interface, you need to supply the DISPIDs for the methods and properties. The DISPID for a parameter of a method is allocated according to the position of the parameter in the method's argument list. You do not need to mark it in the IDL, as MIDL will assign one for you automatically.

Properties' and methods' DISPIDs are specified in the IDL by using the **[id()]** attribute. Here's the IDL from the **Simple** project in Chapter 2:

```
[
    object,
    uuid(3B35F500-7678-11D1-83B0-804F0BC10000),
    dual,
    helpstring("ICalcEaster Interface"),
    pointer_default(unique)
]
interface ICalcEaster : IDispatch
{
    [propget, id(1)] HRESULT Year([out, retval] short *pVal);
    [propput, id(1)] HRESULT Year([in] short newVal);
    [propget, id(2)] HRESULT Month([out, retval] short *pVal);
    [propget, id(3)] HRESULT Day([out, retval] short *pVal);
    [id(4)] HRESULT CalculateEaster();
};
```

Here, the **ICalcEaster** interface has properties **Year**, **Month** and **Day** with DISPIDs 1, 2 and 3 respectively, and a method called **CalculateEaster()** with a DISPID of 4. If the **[id()]** attribute is missed out, MIDL will add a value for you. When you compile this IDL with MIDL, all the information about the interface, including the DISPIDs of the methods and properties, are put into the object's type library.

Standard DISPIDs

The last section showed how you could specify the DISPIDs for members of an Automation interface (in this case, a dual interface). If you have more than one Automation interface on an object, the same DISPID can be used in both interfaces. However, these DISPIDs are not generally polymorphic, and using the same DISPID on different Automation interfaces will not have the same effect. However, Microsoft has defined a few standard DISPIDs, which always have negative values.

> *Note that if you have more than one Automation interface on an object, you will only be able to access the default interface through IDispatch, but you will be able to access all interfaces through their vtables if they are dual.*

The DISPIDs pertinent to control properties are listed in Chapter 7; other values are given in the following table:

Symbol	Value	Description
DISPID_VALUE	0	The default member of the dispinterface
DISPID_UNKNOWN	-1	Value returned by **GetIDsOfNames()** if a name is not recognized.
DISPID_PROPERTYPUT	-3	The DISPID to use when writing a property
DISPID_NEWENUM	-4	The **_NewEnum()** member of a collection
DISPID_EVALUATE	-5	The **Evaluate()** member of an object
DISPID_CONSTRUCTOR	-6	Reserved
DISPID_DESTRUCTOR	-7	Reserved

Of these values, two are of interest to this discussion. The first, **DISPID_UNKNOWN**, we have already seen — it is returned from **GetIDsOfNames()** when the object does not recognize the name. The other one of interest is **DISPID_PROPERTYPUT**. This is used when a client is writing a value to a property. It is necessary because when you write a property value with **Invoke()**, you are calling it as if you are calling a method that has a single parameter but no return value, and so you have to pass two DISPIDs. The first is in **dispIdMember** to indicate the method to call, and the second is used within the **pDispParams** structure. For a single parameter method, the second DISPID is 0, the index of the parameter, but since properties do not have a concept of a 'parameter', this won't work. Instead, you must use **DISPID_PROPERTYPUT**, which is the default DISPID for data sent to assign a value to a property.

GetIDsOfNames

As we've mentioned several times now, this method sends an array of names to the object, and returns an array of DISPIDs for those names. It is the client's responsibility to allocate these arrays. Create a console application in a subdirectory of the **Simple** project, and enter the following program:

```
#include <stdio.h>
#include <tchar.h>
#include "..\simple.h"
#include "..\simple_i.c"
```

173

```
int main()
{
   CoInitialize(NULL);

   IDispatch* pDisp;
   HRESULT hr;
   hr = CoCreateInstance( CLSID_CalcEaster,
                          NULL,
                          CLSCTX_ALL,
                          IID_IDispatch,
                          (void**)&pDisp );

   LPOLESTR pNames = L"CalculateEaster";
   DISPID pDispID;

   hr = pDisp->GetIDsOfNames( IID_NULL,
                              &pNames, 1,
                              LOCALE_SYSTEM_DEFAULT,
                              &pDispID );

   if (pDispID == DISPID_UNKNOWN)
      _tprintf(_T("%ls is not recognized\n"), pNames);
   else
      _tprintf(_T("%ls has a DISPID of %ld\n"), pNames, pDispID);

   pDisp->Release();

   CoUninitialize();
   return 0;
}
```

This code demonstrates the use of **GetIDsOfNames()** on our **ICalcEaster** interface. Notice that the first parameter is **IID_NULL**. This parameter is not used, but a parameter of **IID_NULL** must be passed, or an error code will be returned. The third parameter is the number of names in the array, and also the size of the array is passed in as the final parameter. The fourth parameter is the locale; I have used **LOCALE_SYSTEM_DEFAULT**, which is the locale of the client machine, but you can pass a particular locale if you choose. LCIDs are made up from a combination of language IDs and sub-language IDs, so UK English is:

```
LCID lcidUK = MAKELCID(LANG_ENGLISH, SUBLANG_ENGLISH_UK);
```

You can find these constants in **OleNls.h**.

GetTypeInfoCount and GetTypeInfo

Automation interfaces are described by **type information**. This information is held in one of two ways: either statically (as a type library resource or in a separate file), or dynamically (through type library interfaces). **GetTypeInfoCount()** and **GetTypeInfo()** allow a user to get access to these type library interfaces. Note that in practice, most Automation objects do not implement the type library interfaces, but instead load a type library resource (or file) through **LoadTypeLibEx()** and get COM to return system-generated interfaces.

```
HRESULT GetTypeInfoCount(
    [out] UINT* pctinfo);
```

The **GetTypeInfoCount()** function might just as well be called **SuppliesTypeInfo()**, because it will only return one of two values: 0 if the object does not supply type information, or 1 if it does. The reason why it has this name is for compatibility with its namesake in **ITypeLib**, which is used to get information for an Automation interface from a type library (which can describe many Automation interfaces). If an object does not supply type information, it does not mean that the object doesn't support Automation — it's just that the client must use some other source of type information to find out about the object.

```
HRESULT GetTypeInfo(
    [in] UINT iInfo,
    [in] LCID lcid,
    [out] ITypeInfo** ppTInfo);
```

The **GetTypeInfo()** function returns the **ITypeInfo** interface for the object's type information. The first parameter identifies the type information to return and should always be 0; again, the reason is for compatibility with **ITypeLib**. The second parameter is a locale ID, so that the type information returned can be specific to a locale, and finally the last parameter is an **[out]** parameter that returns the type information for the interface through the pointer you pass in.

The **ITypeInfo** interface has many methods that you can use to query for information about the Automation interfaces, methods and properties that an object supports. In addition to these information-gathering methods, there are two others of interest: **CreateInstance()** and **Invoke()**. The first will create an instance of the coclass described by the type library. Once you have an instance, you can then call **ITypeInfo::Invoke()**, passing a pointer to this instance, to invoke a method or access a property. This version of **Invoke()** can be used to implement **IDispatch::Invoke()**. This means that you can load a type library from a resource or disk file and use it to create an instance of the object that will provide most of the functionality of **IDispatch**. This is how ATL implements **IDispatch** through the **CComTypeInfoHolder** class.

Dual Interfaces

I have described **IDispatch**, which allows clients to query an object for the Automation methods and properties that it supports. Those methods and properties are grouped together as dispinterfaces, but they must be called through **IDispatch::Invoke()**. This adds, at the very least, an extra layer of indirection, since **Invoke()** needs to call a dispinterface method. If the client performs late binding, then access slows to a snail's pace while the client asks the object to resolve method and property names.

Custom interfaces are very efficient. Strictly speaking, a custom interface is a non-standard COM interface; interfaces like **IPersistStream** and **IDropTarget** are standard COM interfaces, and are therefore not custom. However, the term is generally taken to mean a non **IDispatch**-derived interface, which is certainly true when you consider implementing your own interfaces.

COM allows an Automation object to expose its interfaces both through **IDispatch** and through the vtable of a custom interface. Such an interface is called a **dual interface**, and is marked as such by using the **[dual]** attribute in its IDL.

Functions on the interface can be called *either* by using the type library at compile time, *or* by obtaining type information at runtime using the **IDispatch** type information methods. At most, this involves registering the object's type library on the client. The interface can also be called using the vtable, but to enable the call to go across apartment (and process, and machine) boundaries, a proxy object has to be registered on the client. Thus, when you use a dual interface you gain with inproc objects (since interface access is direct), but for local and remote objects you lose in terms of installation because you have to register extra items.

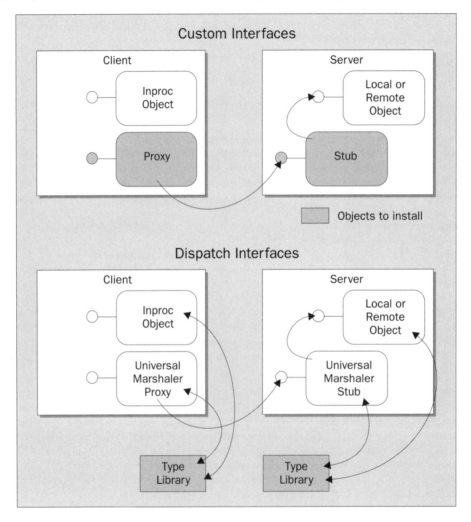

There is one final issue that must be aired here. COM objects allow you to expose multiple interfaces — this is COM's mechanism of providing polymorphism, since different interfaces have the same access to the object, but make the object appear to behave differently. How is this handled with dual interfaces? In the discussion above, I have said that a dual interface is exposed both through **IDispatch** and its vtable, but if there is more than one dual interface, doesn't it mean that there will be more than one implementation of **IDispatch**?

This could be true, and so must be avoided. You will see later exactly how this is handled by ATL, but basically it allows each of the object's dual interfaces to *implement* **IDispatch**, but only one of the interfaces to *expose* it. Each implementation of **IDispatch** provides type information through the *object's* type library and thus has information about the entire object, allowing access to the dispinterface parts of the other dual interfaces. It must be pointed out that since scripting languages like VBScript are untyped, these languages can only access the default interface of the object and so any additional dual interfaces will be inaccessible. There is no 'clean' way to get round this problem: the solutions involve using a metaobject, or providing a custom implementation of **Invoke()**.

Type Libraries

Type libraries are effectively a tokenized form of IDL. You can read a type library by loading it with **LoadTypeLibEx()** to get the system to return a **ITypeLib** interface. You can then call **ITypeLib::GetTypeInfo()** to obtain the **ITypeInfo** interface in order to access the type information.

Type libraries can be separate files, with an extension of **.tlb** or **.olb**, or they can be bound into a module as a resource. Here are some examples from **%systemroot%\system32**:

File	Description
mdisp32.tlb	Type library for OLE Messaging
vbaen32.olb	English type library wrapping the methods in **Vba32.dll**
comctl32.ocx	Inproc server for the Windows common controls that contains a type library as a resource
shdocvw.dll	Inproc server for the Internet Explorer web browser controls that contains a type library as a resource

An Automation object that wants to use the Universal Marshaler must register the type library used for the object. This screenshot shows the registry entry for the Excel 97 **Sheets** interface. The **TypeLib** key gives the type library that the Universal Marshaler uses to determine how to marshal the interface. Any interface that can be described by a type library can utilize the Universal Marshaler, as you'll see later in this chapter.

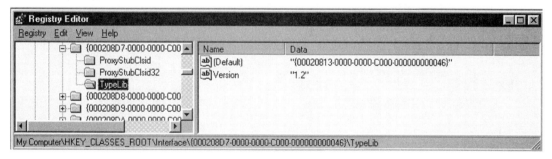

To view a type library, you should use the OLE/COM Object Viewer. This allows you either to specify a file that has type information, or to load a registered type library. Further, if an object has a **IDispatch** interface, you can use OLEView to call **GetTypeInfo()** on that interface and then display the type information. Here are some examples (remember to make sure that Expert Mode is selected in the View menu).

When you select View TypeLib... from the File menu, you can use the file browser dialog to open a file containing type information. Here is the result of loading **shdocvw.dll**:

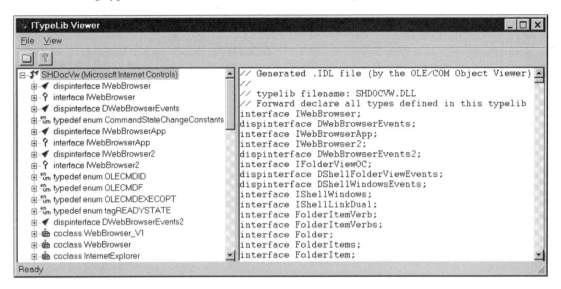

This next screenshot shows all the registered type libraries. Double clicking on the highlighted entry would open the ITypeLib Viewer window for this type library.

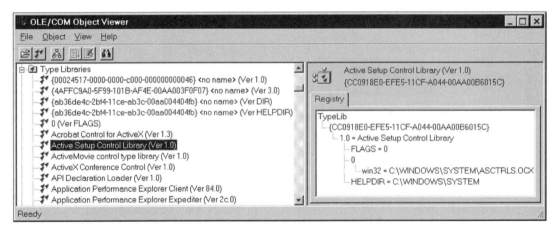

The final screenshot was obtained by clicking on the Microsoft Excel 97 Application entry in the All Objects tree, and then double clicking on the IDispatch entry. Clicking on View TypeInfo... will produce the ITypeLib Viewer for this type library (which is one of several interface viewers provided by OLEView — you can even write your own!).

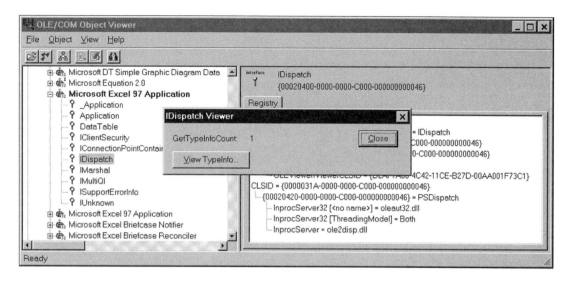

The ATL Wizards add the type library generated from the IDL file into the project as a resource. This type library is used by the module to implement the registration (and unregistration) of the object in response to calls to **DllRegisterServer()** and **DllUnregisterServer()** (or to the command line switches **/RegServer** and **/UnregServer**). ATL uses the type library to implement the default behavior of the **IDispatch** interface.

The type library need not be bound as a resource. Registration is carried out through **AtlModuleRegisterServer()**, which registers the type library (and hence all the interfaces described therein), as well as running a script to register information about the server in the system registry using an ATL-provided object called the Registrar (this script is also held as a bound resource). This function calls **AtlModuleRegisterTypeLib()**, which obtains the server's module name (DLL or EXE) and attempts to load the type library as a resource. If that fails, it attempts to load the type library from a file with the same name (but with the **.tlb** extension) and in the same directory as the module.

IDispatchImpl<>, the ATL class that provides a default implementation of **IDispatch**, loads the type library using **LoadRegTypeLib()**, which uses the type library registration information to locate the type library. This will be correct, since **AtlModuleRegisterTypeLib()** will already have determined whether the type library is a bound resource or a separate type library.

Automation Data Types

Something I've mentioned several times but not yet explained is how you can pass data of different types as parameters to a method to be invoked through **IDispatch::Invoke()**. Consider this interface:

```
interface IWeird : IDispatch
{
   HRESULT SetLong([in] long l);
   HRESULT SetBSTR([in] BSTR bstr);
   HRESULT SetObject([in] IDispatch* pv);
   HRESULT SetFloat([in] float f);
};
```

If the interface has been defined with the **[dual]** attribute, these methods can be called through **Invoke()**, and so when creating the **pDispParams**, you must be able to send a **long**, a **BSTR**, an **IDispatch** pointer, and a **float**. How is this done? Well, the **pDispParams** parameter to **Invoke()** is a pointer to a **DISPPARAMS** structure:

```
typedef struct tagDISPPARAMS
{
    VARIANTARG* rgvarg;
    DISPID* rgdispidNamedArgs;
    UINT cArgs;
    UINT cNamedArgs;
} DISPPARAMS;
```

The **cArgs** member specifies the number of arguments passed, and is the size of the (user allocated) **rgvarg** array. The **cNamedArgs** give the number of parameters that are named, and the DISPIDs of these are passed in the (user allocated) **rgdispidNamedArgs** array.

Named Parameters

What are named parameters? Well, when you write the IDL for an interface, you give the parameters names. Scripting languages like VBA can call the interface methods passing the parameters by position, or by naming each parameter. For example, **Word.Application.8** has a method called **Move()** defined in IDL as:

```
HRESULT Move([in] long Left, [in] long Top);
```

This will move the application by the specified number of pixels. In VB, you can move a Word 97 window 200 pixels to the right and 100 pixels down with:

```
word.Move 200, 100
```

However, VB allows you to write the parameters in any order (and to miss out optional parameters) as long as the passed parameters are named. So the following line has the same effect as the previous one:

```
word.Move Top:=100, Left:=200
```

The script interpreter will have to call **GetIdsOfNames()** on the named parameters to get the DISPIDs, and then place these in the **rgdispidNamedArgs** array. Thus, **rgdispidNamedArgs[0]** is the DISPID of the intended parameter of the value passed in **rgvarg[0]**. (If the client does not use named parameters, then **cNamedArgs** is zero and so **rgdispidNamedArgs** is NULL.)

The script does not have to use names for all the parameters, but parameters that are not named must be positional, so for:

```
HRESULT Method1([in] long param1, [in] long param2,
                [in] long param3, [in] long param4);
```

The following are legal VB:

```
Obj.Method1 1, 2, param4:=4, param3:=3
Obj.Method1 param4:=4, param1:=1, param2:=2, param3:=3
```

The named parameters are always the last parameters in the argument list. Incidentally, this method call in C++ would be:

```
pObj->Method1(1, 2, 3, 4);
```

The consequence of allowing parameters to be named is that the values in the **rgvarg** array are in the *reverse* order to their positions, so that the named parameters are always *first* in the array.

IDL can be used to mark some parameters as **[optional]**. If this is the case, the scripting language need not supply a value for that parameter (remember the example with **Open()** on **Word.Application** you saw earlier?). However, the *interpreter* must pass values for all parameters, including the ones that have not been given a value in the script. If the interpreter does not have a value for a parameter, it indicates this by specifying that the parameter has a type of **VT_ERROR**. The object detects this type, and so uses a default value for the parameter.

VARIANT

The client must be able to pass many different data types in the **rgvarg** array. To do this, the data type of the array is a discriminated union called a **VARIANTARG**, which is **typedef**'d to a **VARIANT** type. The discriminator is called **vt**, and must be set so that the marshaler knows how to marshal the data. The union itself contains one of the following types:

Type	Discriminator	By Ref	Description
BYTE	**VT_UI1**	✓	Unsigned char
USHORT	**VT_UI2**	✓	Unsigned short
UINT	**VT_UINT**	✓	Unsigned integer (size system dependent)
ULONG	**VT_UI4**	✓	Unsigned long
CHAR	**VT_I1**	✓	Signed char
SHORT	**VT_I2**	✓	Signed short
INT	**VT_INT**	✓	Signed integer (size system dependent)
LONG	**VT_I4**	✓	Signed long
FLOAT	**VT_R4**	✓	4 byte floating point
DOUBLE	**VT_R8**	✓	8 byte floating point
VARIANT_BOOL	**VT_BOOL**	✓	A Boolean (transmitted as a **signed short**)
SCODE	**VT_ERROR**	✓	Status code (**HRESULT**)
CY	**VT_CY**	✓	Currency
DATE	**VT_DATE**	✓	Date (transmitted as a **double**)
BSTR	**VT_BSTR**	✓	String
IUnknown*	**VT_UNKNOWN**	✓	Interface pointer

Table Continued on Following Page

Type	Discriminator	By Ref	Description
IDispatch*	VT_DISPATCH	✓	**IDispatch** interface pointer
SAFEARRAY*	VT_ARRAY	✓	Array type
VARIANT*	VT_VARIANT		Pointer to a **VARIANT**
DECIMAL*	VT_DECIMAL		Large decimal type

The table has a column called 'By Ref', which I have used to indicate that the union has a member that allows a pointer to this data type to be put in the **VARIANT**. When data is passed by reference, the discriminator is ORed with the value **VT_BYREF**; this indicates to the marshaler that it should treat the data held in the **VARIANT** as a pointer and so marshal the data that it points to. These members are used when a method returns an **[out]** parameter (what VB calls **ByRef**). Remember from Chapter 1 that the caller must free resources returned by reference.

Two of these types, **BSTR** and **SAFEARRAY**, will be described in the following sections, but there are other types with which you may not be familiar. **CY** is a currency type and is held in 64 bits. **DATE** holds a date and time, and **DECIMAL** holds a large decimal type that has 64 bits for the mantissa and 8 bits for the exponent — truly a large decimal!

In the last section I mentioned that, even if a parameter is optional, there must still be a value in the **pDispParams** parameter of **Invoke()**. This member must have a type of **VT_ERROR** (== **vt**), and it should set the union member to an **SCODE** of **DISP_E_PARAMNOTFOUND**.

Maintaining Data

Some of the data types in a **VARIANT** have to be allocated (**BSTR**s and interface pointers, for example), and these need to be released before a **VARIANT** is released. COM provides a function called **VariantClear()** that will use the discriminator to determine if the resource should be released. Whenever you have finished with a **VARIANT**, you should call this function. There is another function called **VariantInit()** that sets **vt** to **VT_EMPTY**, indicating that a **VARIANT** has no value; this should be called before you use a **VARIANT**.

As you can see, allocating **VARIANT**s, putting data into them, and then ensuring that the resources are properly released is quite a responsibility for a developer. To ease this responsibility, ATL provides a class called **CComVariant**. This class ensures that the **VARIANT** is initialized with **VariantInit()** before it is used, and cleared with **VariantClear()** when it is finally released. To make life easier still, the class also provides overloaded assignment operators and constructors for the most popular data types that a **VARIANT** can take.

In the following code snippet, two methods are defined: one takes a **VARIANT** and the other takes a pointer to a **VARIANT**.

```
HRESULT GetNumberOfMessages(LPVARIANT varNum);
HRESULT LogMessage(VARIANT varMess);

CComVariant varData;
varData = _T("Hello");
LogMessage(varData);
```

```
    varData = 0L;
    GetNumberOfMessages(&varData);
    _tprintf(_T("There are %ld messages\n"), varData.lVal);
```

This code begins by assigning a string to the **VARIANT**. It doesn't matter whether the string is ANSI or Unicode, as there is an assignment operator for both (in fact, the operator for wide characters is the same as for **BSTR**); both operators create a **BSTR** from the string. The **VARIANT** is then passed to the **LogMessage()** function. The next line assigns the **VARIANT** with a value of **0**, ready for the next method call. The assignment operator of **CComVariant** calls **VariantClear()** so that the **BSTR** is released and the variable can be reused.

CComVariant is derived from **VARIANT**, so passing a pointer to a **CComVariant** is the same as passing an **LPVARIANT**. **GetNumberOfMessages()** returns a **LONG** in the **VARIANT**. Note that **CComVariant**'s destructor also ensures that **VariantClear()** is called to release any resources that are held in the **VARIANT**.

BSTR

Passing strings between processes is a problem. The reason for this is that unlike most other data types, there is no predetermined size for strings. "Hello" is smaller than "Goodbye", but the marshaling layer needs to know how exactly much data to send. Further, once a process has determined how much data to transmit and then sent it, the marshaler at the other end will need to create a buffer for the data and pass that buffer to the server. The COM rules state that **[out]** parameters are released by the caller, so such a caller process will need to have access to the same allocator that created the buffer.

Thinking over the first issue, you will come to two possible solutions. Either you can make sure that the marshaling layer checks the length of a string before transmitting it (by doing **strlen()** or **wcslen()** on the string), or the string itself could be some kind of structure that always knows its own length. Automation takes the second option, which has the side effect of allowing **BSTR**s to contain embedded **NULL** characters, and hence to be used to pass binary data if required.

As to the second issue, a process receiving a **BSTR** from another process as an **[out]** parameter must release that data when it has finished with it. COM cannot use **new** (because it is language neutral), and so instead it uses its own memory allocator.

BSTRs are created with **SysAllocString()** and released with **SysFreeString()**. **SysAllocString()** takes a wide character string, and it will do a **wcslen()** on this string and create a buffer for it. The function also keeps the size of the buffer alongside the buffer itself. The pointer that you get back from **SysAllocString()** is a **BSTR**, which is just a wide character (**LPWSTR**) pointer. However, the **DWORD** before this buffer contains the number of bytes taken up by the buffer. To get the length of a **BSTR**, you should pass it to **SysStringLen()**. Once you have created a **BSTR**, you can change it using **SysReAllocString()**. This function takes a pointer to your **BSTR** and to the new string, and will return the new pointer to the **BSTR** in your **BSTR** parameter.

The type **BSTR** is actually a **typedef** for **LPWSTR**, but you should treat it as **LPCWSTR** (i.e. a constant) so that you don't inadvertently write beyond the end of the allocated buffer. There are no functions to allow you to manipulate substrings within a **BSTR**; instead, you should convert it to a convenient data type, like an MFC **CString** or an STL **basic_string**, and then use **SysReAllocString()** when you have finished your manipulations.

Finally, when you have finished using a **BSTR**, you must free it with **SysFreeString()**. This will free the string, returning the memory back to the **BSTR** cache.

Just as with **VARIANT**, there is a lot of maintenance required here, and ATL helps with the **CComBSTR** class. This has two interesting constructors: the first takes a **LPOLESTR** (essentially a wide character string) that can be used to allocate a **BSTR** based on a string. The other constructor takes a length (as an **int**), and the string. However, ATL defines two versions of this constructor — one for Unicode and the other for ANSI strings — and both have a default value of **NULL** for the second parameter. This means that if you call the constructor with just an **int**, the compiler will not know which version to call:

```
CComBSTR bstrAmbiguous(10); // error!
CComBSTR bstrW(10, L"");    // legal
CComBSTR bstrA(10, "");     // legal
```

The first call is ambiguous because the compiler will not know whether to use the **CComBSTR(int, LPCSTR)** or **CComBSTR(int, LPCOLESTR)** constructor. The workaround is given in the last two lines, which although legal, are inelegant.

If you create a buffer with these constructors, the contained **BSTR** can be accessed through a **public** member **m_str**, which can be used either directly or via the **BSTR** conversion operator (**operator BSTR()**). The class also defines various overloaded versions of **Append()** and an operator **+=**. These allow you to add strings together, much like using **strcat()**:

```
CComBSTR bstrGreeting(_T("Hello "));
bstrGreeting.Append(_T("there!"));
_tprintf(_T("%ls"), bstrGreeting.m_str);  // Gives "Hello there!"
```

Notice that **Append()** allocates the resulting **BSTR** and assigns it to the **m_str** data member.

The other interesting thing about **CComBSTR** is that it allows data to be written to or read from an OLE stream (**IStream**). This would be used when a control initializes itself from, or saves itself to, persistent storage, and you'll see an example of this in Chapter 8.

SAFEARRAY

Passing arrays of data between processes requires special handling. The reason for this is that while languages like C and C++ get access through pointers, other languages like VB and Java, which do not have pointers, must still be able to access the same COM arrays. Before I explain about **SAFEARRAY**s, I should point out that in sharp contrast to MFC, which provides the **COleSafeArray** class, ATL does not have a wrapper class for **SAFEARRAY**. If you want to use **SAFEARRAY**s in your ATL object code, you must either use MFC (and suffer the necessary overhead entailed), or access the **SAFEARRAY** functions directly.

Here is the **SAFEARRAY** structure:

```
typedef struct tagSAFEARRAY
{
    USHORT cDims;
    USHORT fFeatures;
    ULONG  cbElements;
    ULONG  cLocks;
```

```
    PVOID   pvData;
    SAFEARRAYBOUND rgsabound[ 1 ];
} SAFEARRAY;
```

The first, third and last members describe the structure of the array: how many dimensions it has, the size of a single element in the array, and information about the number of elements in each dimension. The actual data is pointed to by the **pvData** member.

The **SAFEARRAYBOUND** structure is declared as

```
typedef struct tagSAFEARRAYBOUND
{
    ULONG cElements;
    LONG   lLbound;
} SAFEARRAYBOUND;
```

where **cElements** is the number of elements in an array, and **lLbound** is the lower bound index. For arrays that will only be accessed through C++ you should use a value of 0, since C++ arrays are accessed with a base index of 0. VB arrays, however, can be accessed with a different base index. For example, consider the 11 x 11 array:

```
Dim Values(-5 To 5, 5 To 15) as Integer
```

The **SAFEARRAY** has **cDims** of 2, **cbElements** of 4 and a **rgsabound** with two elements:

```
{{11, -5}, {11, 5}}
```

You do not create **SAFEARRAY**s yourself; instead, you should call the **SafeArrayCreate()** function to do the work:

```
SAFEARRAY* SafeArrayCreate( VARTYPE          vt,
                            UINT             cDims,
                            SAFEARRAYBOUND* rgsabound );
```

The first parameter determines the type of each element; this is followed by the number of dimensions in the array, and then a pointer to a **SAFEARRAYBOUND** that you use to give information about the dimensions. The previous 11 x 11 array is created with:

```
SAFEARRAYBOUNDS rgb[] = {{11, -5}, {11, 5}};
SAFEARRAY* psa;
psa = SafeArrayCreate(VT_I4, 2, rgb);
```

Although superficially similar to the discriminator of a **VARIANT**, the first parameter is restricted to a subset of the types a **VARIANT** may have. It can be one of:

VARTYPE	Description
VT_UI1	Unsigned char
VT_I2	Signed short

Table Continued on Following Page

VARTYPE	Description
VT_I4	Signed long
VT_R4	Float
VT_R8	Double
VT_CY	Currency
VT_DATE	Date
VT_BSTR	String
VT_ERROR	Status code
VT_BOOL	Boolean
VT_VARIANT	**VARIANT** pointer
VT_UNKNOWN	**IUnknown** pointer
VT_DISPATCH	**IDispatch** pointer

Thus, if you want to pass binary data to another process, you can do it with a **SAFEARRAY** of type **VT_UI1**.

When **SafeArrayCreate()** (or a method on an interface) returns a **SAFEARRAY**, you cannot access the buffer created for you immediately. First, you must call **SafeArrayAccessData()**, which returns the **pvData** pointer. When you have finished, you must call **SafeArrayUnAccessData()**. The reason for these two function calls is to lock the safe array to access by other threads.

The pointer returned to you is a **void*** that you need to cast to the appropriate type, and if the array has more than one dimension, you must perform the calculation to access parameters according to the lower bound and dimension size. There are functions called **SafeArrayGetElement()** and **SafeArrayPutElement()** that will get and set a single element from a safe array.

Once you have finished using a safe array, both it and the data it holds must be released. This is carried out by the single function call **SafeArrayDestroy()** that mirrors the **SafeArrayCreate()**.

Note that one of the types that can be put in a **SAFEARRAY** is **LPVARIANT**. This means that a safe array can contain data of various types by wrapping these variables in **VARIANT**s. You are most likely to use this when you want to pass the equivalent of a C-style **struct** to a method as a single parameter rather than as multiple parameters. Of course, this means that the client and server must agree on the order of the elements in the safe array.

Before we move on to a quick example of using safe arrays, there is one final issue that needs to be addressed: how do you describe a safe array in IDL? MIDL supports the data type **SAFEARRAY(type)**, where **type** is one of the types given in the previous table (the type, not the **VT_** value). So, an interface method that returns a **SAFEARRAY** of **BSTR**s is defined as:

```
HRESULT ArrayOfNames([out, retval] SAFEARRAY(BSTR)* pNames);
```

Specifying the type of the elements in the safe array is important because the interface may be marshaled cross-process (or cross-machine) and the marshaler will need to know what the types are in the untyped **pvData** buffer.

Example

Let's look at an example that demonstrates how to expose a **SAFEARRAY** as a property. We'll start by creating a simple object that exposes an array of strings, and then we'll see how to access this property both from Visual C++ (using compiler COM support) and from Visual Basic.

Create a new project with the ATL COM AppWizard and call it Colors (the array that we expose will be a selection of color names). Accept all the default settings in the AppWizard by clicking Finish straight away.

Once the AppWizard has finished, right-click on Colors classes and select New ATL Object. In the Object Wizard, select Objects in the left-hand pane, Simple Object in the right hand pane, and then click on Next >. In the next dialog, select the Names tab, type ColorObject in the Short Name box and click OK to generate the new class.

We want to add a **SAFEARRAY** property to the class, so expand the Colors classes tree in ClassView, right click on the IColorObject entry and select Add Property.... On the ensuing dialog, select VARIANT in the Property Type box and type Colors in the Property Name field.

> *We've chosen to use* **VARIANT** *here because the dialog doesn't allow us to select a* **SAFEARRAY**.

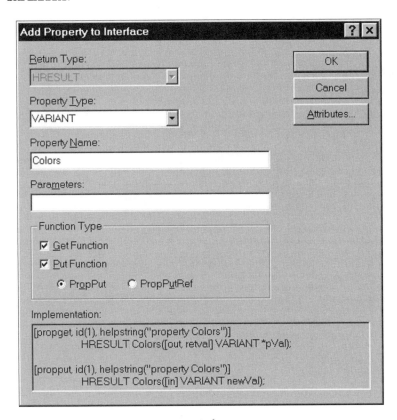

For this example, we'll use the C++ standard library's **vector<>** template to hold the names of the colors, so open **ColorObject.h** and add the following **#include** near the top:

```
#include "resource.h"       // main symbols
#include <vector>           // use the standard library's vector class
```

We can add a **vector<>** member called **m_vecColors** to our class to hold a list of **CComBSTR**s. We'll also add a prototype for **FinalConstruct()**, which we can use to initialize the data, as we discussed in the last chapter. Add the code shown below to the class definition of **CColorObject**.

```
// IColorObject
public:
    STDMETHOD(get_Colors)(/*[out, retval]*/ VARIANT *pVal);
    STDMETHOD(put_Colors)(/*[in]*/ VARIANT newVal);

    HRESULT FinalConstruct();

private:
    std::vector<CComBSTR> m_vecColors;
};
```

Add the implementation of the **FinalConstruct()** function to **ColorObject.cpp**. We'll just initialize the array to hold the seven colors of the visible spectrum:

```
HRESULT CColorObject::FinalConstruct()
{
    m_vecColors.push_back(CComBSTR(L"Red"));
    m_vecColors.push_back(CComBSTR(L"Orange"));
    m_vecColors.push_back(CComBSTR(L"Yellow"));
    m_vecColors.push_back(CComBSTR(L"Green"));
    m_vecColors.push_back(CComBSTR(L"Blue"));
    m_vecColors.push_back(CComBSTR(L"Indigo"));
    m_vecColors.push_back(CComBSTR(L"Violet"));
    return S_OK;
}
```

Now we need to add the code to return the array to callers of **get_Colors()**. Add the following code to the handler for accessing the array:

```
STDMETHODIMP CColorObject::get_Colors(VARIANT * pVal)
{
    VariantInit(pVal);
    pVal->vt = VT_ARRAY | VT_BSTR;
    SAFEARRAY* psa;
    SAFEARRAYBOUND bounds = {m_vecColors.size(), 0};
    psa = SafeArrayCreate(VT_BSTR, 1, &bounds);

    BSTR* bstrArray;
    SafeArrayAccessData(psa, (void**)&bstrArray);
    std::vector<CComBSTR>::iterator it;
    int i = 0;
```

```
      for (it = m_vecColors.begin(); it != m_vecColors.end(); it++, i++)
      {
         bstrArray[i] = SysAllocString((*it).m_str);
      }
      SafeArrayUnaccessData(psa);
      pVal->parray = psa;
      return S_OK;
   }
```

First, we've called **VariantInit()** to initialize the **VARIANT**, then set the type of the **VARIANT** parameter to show that we're using it to hold an array of **BSTR**s. It is important to specify the type of the elements in the array like this, because when the data is marshaled across machine boundaries, the marshaler will need to know how to treat the data held in the **SAFEARRAY**.

After that, a **SAFEARRAYBOUND** is created and initialized to hold the number of colors in the vector, and to indicate that the lower bound is zero (I just can't get out of these C/C++ habits!). **SafeArrayCreate()** is used to create a one-dimensional array that contains **BSTR**s. This will allocate memory for the array of pointers (don't forget that a **BSTR** is a pointer).

The buffer is accessed with the call to **SafeArrayAccessData()**, and then we use the vector's iterator to access the data in the vector and insert a new **BSTR** into the array. After relinquishing access to the array data, we set the **parray** member of the **VARIANT** to the newly created **SAFEARRAY**.

The next step is to add the following code to the handler for setting the array:

```
STDMETHODIMP CColorObject::put_Colors(VARIANT newVal)
{
   if ((newVal.vt & VT_ARRAY) == 0)
      return E_INVALIDARG; // Not an array

   if ((newVal.vt & VT_BSTR) == 0)
      return E_INVALIDARG; // Not an array of BSTRs

   m_vecColors.clear();
   SAFEARRAY* psa = newVal.parray;
   BSTR* bstrArray;
   SafeArrayAccessData(psa, (void**)&bstrArray);

   // Assume just one dimension
   for (int i = 0; i < psa->rgsabound->cElements; i++)
   {
      m_vecColors.push_back(CComBSTR(bstrArray[i]));
   }

   SafeArrayUnaccessData(psa);
   return S_OK;
}
```

First, we check the type of the **VARIANT** to ensure that the data passed in is a **SAFEARRAY** of **BSTR**s. If it is, we clear the vector and then add the new data to the array, using the vector **push_back()** method.

We could compile the code at this point, ready to start creating the clients, but before we do, we'll add a small amount of debugging code. We'll create a simple method called **DumpVector()** that we can use to send the elements of the vector member of our class to the debug window. Add the declaration to the class definition:

```
private:
    std::vector<CComBSTR> m_vecColors;
    void DumpVector();
};
```

And add the implementation to the **ColorObject.cpp** file:

```
void CColorObject::DumpVector()
{
#ifdef _DEBUG
    std::vector<CComBSTR>::iterator it;

    ATLTRACE(_T("[\n"));
    for (it = m_vecColors.begin(); it != m_vecColors.end(); it++)
    {
        ATLTRACE(_T("\t%ls,\n"), (*it).m_str);
    }
    ATLTRACE(_T("]\n"));
#endif
}
```

Here, you can see that we are making use of the **ATLTRACE()** macro. In release builds, this compiles to **(void) 0** (in other words, it does nothing). In debug builds, the macro passes its arguments to the **AtlTrace()** function. **AtlTrace()** takes a variable-length argument list and outputs a **_vstprintf()**-formatted string to the debug window. We've wrapped the implementation in **#ifdef _DEBUG** so that the code isn't executed during release builds.

Finally, add the following code using our new function to the end of the **get_Colors()** and **put_Colors()** methods:

```
STDMETHODIMP CColorObject::get_Colors(VARIANT * pVal)
{
    . . .

    ATLTRACE(_T("Returning SafeArray which has these members:\n"));
    DumpVector();
    return S_OK;
}

STDMETHODIMP CColorObject::put_Colors(VARIANT newVal)
{
    . . .

    ATLTRACE(_T("Changing SafeArray to have these members:\n"));
    DumpVector();
    return S_OK;
}
```

Now you can compile the project. You will find that the compiler complains that **<vector>** uses C++ exceptions and that unwind semantics are not enabled. This is because, by default, the ATL AppWizard turns off C++ exceptions to try and make the code as tight as possible. Still, it is only a warning, and problems will only occur when exceptions occur in the STL allocator. Since these truly are exceptional, you may decide to ignore the warning.

> *To prevent the warning, you can enable C++ exceptions by going to the project settings (Project | Settings...) and on the C/C++ tab selecting C++ Language from the Category box, and checking the Enable exception handling box. If you compile again, the warnings should disappear.*

C++ Client

Let's create a simple C++ client for the object. Create a Win32 Console Application called ColorClient, and place it in the **Colors** project directory. Add a single source code file to the project called **ColorClient.cpp**, and enter the following code:

```cpp
// ColorClient.cpp
#include <windows.h>
#include <stdio.h>
#include <tchar.h>

#import "..\Colors.tlb"

using namespace COLORSLib;

void _tmain()
{
    CoInitialize(NULL);

    try
    {
        IColorObjectPtr pSA(__uuidof(ColorObject));
        _variant_t var = pSA->Colors;
        SAFEARRAY* psa = var.parray;
        BSTR* bstrArray;
        SafeArrayAccessData(psa, (void**)&bstrArray);
        for (UINT i = 0; i < psa->rgsabound->cElements; i++)
            _tprintf(_T("%ls\n"), bstrArray[i]);
        SafeArrayUnaccessData(psa);
    }
    catch(_com_error e)
    {
        _tprintf(_T("Error: 0x%08x %ls\n"), e.Error(), e.ErrorMessage());
    }

    CoUninitialize();
}
```

Once again, we **#import** the type library from the server, and create a **ColorObject** using the smart pointer's constructor. We get the **VARIANT** returned by the **Colors** property and put it into a **_variant_t**. Like **CComVariant**, the **_variant_t** class takes responsibility for freeing the **VARIANT** and its contents in its destructor, so we don't need to worry about explicitly freeing anything. Next, we call **SafeArrayAccessData()** so that we can start looping through the **BSTR** array, and **SafeArrayUnaccessData()** when we've finished.

Here are the results in a console window:

The code isn't too complicated, but it isn't exactly intuitive, either. However, **SAFEARRAY**s are *really* designed for use with VB, so let's see how to use our object in a VB5 application.

VB5 Client

Start Visual Basic 5 and select Standard EXE in the New Project dialog. Add the following controls to the project's form. You can see the names to use in the diagram below:

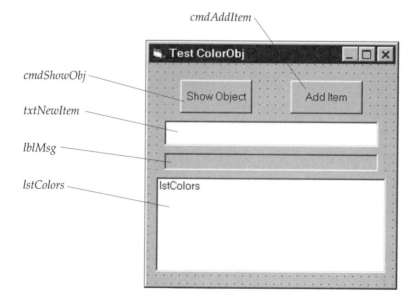

Now add support for the **ColorObject** object by opening the reference dialog (<u>P</u>roject | References...) and selecting the Colors 1.0 Type Library:

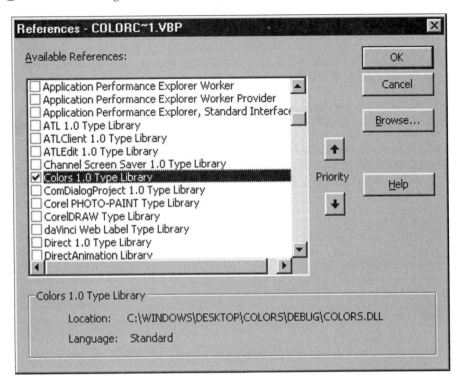

As for the code, begin by declaring a variable for the **IColorObject** interface at module scope:

```
Option Explicit
Private itf As COLORSLib.IColorObject
```

Now create the color object and initialize in the form's **Load** event:

```
Private Sub Form_Load()
    Set itf = New COLORSLib.ColorObject
End Sub
```

Double click on the **cmdShowObj** button and add this code:

```
Private Sub cmdShowObj_Click()
    Dim Size As Long
    Dim ColorArray As Variant
    ColorArray = itf.Colors
    lstColors.Clear
    Size = UBound(ColorArray) - LBound(ColorArray) + 1
    lblMsg.Caption = "There are " & Str$(Size) _
        & " elements in " & TypeName(ColorArray)
    Dim x As Integer
```

193

```
        For x = LBound(ColorArray) To UBound(ColorArray)
            lstColors.AddItem ColorArray(x)
        Next
    End Sub
```

When you click on the **cmdShowObj** button, the number of items is calculated and this, together with information about the type of the array, is put into the **lblMsg** label. Then the code loops through the items in the array and adds them to the list box.

Notice that a copy of the **Colors** property is made by assigning it to the **ColorArray**. This may look unnecessary, but consider this hypothetical code:

```
    For x = LBound(itf.Colors) To UBound(itf.Colors)
        lstColors.AddItem itf.Colors(x)
    Next
```

This results in a call to the **CColorObject::get_Colors()** method, and hence a copy of the array being made for every iteration of the loop. Indeed, wherever a reference to **itf.Colors** is made, there will be a call to **CColorObject::get_Colors()**. This would be even more of a problem if the object were out-of-process — the number of method calls (property accesses) should be kept to a minimum. By acting on your own copy of a property, you can avoid the overhead of frequent method calls.

Add the following code to the **Click** event of the **cmdAddItem** button:

```
    Private Sub cmdAddItem_Click()
        If txtNewItem.Text = "" Then
            Exit Sub
        End If

        ' Read data into an array
        ReDim ColorArray(lstColors.ListCount) As String
        Dim x As Integer
        For x = 0 To lstColors.ListCount - 1
            ColorArray(x) = lstColors.List(x)
        Next
        ColorArray(lstColors.ListCount) = txtNewItem.Text
        itf.Colors = ColorArray
        cmdShowObj_Click
    End Sub
```

The **cmdAddItem** button is used to add a new item to the array. It does this by creating a string array (using **ReDim** so that the size is given at runtime), and then copying all the items from the list box. It then reads the string in the **txtNewItem** edit box and adds this to the end of the array. The object's array property is then set in the single line of code:

```
    itf.Colors = ColorArray
```

To test this, run it (either from the VB IDE or by compiling it first and then running the EXE) and click on the Show Object button.

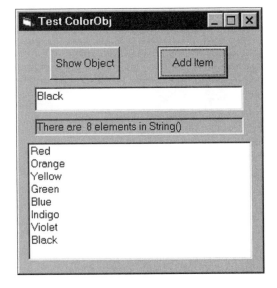

These are the default colors in the array. To add a new color, type the name into the edit box and click on Add Item:

As you can see, **SAFEARRAY** access in VB is simple and natural.

Accessing Automation Objects

Following our little departure into **SAFEARRAY**s, and before moving on to the intricacies of Automation interfaces in ATL, it is worth looking at how to access Automation interfaces in different languages, without assistance.

C++

If the Automation interface is a dual interface, then it can be accessed just like any custom interface. The client must have the MIDL-generated interface definition, so that it can cast the interface pointer returned from **QueryInterface()**. If the object is in a different (and incompatible) apartment from the client, or in a different process, then a proxy must be used. In the following examples, I will use the **CalcEaster** object from the **Simple** project you created in Chapter 2.

Dual Interface Access

Create a Win32 Console Application and place it in a subdirectory of the **Simple** project — I called mine ConsoleClient. Add a new source code file to the project, and enter the following code:

```
#include <stdio.h>
#include <tchar.h>

// Bring in the interface and GUID definitions
#include "..\simple.h"
#include "..\simple_i.c"

int main()
{
   CoInitialize(NULL);
   ICalcEaster* pCalc;
   HRESULT hr;
   hr = CoCreateInstance( CLSID_CalcEaster,
                          NULL,
                          CLSCTX_ALL,
                          IID_ICalcEaster,
                          (void**)&pCalc );
   if (SUCCEEDED(hr))
   {
      short sYear = 1998, sMonth, sDay;
      pCalc->put_Year(sYear);
      pCalc->CalculateEaster();
      pCalc->get_Month(&sMonth);
      pCalc->get_Day(&sDay);
      _tprintf(_T("Easter day in %d is %d/%d/%d\n"),
                                        sYear, sDay, sMonth, sYear);
      pCalc->Release();
   }

   CoUninitialize();
   return 0;
}
```

The client gets access using an interface pointer to call methods in the vtable. This is exactly the same as using a non-dispinterface, and I shall dwell on it here no longer.

Access Through IDispatch

If the interface is derived from **IDispatch** (either a dispinterface or a dual), you can access it using the **IDispatch** interface, but things get a lot trickier. Consider this code, for example:

```
CoInitialize(NULL);
IDispatch* pObj;
HRESULT hr = CoCreateInstance( CLSID_CalcEaster,
                               NULL,
                               CLSCTX_ALL,
                               IID_IDispatch,
                               (void**)&pObj );
short sYear = 1998;

VARIANTARG* pvars = new VARIANTARG[1];
VariantInit(&pvars[0]);
pvars[0].vt = VT_I2;
pvars[0].iVal = sYear;
DISPID dispid = DISPID_PROPERTYPUT;
DISPPARAMS disp = { pvars, &dispid, 1, 1 };

VARIANT varResult;
VariantInit(&varResult);
pObj->Invoke( 0x1,
              IID_NULL,
              LOCALE_USER_DEFAULT,
              DISPATCH_PROPERTYPUT,
              &disp,
              &varResult, NULL, NULL );

delete[] pvars;

// Do other things with the object

pObj->Release();
CoUninitialize();
```

Complicated, huh? First we create the object, and specify that we need the **IDispatch** interface. Then a **VARIANTARG** array with a single member is declared; this member is initialized with a call to **VariantInit()** and then given a value. Remember that **VARIANT**s (and thus **VARIANTARG**) are discriminated unions, so the first task is to set the type of the value (**VT_I2**) in the discriminator, and then the appropriate part of the union is assigned to the value we wish to pass.

The actual data needs to be passed to **Invoke()** in a **DISPPARAMS** structure that has pointers to the array of arguments and the array of parameter DISPIDs as the first two parameters. Notice here that since this is passing a property value to the object, the special value **DISPID_PROPERTYPUT** is used. The call should not return a value, but we still need to pass in a **VARIANT** to **Invoke()**, and this too needs to be initialized. Finally, **Invoke()** is called. The DISPID passed is **0x1** — we know that this is the DISPID of **Year**, and because we do not have to ask the object for it, this method of accessing the property is called **early binding**.

This code is passing a value to a property, so there is only one parameter to pass — if it was a method call with more parameters then there would be even more code to construct the **DISPPARAMS** *parameter passed to* **Invoke()**. *Furthermore, you'll surely have realized that this code has only a quarter of the functionality of our custom interface example. We'd have to go through this rigmarole three more times to retrieve the day and month of Easter 1998!*

The situation gets worse still when you consider **late binding**. Here, the client asks the object for information about the method, which involves calling `GetIDsOfNames()`:

```
// Do other things with the object
OLESTR pszName = L"CalculateEaster";
DISPID dispID;
pObj->GetIDsOfNames( IID_NULL,
                     &pszName,
                     1,
                     LOCALE_USER_DEFAULT,
                     &dispid );
```

This obtains the DISPID for the method to pass to **Invoke()**. If you don't know about the parameters that the method takes, you also need to obtain the type information using `GetTypeInfo()`, and then query that:

```
ITypeInfo* pType;
pObj->GetTypeInfo(0, LOCALE_USER_DEFAULT, &pType);

TYPEATTR* pTypeAttr;
hr = pType->GetTypeAttr(&pTypeAttr);

if (SUCCEEDED(hr))
{
    for (short i = 0; i < pTypeAttr->cFuncs; i++)
    {
        FUNCDESC* pFuncDesc;
        hr = pType->GetFuncDesc(i, &pFuncDesc);
        if (SUCCEEDED(hr))
        {
            if (pFuncDesc->memid == dispid)
            {
                _tprintf(_T("returns %ld\n"),
                    pFuncDesc->elemdescFunc.tdesc.vt);
                for (short n = 0; n<pFuncDesc->cParams; n++)
                {
                    _tprintf(_T("param %ld is type %ld\n"), n,
                        pFuncDesc->lprgelemdescParam[n].tdesc.vt);
                }
            }
            pType->ReleaseFuncDesc(pFuncDesc);
        }
    }
    pType->ReleaseTypeAttr(pTypeAttr);
}

pType->Release();
pObj->Release();
```

I won't go into this code in detail (we'll certainly never have to do anything as long-winded as this using ATL), but it does show how to get information about a method's parameters, and give an idea of just how much help ATL provides for us. Incidentally, if you compile and run this code, the answer you'll get is 24, which is the value of **VT_VOID** in the enumeration that defines the possible values for the **VARIANT** discriminator. This is just what we'd expect: the **CalculateEaster()** method does not return a value.

There is yet another problem with accessing the **IDispatch** pointer: an object can only ever have *one* exposed **IDispatch** pointer, so if you have more than one **IDispatch**-derived interface on an object, only one can be exposed (typically this is the interface marked **[default]**). Thus, only those methods that the interface's **Invoke()** and **GetIdsOfNames()** functions know about can be accessed with this pointer, which means that the other interface is not externally accessible. This is not a problem if the interfaces are accessed through the vtable part of a dual interface (because they will have different vtables), but you should really only have one **IDispatch**-derived interface per object.

Smart Pointers

The previous section showed you how complicated code can be if you want to access **IDispatch** directly. ATL helps with some wrapper classes.

CComPtr

The smart pointer class **CComPtr** (defined in **AtlBase.h**) can be used to help manage the interface pointers. This smart pointer class can be used for custom interfaces, but it is convenient to explain it here. The reason why **CComPtr** is called a 'smart' pointer is that it has an overloaded **operator ->()** that the class uses to allow you to use objects of this class as if they were pointer variables. The class is used like this:

```
void CallEaster(short sYear)
{
    CComPtr<ICalcEaster> pCalc;
    HRESULT hr;
    hr = CoCreateInstance( CLSID_CalcEaster,
                           NULL,
                           CLSCTX_ALL,
                           IID_ICalcEaster,
                           (void**)&pCalc );
    pCalc->put_Year(sYear);
    pCalc->CalculateEaster();
    short sMonth, sDay;
    pCalc->get_Day(&sDay);
    pCalc->get_Month(&sMonth);
    _tprintf(_T("%d/%d/%d\n"), sDay, sMonth, sYear);
}
```

Notice that the interface has not been released at the end of the function. This seems to violate the rules of COM, which state that when an interface pointer is no longer needed, you should release it with a call to **Release()**. In fact, though, this method is being called automatically when the **pCalc** object is destroyed. Let's take a closer look at the code.

The first line declares a local, stack-based variable. It is important that this object is stack based, because it ensures that the object's destructor is called when it goes out of scope. The class takes a parameter that is the type of the encapsulated pointer, so in this code **pCalc** has an **ICalcEaster*** data member (which is **public**, and you can access it as the data member **p**). **CoCreateInstance()** is called, passing the address of the **pCalc** object where you would normally pass the address of an interface pointer. The class has an overloaded **operator &()** that returns the address of the **p** data member, and so this will be initialized with the **[out]** value from **CoCreateInstance()**.

The next line looks more than a little odd:

```
pCalc->put_Year(sYear)
```

pCalc is a stack object, not a pointer, so how can you use the **->** operator? The reason is that **CComPtr** has an overloaded **operator ->()**, which merely returns the value of the encapsulated **p** interface pointer, so the line is the same as **pCalc.p->put_Year()**. When the function finishes and the **pCalc** object goes out of scope, the destructor is called. The **CComPtr** smart pointer class calls **p->Release()** and releases the interface.

Smart pointers are used extensively in the ATL source code, and they can make the code more readable by reducing the levels of indentation required. In the current implementation of **CComPtr**, any method of an encapsulated interface can be called through the smart pointer, including **AddRef()** and **Release()**. You must be very careful when calling these because there is always the implicit call to **Release()** when the object is destroyed. The following code, for example, will raise an exception:

```
void Whoops()
{
   CComPtr<ICalcEaster> pCalc;
   HRESULT hr;
   hr = CoCreateInstance( CLSID_CalcEaster,
                          NULL,
                          CLSCTX_ALL,
                          IID_ICalcEaster,
                          (void**)&pCalc );
   pCalc->Release();
}
```

When **CoCreateInstance()** is called, the interface reference count will be one, the call to **Release()** will reduce this to zero, and the object will be released. However, when the **pCalc** object goes out of scope, **Release()** will be called again. The encapsulated interface pointer will no longer point to a valid interface, and an exception will be thrown. The message is clear: do not call **AddRef()** and **Release()** explicitly through a smart pointer.

CComDispatchDriver

This wrapper class allows you to access the properties of an object. It is used by the ATL property maps and **IPersist*** interface implementations, and is declared in **AtlCtl.h**. The important methods in this class are **GetProperty()** and **PutProperty()**. The class is initialized with an **IDispatch** pointer, and these two methods get and set properties on the object through this pointer. Consider this code:

```
#include <windows.h>
#include <stdio.h>
#include <atlbase.h>
```

```
CComModule _Module;

#include <atlcom.h>
#include <atlimpl.cpp>
#include <atlctl.h>
#include <atlctl.cpp>
#include <tchar.h>

void _tmain()
{
   HRESULT hr;
   CLSID clsid;

   hr = CoInitialize(NULL);
   if (SUCCEEDED(hr))
   {
      CComPtr<IDispatch> pCalc;
      hr = CLSIDFromProgID(L"Wrox.CalcEaster.1", &clsid);
      hr = CoCreateInstance( clsid,
                             NULL,
                             CLSCTX_ALL,
                             IID_IDispatch,
                             (void**)&pCalc );

      CComDispatchDriver pDisp(pCalc);
      short sYear = 1998, sMonth, sDay;
      CComVariant varVal;
      varVal = sYear;
      pDisp.PutProperty(1, &varVal);

      VARIANT varResult;
      VariantInit(&varResult);
      DISPPARAMS disp = { NULL, NULL, 0, 0 };
      pCalc->Invoke( 0x4,
                     IID_NULL,
                     LOCALE_USER_DEFAULT,
                     DISPATCH_METHOD,
                     &disp,
                     &varResult, NULL, NULL );

      pDisp.GetProperty(2, &varVal);
      sMonth = varVal.iVal;
      pDisp.GetProperty(3, &varVal);
      sDay = varVal.iVal;
      _tprintf(_T("%d/%d/%d\n"), sDay, sMonth, sYear);
   }

   CoUninitialize();
}
```

Here, I create the **CalcEaster** object (using **CLSIDFromProgID()** so that I do not have to **#include simple_i.c**), and use this to initialize a **CComDispatchDriver** object. I use this to do all the property 'puts' and 'gets', but to call methods I have to call **Invoke()** directly. It's not hard to figure out that the line

```
pDisp.PutProperty(1, &varVal);
```

puts the data in **varVal** into the object property with a DISPID of 1 (in other words, **Year**). Likewise,

```
pDisp.GetProperty(2, &varVal);
```

gets the value from the **Month** property (which has a DISPID of 2). Notice that in this code I have the **IDispatch** interface on the object, so I have to call **Invoke()** to call a method. This is shown in the code by the call involving DISPID 4, in other words **CalculateEaster()**.

Proxy Generator

In the last section, I showed you a short piece of code for calling **ICalcEaster** through **IDispatch**. The code calls **Invoke()**, but I had to determine the actual parameters to send to the method. This can quickly get complicated, especially if the method you're calling takes many parameters. Is there an easier way to do this? The answer is yes, depending on what interface you are trying to access.

If the interface you are accessing is a dual, like **ICalcEaster**, then the easiest way to access it is through the vtable. If, however, the interface is a dispinterface (i.e. only the **IDispatch** methods appear in the vtable), then you will need to call **Invoke()**. However, you can use the ATL Proxy Generator to create the code to call the interface for you.

Consider this IDL:

```
import "oaidl.idl";
import "ocidl.idl";

[
   uuid(5DC86884-58F2-11D1-A159-04DCF8C00000)
]
dispinterface DCalcEaster
{
properties:
   [id(1)] short Year;
   [id(2), readonly] short Month;
   [id(3), readonly] short Day;
methods:
   [id(4)] HRESULT CalculateEaster();
};

[
    uuid(AD89F7A1-568E-11D1-A159-04D4F8C00000),
    version(1.0)
]
library SIMPLELib
```

```
{
    importlib("stdole32.tlb");
    importlib("stdole2.tlb");

    [
        uuid(5DC86882-58F2-11D1-A159-04DCF8C00000)
    ]
    coclass CalcEaster
    {
        [default] dispinterface DCalcEaster;
    };
};
```

Here, I have changed the `CalcEaster` object to have a dispinterface, using ODL syntax. I can now get Developer Studio to generate a **proxy class** for me. I select Project | Add To Project | Components and Controls..., and then from the Gallery folder I select the Developer Studio Components:

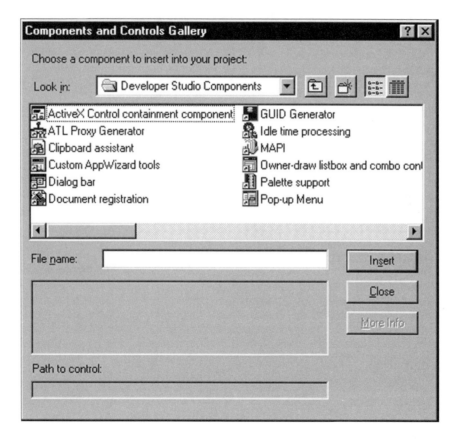

From this dialog, I can select ATL Proxy Generator and then hit Insert. Once I've navigated through the dialogs that inhabit this part of Developer Studio, the following dialog is displayed:

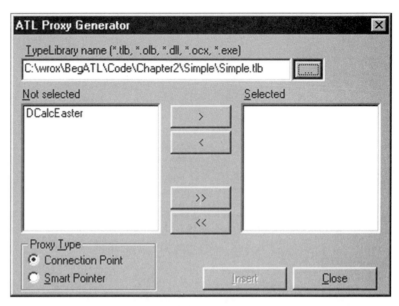

In the screenshot, I have selected the type library generated from the IDL given above. Now I can select the DCalcEaster dispinterface and add it to the Selected box with the > button. To generate a proxy to call the dispinterface, the Smart Pointer proxy type must be selected (the Connection Point type is used for connection points, which feature in Chapter 6). When I click on Insert, the proxy generator will ask me where to save the generated code and then create a header file:

```
//////////////////////////////////////////////////////////////////////////////
// CProxyDCalcEaster
class CProxyDCalcEaster : public CComPtr<IDispatch>
{
// methods:
// DCalcEaster : IDispatch
public:
   HRESULT CalculateEaster()
   {
      VARIANT varResult;
      VariantInit(&varResult);
      DISPPARAMS disp = { NULL, NULL, 0, 0 };
      p->Invoke(0x4, IID_NULL, LOCALE_USER_DEFAULT, DISPATCH_METHOD,
         &disp, &varResult, NULL, NULL);
      return varResult.HRESULT;
   }
};
```

This is a fair attempt at providing a wrapper around the dispinterface, but this code will not work. The line

```
      return varResult.HRESULT;
```

should read

```
        return varResult.scode;
```

Now if I want to call methods on the object, I can include the header generated by the proxy generator and use the **CProxyDCalcEaster** class. This is not without its problems, though. For example, where you would expect to be able to use:

```
    CProxyDCalcEaster pProxy(pCalc.p);
```

the compiler complains about being unable to convert **IDispatch*** to **const   class CProxyDCalcEaster&**. The compiler refuses to accept that there should be a constructor that takes an **IDispatch** pointer. However, since this constructor and the copy constructor use the same code in **CComPtr**, you can use:

```
    CProxyDCalcEaster pProxy((const CProxyDCalcEaster &)pCalc.p);
    hr = pProxy.CalculateEaster();
```

and call the method through the proxy class. (Remember that since the proxy class is derived from **CComPtr**, it will manage reference counting.)

Frankly, there are problems with the Proxy Generator, and it's confusing to have to cast in order to force the constructor to initialize, as I have shown above. However, the code that calls **Invoke()** does work, so you can cut and paste this code to use it elsewhere (which is exactly what I did in the example above).

Visual Basic

VB5 programs can access any interface — through **IDispatch** or through a vtable — provided that the interface is described by a type library. If a type library is not used, VB can only use late binding and therefore can only access an Automation interface. In this case, it must ask the object to resolve textual method names and parameters to DISPIDs, as we have seen earlier on in this chapter with **IDispatch::GetIDsOfNames()**. This is clearly inefficient, because there are many calls required to be made to the object before the actual method can be called.

Late Binding

Late binding is characterized by the use of a variable of type **Object**. This is equivalent to using **IDispatch** pointers in C++. To obtain an object, the client uses **CreateObject()**:

```
    Dim obj as Object
    Set obj = CreateObject("Wrox.CalcEaster.1")
    obj.Year = CInt(txtYear)
    obj.CalculateEaster
    MsgBox "Easter: " & obj.Day & "/" & obj.Month & " in " & obj.Year
```

The call to **CreateObject()** obtains the **IDispatch** pointer, while the call to **CalculateEaster** does the necessary querying of the object for the DISPID of the method and checks that the method takes no other parameters. This is considerably easier than late binding in C++!

Note that the type library does *not* need to be on the client machine. This VB application obtains type information via **GetTypeInfo()**, similar to the C++ code given above.

Early Binding

In early binding, the Visual Basic IDE is told about the object type information at compile time by using the Project | References... menu item.

```
Dim obj As New SIMPLELib.CalcEaster
obj.Year = CInt(txtYear)
obj.CalculateEaster
MsgBox "Easter: " & obj.Day & "/" & obj.Month & " in " & obj.Year
```

In this code, **SIMPLELib.CalcEaster** is the name of the **coclass**, **New** creates an object, and the variable **obj** is assigned to the default interface of the object, in this case **ICalcEaster**. If **ICalcEaster** is not the default interface, then the following code can be used:

```
Dim obj As New SIMPLELib.CalcEaster
Dim itf As SIMPLELib.ICalcEaster
Set itf = obj
itf.Year = CInt(txtYear)
itf.CalculateEaster
MsgBox "Easter: " & itf.Day & "/" & itf.Month & " in " & itf.Year
```

This time, the first line creates the object and returns the default interface. The third line does a **QueryInterface()** for the **ICalcEaster** interface, enabling **CalculateEaster** to be called.

Java

The Java SDK is Microsoft's extension of the Java language. Specifically, it provides extensions to the Java language and classes that allow programmers to get access to the Microsoft Java Virtual Machine (JVM) COM facilities.

Version 2 of the SDK provides a tool called **JActiveX** that takes a type library and creates Java classes for the Automation object's coclass, and Java interfaces for the object's interfaces. These classes and interfaces derive from the Java SDK classes used to access the object, and also have special comments that specify the GUIDs of the coclass and interfaces. The command

```
JActiveX simple.tlb
```

will create an interface for the **ICalcEaster** COM interface, and a class for the **CalcEaster** coclass, putting the Java code in the **simple** directory under **Java\Trustlib**. The Java code to access this object is incredibly straightforward:

```
import simple.*;
class Test
{
    public static void main(String[] args)
    {
        CalcEaster Obj = new CalcEaster();
        ICalcEaster ICalc = Obj;
        ICalc.setYear((short)1998);
```

```
        ICalc.CalculateEaster();
        System.out.println("Easter day is: " + ICalc.getDay() +
            "/" + ICalc.getMonth() + "/" + ICalc.getYear());
    }
}
```

Notice how the **JActiveX** tool generates accessor functions for the properties. The read-only properties **Day** and **Month** only have a **get** method, whereas **Year** has both a **get** and **set** method. This simple code shows how easy COM programming with MS Java is: there is no **CoCreateInstance()** (you just create a new object with **new**), there is no **QueryInterface()** (you just cast to the appropriate **interface**), and there is no call to **Release()** (the Java garbage collector does that).

If you look in the **ICalcEaster.java** file generated by **JActiveX**, you will find an **interface** interspersed with comments:

```
// Dual interface ICalcEaster
/** @com.interface(iid=5DC86881-58F2-11D1-A159-04DCF8C00000, thread=AUTO,
type=DUAL) */
public interface ICalcEaster extends IUnknown
{
  /** @com.method(vtoffset=4, dispid=1, type=PROPGET, name="Year",
        addFlagsVtable=4)
      @com.parameters([type=I2] return) */
  public short getYear();

  /** @com.method(vtoffset=5, dispid=1, type=PROPPUT, name="Year",
        addFlagsVtable=4)
      @com.parameters([in,type=I2] pVal) */
  public void setYear(short pVal);

  /** @com.method(vtoffset=6, dispid=2, type=PROPGET, name="Month",
        addFlagsVtable=4)
      @com.parameters([type=I2] return) */
  public short getMonth();

  /** @com.method(vtoffset=7, dispid=3, type=PROPGET, name="Day",
        addFlagsVtable=4)
      @com.parameters([type=I2] return) */
  public short getDay();

  /** @com.method(vtoffset=8, dispid=4, type=METHOD,
        name="CalculateEaster", addFlagsVtable=4)
      @com.parameters() */
  public void CalculateEaster();

  public static final com.ms.com._Guid iid
    = new com.ms.com._Guid((int)0x5dc86881, (short)0x58f2,
              (short)0x11d1, (byte)0xa1, (byte)0x59, (byte)0x4,
              (byte)0xdc, (byte)0xf8, (byte)0xc0, (byte)0x0, (byte)0x0);
}
```

The comments show that MS Java uses attribute-based programming. The **interface** is marked with the **iid**, **thread** and **type** attributes, while the methods in the interface are marked with attributes that give the offset of the method within the vtable, the DISPID, and the **wFlags** value used in calls to **Invoke()**. Although this is the only current Microsoft tool that uses attribute-based programming in its treatment of COM, it is worth paying attention to, since this is the direction in which COM programming is going.

The attributes show that MS Java uses early binding. The JVM can use the type information at runtime to call these methods through **IDispatch::Invoke()**, or to create the stack frame required to call the methods using the dual interface's vtable.

Automation with ATL

So, how do you create Automation interfaces using ATL?

The first thing you must be aware of is that the Object Wizard will only give you the option of creating custom or dual interfaces — it does not give you the choice of a non-dual Automation interface. If you decide that you want the interface to be non-dual (we'll see an example of when you might do this in Chapter 6), you can edit the IDL to comment out the **[dual]** attribute, or even to declare the interface as a dispinterface.

From the previous discussion, you will be aware that a dual interface needs an implementation of **IDispatch**. For the purpose of looking at how ATL handles dual interfaces, create a simple project called **Automation**. This will be a very simple project; the purpose for now is to learn about what the Wizards do for you.

Crank up the ATL COM AppWizard, enter the name **Automation** and click on OK. In the resulting dialog, accept the defaults and click on Finish, and then dismiss the subsequent dialog. Next, add a new object by using the Insert menu and selecting New ATL Object.... In the next dialog, select Simple Object and then click on Next >. In the Names tab of the next dialog, type **Auto** for the Short Name, ensure that Dual interface is selected on the Attributes tab, and that the Support ISupportErrorInfo check box is checked (you'll see why later).

Here is the header produced by the Object Wizard for the object that has just been created with a single dual interface (**Auto.h**):

```
class ATL_NO_VTABLE CAuto :
  public CComObjectRootEx<CComSingleThreadModel>,
  public CComCoClass<CAuto, &CLSID_Auto>,
  public ISupportErrorInfo,
  public IDispatchImpl<IAuto, &IID_IAuto, &LIBID_AUTOMATIONLib>
{
public:
  CAuto()
  {
  }

DECLARE_REGISTRY_RESOURCEID(IDR_AUTO)
```

```
BEGIN_COM_MAP(CAuto)
   COM_INTERFACE_ENTRY(IAuto)
   COM_INTERFACE_ENTRY(IDispatch)
   COM_INTERFACE_ENTRY(ISupportErrorInfo)
END_COM_MAP()

// ISupportsErrorInfo
   STDMETHOD(InterfaceSupportsErrorInfo)(REFIID riid);

// IAuto
public:
};
```

The significant lines are highlighted. Firstly, the class derives from the **IDispatchImpl<>** template class; if the object implemented the **IAuto** interface as a custom interface, then the **CAuto** class would derive from the **IAuto** interface. The second line to notice is that the **IDispatch** interface has been added to the COM map in addition to the **IAuto** interface.

IDispatchImpl

Why is the class declared like this? For a start, somewhere in the class hierarchy there must be a declaration of the **IAuto** interface. This is achieved through the template, which is declared in **atlcom.h** like this:

```
template <class T,
         const IID* piid,
         const GUID* plibid,
         WORD wMajor = 1,
         WORD wMinor = 0,
         class tihclass = CComTypeInfoHolder>
class ATL_NO_VTABLE IDispatchImpl : public T
{
...
};
```

Rather than deriving from **IAuto** directly, **CAuto** derives from the interface via the template class. But what about the implementation of **IDispatch**? Well, as its name suggests, **IDispatchImpl<>** handles this through the **tihclass** parameter. If you look at the declaration of the template, you can see all the **IDispatch** methods, and that each is implemented in terms of **tihclass**. For example, **GetTypeInfo()**:

```
public:
   typedef tihclass _tihclass;
...
   STDMETHOD(GetTypeInfo)(UINT itinfo, LCID lcid, ITypeInfo** pptinfo)
   {
      return _tih.GetTypeInfo(itinfo, lcid, pptinfo);
   }
...
protected:
   static _tihclass _tih;
```

So, every class derived from **IDispatchImpl<>** delegates its **IDispatch** implementation through to the **tihclass**, which by default is implemented by **CComTypeInfoHolder**. The static member is initialized from the parameters of the **IDispatchImpl**, and in particular the **plibid** parameter that is the GUID of the type library. **CComTypeInfoHolder** uses this to load the type library, and then through the **ITypeInfo*** interface obtains the system implementation of the **IDispatch** methods. If you decide that you want to implement these methods yourself, you can write your own version of **CComTypeInfoHolder**. The following diagram illustrates this chain of command:

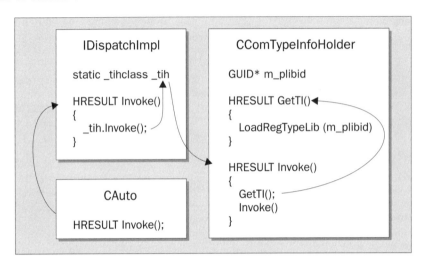

Let's add another dual interface to this object. There is no Wizard to do the work for you, so you'll have to get your hands dirty and edit the IDL file yourself. Along the way, you'll need to generate a new IID, which you can do by running **Guidgen.exe**, just as you did in Chapter 1. Select the fourth option (Registry Format), and then click on Copy. In Developer Studio, open the **Automation.idl** file and add the following interface, pasting in the created GUID as the **[uuid()]** attribute (notice that you will need to remove the braces **{}**):

```
import "oaidl.idl";
import "ocidl.idl";

    [
        object,
        uuid(9542BEB1-6FB8-11D1-A607-00A0C94BC9C3),
        dual,
        helpstring("IAuto Interface"),
        pointer_default(unique)
    ]
    interface IAuto : IDispatch
    {
    };

    [
        object,
        uuid(9542BEB3-6FB8-11D1-A607-00A0C94BC9C3),
        dual,
```

```
      helpstring("IAuto2 Interface"),
      pointer_default(unique)
   ]
   interface IAuto2 : IDispatch
   {
   };

[
   uuid(9542BEA4-6FB8-11D1-A607-00A0C94BC9C3),
   version(1.0),
   helpstring("Automation 1.0 Type Library")
]
library AUTOMATIONLib
{
   importlib("stdole32.tlb");
   importlib("stdole2.tlb");

   [
      uuid(9542BEB2-6FB8-11D1-A607-00A0C94BC9C3),
      helpstring("Auto Class")
   ]
   coclass Auto
   {
      [default] interface IAuto;
      interface IAuto2;
   };
};
```

The second insertion adds **IAuto2** to the coclass, so you will need to add the interface to the implementation of the object, **CAuto**. To do this, open **Auto.h** and add the following lines:

```
class ATL_NO_VTABLE CAuto :
   public CComObjectRootEx<CComSingleThreadModel>,
   public CComCoClass<CAuto, &CLSID_Auto>,
   public ISupportErrorInfo,
   public IDispatchImpl<IAuto, &IID_IAuto, &LIBID_AUTOMATIONLib>,
   public IDispatchImpl<IAuto2, &IID_IAuto2, &LIBID_AUTOMATIONLib>
{
public:
   CAuto()
   {
   }

DECLARE_REGISTRY_RESOURCEID(IDR_AUTO)

BEGIN_COM_MAP(CAuto)
   COM_INTERFACE_ENTRY(IAuto)
   COM_INTERFACE_ENTRY(IAuto2)
   COM_INTERFACE_ENTRY2(IDispatch, IAuto)
   COM_INTERFACE_ENTRY(ISupportErrorInfo)
END_COM_MAP()
```

```
   // ISupportsErrorInfo
      STDMETHOD(InterfaceSupportsErrorInfo)(REFIID riid);

   // IAuto
   public:

   // IAuto2
   public:
   };
```

The first insertion is quite obvious: you want to expose the new interface from the object, and so your object will need to implement the vtable somewhere. Equally understandable is the addition of the **IAuto2** interface to the COM map, but what is the **COM_INTERFACE_ENTRY2()** macro, and why is it used? From our discussion, you will be aware that the object must export a single implementation of **IDispatch**, through the COM map. As you saw in Chapter 3, the COM map holds all the interfaces that the object will export. However, both **IAuto** and **IAuto2** derive from **IDispatch**, and through the **IDispatchImpl<>** class, each will have an implementation of the **IDispatch** methods. If we have two implementations, which will be exposed? This problem is the reason why the **_ENTRY2()** macro is used instead of **_ENTRY()**. It specifies that the **IDispatch** implementation that is exposed comes from **IAuto** and not **IAuto2**.

For new users to ATL, one of the most common mistakes is to forget to use the **COM_INTERFACE_ENTRY2()** macro. If you do forget to do this, and the COM map looks like this:

```
   BEGIN_COM_MAP(CAuto)
      COM_INTERFACE_ENTRY(IAuto)
      COM_INTERFACE_ENTRY(IAuto2)
      COM_INTERFACE_ENTRY(IDispatch)
      COM_INTERFACE_ENTRY(ISupportErrorInfo)
   END_COM_MAP()
```

You will get the following error when you compile the project:

error C2594: 'static_cast' : ambiguous conversions from 'class CAuto *' to 'struct IDispatch *'

Remember this error; it might just save you some debugging time when you come across it.

Adding Functionality

To get a feeling for using Automation interfaces, let's add a method to **IAuto**. Right click on the IAuto interface in ClassView and select Add Method.... Add a method with this name and parameters:

```
   HRESULT Greeting([in] BSTR bstrName, [out, retval] BSTR* bstrGreeting);
```

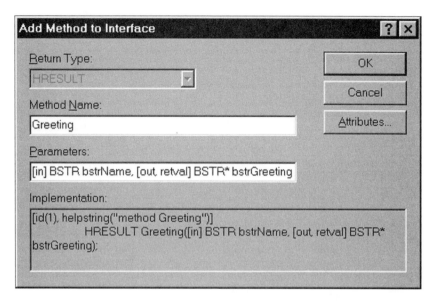

Now click on the Attributes... button, and you'll see the following dialog:

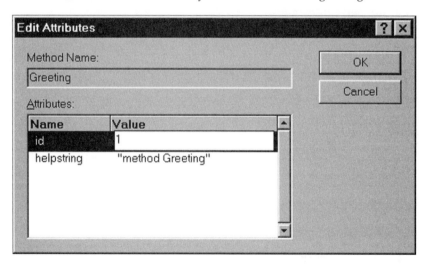

Notice that the Wizard has automatically given the method an id of 1; if you double click on this value, you'll be able to edit it. However, a value of 1 is fine for this example, so don't change it. Click on OK, and then OK again.

The method you have added takes a **BSTR** as an **[in]** parameter, and returns another **BSTR** as an **[out]** parameter. The **bstrGreeting** is also marked as **[retval]**, which means that in VB it will form the return value of a function, rather than having to be retrieved using **ByRef**. Open **Auto.cpp** and implement the method like this:

```
STDMETHODIMP CAuto::Greeting(BSTR bstrName, BSTR * bstrGreeting)
{
```

```
        SYSTEMTIME st;
        GetLocalTime(&st);
        TCHAR strTime[23];
        wsprintf(strTime, _T("The time is %02d:%02d:%02d "),
            st.wHour, st.wMinute, st.wSecond);
        CComBSTR bstrRet(strTime);
        bstrRet += bstrName;
        *bstrGreeting = bstrRet.Copy();
        return S_OK;
    }
```

This function obtains the local time on the machine and formats it into a string. This string is then used to initialize a **CComBSTR**; be aware that if this is not compiled for Unicode, the **CComBSTR** constructor will convert **strTime** to a wide character string. Next, the **+=** operator is used to add the passed-in name to the return string: the **CComBSTR** will reallocate a **BSTR** large enough to hold the extra string data.

Finally, since the **BSTR** will be passed out of the function, we use the **Copy()** method to duplicate **bstrRet** into the **bstrGreeting** pointer. If we didn't do this, and typed this line instead:

```
        *bstrGreeting = bstrRet;
```

we would be asking for trouble, because the **CComBSTR::operator BSTR()** would be called to convert the **CComBSTR** to a **BSTR**. This operator merely returns the encapsulated **BSTR** (*not* a copy), so when the stack variable **bstrRet** goes out of scope and the destructor is called, **SysFreeString()** is called on this encapsulated **BSTR**. The effect of this is that the **BSTR** returned from the method will be invalid. The solution is to do what we've done here, and use the **Copy()** method to make a copy of the **BSTR**.

Once you've compiled the code, the easiest way to test it is to use a VB client. Start VB, and in the New Project dialog select Standard EXE. From the Project menu, select References..., check the Automation 1.0 Type Library and then click OK. Add a label and give it a name of lblRet, and a text box with the name txtName. Finally, add a command button with the name cmdGreeting, double click on it, and add this code:

```
    Private Sub cmdGreeting_Click()
        Dim obj As New Auto
        lblRet = obj.Greeting(txtName)
        Set obj = Nothing
    End Sub
```

Here, a new **Auto** object is created. The **Greeting** method is called directly on this object, which works because VB looks in the type library and, in the absence of an explicitly requested interface, uses the one marked **[default]**, which is **IAuto**. If you use the Object Browser from the View menu, you will find that the **IAuto** interface is missing:

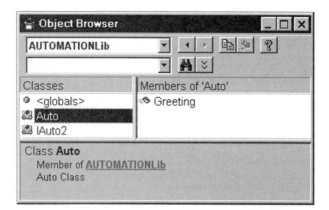

Since it is the default interface, VB will only allow you to access it through instances of the object. Here is an example of the test program running; I have typed Richard in the text box, and then clicked on the Greeting button:

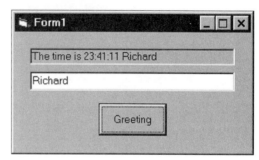

As you can see, the object appends the **BSTR** you pass in to the **Greeting()** method to the end of another **BSTR** that contains the time, and then returns the entire **BSTR** to the VB application.

Now let's add another method. You will need to close VB, because when you added the reference to the **Automation** type library, VB loaded the **Automation.dll**. This prevents you from amending the DLL because the linker will not be allowed access to it.

In ClassView, right click on the IAuto2 entry, select Add Method... and add a method with the following definition:

```
HRESULT GetGender([in] BSTR bstrName, [out, retval] BSTR* bstrGender);
```

This method takes a name with a title, like 'Dr Richard Grimes', and tries to determine the gender from the title. The algorithm is not sophisticated, it just assumes that **Miss**, **Ms** and **Mrs** are female and **Mr** is male. All other titles are treated as indeterminate. This code requires that you extract the first three characters from the **bstrName** and then perform a check.

The **bstrGender** string is formatted to contain the gender and the name, for example: 'The gender of Richard Grimes is unknown'. (This is because there is no gender implied by the title **Dr**). To format this string, the method must extract the name from **bstrName**.

> *As I mentioned earlier, there are no manipulation functions to extract substrings from a* **BSTR***, so instead we will use the C++ standard library's* **basic_string<>** *class.*

215

```
STDMETHODIMP CAuto::GetGender(BSTR bstrName, BSTR * bstrGender)
{
    if (bstrName == NULL)
        return E_INVALIDARG;
    *bstrGender = NULL;

    std::basic_string<WCHAR> strWholeName(bstrName);
    std::basic_string<WCHAR> strTitle;
    std::basic_string<WCHAR> strName;

    strTitle = strWholeName.substr(0, 3);
    std::basic_string<WCHAR>::size_type pos;
    pos = strWholeName.find(L' ');
    if (pos == std::basic_string<WCHAR>::npos)
        return E_INVALIDARG;
    strName = strWholeName.substr(pos + 1);

    CComBSTR bstrRet(L"The gender of ");
    bstrRet += strName.c_str();
    bstrRet += L" is ";

    if (strTitle.compare(L"Mr ") == 0)
        bstrRet += "male";
    else if (strTitle.compare(L"Mrs") == 0 ||
             strTitle.compare(L"Mis") == 0 ||
             strTitle.compare(L"Ms ") == 0)
        bstrRet += "female";
    else
        bstrRet += "unknown";

    *bstrGender = bstrRet.Copy();
    return S_OK;
}
```

In this code, the **basic_string** is based on **WCHAR** so that we can initialize it with a **BSTR**. Then we use **basic_string::substr()** to get the first three characters, so that we can test for a title. After that, **find()** is used to get the position of the first space in the string.

As it stands, the code assumes that the name will follow the first space, so if I enter 'Richard Grimes', the method will take the name to be 'Grimes'. (I leave it as an exercise to the reader to fix this problem.)

> *Notice that the position is returned as a value of type* **std::basic_string<WCHAR>size_type**. *It's longwinded types like these that put many people off the C++ standard library, which is a great shame because the library provides many useful classes.*

If **find()** fails, it returns a value of **std::basic_string<WCHAR>::npos** (which is actually -1), and we use this to return an error back to the user. Next, **substr()** is used again to retrieve the name, which is added to the **CComBSTR** that's used to construct the return value.

The final part of the algorithm checks the **strTitle** string for a known title — this is done with the **compare()** method, which returns values in a similar way to the CRT **wcscmp()** function.

Before you can compile this code, you will need to add the appropriate STL header to **Auto.cpp**:

```
#include "Auto.h"
#pragma warning(disable : 4530)
#include <string>
```

The code in the **<string>** header uses C++ exception handling, but exceptions are turned off by default, and this will cause the compiler to issue warning **C4530**. The **#pragma** prevents this warning from appearing in the output window. The code should now compile and link cleanly.

To test the new method, you need to alter the VB project. Add another button to the form and call it cmdGetGender. Double click on the button and enter this code:

```
Private Sub cmdGetGender_Click()
    Dim obj As New Auto
    Dim itf As IAuto2
    Set itf = obj
    lblRet = itf.GetGender(txtName)
    Set obj = Nothing
    Set itf = Nothing
End Sub
```

This time, we cast to the **IAuto2** interface to get access to the **GetGender()** method. Here is an example of running this example code:

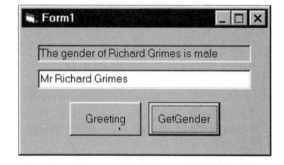

If you type in an invalid name, like 'Richard', you'll get the following dialog if you run the application from the VB IDE:

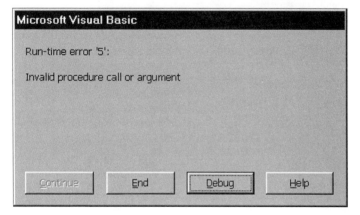

217

And you'll get this dialog if you compile and
then run the application:

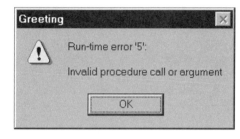

These dialogs indicate that an error was returned, and in this case it came from the
E_INVALIDARG returned by **GetGender()** when it cannot find a space in the string. This error
is not very clear — it is just one of the standard error codes — and it gives no indication of
which parameter is incorrect or what was incorrect about it. To do better, we need to use **rich
error information**.

Handling Errors

Do you remember checking the Support ISupportErrorInfo box in the Object Wizard? Well, here's
why you did it. If an error occurs when you access an Automation interface method through
IDispatch, the implementation can return error information through the **EXCEPINFO** parameter
of **Invoke()**. But what if the very same method is accessed through the vtable part of a dual
interface? There is no **EXCEPINFO** parameter, so how can the client access this rich error
information? To get this information back to the client, the server must create an error object and
give the client access to it. This is the purpose of **ISupportErrorInfo**.

> *Error objects are important for returning rich error information from Automation
> objects, but they are not confined to Automation objects — they can be applied to
> any COM object. This is why the* Support ISupportErrorInfo *check box is available
> for both dual and custom interfaces in the Object Wizard* Attributes *tab.*

To see how error objects work, let's get back to error handling with **Invoke()**. If a client wants
to receive rich error information when it calls **Invoke()**, it can pass in a pointer to an
EXCEPINFO structure as the 7th parameter. This structure has the following members:

```
typedef struct tagEXCEPINFO
{
  USHORT wCode;
  USHORT wReserved;
  BSTR bstrSource;
  BSTR bstrDescription;
  BSTR bstrHelpFile;
  ULONG dwHelpContext;
  void* pvReserved;
  HRESULT (*pfnDeferredFillIn)(struct tagEXCEPINFO*);
  SCODE scode;
} EXCEPINFO;
```

The **scode** or **wCode** member (but not both) holds a code that determines what error occurred.
There are two ways to return error codes because VB typically uses just the **wCode**, which can't

be used to return **HRESULT**s (**unsigned short** is only 16-bit). Having the **scode** available as well gives you this option. The client that receives this structure should check both **scode** and **wCode** to see which is non-zero.

The **pfnDeferredFillIn** member can either point to a function that will fill an **EXCEPINFO** structure, or it can be **NULL**. If it has a non-**NULL** value, then the client can choose when to ask the object for error information, but note that the rest of the members in the structure will be empty. If deferred error info is not used (the member *is* **NULL**) then the other members of the structure *are* filled. The three **BSTR** members are strings that indicate the source (its ProgID), a description of the error, and the name of a help file that contains further information. The appropriate position in the help file is indicated by the **dwHelpContext** member.

A server can use this structure to provide rich error information to a client. Not only can the client process display a dialog with the name of the object that caused the problem and a description, but also it can start **WinHelp** and load the appropriate file and context. If you look back to the dialog produced by the VB IDE when an error occurs, you will see that there is a Help button. If you click on this button, VB will use the information in the **EXCEPINFO** structure to start up **WinHelp**.

An **error object** is essentially a wrapper around the **EXCEPINFO** structure. These objects implement two interfaces: **ICreateErrorInfo** to set values, and **IErrorInfo** to get them.

```
interface ICreateErrorInfo: IUnknown
{
    HRESULT SetGUID([in] REFGUID rguid);
    HRESULT SetSource([in] LPOLESTR szSource);
    HRESULT SetDescription([in] LPOLESTR szDescription);
    HRESULT SetHelpFile([in] LPOLESTR szHelpFile);
    HRESULT SetHelpContext([in] DWORD dwHelpContext);
}

interface IErrorInfo: IUnknown
{
    HRESULT GetGUID([out] GUID* pGUID);
    HRESULT GetSource([out] BSTR* pBstrSource);
    HRESULT GetDescription([out] BSTR* pBstrDescription);
    HRESULT GetHelpFile([out] BSTR* pBstrHelpFile);
    HRESULT GetHelpContext([out] DWORD* pdwHelpContext);
}
```

These methods get and set the appropriate members of the error object; the new item not present in **EXCEPINFO** is the GUID. This item is used to hold the IID of the interface that the error object is associated with. There will often be more than one interface callable on a single thread, so the GUID indicates which interface generated the error. Note that each thread of execution has an associated error object — if this were not the case, then a client using an object on one thread could access the error object while another thread was setting it.

The **ISupportErrorInfo** interface has a single method:

```
interface ISupportErrorInfo: IUnknown
{
    HRESULT InterfaceSupportsErrorInfo([in] REFIID riid);
}
```

A client calls this method to determine whether the object supports rich error information for a particular interface. The client passes in the IID of the interface that it is interested in, and the method returns **S_OK** if the interface has an error object, or **S_FALSE** if it doesn't.

Your objects must keep a list of all the interfaces and the error objects that they support. If you look in the implementation file for the **CAuto** class, **Auto.cpp**, you will find that the Object Wizard has added the following method:

```
STDMETHODIMP CAuto::InterfaceSupportsErrorInfo(REFIID riid)
{
    static const IID* arr[] =
    {
        &IID_IAuto,
    };
    for (int i=0;i<sizeof(arr)/sizeof(arr[0]);i++)
    {
        if (InlineIsEqualGUID(*arr[i],riid))
            return S_OK;
    }
    return S_FALSE;
}
```

Notice that the array contains only the **IAuto** interface; this is because the Object Wizard did not know about the new interface **IAuto2** when it generated this code. To allow **IAuto2** methods to return rich error information, you need to add its IID to the map:

```
static const IID* arr[] =
{
    &IID_IAuto,
    &IID_IAuto2
};
```

The code is pretty self-explanatory: it just goes through every item in the array and compares the IID with the parameter passed to the method.

Note that the Wizard derives the object class from **ISupportErrorInfo**, which is fine in our case, because we want to provide error objects for two interfaces. If the object has a single interface, then you can derive the object class from **ISupportErrorInfoImpl<>** instead. This template takes the IID of the interface that supports error objects, provides an even more trivial implementation of the **InterfaceSupportsErrorInfo()** method.

How do you set one of these error objects, and how does a client use one? To see how they work, add a method to each of the interfaces on the **Auto** object. Right click on the **IAuto** interface in ClassView and select Add Method.... Add a method called **Value()** that takes a single **[in]** parameter of type **LONG**:

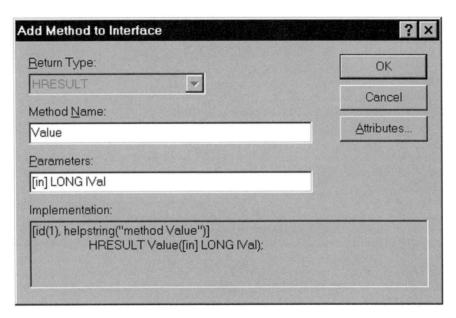

Do the same for the **IAuto2** interface, but call the method **Value2()**. These methods will check the passed parameter and generate an error if the value is less than 0 (in the case of **Value()**) or if it is greater than 0 (in the case of **Value2()**).

> *You cannot call the method in **IAuto2 Value()** because of the way that ATL uses multiple inheritance to implement interfaces (there would be two methods called **Value()** with the same parameters in the **CAuto** class, which would therefore not compile). This is one area where MFC is better than ATL: MFC uses nested classes to implement interfaces in a C++ class, and this would enable you to have two interfaces with the same method signatures.*

```
STDMETHODIMP CAuto::Value(LONG lVal)
{
    if (lVal < 0)
    {
        TCHAR str[256];
        wsprintf(str, _T("IAuto: %ld is too small, use a value > 0"),lVal);
        Error(str, IID_IAuto);
        return E_FAIL;
    }
    return S_OK;
}

STDMETHODIMP CAuto::Value2(LONG lVal)
{
    if (lVal > 0)
    {
        TCHAR str[256];
        wsprintf(str, _T("IAuto2: %ld is too big, use a value < 0"), lVal);
        Error(str, IID_IAuto2);
```

```
        return E_FAIL;
    }
    return S_OK;
}
```

These functions both call the inherited **CComCoClass** method **Error()**. There are several overloaded versions of this method, depending on whether you want to pass the descriptive text as an **LPCSTR**, an **LPCOLESTR** or an ID to a string resource; and on whether you want to pass information about a help file and help context. These overloaded methods call various file-scope overloaded functions called **AtlReportError()**. Finally, these methods in turn call the single function **AtlSetErrorInfo()** which actually does the work. You can find this function in **AtlImpl.cpp** — take a look: the code is straightforward and creates an error object from the CLSID, IID and descriptive text.

To test our error-handling code, add another command button to the VB form and call it cmdSetVal. Double click on the button and add the following code:

```
    Private Sub cmdSetVal_Click()
        Dim obj As New Auto
        Dim itf As IAuto2
        Set itf = obj
        lblRet = ""
        obj.Value Val(txtName)
        itf.Value2 Val(txtName)
        Set obj = Nothing
        Set itf = Nothing
    End Sub
```

Now when you run the client, enter a (positive) number in the text box and click on the SetVal button, you will get the following dialog from the VB IDE:

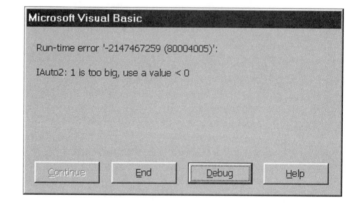

Alternatively, if you compile the project and then run it, you'll get this dialog:

Notice that in both cases, the error number returned from the **Value()** (or **Value2()**) method is **E_FAIL**. VB also gives the string that you constructed in the method.

The problem with allowing VB to handle the error object is that when you dismiss the dialog, it will stop the application. So just to finish off this example, let's handle the error:

```
Private Sub cmdSetVal_Click()
    On Error GoTo except
    Dim obj As New Auto
    Dim itf As IAuto2
    Set itf = obj
    lblRet = ""
    obj.Value Val(txtName)
    itf.Value2 Val(txtName)
    Set obj = Nothing
    Set itf = Nothing
    Exit Sub
except:
    Dim str As String
    str = "Error from " + Err.Source + Chr$(10) + Chr$(13)
    str = str + Err.Description + Chr$(10) + Chr$(13)
    str = str + "HRESULT: " + Hex$(Err.Number)
    MsgBox str
End Sub
```

The **On Error** line catches the error, and in the handler we use the VB **Err** object to extract information from the error object:

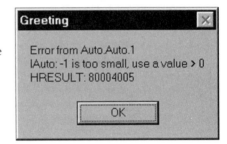

C++ Error Client

The VB client caught the error object generated when an error occurred, but Visual Basic hid the full details of what was going on. This next example will show you how to catch error objects in a C++ project.

To do this, the client should query the object for the **ISupportErrorInfo** interface. If a valid interface pointer is returned, it means that the object supports error objects. Next, the client must call the **InterfaceSupportsErrorInfo()** method, passing the IID of the Automation interface it is interested in. If this method returns **S_OK**, the client can obtain the error object for the current (server) thread of execution for this Automation interface.

To obtain the error object itself, the client must call **GetErrorInfo()**. I find this function rather odd, because it is a global function; it is not a method on an interface implemented by the server object. You don't pass any sort of reference to an object to this method: it just *knows* that you want to get the current error object on the current object for the current thread of execution.

In fact, the Microsoft documentation states that the function returns the most recently set error object in the current logical thread. If the current client thread has more than one Automation object (and each object may have more than one Automation interface), COM on the client side will only maintain the error object that was most recently set.

Still, you really don't need to worry about all this, because if you use the COM native support classes, they will do all the work for you. Now you'll understand why I like them so much!

Creating a client is straightforward. You could create a GUI project, but it is much easier to write a console application. Start up Developer Studio and create a new Win32 Console Application. I called my project **AutoClient**. Add a source file to the project, and enter the following code:

```
#include <windows.h>
#include <stdio.h>
#include <tchar.h>

#import "..\automation\automation.tlb"

using namespace AUTOMATIONLib;

int _tmain(int argc, _TCHAR** argv)
{
   CoInitialize(NULL);

   try
   {
      IAutoPtr pAuto(__uuidof(Auto));
      IAuto2Ptr pAuto2 = pAuto;

      // Get the user to pass values to the object
      TCHAR str[256];
      LONG lVal;
      while (true)
      {
         _tprintf(_T("(enter 0 to stop)> "));
         _tscanf(_T("%s"), str);
         lVal = _ttol(str);
         if (lVal == 0)
            break;
         try
         {
            pAuto->Value(lVal);
            pAuto2->Value2(lVal);
         }
         catch(_com_error e)
         {
            _tprintf(_T("There is an error")
            _T(" (%08x) in %s: \n\t\"%s\"\n"),
            e.Error(), (LPCSTR)e.Source(),
```

```
                (LPCSTR)e.Description());
            }
        }
    }
    catch(_com_error e)
    {
        _tprintf(_T("There is an error (%08x):")
            _T(" %s\n"), e.Error(),
            e.ErrorMessage());
    }

    CoUninitialize();
    return 0;
}
```

This code uses the VC++ COM compiler support smart pointers, so it needs to import the type library from the **Automation** project right at the top of the code.

Type in and compile this code and then look in the **Debug** (or the appropriate **Release**) directory for the two files **automation.tlh** and **automation.tli** generated by the **#import** line from the type library. In the **.tlh** file, you will find the wrapper **structs** for the interfaces. As an example, look for the **struct IAuto** — it declares the **virtual** method **raw_Value()**, which is the actual vtable method that the IDL file calls **Value()**, and also a wrapper **Value()** method that you call in the client code. Take a look in the **.tli** file, and you'll find:

```
inline HRESULT IAuto::Value ( long lVal ) {
    HRESULT _hr = raw_Value(lVal);
    if (FAILED(_hr)) _com_issue_errorex(_hr, this, __uuidof(this));
    return _hr;
}
```

So, when you call **IAuto::Value()** in the client code, the wrapper method actually calls the object vtable method **raw_Value()**. If this returns a non-success **HRESULT**, it goes on to call **_com_issue_errorex()**. This method creates a **_com_error** object and throws it as an exception.

The interesting thing from our point of view is that this function will do all the work of querying for **ISupportErrorInfo** and testing to see if the error supports rich error information for the interface that we discussed above. If everything's OK, then the **_com_issue_errorex()** function will get access to the error object for the logical thread and hold this in the **_com_error** object. When the exception is caught, you can use this exception object's convenient methods to access the error object's values. This is shown later in the code, but first let's look at how the object is created.

Within the outer **try**/**catch** block, we have the line:

```
IAutoPtr pAuto(__uuidof(Auto));
```

This creates the **Auto** object, obtains the **IAuto** interface, and wraps it in a **_com_ptr_t**-derived smart pointer. We want to test both the **IAuto** and **IAuto2** interfaces, so the next line creates a smart pointer for the **IAuto2** interface and uses the assignment operator to initialize it. This operator will do a **QueryInterface()** to get the interface.

225

Next, the code goes into a loop getting input from the user, which is broken if the user enters 0. The code converts the string to a number, and then passes this to the **Value()** and **Value2()** methods of the **IAuto** and **IAuto2** interfaces via calls to the wrapper methods. These calls are wrapped in a **try/catch** block to catch any exceptions thrown by these wrapper methods.

The exception handler just prints out the data in the error object. Here are some test results:

```
AutoClient                                                    _ □ ✕

<enter 0 to stop>> 25
There is an error (80004005) in Auto.Auto.1:
       "IAuto2: 25 is too big, use a value < 0"
<enter 0 to stop>> -50
There is an error (80004005) in Auto.Auto.1:
       "IAuto: -50 is too small, use a value > 0"
<enter 0 to stop>> 0
Press any key to continue
```

As expected, when **IAuto2::Value2()** is called with a positive number, an exception is thrown. The **HRESULT** is **E_FAIL**, which is just the return value from the **Value2()** method. The source of the error is given as 'Auto.Auto.1', which is the ProgID of the object, and the description is 'IAuto2: 25 is too big, use a value < 0', indicating that it did indeed come from **IAuto2**.

When I enter a negative number, **IAuto::Value()** complains, telling me that I should use a positive number. Lastly, I stop the process by entering a value of 0.

This is just as you would expect — the error object is being propagated from the **Auto** object to the client. One thing that is not immediately obvious from this code, though, is that error objects can be propagated across process and machine boundaries and still be associated with their logical thread.

But what if the client accesses the object through **IDispatch**? Try this code. First, add an **IDispatch** smart pointer:

```
IAutoPtr pAuto(__uuidof(Auto));
IAuto2Ptr pAuto2 = pAuto;
IDispatchPtr pDisp = pAuto;
```

And after the inner exception block, add:

```
HRESULT hr;
VARIANT varResult;
VariantInit(&varResult);

VARIANTARG vars;
VariantInit(&vars);
vars.vt = VT_I4;
vars.lVal = lVal;

DISPPARAMS disp = {&vars, NULL, 1, 0};
EXCEPINFO excepInfo;
```

```
        hr = pDisp->Invoke(0x2, IID_NULL,
                           LOCALE_USER_DEFAULT,
                           DISPATCH_METHOD, &disp,
                           &varResult, &excepInfo,
                           NULL);

        if (hr == DISP_E_EXCEPTION)
        {
           _tprintf(_T("There is an error in Invoke()")
              _T(" (%08x) in %ls: \n\t\"%ls\"\n"),
              excepInfo.scode, excepInfo.bstrSource,
              excepInfo.bstrDescription);
           SysFreeString(excepInfo.bstrSource);
           SysFreeString(excepInfo.bstrDescription);
           SysFreeString(excepInfo.bstrHelpFile);
        }
```

Make sure that the call to **Invoke()** has the DISPID of **Value()** as given in the IDL; the code above uses **0x2**. When **IAuto::Value()** is called, and when a negative number is passed, **Invoke()** will return **DISP_E_EXCEPTION** and you can then print out the rich error information. Notice that you have not changed the object at all. The system-generated version of **Invoke()** will check for an error object and use the values therein. Here's some results:

This calls the **Value()** method on **IAuto**, but what about **Value2()** on **IAuto2**? Add some more code:

```
        IDispatchPtr pDisp = pAuto;
        IDispatchPtr pDisp2 = pAuto2;
```

And:

```
        hr = pDisp->Invoke(0x2, IID_NULL,
                           LOCALE_USER_DEFAULT,
                           DISPATCH_METHOD, &disp,
                           &varResult, &excepInfo,
                           NULL);

        if (hr == DISP_E_EXCEPTION)
        {
           _tprintf(_T("There is an error in Invoke()")
              _T(" (%08x) in %ls: \n\t\"%ls\"\n"),
```

```
                       excepInfo.scode, excepInfo.bstrSource,
                       excepInfo.bstrDescription);
               SysFreeString(excepInfo.bstrSource);
               SysFreeString(excepInfo.bstrDescription);
               SysFreeString(excepInfo.bstrHelpFile);
           }
```

```
       hr = pDisp2->Invoke(0x2, IID_NULL,
                           LOCALE_USER_DEFAULT,
                           DISPATCH_METHOD, &disp,
                           &varResult, &excepInfo,
                           NULL);

       if (hr == DISP_E_EXCEPTION)
       {
           _tprintf(_T("There is an error in Invoke()")
               _T(" (%08x) in %ls: \n\t\"%ls\"\n"),
               excepInfo.scode, excepInfo.bstrSource,
               excepInfo.bstrDescription);
           SysFreeString(excepInfo.bstrSource);
           SysFreeString(excepInfo.bstrDescription);
           SysFreeString(excepInfo.bstrHelpFile);
       }
```

Here are the results:

This is clearly not what we want. In the first test (with a parameter of **1**) you would expect an exception from **IAuto2::Value2()**. This is happening, but only for the call through the smart pointer. To work out what's happening, you have to look at the next text. This time the parameter is **−1**, so you would expect **IAuto::Value()** to throw an exception. It does so *three* times: once for the call through the smart pointer, a second time when a call is made through **pDisp->Invoke()** and a third time when there is a call through **pDisp2->Invoke()**.

The reason for this behavior stems from something we looked at right at the start of the chapter. As I said then, there is just one implementation of **IDispatch**, so **pDisp** and **pDisp2** point to the same interface! Since the same DISPID is passed to **Invoke()**, the same method will be called (**IAuto::Value()**).

You may think that the solution is to change the DISPID of **Value2()** to a different value (say 4), but this will not work because the call to **pDisp2->Invoke(0x4, ...)** will return **DISP_E_MEMBERNOTFOUND** — in other words, a method with a DISPID of **0x4** can not be found on **IAuto**. The reason for this return value is that the implementation of **GetIdsOfNames()** that is used internally only recognizes the DISPIDs of **IAuto**. There is no way to specify which Automation interface should be called through **IDispatch**, and the only solution would be to provide a custom implementation of **Invoke()** and **GetIdsOfNames()**.

Summary

At the start of the chapter, I explained what Automation interfaces are and why they are used. I explained that they are implemented using the **IDispatch** interface, and that COM can implement the methods of this interface if it is supplied a type library describing the object.

I also explained what a dual interface is, and how to create and view type libraries. I described the data types that can be passed to an Automation interface method, and the helper classes provided by ATL: **CComBSTR** and **CComVariant**.

I showed you how to create an object with a dual interface, and how to add a second dual interface to an object that already has an Automation interface. I demonstrated how to call the object from C++, VB and Java. In the C++ code, I gave examples of calling the interface directly (using the vtable part of a dual interface), and by using **IDispatch::Invoke()**.

Finally, I showed you how to use rich error reporting using error objects, and how to access error objects in the client.

Marshaling and Threading

Previous chapters have shown how to create simple in-process and local objects. You've also seen in a general way how **marshaling**, provided by **proxies** and **stubs**, enables communication between objects in different locations without causing any changes in the client code. In all cases, the client code accesses methods on COM objects via pointers to their interfaces.

In this chapter, we're going to take a more detailed look at the different types of marshaling available. We'll discuss the pros and cons of packaging your components as DLLs and EXEs, and we'll look at setting up your components to allow clients on a different machine to access them. We'll also take a quick look at debugging your components, and finally we'll examine threading.

DLL and EXE Servers

We'll start with a quick reminder of the two module types available to COM servers: DLLs and EXEs. In ATL, the module type is chosen when the ATL COM AppWizard generates the project.

DLLs

DLLs are dynamic-link libraries that are loaded into the process space of an application.

- The thread in the client that loads the DLL calls **CoInitialize()** or **CoInitializeEx()**. The DLL doesn't initialize COM for itself (nor must the DLL call **CoUninitialize()**).

- DLLs do not have any direct control over their own lifetime — they are loaded and unloaded by an external force: the client process.

- *But* COM shifts control over a DLL server's lifetime back to the DLL itself through the use of a protocol based around the **DllCanUnloadNow()** function, which all COM DLLs must export. Client processes must never unload DLLs without checking the **DllCanUnloadNow()** function. Typically, client processes can call **CoFreeUnusedLibraries()** to free unused DLLs. This function calls **DllCanUnloadNow()** internally.

▶ DLL servers can delay creating their class objects until **DllGetClassObject()** is called for that particular class object. Clients get pointers to the server's class objects from (indirect) calls to **DllGetClassObject()**.

▶ DLL servers are efficient in terms of clients accessing their interfaces' methods. In the best case, no proxy will be used to access the object's interfaces; compared with creating a C++ stack-based object, there is just one extra level of indirection to get to the object.

▶ DLL servers are risky. They are loaded into the memory space of the client, so they have complete access to the client's memory. A badly written server could write over the client's memory, causing the process to crash. A malicious server could wreak havoc.

▶ DLL servers run in the security context of the client process. This means that the objects from the DLL have the same security clearance and identity as the client process. This is fine if you trust the object to use your identity responsibly, but if the object has been written by an unknown third party, you may feel a little reticent about this, preferring the object to be run under a less privileged account.

▶ If multiple client processes create objects from the DLL, the in-process server is loaded into each process. Code from the DLL is shared between the processes, but data is not. As we saw in Chapter 3, this limits ATL singletons to being per-process.

EXEs

EXEs are executables. Each executable has/is/defines its own process.

▶ EXE servers call **CoInitialize()** or **CoInitializeEx()** for themselves (and, ultimately, **CoUninitialize()**).

▶ EXEs have control over their own lifetime. An executable will unload when its code finishes running. In C++, that means it will unload whenever it returns from its **main()** or **WinMain()** function.

▶ EXE servers create their class objects when the process is first loaded, and register them with the class table. Clients get pointers to interfaces on the class objects (indirectly) from the class table.

▶ EXE servers are usually less efficient than DLL servers, because communication with an EXE always involves a proxy-stub.

▶ EXE servers offer more protection to the client application than DLLs — EXEs have their own memory address space, so they can't write across the client's memory.

▶ EXE servers have their own security context.

▶ Multiple clients can connect to the same instance of an EXE server (if the server will allow it). This allows singletons to be WinStation-wide, as explained in Chapter 3.

Marshaling

Marshaling is the process of packaging and sending data across apartment, process, or machine boundaries, and is carried out by proxies and stubs, which are always implemented as in-process servers. Each proxy is loaded into the client process, and communicates with a corresponding stub in the server process. The proxy and stub are usually implemented in the same DLL. Each proxy object is responsible for marshaling the methods on a single interface, but each DLL can serve the proxy objects for a number of different interfaces.

This in-process nature of the proxy and stub is what allows the feature of COM known as **location transparency**. Location transparency means that the server programmer can write essentially the same code for their coclasses, regardless of the relative locations of the client and server at runtime. Logically, it also means that the client programmer can do the same. The basis of COM is that clients always call methods on pointers in their own address space. These pointers may be directly to a server's interfaces, or to a proxy's. COM handles the loading of proxies and stubs as necessary; it's up to the proxies and stubs themselves to handle the inter-process communication behind the scenes.

You don't really need to know a great deal about marshaling in order to use it successfully, but you do need a basic understanding of the different mechanisms and terms involved. There are three main types of marshaling, which we'll examine in the following sections:

> **MIDL-Produced Marshaling**
>
> **Type Library Marshaling**
>
> **Custom Marshaling**

MIDL-Produced Marshaling

MIDL-produced marshaling is marshaling code produced by **MIDL**. In other words, **MIDL**-produced marshaling is what you get for free when you write an IDL file (or allow the Wizards to do it for you), and then run it through the **MIDL** compiler.

In ATL AppWizard-produced projects, the marshaling code is generated automatically from your project's IDL file whenever the project is built. Each ATL project has a custom build step applied to the IDL file to generate all the files necessary for the marshaling code:

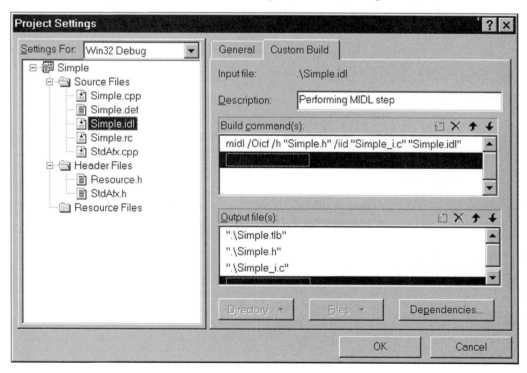

If your file is called **Simple.idl**, the custom build step will cause **MIDL** to produce the following files:

Filename	Description
Simple.h	The interface header file
Simple.tlb	The type library
Simple_i.c	Constant definitions
Simple_p.c	Proxy and stub code
dlldata.c	Start-up code for the proxy-stub DLL

In addition to these files, the AppWizard will create the following files when your project is created:

Filename	Description
Simpleps.mk	Makefile to produce the proxy-stub DLL
Simpleps.def	Module definition file to export inproc server methods (**DllGetClassObject()**, etc.)

Although the custom build step produces all the necessary files, it is up to you to build the proxy-stub DLL from the makefile. The makefile compiles all C files in the project directory, but links together only the object files produced from the **.c** files listed above. You can build the proxy-stub DLL using the following command line (replacing **Simpleps.mk** with the name of your own makefile!):

```
nmake Simpleps.mk
```

> *To enable command line builds, you should run the **Vcvars32.bat** file located in your installation's **\bin** directory, to modify the **PATH**, **LIB** and **INCLUDE** environment variables.*

To register the proxy-stub DLL as the handler for a particular interface, you can just pass the name of the DLL to **regsvr32**, just as you would with any other DLL COM server:

```
regsvr32 Simpleps.dll
```

The proxy-stub DLL is self-registering, adding the necessary entries to the registry to hook it up to a particular interface. This means that it adds a CLSID entry and, beneath that, an **InprocServer32** entry to **HKEY_CLASSES_ROOT\CLSID**, just like any COM server would.

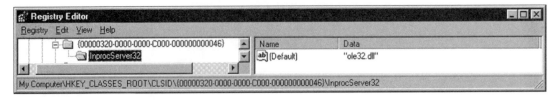

> *The screenshot shows the registry entry for* **Ole32.dll**, *which provides the proxy-stub implementation for many of the standard interfaces.*

Registering the proxy-stub DLL also adds an entry for the IID in the **HKEY_CLASSES_ROOT\Interface** key, and beneath that a **ProxyStubClsid32** key, which relates the interface to the CLSID.

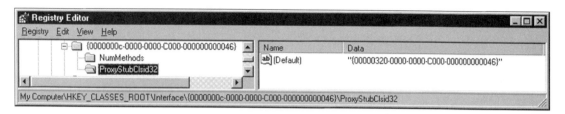

> *This screenshot shows the interface entry for* **IStream**, *one of the standard interfaces handled by* **Ole32.dll**.

MIDL-produced proxy-stubs register themselves with the same CLSID as the IID of the first interface for which they provide the proxy.

Remember that whenever an interface changes, so must the proxy-stub; you will need to rebuild the proxy-stub DLL and reregister it. Also remember that the proxy-stub DLL must be registered on all machines that use that interface, whether as client or server.

Type Library Marshaling

COM provides a proxy-stub DLL called the **Universal Marshaler**, which is implemented in **Oleaut32.dll**. This marshaler can be used to marshal any interface described in a type library.

> *Note that not all interfaces can be described in type libraries. Interfaces that can, only use a subset of the data types supported by* **MIDL** — *the Automation types described in the last chapter.*

The only requirements for an interface to use the Universal Marshaler are that **Oleaut32.dll** must be registered as the proxy-stub for that interface (on both client and server machines), and that the interface's type library must be registered. In practice, when you register the object on the server machine, these two criteria will be met. On the client machine, you will need to register the type library some other way.

> *The tools* **RegRgs32** *and* **RegTlb32**, *available for download from the World of ATL web site, could be used to register the type library on the client.*

When the client accesses an object's interface, COM will read the interface's registry entry to see what proxy-stub to use. This entry will give the CLSID of the Universal Marshaler, so COM will then look into the interface's registry entry for a **TypeLib** entry. This allows the Universal Marshaler to read the type library and hence determine the types of all the parameters of all the methods. When the client makes a method call, the Universal Marshaler can determine the types of the parameters on the stack, and construct an appropriate package to marshal to the server.

Note that the Universal Marshaler still requires information to be registered on the client, but it is particularly useful in one niche area: interoperability between 16-bit and 32-bit machines. 16-bit COM also has a Universal Marshaler (although somewhat restricted compared to the 32-bit version), and it can talk to the 32-bit Universal Marshaler using remote Automation. If you have a 16-bit COM application, you can write 32-bit code to talk to it over the network. Of course, if you have a 16-bit *and* a 32-bit proxy-stub registered for a 16-bit local server, this will allow you to use the object in a 32-bit process. However, you do need to make sure that you do not use 32-bit-only data types like **wchar_t** strings, because a 16-bit object will not know how to use them. This is another area where the Universal Marshaler adds value: it knows that **BSTR**s are **char** strings on 16-bit systems but **wchar_t** on 32-bit systems, and will do the necessary conversion for you.

To use type library marshaling, the type library must be registered, which is usually done with a call to the **RegisterTypeLib()** API. In addition to adding an entry under the **HKEY_CLASSES_ROOT\TypeLib** key, **RegisterTypeLib()** adds registry entries for all the Automation-compatible interfaces in the library, hooking them up to the Universal Marshaler. This means that all dispinterfaces, dual interfaces, and interfaces with the **[oleautomation]** attribute will be registered along with the type library.

ATL AppWizard-generated projects register the type library by default when the server is registered. The first parameter to **CComModule::RegisterServer()** is a **BOOL** value that indicates whether the type library should be registered at the same time as the server. If the value is **TRUE**, **CComModule::RegisterServer()** uses the **RegisterTypeLib()** API to register the type library. If you don't want the type library to be registered at this time, you should set the value to **FALSE** when the function is called. **CComModule::RegisterServer()** is called in the **_tWinMain()** function of an ATL EXE, and in the **DllRegisterServer()** function of an ATL DLL.

It is this behavior that has allowed us to avoid explicitly registering a proxy-stub DLL for the interfaces that we have created up to this point. All our interfaces have been Automation-compatible, so registering the server has automatically registered the type library and the interfaces in it, so that they can be marshaled by **Oleaut32.dll**.

So, in which situations would you want to use type library marshaling, and when would you use **MIDL**-produced marshaling?

Well, if you want to use data types that aren't supported by the Universal Marshaler, you'll have to use **MIDL**-produced marshaling code, because you can't use type library marshaling.

If you want to minimize the number of files distributed with your server, you'll probably prefer type library marshaling since the type library can be compiled into your server as a resource. It is possible to combine the **MIDL**-generated proxy-stub code into the module for a DLL server, but this is not possible for an EXE server (since the proxy-stub must be in-process).

If performance is an issue, you may choose **MIDL**-generated marshaling code over type library marshaling. There is a slight overhead in the Universal Marshaler having to load and consult the type library.

> Both **MIDL**-*produced marshaling and type library marshaling are forms of* **standard marshaling**.

Custom Marshaling

Standard is adequate for most needs, but occasionally you may seek better performance. Custom marshaling allows you to replace the existing marshaling mechanism with one of your own.

We won't look at custom marshaling in detail, because it's an advanced optimization technique, but we will explain enough so that you won't be surprised by the behavior of your components, and so that you can choose to investigate further if you find custom marshaling of interest. ATL provides no special help for implementing custom marshaling.

Standard marshaling has to be generic, which means that the marshaling mechanism is not necessarily the most efficient for all circumstances. Typical situations in which you might want to implement custom marshaling are:

▶ You're marshaling a data type that standard marshaling doesn't handle well, or where some of the values you're transmitting are irrelevant in the other process. An example might be a node in a doubly-linked list, for which the process you're sending data to isn't interested in the pointer to the next node.

▶ You're marshaling a constant property across the network. With standard marshaling, the data would need to flow across the network each time the property is read by a client. By implementing custom marshaling, you can cache the state of the property on the client machine for speedier access. This is known as **pickling**.

▶ You want to optimize the marshaling according to the context of the server (inproc, local, or remote).

An object that uses custom marshaling must implement the **IMarshal** interface. When COM gets a request to create an object, and the class object has returned an instance of the class, COM **QI()**s the object for **IMarshal**. If the object returns an **IMarshal** interface pointer, COM knows that custom marshaling is being used (if an error is returned, COM will use standard marshaling instead). This extra call to **QueryInterface()** for the **IMarshal** interface is often a cause of confusion to people; now you know what it is if you see it when you're **QI()** debugging! **IMarshal** has an IID of 00000003-0000-0000-C000-000000000046.

In addition to supporting **IMarshal** on your object, you still need to implement a proxy object (you do not need a separate stub object, because the proxy object will talk directly to the object through whatever IPC mechanism you choose). This in-process object also needs to implement **IMarshal**, plus all the interfaces that the object supports. The **IMarshal** interface has some methods that are specific to the proxy and others that are specific to the object, but basically it is used to set up the connection between these two objects.

Now, when the client calls methods on the interface, it will actually be calling methods on the proxy. These methods will use whatever scheme is appropriate for the interface to package up the method requests and parameters and send this data to the server. The server unpackages this data and dispatches the request to the appropriate handling routine, which can then return a reply back to the proxy, again in a packaged form. The proxy unpackages the data and returns it to the client.

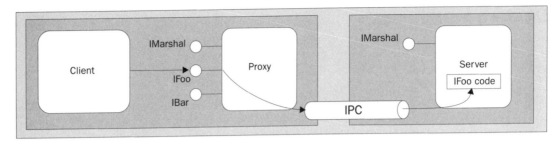

Note that in this mechanism the object doesn't actually have to implement the interfaces that the client thinks it does — it is up to the proxy to decide how to dispatch the method requests. In the example shown in the diagram, the server only implements **IMarshal**, but the client's calls on the **IFoo** interface result in the proxy telling the server to perform an action via a non-COM call.

Remote Servers

Remote servers are simply servers running on a different machine from the client. Although COM has allowed cross-process calls for many years, it wasn't until the introduction of DCOM (Distributed COM) with the release of NT 4.0 that cross-machine calls were realized. Although DCOM is really just the latest version of COM, its relative newness still ensures it gets separate billing.

> *DCOM comes as standard with NT 4.0, and as an add-on for Windows 95. It is also installed automatically as part of the Internet Explorer 4.0 package. To get the most out of COM, and to run the examples in this chapter, we recommend that you install the latest version, even if you're not interested in remote servers — enhancements and bug fixes in the latest versions are relevant to single machine users too. Microsoft provides service packs and updates for Windows 95 and Windows NT free of charge on its web site. DCOM for Windows 95 can be downloaded from:*
>
> *http://www.microsoft.com/com/dcom95/download-f.htm*
>
> *Note that DCOM for Windows 95 only runs over TCP/IP and requires user-level access control to use it for hosting servers.*

Surrogates

Both DLL and EXE servers can be accessed remotely, but a DLL needs the support of a **surrogate** process. As we mentioned earlier in the chapter, a DLL must be loaded into a process in order for it to run. When that process is designed to allow a DLL server to be accessed remotely (or even to be accessed from another process on the same machine), it's known as a surrogate.

Surrogates were introduced in NT 4.0 service pack 2. The system provides a standard surrogate called **DllHost.exe**, which can be used as the surrogate for any DLL server. Alternatively, you can write your own, which you may decide to do if you want to apply special security code. Writing a custom surrogate is beyond the scope of this book, but we'll look at an example of using the standard surrogate later in the chapter.

Surrogates are associated with DLLs via entries in the system registry. The server needs an AppID value beneath its CLSID key, which relates the server back to a key under **HKEY_CLASSES_ROOT\AppID**. This related key contains a string value named **DllSurrogate**, which may be the path to the surrogate to use, or it may be blank, in which case the system surrogate is used. We'll look in detail at the registry entries required when we come to create an example later in the chapter.

When a client requests an object from a remote machine, and that machine finds that the server is inproc and marked as running in a surrogate, the surrogate is started and given the CLSID of the in-proc server.

Accessing Remote Servers

There are two options for accessing remote servers. The first is to configure the registry on the client machine to create an object on another, specified, machine. The second is to pass a machine name to the **CoCreateInstanceEx()** function when you create an object.

The advantage of the first method is that your client code can continue to call **CoCreateInstanceEx()**. It doesn't need to know anything about the machine that the object will be created on, and you can change the way in which the server is created without recompiling the client. The disadvantage of the registry method is that the settings affect all the clients on that machine, which may not be appropriate. For example, you may have several objects on different machines across a network, and the client may want to access a particular object depending on some runtime criteria (for load balancing, perhaps).

The second method gives the client application fine control over the way in which the server is created, and allows it to make use of some optimizations provided by the **CoCreateInstanceEx()** function.

We'll look at each of these methods in turn.

Registering a Server for Remote Access

To register a server for remote access, it first requires an AppID value beneath its CLSID key. In this figure, you can see the AppID entry for the **MSDEV.APPLICATION** coclass. (This coclass represents the Developer Studio application — even your development environment is a COM server!)

The AppID value's data is a GUID that also appears as a subkey under the **HKEY_CLASSES_ROOT\AppID** key.

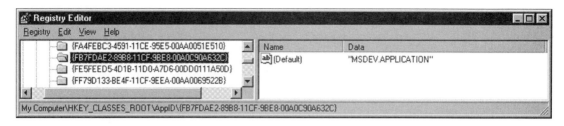

The AppID subkey is used to control configuration options for a single executable. Since an executable can serve many different coclasses, the configurations applied to the AppID key could affect many coclasses.

ATL AppWizard-generated EXE projects will automatically add the AppID key and value to the project's coclasses. The registry entries come from the RGS files that we examined in Chapters 2 and 3. The (Default) named value of the AppID key is meant as a description of the application. Wizard-generated projects will use the name of the project for this value. Note that Wizard-generated DLL projects won't register any AppID information, so if you want to use a surrogate, you will have to edit this file yourself.

To get the application to be activated on another machine, you need to add a **RemoteServerName** string value under the AppID subkey for your object server. However, you don't need to do this by hand, because **DCOMCnfg**, a utility supplied with DCOM, enables you to set the required registry entry using a simple dialog.

If you run **DCOMCnfg** by typing its name into the Run dialog accessible from the Start menu, you'll see the dialog shown here. The first tab lists the applications registered on your system:

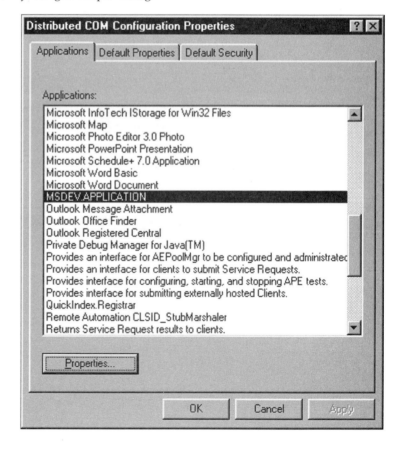

If you double-click on one of the entries in the list (or select one and hit the <u>P</u>roperties... button), you'll bring up a new dialog displaying the properties dialog for that application. The Location tab allows you to set the location at which the server will run.

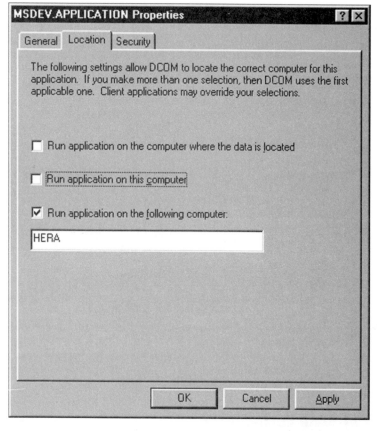

The name that you use for the remote server depends on the network transport used, but all UNC names like **\\HERA** and **HERA**, as well as DNS names like **hera.com**, and IP addresses like **194.222.147.74** are accepted.

Note that the Location page also shows two other non-exclusive options. We'll ignore the first of these. The second option specifies that the server can be run on the local machine. The options on this page are non-exclusive, so that you can allow a server to be launched locally *or* remotely depending on the context supplied to the creation function. COM will check the contexts specified by the client and will access the server according to the preferred order given below.

▶ If the CLSID has an **InprocServer32** or **InprocHandler32**, the specified DLL is used.

▶ If the AppID has a **LocalService** value, COM checks to see if there is a registered class object and if not it starts an NT service on the local machine. (This step only applies to COM on NT.)

▶ If the CLSID has a **LocalServer32** value, COM checks to see if there is a registered class object, and if not starts the specified process.

▶ If the AppID has a value **DllSurrogate**, but the value is empty, **DllHost** is used.

▶ If **DllSurrogate** is present and gives a path to a server, the specified surrogate is used.

▶ If the AppID has a **RemoteServerName** then the request is forwarded to COM on the specified machine.

Note that if the object is launched on a remote machine, then it will use the same search order, except it starts the search with the check on **LocalService**. If the remote machine tries to delegate the activation to yet another machine, it will fail because all activations require a security context (an access token) which cannot be passed from machine to machine under NT 4.0. Such a facility will be available with the distributed security features of NT5.

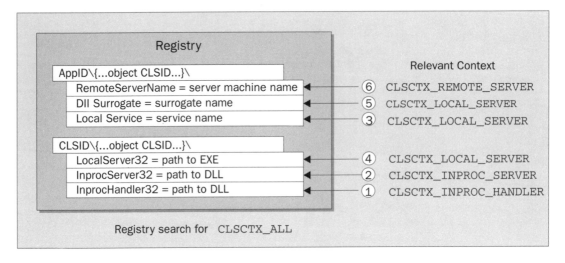

Note that only Windows NT allows remote activation. Windows 95's weaker security model only allows remote access to COM servers that have been pre-launched.

CoCreateInstanceEx()

The second way to access remote objects is to use **CoCreateInstanceEx()** and its parameters to specify the name of the server machine.

```
HRESULT CoCreateInstanceEx(
    REFCLSID rclsid,              // CLSID of the object to be created
    IUnknown* punkOuter,          // If part of an aggregate, the controlling
                                  // IUnknown
    DWORD dwClsCtx,               // CLSCTX values
    COSERVERINFO* pServerInfo,    // Machine on which the object is to be
                                  // instantiated
    ULONG cmq,                    // Number of MULTI_QI structures in
                                  // rgmqResults
    MULTI_QI rgmqResults[]        // Array of MULTI_QI structures
    );
```

Like **CoCreateInstance()**, this function takes parameters for the CLSID of the object to be created, the outer unknown (if the object is being created as part of an aggregate, which is only for inproc objects), and context values for the server. The context values can be a combination of flags from the **CLSCTX** enumeration:

```
typedef enum tagCLSCTX
{
```

```
      CLSCTX_INPROC_SERVER = 1,
      CLSCTX_INPROC_HANDLER = 2,
      CLSCTX_LOCAL_SERVER = 4,
      CLSCTX_REMOTE_SERVER = 16
  } CLSCTX;
```

The system headers also define a couple of frequently used constants: **CLSCTX_SERVER** (which combines all the **_SERVER** contexts) and **CLSCTX_ALL** (which represents *all* the possible contexts).

Unlike **CoCreateInstance()**, **CoCreateInstanceEx()** takes a **COSERVERINFO** parameter, which is used to determine the security settings used to connect to the server, and the name of the server to connect to. It also takes an array of **MULTI_QI** structures (with a related **ULONG** parameter) that is used to request and return a number of interfaces from the newly created object.

The **COSERVERINFO** parameter is a **struct** that looks like this:

```
  typedef struct _COSERVERINFO
  {
     DWORD dwReserved1;
     LPWSTR pwszName;
     COAUTHINFO* pAuthInfo;
     DWORD dwReserved2;
  } COSERVERINFO;
```

The reserved parameters, **dwReserved1** and **dwReserved2**, must be set to 0. In the future, these parameters may be used, but at the moment they do nothing. **pwszName** is a null-terminated Unicode character string that gives the name of the server host machine. It follows the same conventions as the **RemoteServerName** registry entry we looked at earlier in the chapter.

pAuthInfo passes security information to the server. This is required because a remote server machine should not allow just anyone to launch or access a process. Instead, the server machine should be more careful. It should check that the client is who they say they are (known as **authentication**), and then check that the client can do what it asks (**authorization**). The **COAUTHINFO** parameter depends on the authentication authority that is used. You can use the default security authority (NTLM security for NT 4.0 and Kerberos for NT 5.0), by passing a **NULL** value for this parameter. This will be adequate for most needs.

> For full details on DCOM security, take a look at Professional DCOM Programming
> (Wrox Press, 1997).

Note that if the **COSERVERINFO** parameter passed to **CoCreateInstanceEx()** is **NULL**, then COM will consult the value of the corresponding **RemoteServerName** in the registry. If that is empty, COM will create the object on the local machine.

The **MULTI_QI** parameter allows you to request several interfaces in one go. **CoCreateInstance()** allows you to ask COM to create an instance of a COM object and return a single interface on that object. If you want more than one interface, you must make multiple calls to **QueryInterface()**, and if the object is remote, that means multiple calls across the network. Calls across a network are relatively slow, so it's more efficient to request a number of interfaces with a single call — **CoCreateInstanceEx()** allows you to do just that.

The **MULTI_QI** structure looks like this:

```
typedef struct _MULTI_QI
{
    const IID* pIID;
    IUnknown*  pItf;
    HRESULT    hr;
} MULTI_QI;
```

You pass in the IID of the interface that you want in **pIID**, and **CoCreateInstanceEx()** will return the status code in **hr**. If the interface request was successful, the interface pointer will be in **pItf**.

The **cmq** parameter must be set by the caller to the number of elements in the **rgmqResults** array.

> *Note that the compiler COM support smart pointers don't provide a wrapper function for* **CoCreateInstanceEx()** *(although they provide a* **CreateInstance()** *method that wraps* **CoCreateInstance()**)*. You can still use smart pointers when creating remote servers. We'll show you how in the example later in the chapter.*

Remote Objects with ATL

Now that we've seen the theory of remote objects, let's look at what it takes to get some ATL components communicating with clients on another machine. We'll create a DLL server and hook it up to the standard surrogate, and we'll create a EXE server. In each case, we'll show how the client can talk to a server on another machine via registry entries or a call to **CoCreateInstanceEx()**. You'll also see how to set up separate projects to share the definition and implementation of a coclass.

This example implements a simple object that exposes one method — **GetFreeDiskSpace()** — to return the amount of free disk space on the machine. The chances of two machines having the same amount of free disk space are very small, so it is a useful object to show that remote activation is working.

For our example, we want to create a DLL project and an EXE project that expose the same coclass with the same interface and implementation. Clearly, we don't want to duplicate code or interface definitions between the projects, so we'll set up the projects so that they refer to the same files as much as possible. In this small example, the effort required to share the files is quite large in proportion to the size of the project, but the benefits of minimizing effort and increasing maintainability quickly grow along with the size of the project.

The first step is to create a new folder with the name **ServerInfo**. We'll use this folder to store all the files to be shared between the projects. That will include the IDL file (and the files that **MIDL** will produce from it), as well as the header and implementation files that will be common to both projects.

DLL Server

The next step is to create the DLL version of the project. Fire up Developer Studio and create a new ATL COM AppWizard project called **ServerInfo**, store it in a subdirectory of the **ServerInfo** directory you just created, and call this subdirectory **ServerInfoDll**. (Use the ... button to select the **ServerInfo** directory, then type **ServerInfo** as the Project name and finally add **Dll** to the end of the text in Location). You can see the settings you need to make in the screenshot below:

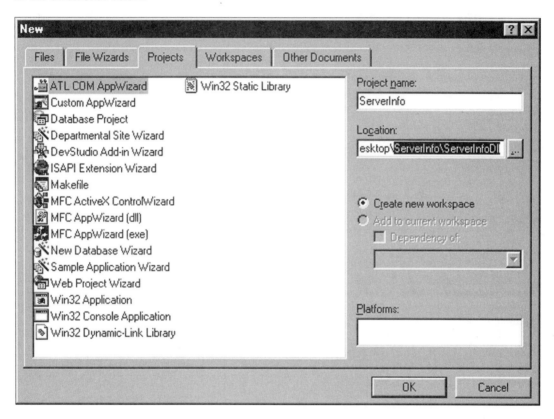

Choose Dynamic Link Library (DLL) as the server type on Step 1 of the AppWizard and press Finish, then click OK on the next dialog.

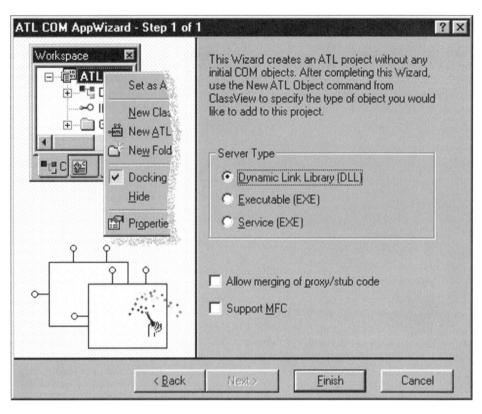

Next, add a new Simple Object to the project using the ATL Object Wizard. Click Next > and enter the details of the object on the Names tab. The Short Name should be **DiskInfo**, and the remainder of the fields can be left with their default values:

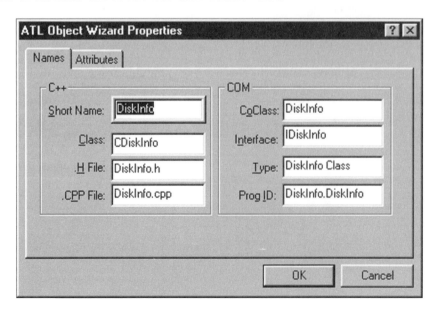

On the Attributes tab, ensure that the <u>C</u>ustom interface radio button is selected, and click on OK:

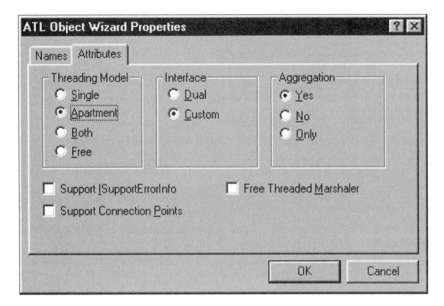

Now in the ClassView for the project, right-click on the IDiskInfo interface and select Add Method...

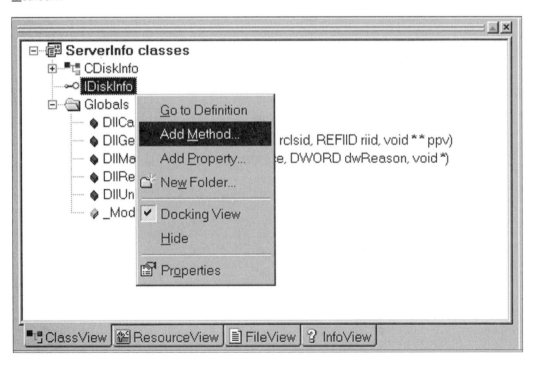

Now enter the name of the method and its parameters and click on OK:

```
GetFreeDiskSpace( const wchar_t* wszDrive,
                  hyper*          hypFreeBytes )
```

Here, **wszDrive** is the name of the drive on the machine on which the object is running, and is an **[in, string]** parameter. Note the use of **[string]**; **wchar_t*** could be treated by the marshaling code as a pointer to a single **wchar_t**, so this attribute tells the marshaler to call **wcslen()** on the parameter to find out exactly how many characters to marshal. The results are returned in the **[out]** parameter **hypFreebytes**. The 64-bit integer **hyper** is used here because the Win32 function that we will use returns this data type to accommodate very large disks. Because the method uses this data type, which is an IDL-specific data type and not one of the Automation types, you cannot implement the interface as a dual.

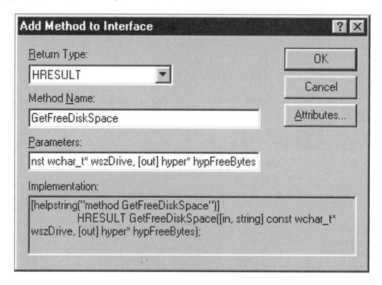

Now in ClassView open the CDiskInfo tree and then the IDiskInfo tree, and then double-click on the GetFreeDiskSpace() method. Enter the following code:

```
STDMETHODIMP CDiskInfo::GetFreeDiskSpace(const wchar_t * wszDrive,
                                         hyper * hypFreeBytes)
{
    USES_CONVERSION;

    DWORD dwSectorsPerCluster;
    DWORD dwBytesPerSector;
    DWORD dwNumberOfFreeClusters;
    DWORD dwTotalNumberOfClusters;

    // GetDiskFreeSpaceEx() is not available
    // before Win95 OSR2, so we'll use GetDiskFreeSpace()
    GetDiskFreeSpace(W2T(wszDrive), &dwSectorsPerCluster,
        &dwBytesPerSector, &dwNumberOfFreeClusters,
        &dwTotalNumberOfClusters);
```

```
    // The number of bytes per cluster should fit into a DWORD
    DWORD dwBytesPerCluster;
    dwBytesPerCluster = dwSectorsPerCluster * dwBytesPerSector;

    // But the number of bytes on the disk needs careful handling
    *hypFreeBytes =  UInt32x32To64(dwNumberOfFreeClusters,
        dwBytesPerCluster);

    return S_OK;
}
```

Finally, open **DiskInfo.rgs** and edit it to ensure that registry entries used by both the DLL and EXE server have the **NoRemove** keyword applied. This means that the shared entries won't be removed when one of the servers is unregistered. The registry script should now look like this:

```
HKCR
{
    NoRemove DiskInfo.DiskInfo.1 = s 'DiskInfo Class'
    {
        NoRemove CLSID = s '{DF03FEF1-6BC7-11D1-B28D-00A0C94515AD}'
    }
    NoRemove DiskInfo.DiskInfo = s 'DiskInfo Class'
    {
        NoRemove CurVer = s 'DiskInfo.DiskInfo.1'
    }
    NoRemove CLSID
    {
        NoRemove {DF03FEF1-6BC7-11D1-B28D-00A0C94515AD}
                                            = s 'DiskInfo Class'
        {
            InprocServer32 = s '%MODULE%'
            {
                val ThreadingModel = s 'Apartment'
            }
            NoRemove ProgID = s 'DiskInfo.DiskInfo.1'
            NoRemove VersionIndependentProgID = s 'DiskInfo.DiskInfo'
        }
    }
}
```

You can see that the **NoRemove** keyword has been applied to every entry except **InprocServer32**. Only the **InprocServer32** entries will be removed when the DLL server is unregistered. Notice that the **ProgID** and **VersionIndependentProgID** lines have been moved to the bottom of the registration block. The reason for this is that the registrar uses a recursive routine to register keys, which detects when **NoRemove** is used. After this, no other subkey can be removed from this key. If the **ProgID** line was above the **InprocServer32** line, neither key would be removed (even though **InprocServer32** has *not* been marked **NoRemove**); the solution is to put all items that need to be removed before those that must not be removed.

Because we're also going to be using this DLL server with a surrogate, we need an AppID value for it. Although ATL EXE projects are automatically set up to register AppIDs, ATL DLL projects aren't. To rectify this, we need to generate a new GUID for the AppID using the GUID Generator, and then we can add the AppID value to the **DiskInfo.rgs** file, just below the closing brace of the **InprocServer32** entry. Once again, we use the **NoRemove** keyword because this entry will be shared with the EXE server

```
        val ThreadingModel = s 'Apartment'
    }
    NoRemove ProgID = s 'DiskInfo.DiskInfo.1'
    NoRemove VersionIndependentProgID = s 'DiskInfo.DiskInfo'
    NoRemove val AppID = s '{35035403-6C02-11D1-B28D-00A0C94515AD}'
}
```

This registers the coclass with the AppID, but the AppID itself also needs some registry settings. In EXE projects, these are generated as a separate RGS file. We'll follow that convention in our DLL project.

Create a new text file and save it in the **ServerInfoDll** directory as **ServerInfo.rgs**. Add the following text to this file, and save it again:

```
HKCR
{
    NoRemove AppID
    {
        NoRemove {35035403-6C02-11D1-B28D-00A0C94515AD} = s 'ServerInfo'
        'ServerInfo.dll'
        {
            val AppID = s {35035403-6C02-11D1-B28D-00A0C94515AD}
        }
    }
}
```

The two GUIDs in this file are the same as the AppID we added to the **DiskInfo.rgs** file.

Now import this file as a **"REGISTRY"** resource. Go to ResourceView and right-click on the **"REGISTRY"** folder and hit Import... Set the Files of type list to show All Files (*.*) and the Open as list to show Custom, then select **ServerInfo.rgs**. Set the resource type to be **"REGISTRY"** then hit OK. Once the resource has been imported, bring up its properties dialog and set its ID to **IDR_ServerInfo**.

Since we have an additional registry script in the project, you need to make sure that it gets run during registration and unregistration. Add these lines of code to **DllRegisterServer()** and **DllUnregisterServer()** in **ServerInfo.cpp**:

```
STDAPI DllRegisterServer(void)
{
    // registers object, typelib and all interfaces in typelib
    _Module.UpdateRegistryFromResource(IDR_ServerInfo, TRUE);
    return _Module.RegisterServer(TRUE);
}
```

```
STDAPI DllUnregisterServer(void)
{
    _Module.UpdateRegistryFromResource(IDR_ServerInfo, FALSE);
    _Module.UnregisterServer();
    return S_OK;
}
```

This code just registers the information in the new RGS file whenever the server is asked to register itself, and unregisters it when the server is asked to unregister itself.

Moving the Files

At this stage we have a fairly standard, DLL server project (which also registers its own AppID). However, before we compile the project, we need to move files that will be common to both the EXE server and the DLL server into the **ServerInfo** folder.

First, move the **ServerInfops.def** and **ServerInfops.mk** files, so that we can make the proxy-stub using files from the **ServerInfo** folder. The proxy-stub DLL will be used by both versions of the server.

Next *copy* the **ServerInfo.idl** file from the **ServerInfoDll** folder to its parent, **ServerInfo**. The reason that we're copying this file, rather than moving it, is that the ATL Wizards automatically add their interface definitions to the *ProjectName*.**idl** file. If we ever needed to run the Wizards again, we could do so. We'd then have to copy the Wizard-generated IDL from the file in the **ServerInfoDll** folder into the IDL file in the **ServerInfo** folder.

However, we don't want the original IDL file to be 'live', so we need to remove it from the project. The easiest way to do that is to go to FileView, select the IDL file and hit the *Delete* key. Once you've done this, the file will no longer appear in FileView, and it will no longer be run through **MIDL** when the project is built. You would only ever need to look at that file again if you ran a Wizard that changed it. We don't have to worry about that in this example.

Now we need to hook up the new IDL file to the project. The first step is to add the file by right-clicking on the Source Files icon in FileView, and selecting the Add Files to Folder... menu item. This will bring up the Insert Files into Project dialog. Set the Files of type to All Files (*.*) then navigate to the **ServerInfo** folder, select the IDL file and hit OK.

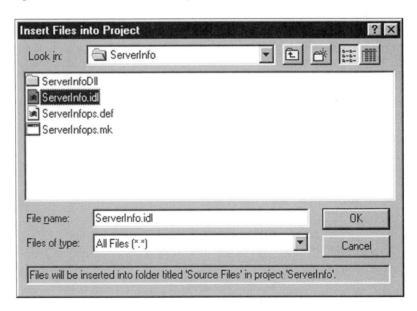

Once the IDL file has been added to the project, we need to set up a custom build step for it. This build step will run the file through the **MIDL** compiler to produce the marshaling code, type library, interface header and GUID definition files. All these files need to be output in the **ServerInfo** directory, since they will be shared by both of our server projects.

Right-click on the IDL file in FileView and select the Settings... menu item. Make sure that the Settings For list at the top-left of the Project Settings dialog displays All Configurations, then click on the Custom Build tab.

Give the custom build step a description of Performing MIDL step... and add the following command line to the Build command(s) list:

```
midl /Oicf /out ".." /h "ServerInfo.h" /iid "ServerInfo_i.c"
"..\ServerInfo.idl"
```

Add **..\ServerInfo.tlb**, **..\ServerInfo.h** and **..\ServerInfo_i.c** to the list of Output file(s). The dialog should appear as shown below:

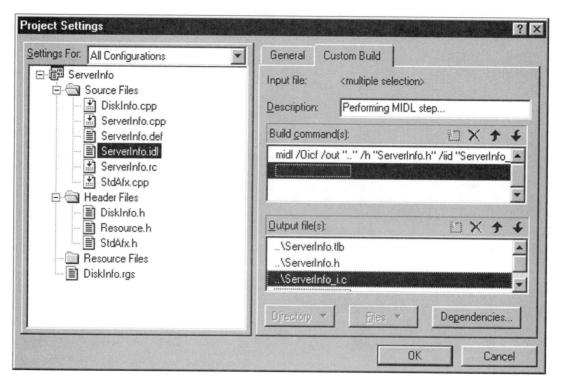

This custom build step is very similar to the build step for the original IDL file. The differences are purely to do with the new location of the IDL file and its output. The result of this build step is that all the **MIDL**-generated files will be produced in the parent directory of this project, the **ServerInfo** directory.

As a result of these changes, we need to make a few changes to the files in the project so that they refer to the new location of the **MIDL**-generated files. In **ServerInfo.cpp**, we need to change the **#include**s for **ServerInfo.h** and **ServerInfo_i.c**, so that they point to the project's parent directory where the files now live. We're going to move the **resource.h** and **DiskInfo.h** files into the **ServerInfo** directory, so we might as well change the **#include**s for these now, too.

```
#include "stdafx.h"
#include "..\resource.h"
#include "initguid.h"
#include "..\ServerInfo.h"

#include "..\ServerInfo_i.c"
#include "..\DiskInfo.h"
```

Move the symbol header file, **resource.h**, to the **ServerInfo** directory and remove this file from the project by clicking on its icon in FileView and hitting the *Delete* key. Now we need to point the resource script to the new location of the type library. We'll do this using the Resource Includes dialog box, which you can bring up via the View | Resource Includes... menu item. Change the symbol header file to ..\resource.h and change the **TYPELIB** resource in the compile-time directives box to point to the new location of the type library, as shown:

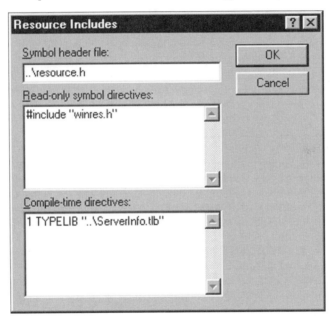

When you click OK, Developer Studio will warn you about the action that you're about to take, but you can safely ignore this and press the OK button on the message box:

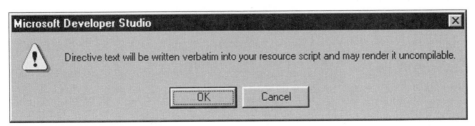

The final step to moving the common files into the **ServerInfo** directory is to move the header and implementation of the **CDiskInfo** class. First, close all open files, then remove the **DiskInfo.h** and **DiskInfo.cpp** files from the project by clicking on their icons in FileView and hitting the *Delete* key. Now move the files from the **ServerInfoDll** directory to the **ServerInfo** directory. Add these files (and **Resource.h**) back into the project by using the Project | Add To Project | Files... menu item.

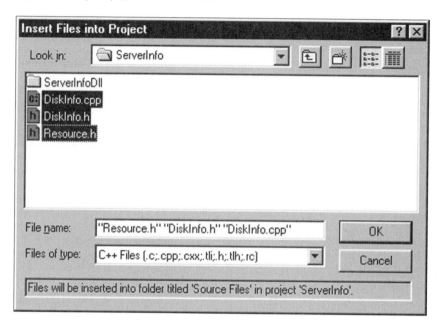

Compile the project now to see that everything is still working after all our changes, and to ensure that the type library gets built.

You may get a dialog suggesting that **Resource.h** will be overwritten, but don't worry. This is Developer Studio adding the resource ID for **IDR_ServerInfo** to this file. Click on Yes to continue the build.

EXE Server

The next step is to create the EXE version of our COM server. Create a new ATL COM AppWizard project called **ServerInfo** (this time generate it in the **ServerInfo\ServerInfoExe** directory), and make sure that the server type is set to Executable (EXE).

Now go to FileView, select the IDL file, and hit the *Delete* key. Use the Project | Add To Project | Files... menu item to add the **ServerInfo.idl**, **DiskInfo.cpp** and **DiskInfo.h** files from the **ServerInfo** directory into the project.

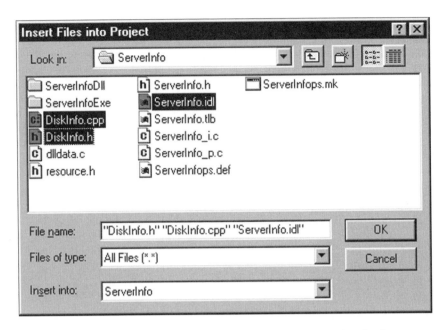

Right-click on the icon for the new IDL file in FileView and select the Settings... menu item. Give the IDL file the same custom build step as the IDL file we added to the DLL project. The easiest way to get the settings across is to have both projects open at once, then copy and paste the settings. Don't forget to set the build step for *all* the project's configurations:

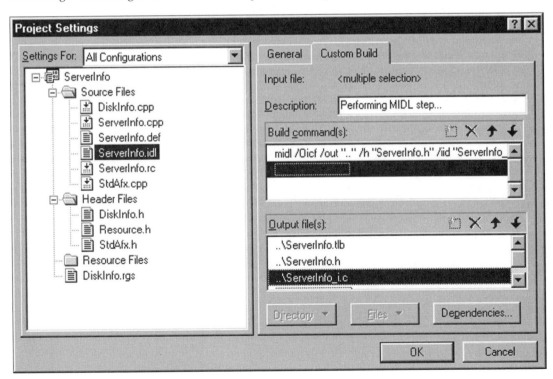

In **ServerInfo.cpp**, we need to change the **#include** paths just as we did in the DLL server. Since we did not use the ObjectWizard to add the object to the project, you need to do the work that it would have done. So, add a **#include** for **..\DiskInfo.h**:

```
#include "stdafx.h"
#include "..\resource.h"
#include "initguid.h"
#include "..\ServerInfo.h"

#include "..\ServerInfo_i.c"
#include "..\DiskInfo.h"
```

and add an entry for the **CDiskInfo** class to the object map in the same file; in the DLL project, this entry was automatically added by the Wizard.

```
BEGIN_OBJECT_MAP(ObjectMap)
    OBJECT_ENTRY(CLSID_DiskInfo, CDiskInfo)
END_OBJECT_MAP()
```

Next, we need to add the component's resource script to the project. The registry entries are slightly different between the DLL and EXE projects, but similar enough that we can use the RGS file from the DLL project as a starting point. Copy **DiskInfo.rgs** from the **ServerInfoDll** directory into the **ServerInfoExe** directory, and replace the **InprocServer32** block with a **LocalServer32** entry, as shown:

```
LocalServer32 = s '%MODULE%'
NoRemove ProgID = s 'DiskInfo.DiskInfo.1'
```

We also need to edit the Wizard-generated **ServerInfo.rgs** file to ensure that the AppID is exactly the same as the AppID used for the DLL, and we'll apply the **NoRemove** keyword so that it won't be removed when the server unregisters itself:

```
HKCR
{
    NoRemove AppID
    {
        NoRemove {35035403-6C02-11D1-B28D-00A0C94515AD} = s 'ServerInfo'
        'ServerInfo.EXE'
        {
            val AppID = s {35035403-6C02-11D1-B28D-00A0C94515AD}
        }
    }
}
```

You will need to add the **DiskInfo.rgs** to the project as you did for **ServerInfo.rgs** in the DLL project. So, go to ResourceView, right-click on the **"REGISTRY"** folder and hit Import.... Set the Files of type list to show All Files (*.*) and the Open as list to show Custom, then select **DiskInfo.rgs** from **ServerInfoExe**. Set the resource type to be **"REGISTRY"** then hit OK. Once the resource has been imported, bring up its Properties dialog and set its ID to **IDR_DISKINFO**. Now the resources should have the same IDs as for the DLL project.

Finally, we need to set the resource
script up with the new location of
the type library and symbol header
file, just as we did in the DLL
project. Use the View | Resource
Includes... menu item to bring up
the Resource Includes dialog box,
and change the dialog as shown.

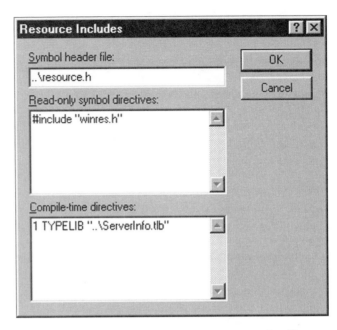

You may get warnings about the changes that you've made when it comes to saving the files.
Once again, you can safely ignore them, and just click OK on the dialogs. So that the
dependencies are correctly set up, remove **Resource.h** from the FileView and add it back again
from the **ServerInfo** directory.

Proxy-Stub DLL

Now that we've got our servers set up, we're almost ready to try them out with a client. Make
sure that you've compiled the **ServerInfoDll** and **ServerInfoExe** projects.

Build the proxy-stub DLL by opening a command prompt at the **ServerInfo** directory and
using the following command line:

```
nmake ServerInfops.mk
```

Register the DLL with:

```
regsvr32 ServerInfops.dll
```

If you run **RegEdit** and look at the CLSID for the class, you will find that the class will have
both **InprocServer32** and **LocalServer32** keys, as well as having an AppID named value:

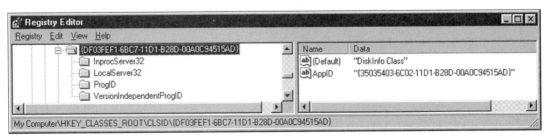

You can also see the entry for the **IDiskInfo** interface in the **Interface** section of the registry:

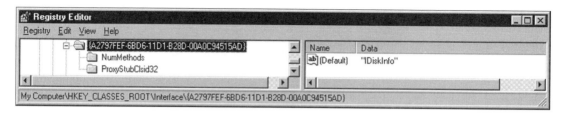

Client

Now we'll create the client for these servers. Create a new Win32 Console Application called **GetDiskSpace** and save it in a subdirectory of **ServerInfo**.

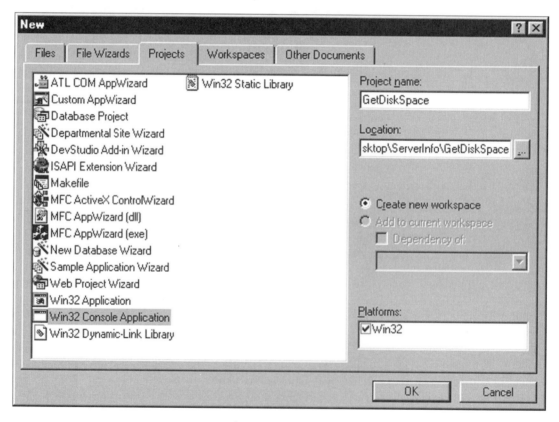

Create a new text file and save it in the project directory as **GetDiskSpace.cpp**. Add the file to the project, then type in the following code:

```
#include <windows.h>
#include <stdio.h>
#include <tchar.h>
```

```
#import "..\ServerInfo.tlb"
using namespace SERVERINFOLib;

int _tmain(int argc, _TCHAR** argv)
{
   CoInitialize(NULL);

   try
   {
      IDiskInfoPtr pDiskInfo(__uuidof(DiskInfo));
      hyper hypDiskSize;
      pDiskInfo->GetFreeDiskSpace(L"C:\\", &hypDiskSize);
      _tprintf(_T("There are %I64d free bytes\n"), hypDiskSize);
   }
   catch (const _com_error& e)
   {
      _tprintf(_T("There is an error (%08x): %s\n"),
         e.Error(), e.ErrorMessage());
   }

   CoUninitialize();
   return 0;
}
```

This file has been set up to work with both Unicode and ASCII builds, hence the **_T()**
macros around the string literals, and the use of **_tmain()** *and* **_tprintf()**. *Note that*
the disk's root directory is passed to **GetFreeDiskSpace()** *as a wide character string*
whether Unicode is being used or not.

We have used a relative path to the type library of the object in the **#import** statement, and it's
this directive that generates the smart pointer wrapper for the **IDiskInfo** interface we use in
the code. As usual, we use the smart pointer's constructor to create an instance of the **DiskInfo**
coclass:

```
explicit _com_ptr_t( const CLSID& clsid,
                     DWORD dwClsContext = CLSCTX_ALL ) throw( _com_error );
```

This version of the constructor makes a call to **CoCreateInstance()** using the second
(optional) parameter as the context of the component to create. In this case, we're using
CLSCTX_ALL because we haven't specified anything else, so COM will use the search order that
we examined earlier in the chapter to decide how to activate our server. Our server has both a
LocalServer32 and **InprocServer32** entry, so we'd end up using the in-process server if we
compiled and ran the code at this point. You can do exactly that to see that the code works as
advertised: run the tool from the command line, and it will print out the number of free bytes
on your **C:** drive. Check this value with the value given by the **dir** command (note that if you
are running low on conventional memory, running **GetDiskSpace** may result in the virtual
memory swap file grabbing an extra chunk of disk space, which may make the two disk space
sizes appear different).

With the client code as supplied, you could force the client to load the EXE server by unregistering the DLL. However, a more flexible client would be able to get the desired context from the command line and load the appropriate server. Let's change our client to do that. The changes to make are shown highlighted below:

```
int _tmain(int argc, _TCHAR** argv)
{
    CoInitialize(NULL);

    try
    {
        HRESULT hr = S_OK;
        IDiskInfoPtr pDiskInfo;
        if (argc == 2 && argv[1][0] == _T('L'))
            hr = pDiskInfo.CreateInstance(__uuidof(DiskInfo),
                NULL, CLSCTX_LOCAL_SERVER);
        else
            hr = pDiskInfo.CreateInstance(__uuidof(DiskInfo),
                NULL, CLSCTX_INPROC_SERVER);

        if (FAILED(hr))
            _com_issue_error(hr);

        hyper hypDiskSize;
        pDiskInfo->GetFreeDiskSpace(L"C:\\", &hypDiskSize);
        _tprintf(_T("There are %I64d free bytes\n"), hypDiskSize);
    }
    catch (const _com_error& e)
    {
        _tprintf(_T("There is an error (%08x): %s\n"),
            e.Error(), e.ErrorMessage());
    }

    CoUninitialize();
    return 0;
}
```

In this code, we're using **_com_ptr_t<>::CreateInstance()** to create the object with a specific context. If our client is executed with a single command line parameter, then **argc** will be **2** because the first argument that gets counted is the name of the client executable. If this command line parameter begins with the letter **L** (case sensitive), we create the local server. In all other cases, we create the in-process server.

Now you can compile the project again. To convince yourself that the client can call either the in-process or the local server, run this project under the debugger. Place a breakpoint on the line that calls **GetFreeDiskSpace()**, then press *F5* (or use Build | Start Debug | Go). When the debugger stops, we know that the server object has been created and the module for it must be loaded. If you're running Windows 95 bring up Process Viewer, otherwise use the NT Task Manager (right click on the Task bar and select Task Manager) and look for ServerInfo.exe in the list of running processes. You won't see it, because in this case we're creating our object from the in-process server. Run the client to completion.

Now go to the project settings (Project | Settings...), switch to the Debug tab, and add Local to the Program arguments (notice the capital 'L'). Now press *F5* to debug the process again. When the debugger stops this time, you can run Process Viewer and you'll see that ServerInfo.exe is in the list of running processes, proving that we're creating our object from the EXE server. The Windows 95 Process Viewer will look something like this:

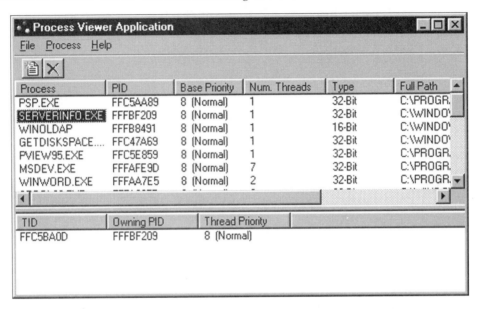

Meanwhile the NT Task manager will show:

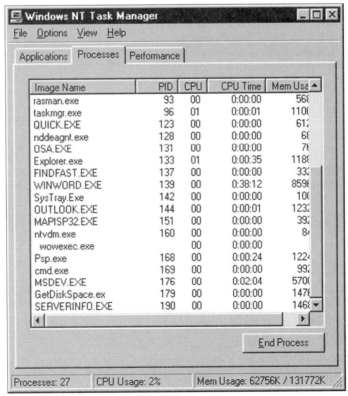

You will also notice that **GetDiskSpace** will take a little longer to run, since it has to load the object in a separate process.

Distributed COM

Now we have all the server code we need to run the object on a remote machine. In this section, we'll look at three ways to do this:

▶ How to use the existing client to communicate with the EXE server on another machine by changing some registry settings on the client machine

▶ How to create a new client to communicate with the EXE server on a machine specified by a command line argument

▶ How to use the new client to communicate with the DLL server on another machine by using a surrogate

RemoteServerName

First, we need to copy **ServerInfo.exe** and **ServerInfops.dll** to a local drive on the remote host machine of your choice (if you have a choice!). It's obvious why the EXE server needs to be on the host machine; it's also vital that the proxy-stub information be available so that the interfaces used by the server can be properly marshaled.

You can register the proxy-stub DLL straight away by using **regsvr32**:

```
regsvr32 ServerInfops.dll
```

You'll also need to register the EXE server. If you haven't built the EXE server with a MinDependency build, you'll need to ensure that **Atl.dll** (which contains ATL's registrar code) is available and registered on the host machine. **Atl.dll** should be in the **System** (on Windows 95) or **System32** (on Windows NT) directory. If it isn't there, copy it to the correct location from your Visual C++ product CD and register it with:

```
regsvr32 Atl.dll
```

> *Note that there are two versions of* **Atl.dll**. *For Windows NT, use the one in the* **DevStudio\Vc\Redist** *directory on the Visual C++ product CD. This is a Unicode DLL, so it won't work on Windows 95. For Windows 95, use the version in the* **DevStudio\Vc\Redist\Ansi** *directory.*

Once you're sure that **Atl.dll** is available if necessary, you can register the server by typing the following at a command prompt:

```
ServerInfo.exe /regserver
```

Now you need to make sure that the client has permission to launch and access the remote object. On the *host* machine, run **DCOMCnfg**. Double-click on the DiskInfo Class, and select Use custom access permissions from the Security tab. Next, click on the Edit button, then the Add... button, and add Everyone to the list (if you're using Windows NT) or grant access to The World (if you're using Windows 95).

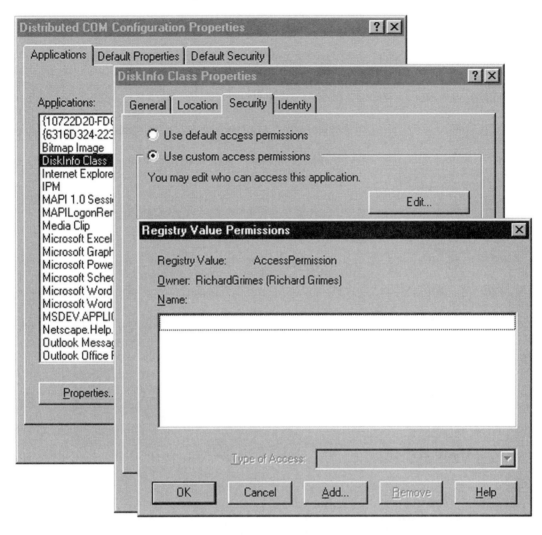

If you're using Windows NT, perform the same procedure for the launch permissions. If you're using Windows 95, you won't be able to edit launch permissions, because Windows 95 doesn't allow servers to be launched remotely. If you want a COM server to be accessed remotely, it must be launched before a client tries to connect to it.

Exceptions apart, this will allow any user account to launch and then access an object. Typically, you would be more careful in choosing users or groups to whom you would give permissions. For this example, giving access to everyone will be safe enough, unless you're overcome with paranoia at the thought of letting the world know how much free disk space you have.

The final step on the host machine is to make sure that DCOM itself is enabled by ticking the checkbox labeled Enable Distributed COM on this computer on the Default Properties page of the main **DCOMCnfg** dialog. On Windows 95, you must make sure that remote connections are enabled by checking the Enable remote connection checkbox on the Default Security page.

Now we'll turn our attention to the client machine.

First, make sure that **GetDiskSpace.exe** is available on the client machine, and that **ServerInfops.dll** is registered on that machine. Also ensure that **ServerInfo.exe** is registered on that machine — although we don't need the server EXE to be on the client machine (in fact, you can remove it as soon as it's been registered), we *do* need the AppID entry that its registration creates.

On the *client* machine, run **DCOMCnfg** and double-click the DiskInfo Class to bring up the DiskInfo Class Properties dialog, and select the Location tab. On this page, deselect Run Application on this computer and select Run application on the following computer. In the edit box, add the name of the remote computer (the screenshot shows that my remote computer is called **HERA**; you should use the name of the computer you set up as the server's host machine).

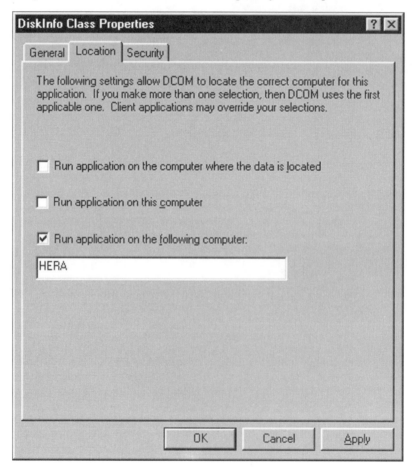

If you're using Windows NT as the server machine, that's all you need to do! Run the client application as if you want to use a local server:

```
GetDiskSpace Local
```

One thing you will notice immediately is that the client now takes much longer to run. Part of this delay is due to the security checks that ensure you can launch and access the server, while the rest is attributable to the time it takes to transmit data across the network.

If you're using Windows 95, you need to launch the server on its host machine manually (just double-click **ServerInfo.exe**) before running the client. Note that you will need to manually relaunch the server each time you want to run the client. When the client finishes and releases its reference to the **DiskInfo** object, the server will shut down, and Windows 95 won't allow you to reactivate it remotely.

When you run the client as described, you'll now be able to see the free space on the **C:** drive of the remote machine. Because you have disabled the launching of the server on the client machine, COM searches for and finds the **RemoteServerName** entry for the remote host and asks that host to run the server.

```
C:\>GetDiskSpace
There are 434995200 free bytes
C:\>GetDiskSpace Local
There are 128532480 free bytes
C:\>
```

This screenshot shows an example of what you should get. My client machine (Zeus) has 435Mb free, whereas Hera has only 129Mb free.

Before we move on to the next test, undo the changes you made on the client with **DCOMCnfg**. Check Run Application on this computer and uncheck Run application on the following computer:

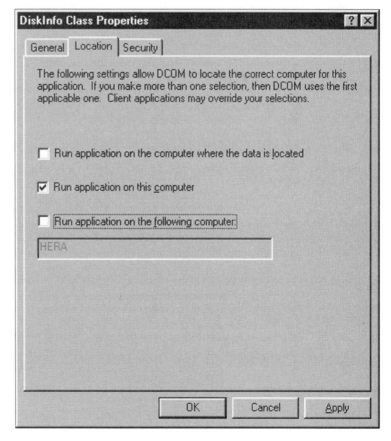

CoCreateInstanceEx

Now we're going to show how to pick the server host name programmatically. Open the **GetDiskSpace** project and edit the source file. The changes to make are shown highlighted:

```
#define _WIN32_DCOM
#include <windows.h>
#include <stdio.h>
#include <tchar.h>
#include <atlbase.h>
#include <atlimpl.cpp>

#import "..\ServerInfo.tlb"
using namespace SERVERINFOLib;

int _tmain(int argc, _TCHAR** argv)
{
   CoInitialize(NULL);

   try
   {
      HRESULT hr = S_OK;
      IDiskInfoPtr pDiskInfo;
      if (argc == 3 && argv[1][0] == _T('R'))
      {
         USES_CONVERSION;
         COSERVERINFO csi = {0, T2W(argv[2]), NULL, 0};
         MULTI_QI qi = {&__uuidof(IDiskInfo), NULL, S_OK};
         hr = CoCreateInstanceEx(__uuidof(DiskInfo), NULL,
                             CLSCTX_REMOTE_SERVER, &csi, 1, &qi);
         if (FAILED(hr))
            _com_issue_error(hr);
         IDiskInfo* pInt = static_cast<IDiskInfo*>(qi.pItf);
         pDiskInfo.Attach(pInt);
      }
      else if (argc == 2 && argv[1][0] == _T('L'))
         hr = pDiskInfo.CreateInstance(
            __uuidof(DiskInfo), NULL, CLSCTX_LOCAL_SERVER);
      else
         hr = pDiskInfo.CreateInstance(
            __uuidof(DiskInfo), NULL, CLSCTX_INPROC_SERVER);

      if (FAILED(hr))
         _com_issue_error(hr);

      hyper hypDiskSize;
      pDiskInfo->GetFreeDiskSpace(L"C:\\", &hypDiskSize);
      _tprintf(_T("There are %I64d free bytes\n"), hypDiskSize);
   }
   catch (const _com_error& e)
   {
      _tprintf(_T("There is an error (%08x): %s\n"),
         e.Error(), e.ErrorMessage());
```

```
    }

    CoUninitialize();
    return 0;
}
```

The first change is to define the **_WIN32_DCOM** symbol. This allows us to use the **CoCreateInstanceEx()** API.

The next change is the inclusion of two ATL files, **Atlbase.h** and **Atlimpl.cpp**. These files contain the definition of a text conversion macro that we make use of in the new code. The macro, **T2W()**, converts a text string (which may be ANSI or Unicode) into a wide character string that we need for the name of the server in the **COSERVERINFO** parameter to **CoCreateInstanceEx()**. If you are compiling for Unicode, this macro expands to nothing; otherwise it converts an ANSI string to Unicode. To do this, the **T2W()** macro creates a temporary buffer by using the **_alloca()** CRT function to allocate memory *on the stack*. Since the memory is allocated locally (in the function's stack frame), it is automatically freed when the function returns.

To be able to allocate memory, **T2W()** needs to know how big the buffer should be. The macro could define a code block (within braces **{}**) and a local variable, but this would restrict its use in a function's parameter list, so instead a variable needs to be declared that's local to the entire code block where the conversion macros will be used. This is done by the **USES_CONVERSION()** macro.

The new code checks for the presence of two command line parameters (the '3' value you see in the **if** statement includes the name of the EXE). The first of these parameters should be **Remote** (or any other word beginning with a capital 'R'), while the second parameter should be the name of the remote host.

We initialize the **COSERVERINFO** and **MULTI_QI** structures to pass to **CoCreateInstanceEx()** with the name of the server and the interface to return. After the call to **CoCreateInstanceEx()** (in which we specify the context of the server to be remote), we extract the interface pointer from the **pItf** member of the **MULTI_QI** structure, then attach it to the smart pointer.

Now you can build the new version of the client, and run it with the **Remote** command line argument and the name of the remote host, like this:

GetDiskSpace Remote Hera

If you have Task Manager open on the remote host, you should see **ServerInfo.exe** appear briefly in the list of processes.

```
C:\>GetDiskSpace
There are 451706880 free bytes
C:\>GetDiskSpace Local
There are 451706880 free bytes
C:\>GetDiskSpace Remote HERA
There are 128532480 free bytes
C:\>_
```

If you're running on Windows 95, don't forget to prelaunch the server!

267

Surrogate

The final test of our remote server is to show that we can remote the DLL version of the server using the system-supplied surrogate process. We don't need to write any new code for this test.

First, install the DLL server, **ServerInfo.dll**, on a remote host. Copy it to the machine and run **regsvr32** on it.

Ideally, this should be a different machine from the one you were using for the previous remote object tests. If you cannot get access to another machine then use the same one, but make sure that you unregister **ServerInfo.exe** on that machine. To test that the server has been unregistered, you can go to the client machine and run **GetDiskSpace** for a *remote* object. This should fail with the error code of **0x80040154**:

```
C:\>GetDiskSpace Remote HERA
There is an error (80040154): Class not registered

C:\>
```

If you are using a fresh host machine, make sure that you install **ServerInfops.dll** on it. The proxy-stub DLL must be registered on *all* machines that use the **IDiskInfo** interface, whether as servers or clients.

Now run the OLE/COM Object Viewer (**OleView.exe)** on the remote host. Make sure that Expert Mode is selected in the View menu. Open the All Objects tree and look for DiskInfo Class.

Select the class in the tree view and then select Implementation and Inproc Server in the right hand pane.

> *Don't click on the + when you select* DiskInfo Class. *That will create an instance of the object. If you have done this, use* Release Instance *from the* Object *menu to release the object.*

Check the Use Surrogate Process box; however, the Object Viewer will not add the **DllSurrogate** value unless it detects a change in the Path to Custom Surrogate box, so type a space in this box and then delete it. This will hook the server up to the system-supplied surrogate, **DllHost.exe**. To update the registry, click on an entry for another object.

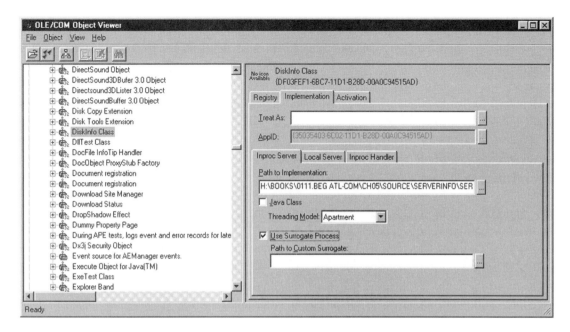

If you are running NT on the remote host, start up Task Manager and move to the Processes tab. Now on the client machine, try running **GetDiskSpace** for the remote object. While you're doing this, check Task Manager on the remote host. You will find that the call will succeed, and on the host you will see **DllHost.exe** appear momentarily in the Task Manager.

If you are running the object on Windows 95, you need to start **DllHost** with the inproc server. To do this, you need to pass the CLSID of the object as a command line parameter. Type the follwing command line into the Run box on the server machine:

```
DllHost {DF03FEF1-6BC7-11D1-B28D-00A0C94515AD}
```

If this still doesn't convince you, you can use the Visual C++ debugger as before. On the machine where you have Visual C++, open the **GetDiskSpace** project and place a breakpoint on the line that calls **GetFreeDiskSpace()**, just as you did earlier on in the chapter. Set the Program arguments to 'Local'. Since you do not have a local server for this class, COM will check the AppID for the class server for either the **LocalService** (for an NT Service) or **DllSurrogate** value.

Now when you run **GetDiskSpace** under the debugger, the execution will stop at the call to **GetFreeDiskSpace()** and you should now task switch to Process Viewer or the NT Task Manager to confirm that **DllHost.exe** is running.

Security

When a client calls `CoCreateInstanceEx()` to get access to a remote object, this may mean that another process (a local server, or a surrogate) will be launched on another machine. Think about this. If you have a server on your machine, do you want anyone to launch it whenever they like? More worrying still, if the object has access to your machine's resources (as in the case of the `DiskInfo` object), do you want just anyone to use that object? I think not.

Reassuringly, COM can apply security when launching or accessing COM objects. This applies to remote objects *and* local objects, because both are implemented in a different process from the client. However, COM security does not apply to inproc objects because they are created in, and take on, the security context of the client process.

You can apply security in two ways: declarative or programmatic. In the first case, the security settings are held as part of the object server's registry values. These values are in the AppID for the object server, and thus do not allow for security on a fine grain, per-coclass or per-object call basis. To do that, you need to apply security programmatically.

ATL effectively assumes that you will apply declarative security, in that there is currently no support for programmatic security. However, if you want to apply programmatic security you are free to do so yourself.

In this section, I will explain how to use `DCOMCnfg` to apply declarative security to an object server.

Authentication and Authorization

Authentication is a mechanism whereby a security authority determines whether a user is who they say they are. Authentication typically involves asking for a password and then comparing it with the password for the user account. NT does this using a challenge-response scheme where passwords are passed over the network in an encrypted form to prevent eavesdroppers from obtaining them.

Authentication can be carried out when a client first connects, when a method call is made, or on every packet of data passed from the client to the server machine. `DCOMCnfg` allows you to determine the default authentication level for all servers on the Default Properties tab.

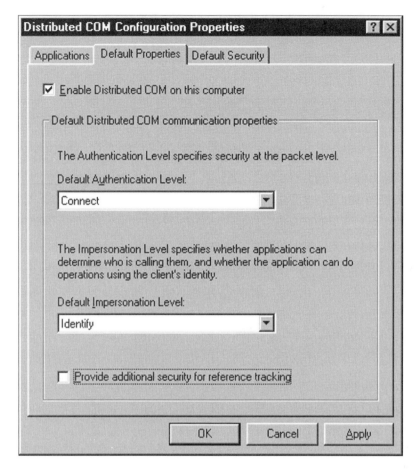

You may decide to turn off authentication entirely, but this is obviously very risky. Note that the default authentication level is applied only when there is not a server-specific value; currently the only way to apply this on a per-server level is programmatically, or by editing the registry by hand. If the client and server use two different authentication levels, the higher of the two is used.

This screenshot also shows the default *impersonation* level used by servers on this machine. The impersonation level is only available on NT. If enabled to a sufficient level, an object can get the identity of a connected client and use this identity (the server impersonates the client) to access server resources as if the object is running under that client's user account. The options are:

- Anonymous, where the client's identity is not available.
- Identify, where the object can impersonate the client only for the purposes of obtaining its identity.
- Impersonate, where the object can impersonate the client in order to access secured objects.
- Delegate, where the object can impersonate the client to call a remote object, and that object will get the security of the original client. This requires distributed security and so will only be available in NT5.

Both the client and the server can specify an impersonation level, but if these are different then the client value takes precedence.

Authorization is the process whereby a security authority checks that a user (who has been authenticated) is allowed to perform the task that they are attempting to do. COM applies authorization on two tasks: *launching* a server and *accessing* a server. Default authorization can be applied through the Default Security tab, and these values are used whenever a server does not have a list of authorized accounts. The default values are to disallow all users from launching a server, and allowing only the Administrators, the Interactive user and the System accounts to access an object in a running server.

The Interactive account is any account that is currently logged onto the local machine, and so does not apply to remote access of objects. The System account is a special account used by NT. It has complete access over the local machine, but it does not have access to remote resources. The System account is typically used by services.

Server Authorization

The Applications tab lists all the servers that have an entry in the AppID key. Despite the fact that **DCOMCnfg** provides a list of what appears to be coclasses, remember that the settings are applied to the AppID and not to a coclass. **DCOMCnfg** displays the name of the first coclass that it finds that is associated with a particular AppID, but it's unclear why it does this since a server can have several coclasses. The values that you change with **DCOMCnfg** on a server will apply to all coclasses in that server.

When you double-click on an entry, you'll get another dialog that allows you to change the security settings for that server. Let's look at the information it provides.

The General tab gives information about the server: the name of the server file, and details about whether an EXE, a service, or a surrogate will be used. You have already seen the Location tab, and it is used to set the **RemoteServerName** value. The Security tab allows you to specify the user accounts that are authorized to launch and access the server. Finally, the Identity tab sets the account that a server will use (and is discussed in the next section).

The following figure shows the Security tab for **DCOMCnfg** on NT. Since Windows 95 does not allow remote activation of servers, its Security tab just has a button to allow you to edit the custom access permissions (effectively the top third of the NT tab).

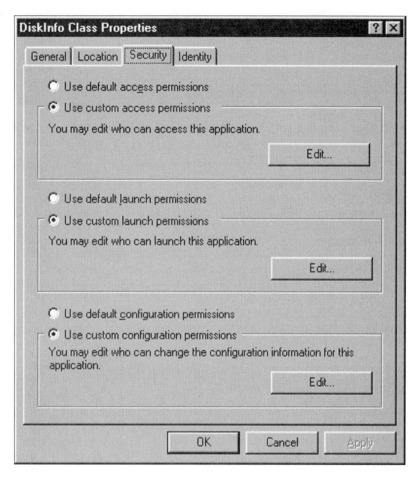

To specify who can launch a server, click on Use custom launch permissions and then on the Edit... button. This will bring up a standard NT dialog that gives the accounts and groups of accounts that can launch the server. You may edit these values to allow some users to launch the server and to deny others that right. Accounts are added from lists of accounts obtained from the local NT machine and any domains that the machine may be a member of.

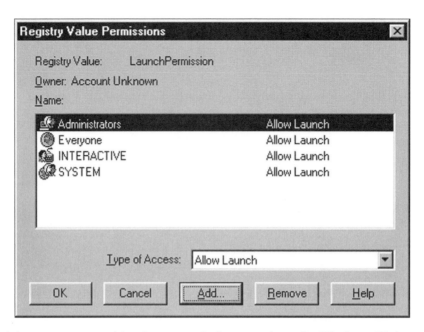

On NT, giving access to an object is a very similar procedure. On Windows 95, however, this is the only security that you can set, and you'll be presented with a list of accounts and groups from a specified security authority:

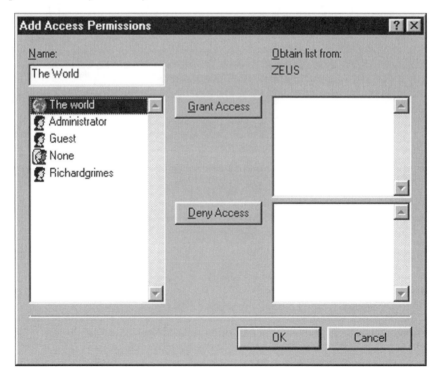

This screenshot shows the groups and users available on the NT machine **ZEUS**. You specify this security authority using the Network applet in the control panel:

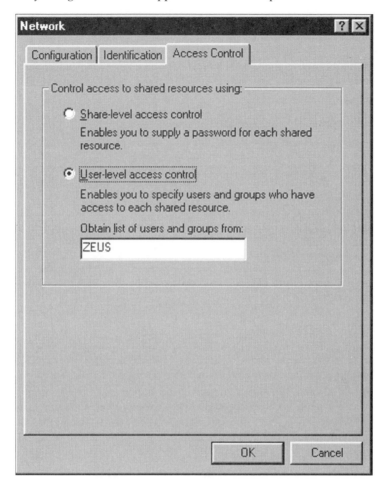

When you're developing an object, it's often convenient to give access to Everyone (NT) or The World (Windows 95), but for final system testing, and in production code, you should use an appropriate account or group.

Identity

The final tab in the NT version of **DCOMCnfg** (not available in the Windows 95 version) is the Identity tab. This specifies the account that will be used when the server is launched. There are four options here: interactive user, launching user, this user and System. The final option is only available for COM servers implemented in a service.

When a user logs on to an NT machine (either locally or over a network), NT creates a secured object called a WinStation. This holds the desktop for that user, so if the user launches a process on the remote machine, and this process has a user interface, the UI will appear in the desktop of the WinStation of the user. Obviously, only the desktop of the interactive user is visible on the monitor. This is a particular problem if the process creates a modal dialog, because if this process is running in a desktop other than the interactive user's, the dialog will not be visible and no one will be able to dismiss it, effectively blocking that particular thread of the process. (There are ways to get modal dialogs shown on the interactive desktop, but generally it is a bad idea to use them.) Let's look at how the identity helps this situation.

If you use **DCOMCnfg** to specify that the server runs as the interactive user, this means that it will take on the security of the user who's currently logged on, and use the interactive WinStation. If any objects created by the server need access to secured objects on the host machine, it will use the interactive user's security (although the object developer can change this by using impersonation). Since the server will use the interactive WinStation, it means that any UI *will* be visible on the host machine's desktop.

The problem with this identity, however, is that there must be a user logged onto the host machine. This will not be the best choice in many situations, since it is clearly a security risk to leave a machine unattended with a user logged on — anyone with physical access to that machine will be able to use it.

If there is no logged-on user, you can still access a server if it uses the identity of the launching user. In this case, the host machine will create a WinStation for the user, and this WinStation will not have a visible desktop. Now the server will have the security of the client that launched it and so (as long as the object does not decide to impersonate another user) this security will be used whenever the object attempts to access a secured NT object. However, WinStations are quite expensive in terms of system resources, so you will be restricted in the number of clients that can connect.

> *Secured NT objects are things like files (if you are using NTFS), registry keys, processes, threads and synchronization objects like events, semaphores and mutexes.*

Finally, we come to This user. This option allows you to specify a particular user that will be used whenever the server is launched. The advantage of this approach is that only one WinStation will be created, and thus resources are conserved. It also simplifies security administration, since if the object uses secured NT objects you only need to allow access to these objects from this single account.

Debugging Local Objects

Now that we've seen how COM objects can communicate across process boundaries, how can you debug local servers when they go wrong?

In fact, this is fairly easy to do. One way is to set break points in your server and set it running. When a local server process starts, it registers its class objects and then goes into a loop waiting to be told to die. When a client gets an object and calls its methods, the breakpoints will be hit.

Another way to debug a local server is to step from the client into the server code using the debugger. If you have OLE RPC Debugging selected (Tools | Options..., Debug tab), then when you step into a method call on a local object, Developer Studio will run the local object under the debugger and if necessary start a new copy of Developer Studio. Of course, for this to work best, the registered server must be the debug version.

While single stepping like this, you may find that when you get access to the object, the debugger has placed you somewhere in the murky depths of **OLE32.DLL**. Don't worry, just single-step a few times and eventually you will step into your object code and Developer Studio will bring up the C++ source. Similarly, once an object method has finished, if you single step past the **return** statement you will end up stepping through **OLE32.dll** again. At this point it is best just to press *F5* and wait for a breakpoint to be hit in the client.

Threading

Threading is a complicated topic. In this section, we aim only to give you a quick overview of the issues related to COM threading. This is certainly not intended as an exhaustive treatment of the subject.

We'll start by examining one of the most important concepts of COM threading, **apartments**, before taking a quick look at the requirements that different types of apartment place upon the developer.

Apartments

An **apartment** is a conceptual unit that contains one or more threads running in the same process. There are (currently) two types of apartment: **single-threaded apartments** (**STAs**) and **multi-threaded apartments** (**MTAs**).

Single-threaded apartments only ever contain a single thread. That thread initializes itself in an STA by calling **CoInitialize(NULL)** or **CoInitializeEx(NULL, COINIT_APARTMENT_THREADED)**. (These calls are identical, since **CoInitialize()** just calls **CoInitializeEx()**.) There can be zero or many STAs in a single process.

Multi-threaded apartments can contain one or more threads. Each thread must initialize itself in the MTA by calling **CoInitializeEx(NULL, COINIT_MULTITHREADED)**. There can only be zero or one MTAs in a single process.

> *You may see multi-threaded apartments referred to as 'free-threaded apartments', but this term has largely fallen out of use.*

COM calls that are made across apartment boundaries need marshaling, and interface pointers from one apartment won't work in another apartment unless they are marshaled first.

This marshaling is designed to protect code that has been written with one threading model from being called by code that has been written with an incompatible threading model. In other words, the act of initializing a thread to live in an STA prevents multiple threads from simultaneously accessing objects in that apartment/thread. This means that the code running in an STA does not need to be written to be thread-safe. The act of initializing a thread to live in the MTA allows multiple simultaneous access, so in this case, the code must be thread-safe.

> *Now you can see why DLL servers need marshaling code too. The possibility of inter-apartment marshaling means that you need to supply marshaling code (proxy-stub DLL or type library) no matter how your components are packaged.*

Here you can see a diagram showing some of the interactions between threads and apartments. You can see that there is one MTA and many STAs in this example, and that marshaling is used for calls between threads, except where both threads are part of the MTA.

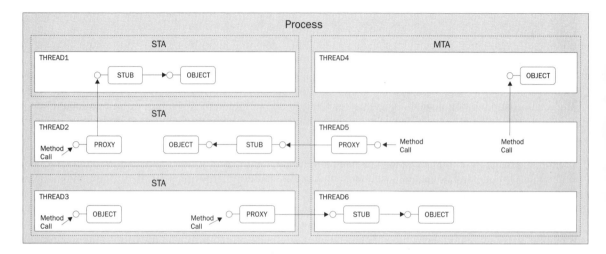

STAs and Message Pumps

When an object is run in an STA, access from multiple threads must be synchronized to prevent corruption of the object's state. The developer can feel reassured that the object's state will be protected from multi-threaded access, because no other thread has direct access to the object. All other threads must communicate with the object through a proxy-stub. It's up to COM and the marshaling code to provide synchronization, which is done using the STA's Windows message queue. When a method request is made, a message is posted to the message queue. Since the messages are read and dispatched from the queue one at a time, this ensures that access to an object is from a single thread at any one time.

The corollary of this is that each STA must have a message pump.

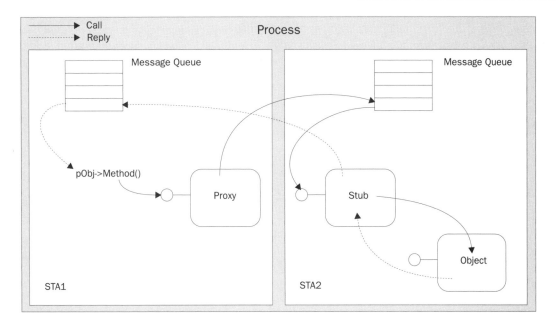

MTAs and Thread Safety

When an object is running in an MTA, any other thread in the MTA can access it directly; because of this, any internal state of the object must be protected from concurrent access, and all methods must be reentrant. This protection must be provided by the creator of the object.

Writing thread-safe code is quite a subtle business, but at the very least, the reference count must be changed with **InterlockedIncrement()** and **InterlockedDecrement()**, rather than the C++ **++** or **--** operators, which may be preempted by another thread before the operation has completed.

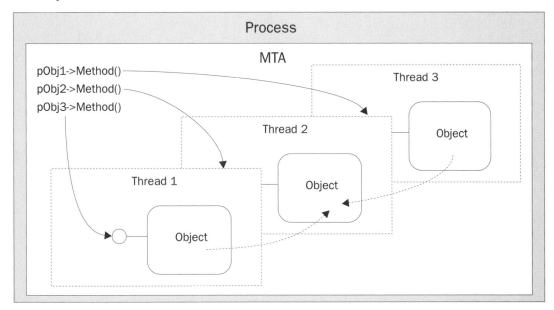

The advantage of this direct access is that well written thread-safe code running in an MTA should be faster than the equivalent code in an STA, since it gets round the potential bottleneck of the Windows message queue we're forced to use in the case of STAs. However, it does put the onus on the developer to make sure that object state access is thread safe, and that methods are reentrant.

Threading and Inproc Servers

In-process servers do not call **CoInitializeEx()** because the COM libraries will already have been initialized before the server is loaded. There is obviously a potential conflict here: what if a client thread is part of an MTA, and it attempts to create an in-process object that is written to run in an STA? Without some extra mechanism, a non-thread-safe object could be created in an MTA.

To avoid such problems, COM requires in-process components to register their threading model in the registry. COM will use this information to ensure that the component is created in an appropriate apartment.

In this case, COM will create a new STA thread in the client process and run the object there. The client thread will be in a different apartment, so the access will require a proxy. Since an STA is used, synchronization will be applied.

COM knows what threading model the object uses by checking a named value in the CLSID key of the object's coclass. This value, **ThreadingModel**, takes one of four values: **Single** (which is equivalent to the value being missing), **Apartment**, **Free**, or **Both**.

Single means that the object knows nothing at all about threads; this is the case for COM objects that were written before the new threading models were introduced. The object will be run in the main STA of the process (the main STA is the first STA that is created) — if necessary, COM will create an STA if one has not already been created.

Apartment means that the object can run in any STA in a process (not just the main STA).

Both means that the object can run in either an STA or an MTA, which implies that all methods are reentrant and object state is protected from concurrent access. Such an object is designed to run in an MTA, but it will work fine in an STA. Although there will be more synchronization code than necessary when such an object runs in an STA (the message loop, and the object's own synchronization code), this won't degrade performance greatly. The STA synchronization will ensure that two threads can never access the object at one time, so the object's synchronization code will have little effect.

Free means that the object should only run in an MTA, and is used to indicate that the object will create and use worker threads. Doing this indicates to COM that efficient execution of the object will only happen if the object is created in an MTA. If the object is created in an STA (which would be possible if it was marked as **Both**), then as the worker threads are created and enter an MTA (with a call to **CoInitializeEx()**), access to the object will be through a proxy loaded by COM, degrading performance. When an object is marked as **Free**, the client *must* create the object in an MTA, which ensures that the worker threads have direct access to the object. The client, on the other hand, may be in a different apartment and thus require access through a proxy.

Generally, an object that uses worker threads should be marked as **Free** to enable direct access between object and workers. However, if the client makes more calls to the object than the object makes to the worker threads (or the threads to the object), it may be more efficient to mark the object as **Both** so that the client has direct access to the object.

If the client apartment is incompatible with the threading model of the object COM will silently create a proxy to do the cross-apartment access. In the following table, you can see the threading model of the object and the client apartment that called **CoCreateInstance()** to create the object. The values in the table indicate whether the client has direct access or whether a proxy is used.

		Object Threading Model			
		Single	Apartment	Both	Free
	Main STA	Direct	Direct	Direct	Proxy
Client Apartment	**STA**	Proxy	Direct	Direct	Proxy
	MTA	Proxy	Proxy	Direct	Direct

ATL and Threading Models

Let's look at the ways that threading interacts directly with ATL code. The first and most obvious way is the Threading Model frame of the Attributes tab provided by the Object Wizard. When you create a new class, you have the choice of setting the threading model to one of four values.

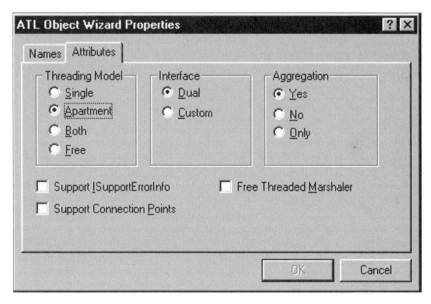

The value that you choose has two main effects: it sets the threading model class used as the template parameter to **CComObjectRootEx<>**, and (for DLL servers only) it sets the **ThreadingModel** registry entry in the RGS file.

CComObjectRootEx<> is the base class used to handle the **IUnknown** methods of your generated class and is therefore responsible for reference counting. If you pick Single or Apartment, **CComObjectRootEx<CComSingleThreadModel>** is used as the base class. If you pick Both or Free, **CComObjectRootEx<CComMultiThreadModel>** is used.

CComSingleThreadModel is used to implement **AddRef()** and **Release()** using the C++ **++** and **--** operators. The **CComMultiThreadModel** class ensures that **AddRef()** and **Release()** are implemented using **InterlockedIncrement()** and **InterlockedDecrement()**, thus preventing concurrent access to the reference count when it is being changed.

For DLL servers, a **ThreadingModel** value is also added to the object's **CLSID** key in the generated RGS file, with the appropriate data value (except in the case of Single, in which case, the **ThreadingModel** entry is omitted).

Initializing COM

The **ThreadingModel** registry entry is all that the objects in a DLL need to ensure that they get created in the right sort of apartment. COM will either load them into the apartment of the client, if it's compatible with the threading model, or a different apartment if it's not.

EXE servers, on the other hand, are responsible for creating their own apartments. By default, ATL EXE servers consist of a single thread (and therefore a single apartment), and all the objects are created on this thread. The AppWizard initializes this thread to live in an STA, in the **_tWinMain()** function, but you can follow the directions given in the comments (i.e. use **CoInitializeEx()**) to create your objects in an MTA.

```
extern "C" int WINAPI _tWinMain(HINSTANCE hInstance,
    HINSTANCE /*hPrevInstance*/, LPTSTR lpCmdLine, int /*nShowCmd*/)
{
    lpCmdLine = GetCommandLine(); //this line necessary for _ATL_MIN_CRT
    HRESULT hRes = CoInitialize(NULL);
//  If you are running on NT 4.0 or higher you can use the following call
//   instead to make the EXE free threaded.
//  This means that calls come in on a random RPC thread
//   HRESULT hRes = CoInitializeEx(NULL, COINIT_MULTITHREADED);
```

*Note that you cannot remove the message loop from_ **_tWinMain()** *even if you do convert the EXE to run in an MTA. Although the message pump is not used for synchronization (as it would be when running in an STA), it is still used to close down the server when all objects are released.*

The Global Threading Model

The global threading model for an ATL project is defined in **StdAfx.h** by one of the following symbols:

> **_ATL_SINGLE_THREADED**
>
> **_ATL_APARTMENT_THREADED**
>
> **_ATL_FREE_THREADED**

The default is **_ATL_APARTMENT_THREADED**.

These symbols are used to **typedef** one of the threading model classes
(**CComSingleThreadModel** or **CComMultiThreadModel**) to **CComObjectThreadModel** and
CComGlobalsThreadModel, as you can see from this code taken from **Atlbase.h**.

```
#if defined(_ATL_SINGLE_THREADED)
    typedef CComSingleThreadModel CComObjectThreadModel;
    typedef CComSingleThreadModel CComGlobalsThreadModel;
#elif defined(_ATL_APARTMENT_THREADED)
    typedef CComSingleThreadModel CComObjectThreadModel;
    typedef CComMultiThreadModel CComGlobalsThreadModel;
#else
    typedef CComMultiThreadModel CComObjectThreadModel;
    typedef CComMultiThreadModel CComGlobalsThreadModel;
#endif
```

We can ignore **CComObjectThreadModel**, because this **typedef** is only used for compatibility
with ATL 1.1 code, but **CComGlobalsThreadModel** is more important since it controls the
increment and decrement method used for both the lock count and reference counts of the
module and the class factories in your project. The default global threading model results in
thread-safe code, so you don't actually need to worry about this, but now you know precisely
what that **#define** in **StdAfx.h** means.

Manual Marshaling

There are times when it is necessary to manually marshal interface pointers. Whenever you want
to pass an interface pointer from one thread to another across an apartment boundary without
doing it via a COM method call, you'll need to marshal that pointer yourself. For example, you
may have two threads, each in a different STA, and each with an (already created) object. You'll
need to manually marshal the interface pointers if one object is to get access to the other.

There are a couple of ways to marshal an interface pointer across apartments. One way requires
the use of the **CoMarshalInterThreadInterfaceInStream()**, and
CoGetInterfaceAndReleaseStream() functions, but this is pretty complicated. The second
way is much simpler, and uses an object called the Global Interface Table (GIT), but this is only
available on NT with service pack 3.

This kind of manual marshaling is beyond the scope of this book. You'll only need to find out
about manually marshaling interfaces if you're creating multithreaded servers. We'll limit our
discussions to single-threaded servers for this book.

In general, you can lead a trouble-free life, by sticking to the apartment threading options that
ATL uses by default. Your code will be reasonably efficient and you don't need to worry about
making it thread-safe, because ATL and COM handle that for you.

Summary

This chapter has introduced you to local COM and remote DCOM objects. It has demonstrated to you that remote objects are just local objects on another machine, and that making them remote is either an administrative task performed with a tool like **DCOMCnfg** or **OLEView**, or a programmatic task that the client can perform with **CoCreateInstanceEx()**.

We introduced you to surrogate processes (in particular the system-provided **DllHost.exe**), and led you through an example to allow an inproc object to be activated on a remote host.

You've also seen how to adjust an ATL project to use a common source to produce both DLL and EXE versions of a component.

Finally, you gained just enough insight into security and threading to allow you to follow those paths further if you choose.

Connectable Objects

The term **ActiveX control** actually means any COM object that has the **IUnknown** interface and is self-registering. A **full control**, on the other hand, implements many interfaces to enable it to interact with the user and the program in which it is shown. Full controls are inproc objects, and as such they can only be created as part of another process. Such a process is called a **container** and examples of these are Internet Explorer, Word97, and applications created with Visual Basic 5.0.

What makes a process a control container? Well, it must understand the standard interfaces that a full control implements (**IOleControl** etc), and it must also implement COM interfaces that allow a contained control to inform the container when some event occurs in the control (the control's data changes, or maybe a user clicks on the control). This implies that the communication between the control and the container is two-way. The control is **connected** to the container.

However, the process can be quite complicated, since the container may make several connections to a single control, or even to several controls, and so there must be a way to manage all these connections. This is the reason for **connection points**, and this chapter is the first of three that will lead you to the goal of creating a full control yourself.

Connection Points and Connectable Objects

At this point, you have learned how to create a COM object without a user interface that can be created in-process, in another process, or on another machine. You have also seen how to apply the **IDispatch** interface so that scripting languages like VBScript can access a COM object. However, one of the great things about COM is that you can create objects that have a user interface, allowing them to react to user interaction. These objects are called **controls**.

A History of Controls

First, let's set the scene with a little history. 'Control' is a label that has been applied to a number of different things as technologies have changed, so having some kind of perspective is no bad thing. Windows has always had controls; most of the interaction you have with applications is through controls, particularly when you're using applications that employ dialogs or forms. The Windows Common Controls include simple controls like edit boxes, list boxes and buttons, and more complicated controls such as the list and tree controls that are used in Windows Explorer.

These are all visible controls, characterized by the fact that they have a window. They need to have a window because they have to react to user actions, and to provide notifications. When you click on a button, for example, the button changes its appearance to make it look as if it has been depressed — this is the control reacting to user input. However, the button must do more than just *look* as if it has been pushed; it must inform the application that the user has clicked it, and it does this with a **notification**.

All of these operations are done with Windows messages. When you left-click on a button, its window gets a **WM_LBUTTONDOWN** followed by a **WM_LBUTTONUP**, telling it that the user has clicked the mouse on it. To handle these messages, the button needs to have a **Windows procedure**, in which it can test for the button-down/button-up sequence and perform the change of appearance. In addition, since the button knows the parent window handle of the process in which it is being used, it can tell its parent that it has been clicked by sending it a **BN_CLICKED** notification as part of a **WM_COMMAND** message.

These are controls at their most basic: if the parent window wants the control to do something, it has to send the control a message — there is no equivalent of a COM method call. If the control holds some data and the parent window wants to access that data, it has to send a message to tell the control to change the data or return it — without COM method calls, what else is there to do? As a developer, you have to manage all these messages and notifications. Furthermore, the model is not very extensible, as there is no standard way that a parent window can ask a control what it can do — whether it is capable of sending notification messages like **BN_CLICKED**, for example. Also, since the notifications are handled through Windows messages, it means that the parent window developer must program in a language that provides access to the Windows procedure. A language that hides the Windows procedure prevents the handling of these notifications.

To get round these problems, Microsoft introduced Visual Basic eXtension controls (**VBXs**) in Visual Basic 3.0. VBXs were DLLs that could contain more than one control, and each of these could have properties and methods, just like you can have on a COM object today. Through a convoluted mechanism, VB hooked the VBX notifications into a VB form's Windows procedure and exposed the notifications as VB events. A VBX container (usually your VB3 project) could read and write control properties, and call control methods. This was a great boon, because the VB programmer could write some code that would be called when, for example, a control was clicked. Because VB had its own notification mechanism, he didn't have to worry about implementing a Windows procedure or handling Windows messages.

However, there were several problems with VBXs. First of all, they were firmly fixed to the 16-bit Windows architecture, and it was not possible to write 32-bit VBXs. Second, although VBX controls could implement methods, they could only be chosen from a range of *eight* standard methods, which was extremely restrictive. The only way to get round this was to define an **Action** property that would direct the control to perform a custom method; an ugly compromise. Thirdly, the model for generating events was inflexible.

Then came COM. This allowed controls to have properties and methods, and type libraries allowed a control to say what properties and methods it supported. A tool like VB can query a control to find out what it can do, and then present the developer with a list of the properties and methods that they can work with. However, properties and methods provide only a one-way communication, from the container to the control. To achieve two-way communication, the control must also be able to talk to the container.

To standardize their burgeoning technologies, Microsoft produced the OCX specification. OCXs are inproc Automation objects, and therefore have properties and methods that are described by a type library. In addition to the controls themselves, the specification also describes OCX containers. These too are COM objects, and so a control can call methods on a container. Typically, this happens when an event occurs in the control and it wants to inform the container about it.

If a control has properties (which could be simple data like the background color, or the font used to draw text), then implementing controls as Automation objects makes it easy for a tool to change these properties at design time in response to actions from the VB developer. However, when the developer saves a form or compiles the application, VB must be able to save all these property values in one go. The specification indicated how this should be done, using **persistence interfaces** and **property sets**. Of course, if a member of a property set changes, the container will want to know about it. The specification defined a mechanism whereby the control could inform the container.

It's not hard to see that there's a lot of communication going on here, and since there may be more than a single channel of communication, this two-way conversation has to be managed. For example, there may be two or more places in the container that require notifications when a single property changes, or a control could provide notifications of many different types. To manage all these notifications, Microsoft provided **connection points**, the subject of this chapter.

Callbacks

Callbacks are a technique used extensively in 16- and 32-bit Windows. They improve on a message-based notification mechanism because they involve passing the address of a handler function to a function that provides notifications. This notifying function then 'calls back' through this handler function pointer when it needs to inform it of some event or change of data. The great advantage of using a function instead of a message is that it can take typed parameters, so the notifying function can pass data to the handler specific to the event that has occurred. Although you can do this with a Windows message, it is cumbersome because the parameters to Windows messages are typeless.

As a Windows programmer, you will be most familiar with using callbacks when registering a window class, where the address of the Windows procedure is passed (via the **WNDCLASS** structure) to **RegisterClass()**. When you've created a window of this class, Windows will call the Windows procedure any time you dispatch messages (obtained from the message queue) with **DispatchMessage()**. Another example of a callback is when you want to enumerate Windows objects — the windows on the desktop, for example. To do this, you call **EnumWindows()** passing the address of a callback function. Windows will then call this function for every window it can find.

These callbacks have two important characteristics. The first is that the callback address is the address of a single function, and the second is that in 32-bit Windows, the function accepting the callback address must be implemented in process (most likely in a DLL) — otherwise, the callback address will be invalid.

289

COM both extends and restricts this idea. You have already seen that COM marshaling allows an interface pointer in one process to be used in another process — this improves on Windows callbacks, because it means that callbacks can be made cross process. However, marshaling also applies a restriction (albeit a small one): marshaling can only be done on an interface, and not just on a single method. Callbacks in COM require the process requiring a notification to implement an interface and then pass a pointer to it to the notifying object. This interface may have just a single method, or it could have many methods to handle many different events.

Incoming and Outgoing Interfaces

The COM terms for callback interfaces can be a little confusing, so I shall try and explain them. An interface that's designed to be used as a callback is called a **sink interface**, because it *sinks* event notifications. Sink interfaces are one type of **incoming interface**; these are interfaces containing methods that are called by clients, and so the calls are 'coming in' to the server. All the interfaces you have come across so far have been incoming interfaces.

For a COM object to notify another object of an event, it must make calls on the other COM object's sink interfaces. To enable this, the client wanting the notifications must pass its sink interface pointer to the object generating the events. This leaves the client in a bit of a dilemma: does the server know about its sink interface? After all, the pointer it will pass will be an **IUnknown** pointer, so how can a client be sure that an object will know about the particular sink interface it should **QI()** for?

The server object supports connections to sink interfaces by implementing **connection points**, and it indicates the connection points it has by exposing the **IConnectionPointContainer** interface. The client can **QI()** for this interface to see if the object supports connection points, and then call a method on this interface to determine if a connection point exists for the specific sink interface. In addition to this, the server object designer lists the sink interfaces that it will call through the connection point mechanism as **outgoing interfaces** in the object's IDL. This is done by using the **[source]** attribute: the server object is indicating that the interface is a *source* of events, and that another object can implement the interface to *sink* the notifications.

This picture explains the terminology:

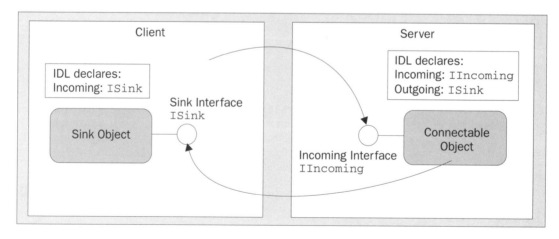

In this picture, the 'connectable object' uses connection points to manage connections between the server and client. The client implements a sink object, **QI()**s for **IConnectionPointContainer**, and then asks for the connection point object for the particular sink interface. The client passes the sink interface pointer to the connection point object to make the connection; it can then continue to call methods on the object's incoming interface. However, at some point the connectable object will need to callback on the client, which it does by looking up the right connection point object and accessing it for the client's sink interface pointer. At some later stage, the client may decide that it no longer needs notifications, and so it can get access to the connection point object again, this time to tell it to stop providing notifications.

Connection Topologies

All the details of how the client obtains connection point objects and tells the object that it wants (or doesn't want) notifications are given in the next section, but first let's look at the different ways of connecting clients and objects through connection points.

The example above demonstrated a one-to-one relationship — a single client connection to a single object — but this may not be the model that the designer requires. For example, there may be many clients (or many places in a single client's code) that will want to be informed by a single connectable object when an event occurs (many-to-one); or a single client could pass its sink interface to get notifications from many connectable objects (one-to-many).

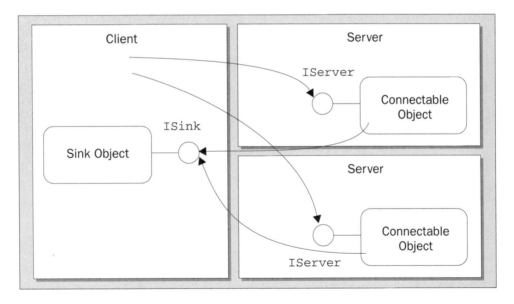

The above diagram shows the one-to-many case: the client has a single sink object, and it passes the sink interface pointer to two connectable objects, so that notifications from both objects are handled by the same client code. An example of this is a client that has two buttons on a form: the client sink object is used to handle click events, so when the user clicks on either button, it is handled by the same method in the client.

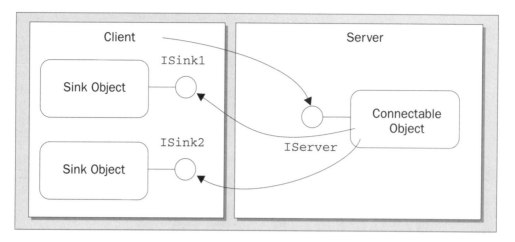

This picture shows the many-to-one case. Here, a single object may support callbacks to many different sink interfaces. The client in the picture has created two different sink objects, each with a different sink interface. An example of this would be a control that informs the client on one outgoing interface when the control is clicked, and on another when its internal state changes. To support this, the connectable object will have to support (at least) two different outgoing interfaces.

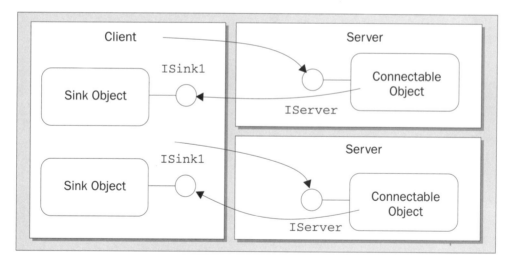

This third topology is a combination of the first two, and shows the client creating more than one sink object, with each implementing the *same* sink interface. The client passes these to different connectable objects, and so the notifications from the objects will be handled differently by the client.

As you can see, there is plenty of flexibility in how clients and objects can connect. These different topologies are difficult to maintain, and the mechanism is rationalized using **connection point objects**.

Connection Points

For each outgoing interface that the connectable object supports, the object should implement a connection point object. This object is used to maintain an array of the client sink interfaces for the clients that are connected. So, if the connectable object can callback to (say) the **ISink** interface, then it will have a connection point object specifically for this outgoing interface. Whenever a client that has a sink object that supports the **ISink** interface makes a connection to the connectable object, it does so by registering itself with the appropriate connection point object. Now when the connectable object generates an event that is handled by the **ISink** interface, it can use the connection point object to get access to all of the connected clients and then fire the event.

Connection point objects expose the **IConnectionPoint** interface. Of its five methods, three are of particular interest to us here. The **Advise()** and **Unadvise()** methods are used by clients to register their sink interfaces with the connectable object: when a client calls **Advise()**, the connection point object will add the sink interface pointer to its list of interface pointers. When the connectable object needs to notify the connected clients, it should obtain the appropriate connection point object and then use its **EnumConnections()** method to get an enumeration object through which it can access all these client sink interfaces. The connectable object should then iterate through these interfaces and call the appropriate method.

The **EnumConnections()** method returns a pointer to an **IEnumConnections** interface. This interface enumerates the current connections for a connectable object in **CONNECTDATA** structures — you can call the **Next()** method to get back an array of **CONNECTDATA** structures. **CONNECTDATA** looks like this:

```
typedef struct tagCONNECTDATA
{
    IUnknown*  pUnk;
    DWORD      dwCookie;
} CONNECTDATA;
```

The **pUnk** is the client sink interface, and **dwCookie** is a unique identifier for this interface pointer. When the client calls **Advise()** on the connection point object, the latter should create a new **CONNECTDATA** structure filled with the sink interface pointer, and add it to its internal array of sink interfaces. The connection point object should then return the **dwCookie** back to the client through the **[out]** parameter of A**dvise()** with the same name. The client should hold on to this cookie so that it can identify the interface when it decides it no longer wants to receive notifications and calls **Unadvise()**.

Notice how the connection point object receives a sink interface pointer (for example **ISink**), but saves it internally as an **IUnknown** pointer. It needs to do this so that it can implement the enumerator object (which we shall cover in the next chapter). When the connection point object saves the sink interface, it upcasts to get the **IUnknown** pointer. This means that the pointer still points to the sink interface, but that only the **IUnknown** methods can be called through it.

When the object wants to notify the client and obtains a **CONNECTDATA** structure for it, it will need to downcast the **pUnk** back to the sink interface, so that it can call the appropriate method. This is perfectly fine, even for sink interfaces on clients that are out of process, since the upcasting does not change the pointer: it merely slices off the methods not described by the upcast interface. The downcast restores access to those methods.

Interface pointers in **CONNECTDATA** are held typeless, but connection point objects are typed — that is, they are specific to a particular outgoing interface. The IID of the connection point's outgoing interface can be obtained by calling **GetConnectionInterface()**.

Connection Point Container

As we've already discussed, a connectable object can fire events to more than one outgoing interface. Each outgoing interface is handled by a connection point object, and to maintain all these connection point objects, the connectable object has a single connection point container. Connection point container objects expose the **IConnectionPointContainer** interface, which has two methods. The first, **FindConnectionPoint()**, allows a client to ask the connectable object for an interface pointer to the connection point object that is managing events for a particular outgoing interface: the method takes a parameter that is the IID of the client's sink interface. The other method is called **EnumConnectionPoints()**, and this returns an interface pointer to an enumeration object that a client can use to iterate through all the connection point objects that exist in the container.

The following diagram shows the relationship between the connectable object, the connection point container and the connection point objects:

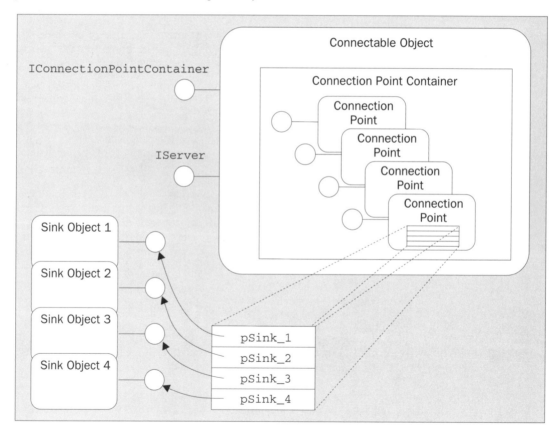

If a client wants to determine whether an object supports connections, it should first **QueryInterface()** for the **IConnectionPointContainer** interface. If a valid pointer is returned, the client knows that the object is connectable.

To determine whether the connectable object supports connections to a *particular* outgoing interface, the client has two choices. The first option is to iterate though all the connection point objects using the enumerator object obtained by calling **EnumConnectionPoints()** on the container, and then on each connection point object it can call **GetConnectionInterface()** to get the IID of the outgoing interface. The second option is to call **FindConnectionPoint()** on the container, passing the IID of the sink interface to see if there is a connection point for this as an outgoing interface.

ATL and Connection Points

The last diagram showed that the connection point container object and the server object are one and the same thing, in which case it's the server object that needs to implement the **IConnectionPointContainer** interface. ATL provides a default implementation of this interface with the **IConnectionPointContainerImpl<>** template. The single parameter of the template is the ATL class for the connectable object. For your ATL object to implement this interface it must derive from this template and, of course, the **IConnectionPointContainer** interface must be added to the COM map.

A connection point container object must have access to the connection point objects that it supports, and ATL does this through a **connection point map**. This map is declared in your ATL class, and is the reason why your class is a parameter of the container template — normally in C++, a base class can only have access to a member in a derived class if the member is declared in the base class. However, for data members this would mean that every instance of the derived class would have a copy of this data. This is unnecessary for the connection point map, because a single connection point object should handle *all* connections to a particular outgoing interface. The map should be static — in other words, there should be just one copy for all instances of the derived class. Passing the derived class as a parameter of the template gives the **IConnectionPointContainerImpl<>** template access to this static member.

The connection point map is declared using the macros:

```
BEGIN_CONNECTION_POINT_MAP()
END_CONNECTION_POINT_MAP()
```

The first macro takes the ATL class as its only parameter. Connection point objects are added to the map using the **CONNECTION_POINT_ENTRY()** macro, which takes the IID of the outgoing interface that the connection point object supports.

If, for example, the **CEvents** class supports connections to the outgoing **IEventSink** interface, it must derive from **IConnectionPointContainerImpl<CEvents>**, and the connection point map is implemented like this:

```
BEGIN_CONNECTION_POINT_MAP(CEvents)
   CONNECTION_POINT_ENTRY(IID_IEventSink)
END_CONNECTION_POINT_MAP()
```

Before we move on to the main example in this chapter, let's create a lightweight application that consolidates what we've seen so far. In Developer Studio, create a new ATL COM AppWizard project called Clicker, accepting all the default options.

From the Insert menu, select New ATL Object..., Controls, and then Full Control. After clicking on Next >, give the object the Short Name of ClickIt; on the Attributes tab, make sure that Support Connection Points is checked.

Our control will respond to mouse clicks by firing an event in its container. Message maps will be explained fully in Chapter 8, so for now just change the code by adding a handler for the **WM_LBUTTONDOWN** message, and trust me! Open the **ClickIt.h** file and add this line to the message map:

```
BEGIN_MSG_MAP(CClickIt)
    MESSAGE_HANDLER(WM_PAINT, OnPaint)
    MESSAGE_HANDLER(WM_SETFOCUS, OnSetFocus)
    MESSAGE_HANDLER(WM_KILLFOCUS, OnKillFocus)
    MESSAGE_HANDLER(WM_LBUTTONDOWN, OnClick)
END_MSG_MAP()
```

Add the declaration of the message handler:

```
// IClickIt
public:
    HRESULT OnDraw(ATL_DRAWINFO& di);
    LRESULT OnClick(UINT uMsg, WPARAM wParam, LPARAM lParam,
                                              BOOL& bHandled);
```

Now open **ClickIt.cpp** and add the implementation of the handler:

```
LRESULT CClickIt::OnClick(UINT uMsg, WPARAM wParam,
                                LPARAM lParam, BOOL& bHandled)
{
    ::MessageBox(NULL, _T("Handled in control"), _T("ClickIt"), MB_OK);
    return 0;
}
```

All this does is handle the user clicking on the control by producing a message box. Compile the control.

The next thing to do is create a simple VB project to test the control. Start VB and select a Standard EXE project, then from the Project menu select Components... and check Clicker 1.0 Type Library. This will add an icon to the toolbox, so double click on it to add the **ClickIt** control to the form. You will see something like this (remember, you have added no drawing code, so the image you see is the default provide by the Object Wizard):

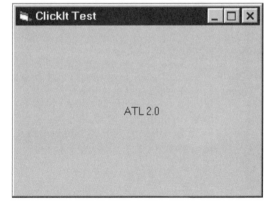

Now run the project and click in the middle of the form. You will get the following dialog:

As the text suggests, the click event has been caught and handled in the control; you did not add any code to the VB form to handle the event. To illustrate our discussion, we need to change the control to generate events. There are three steps: you need to change the IDL to declare the outgoing interface, you need to add support for a connection point container, and you need to generate the event. These are carried out in the following sections.

Adding an Outgoing Interface

When you add an outgoing interface to an object, you need to start with an existing interface. There are two ways to do this: either you can declare the interface in the object's IDL, or you can declare it in the IDL of the client and refer to that IDL through either a **#import** or **#importlib** statement. We will look at both possibilities in this chapter.

The **ClickIt** object will use VB as a client, but the obvious problem here is that when you create a VB application, you do not have any IDL for the project. How then can you declare the sink interface?

If the connectable object is written in VB5, it can use the **Event** keyword to declare a method that will be called when an event is generated. However, we're *not* using VB for the connectable object, so we'll have to declare the sink interface in the object's IDL. Open **Clicker.idl** and add a new dispinterface:

```
library CLICKERLib
{
    importlib("stdole32.tlb");
    importlib("stdole2.tlb");


    [
        uuid(B0E1CEB0-778E-11D1-9A76-0060973044A8)
    ]
    dispinterface IClickEvent
    {
        properties:
        methods:
    };
```

Here, the IID has been generated with the GUID generator. A dispinterface is used because although VB does not implement **IClickEvent**, it most certainly does implement **IDispatch**. Declaring a dispinterface in the object's type library means that VB can read the type library, look for the interfaces on the coclass that are marked as outgoing interfaces, and then read the definition of the dispinterface. In this way, VB can make sure that its implementation of **Invoke()** can handle calls to this dispinterface.

297

VB is not the only application that only uses dispinterfaces as sink interfaces. IE and the ActiveX Control Test Container are two other examples. If you write your own client, as you'll do later in the chapter, you can implement any kind of sink interface on the client. Add the interface to the coclass:

```
coclass ClickIt
{
    [default] interface IClickIt;
    [default, source] dispinterface IClickEvent;
};
```

The interface is marked with **[default, source]** to indicate that it is an outgoing interface, and the *default* outgoing interface. Notice that the interface has been declared within the **library** block. This is to make sure that MIDL generates the constants for the interface. If the declaration is made outside of the library block, MIDL will see that the interface is declared in the **coclass** as **[source]**, assume that a client has already generated the **IID_** constant for this interface, and not do it again.

When you save the IDL file, you should find that **IClickEvent** appears in the ClassView. Right click on it and add a method:

```
HRESULT OnClick([in] BSTR bstr);
```

Now compile the code again.

Adding ATL Connection Point Support

When you indicate that you want to use connection points in Object Wizard, it will derive your class from **IConnectionPointContainerImpl<>** and add a connection point map. However, it does not know about your outgoing interface (how could it?), so you will need to edit the header file. Open **ClickIt.h** and edit it:

```
public IDispatchImpl<IClickIt, &IID_IClickIt, &LIBID_CLICKERLib>,
public IProvideClassInfo2Impl<&CLSID_ClickIt,
                              &DIID_IClickEvent, &LIBID_CLICKERLib>,
public IPersistStreamInitImpl<CClickIt>,
```

As its name suggests, the **IProvideClassInfo2** interface is used to provide information about the GUIDs used by the class. Since the class now has a default outgoing interface, you need to make sure that this is reflected in the **IProvideClassInfo2Impl<>** template.

> *The constant for the* **IClickEvent** *is prefixed with* **D** *because MIDL has noticed that the interface is a dispinterface.)*

Next, so that ATL will create a connection point object for the outgoing interface, you need to add it to the connection point map:

```
BEGIN_CONNECTION_POINT_MAP(CClickIt)
    CONNECTION_POINT_ENTRY(IID_IPropertyNotifySink)
    CONNECTION_POINT_ENTRY(DIID_IClickEvent)
END_CONNECTION_POINT_MAP()
```

However, doing this tells ATL that the **CClickIt** C++ class can fire events to the **IClickEvent** outgoing interface, which of course it can't... yet!

Event Firing Code

This is the final step. You need to add code to the **CClickIt** class to fire events, so that the connection point map will compile. You also need to fire those events somewhere in your code. To add code to fire events you need to use the ATL Proxy Generator. From the Project menu, select Add To Project | Components and Controls....

From there, double click on Developer Studio Components, and then select the ATL Proxy Generator and click on Insert, followed by OK:

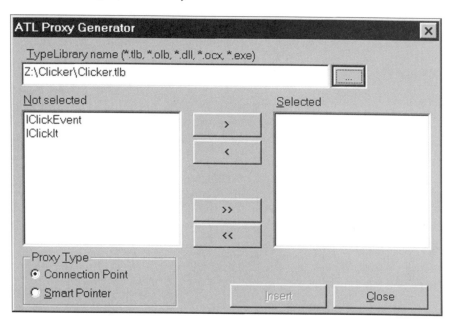

In the TypeLibrary name field at the top, type the name of (or browse for) the type library of the **Clicker** project — it should be in the control's project directory. Make sure that Connection Point is selected and click on IClickEvent, and then on >, followed by Insert. This will produce a dialog giving a default name for the proxy file (**CPClicker.h**), and suggesting that it should be saved in the project directory. Click Save. You can then close the proxy generator and the Component Gallery.

The proxy generator has created a class called **CProxyIClickEvent<>**, derived from **IConnectionPointImpl<>**, the ATL template that implements connection points. The class has a single method:

```
HRESULT Fire_OnClick(BSTR bstr)
```

that will be called when the control wants to generate an event. Here is the relevant code:

```
IUnknown** pp = m_vec.begin();
while (pp < m_vec.end())
```

```
{
   if (*pp != NULL)
   {
      pvars[0].vt = VT_BSTR;
      pvars[0].bstrVal= bstr;
      DISPPARAMS disp = { pvars, NULL, 1, 0 };
      IDispatch* pDispatch = reinterpret_cast<IDispatch*>(*pp);
      pDispatch->Invoke(0x1, IID_NULL, LOCALE_USER_DEFAULT,
         DISPATCH_METHOD, &disp, &varResult, NULL, NULL);
   }
   pp++;
}
```

The ATL code uses a vector, and this routine is iterating through all the **IUnknown** pointers in this vector. These pointers are converted to **IDispatch** pointers with **reinterpret_cast<>** — **QueryInterface()** is not required, because the pointers are indeed **IDispatch** pointers that have been previously cast (when they were added to the vector) to **IUnknown***. The code then calls **Invoke()**, passing the DISPID of the sink method that will handle the event.

While you're looking at **CPClicker.h**, notice the proxy generator bug we saw in the last chapter. At the bottom of the method there is:

```
return varResult.HRESULT;
```

Replace this with:

```
return varResult.scode;
```

The example is almost finished. All you need to do now is derive your class from this proxy class in **ClickIt.h**:

```
   public IDataObjectImpl<CClickIt>,
   public CProxyIClickEvent<CClickIt>,
   public IConnectionPointContainerImpl<CClickIt>,
```

And include the header:

```
#include "resource.h"        // main symbols
#include "CPClicker.h"
```

To fire the event, you need to call **Fire_OnClick()**, so do this in **OnClick()**:

```
LRESULT CClickIt::OnClick(UINT uMsg, WPARAM wParam,
                                    LPARAM lParam, BOOL& bHandled)
{
   ::MessageBox(NULL, _T("Handled in control"), _T("ClickIt"), MB_OK);
   Fire_OnClick(CComBSTR("Fired from control"));
   return 0;
}
```

Now you need to compile the project, but before you do so, make sure that the VB project has been closed (and if it hasn't, save the project and shut down VB). This is because VB will have a reference to the object's DLL to get access to the type library, and this will prevent the linker from overwriting it.

Once the control is built, reopen the VB client project. Open a code window for the form, and select the **ClickIt** control from the Object pull-down list box (it will probably be called **ClickIt1**). Look in the Procedure pull-down list box, and you will see that the **OnClick** event has been magically added to the list of events you can handle.

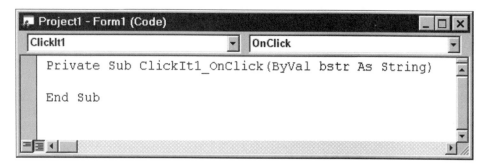

Since it is the default outgoing interface for the control, VB will add an event handler for you. Add the following code:

```
Private Sub ClickIt1_OnClick(ByVal bstr As String)
    MsgBox bstr + " and handled in VB"
End Sub
```

The theory goes that when the event is fired from the control, it is handled by the event code in the VB application. This should take the string passed from the control and display it in a message box. To test out the code, run the application and click on the control. First of all, you'll get the message box we had earlier that said Handled in control. However, when you click on OK, you will get this message box:

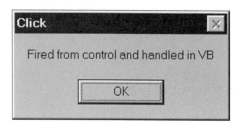

This is the result of the code that you added to the VB application, proving that you caught the event fired from the control when you clicked on it.

Example: The EventWatcher Class

The last example used VB to sink events, so now let's try a beefier project: one that not only sinks events in a C++ control, but also involves *three* projects (see if your virtual memory can handle that many instances of Visual C++ at one time!).

This example demonstrates connection points that use custom interfaces. There are three parts to it, with a Visual C++ project for each.

▶ Firstly, you need a server object that implements the object to which you want to connect, and the connection point object that manages the connection.

▶ Secondly, you need a client, which in this case will be an ActiveX control. This does not have to be so, but an ActiveX control is used here as a convenient vehicle to get visual feedback when events occur.

▶ Finally, you need something to generate the event that will trigger the server object to notify the client.

These three projects will be called **EventWatcher**, **EventCtrl** and **SetEvent** respectively.

I have chosen to use Win32 kernel event objects as the trigger for the server object. In case you haven't come across them before, a Win32 event object is used for synchronization, and is particularly useful when used cross process.

You may have your own trigger to tell the server to notify the client (a clock tick, perhaps), but an event object is quite common. Win32 allows you to wait on a change to the NT event log or the system registry by calling **NotifyChangeEventLog()** and **RegNotifyChangeKeyValue()** respectively. Both of these take a handle to an event object that the system sets to the 'signaled' state when the appropriate event happens, and the process calling these functions waits on the event object to change state using the Win32 **WaitForSingleObject()** function.

Similarly, you can detect that a directory has changed by getting a notification handle with calls to **FindFirstChangeNotification()** and **FindNextChangeNotification()**. This handle can be used with the **WaitForSingleObject()** as well, just like waiting on an event object.

This example will show you how to wait on a Win32 event object, and to use this to generate a control event. You can change it according to the type of notification that you want to receive.

The EventWatcher Server Object

This is the object that waits upon the Win32 kernel event object. An event object can be in one of two states, signaled and non-signaled, and you can set this state with the Win32 **SetEvent()** and **ResetEvent()** functions. In this example, the **EventWatcher** object will notify the control client when the event changes state from non-signaled to signaled (and vice versa). My example is a little contrived, since I'm checking for the state change in both directions — you will more likely check for the event object to change from non-signaled to signaled, indicating (say) that a file has been added to a directory.

The **EventWatcher** object will support the **IEvents** interface:

```
interface IEvents : IUnknown
{
    HRESULT WatchEvent([in, string] wchar_t* strEventName);
    HRESULT SetInterval([in] LONG lInterval);
};
```

The client control should establish a connection with the **EventWatcher** object. This object will check on the state of a named event object, and the control client can start the process by calling **WatchEvent()**, passing the event object's name. This check will be carried out every 500ms, and to change this interval the client can call **SetInterval()**.

I said in the earlier discussion that to make the connection, the client must get hold of the connection point container interface, ask it for the connection point object for the sink interface, and then call **Advise()**. The reverse process, of telling the connectable object that the client no longer needs notifications is similar, except it should call **Unadvise()**. All this is a lot of work, and ATL has simplified it with two functions: **AtlAdvise()** and **AtlUnadvise()**.

ATLAdvise() looks like this:

```
ATLAPI AtlAdvise( IUnknown*  pUnkCP,
                  IUnknown*  pUnk,
                  const IID& iid,
                  LPDWORD    pdw );
```

ATLAPI sets up the calling convention appropriately whether the function is linked statically or dynamically, and defines the function as returning a **HRESULT**. The first parameter is the **IUnknown** of the connectable object that the client wants to connect to, while the second parameter is the **IUnknown** on the sink object in the client. The third parameter is the IID of the sink interface, and the final parameter is the address of a **DWORD** that will take the cookie that uniquely identifies the connection.

When the client no longer wants to receive events, this cookie is used in a call to:

```
ATLAPI AtlUnadvise( IUnknown*  pUnkCP,
                    const IID& iid,
                    DWORD      dw );
```

After making the connection, the client should call **WatchEvent()** on the **IEvents** interface of the object, telling it to watch a particular event object. The **EventWatcher** will create a new thread in the server object and return immediately. The client can then continue doing its work. This is an example of performing an asynchronous method call with COM. By nature, COM is synchronous — the calling thread is blocked while the callee is processing the call. By spinning a new thread, the **EventWatcher** object frees the client thread to continue its work. Using the connection point mechanism, the object can inform the client when an event has occurred.

This new server thread will go into a loop checking the state of the event object to see if it changes. When this happens, the object thread should obtain the connection point for this outgoing event interface, and then generate the appropriate event. After doing this, the server object thread will continue to check the state of the event.

The process of obtaining the array of sink interface pointers and then going through each pointer and calling the appropriate method on the sink is tedious, so Visual C++ supplies a Wizard — the **proxy generator** — to write this code for you, as you saw earlier in the chapter.

Although calling **Unadvise()** will tell the object not to notify the client of the event object's state changes, it does not stop the worker thread. To kill this thread, the client should release the object, and the **FinalRelease()** method on the object should tell the thread to die.

Before we go any further, there's one more choice to make. Our server needs to create a new thread, and we have two options. Either the server object thread is in an STA, and the client sink interface would have to be marshaled to the apartment that owns the worker thread; or the server and worker thread are part of the same MTA, in which case marshaling is not required. For simplicity, let's go for the second option.

Now you have an idea of how this object works, let's go through the steps of creating it.

Creating the Project

Start up the ATL COM AppWizard and create a new project called EventWatcher. On the dialog, select Executable (EXE) and click on Finish.

Next, you need to add a new object and create the **IEvents** interface. So, select New ATL Object... from the Insert menu, and from the resulting dialog select Objects and then Simple Object and Next >. In the following dialog, type Events for the Short Name:

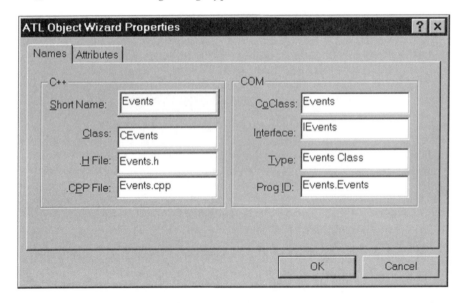

Click on the Attributes tab and select Free for the Threading Model, and also select Support Connection Points. Free threading is required because we want the connectable object to be part of an MTA: remember, to an ATL object 'free threading' means a multithreaded apartment.

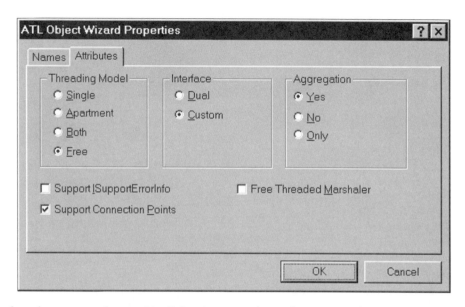

The other change to make on this dialog is to opt for a Custom interface — you can use a dual interface if you like, but it would be less efficient. You don't have to use an Automation interface because in this example, you will implement both ends of the connection point.

Editing the Class

The next task is to edit the **CEvents** class to make the object do something. In the project's ClassView, right-click on the IEvents entry and select Add Method...

In the resulting dialog, type **WatchEvent** for the Method Name and **[in, string] wchar_t***
strEventName for the Parameters (if you click out of the Parameters edit box, you'll see the
Implementation updated):

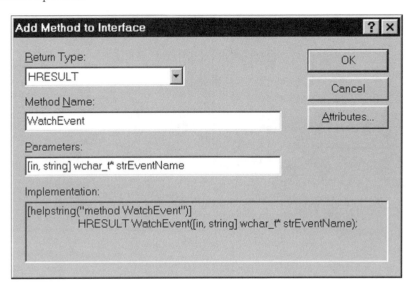

Click on OK, and then repeat this process for the **SetInterval()** method (which has a
parameter of **[in] LONG lInterval**). The ClassView should now look like this:

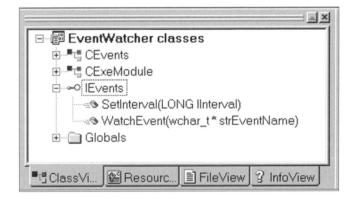

Our next responsibility is to add the code for these methods. The first task is to handle the
interval that specifies how often our object should check the event. Open **Events.h** and add a
new private data member called **m_dwInterval**, initializing it in the constructor:

```
class ATL_NO_VTABLE CEvents :
    public CComObjectRootEx<CComMultiThreadModel>,
    public CComCoClass<CEvents, &CLSID_Events>,
    public IConnectionPointContainerImpl<CEvents>,
    public IEvents
```

```
{
public:
    CEvents() : m_dwInterval(500)
    {
    }

    DECLARE_REGISTRY_RESOURCEID(IDR_EVENTS)

    BEGIN_COM_MAP(CEvents)
        COM_INTERFACE_ENTRY(IEvents)
        COM_INTERFACE_ENTRY_IMPL(IConnectionPointContainer)
    END_COM_MAP()

    BEGIN_CONNECTION_POINT_MAP(CEvents)
    END_CONNECTION_POINT_MAP()


    // IEvents
public:
    STDMETHOD(SetInterval)(/*[in]*/ LONG lInterval);
    STDMETHOD(WatchEvent)(/*[in, string]*/ wchar_t* strEventName);

private:
    DWORD m_dwInterval;
};
```

Notice that because we chose to Support Connection Points, the Object Wizard has derived the class from the **IConnectionPointContainerImpl<>** template, with the class as its parameter. The Object Wizard has also created a connection point map, which at the moment is empty.

Now open **Events.cpp** and add the code for **SetInterval()**, so that the client can change the interval between the times that the server checks the event object:

```
STDMETHODIMP CEvents::SetInterval(LONG lInterval)
{
    if (lInterval < 100)
        return E_FAIL;

    m_dwInterval = lInterval;
    return S_OK;
}
```

Notice that I have put a check in here — the interval is in milliseconds, so I am making sure that the object does not check the event more often than once every 100ms. If that happened, the object could take up too much CPU time. The default interval is 500ms, as set in the constructor's initialization list.

Creating the Worker Thread

When the client calls **WatchEvent()**, the server creates a new thread to watch for the specified event object to change state. This worker thread will tirelessly watch the event, and will only die when it is told to, which happens when the **EventWatcher** object itself dies. However, since there are (at least) two threads trying to die, there must be some communication between them to make sure that they are destroyed in the correct order. The nature of threads is that they run independently of each other and so, in the few cases when one thread depends on what another is doing, the two must be able to indicate to each other what stage they are in.

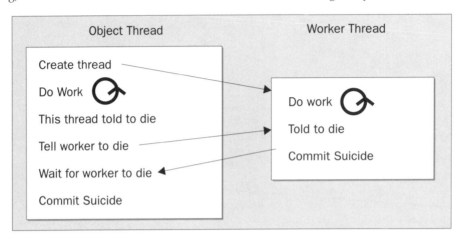

The two messages sent between the two threads are:

- The object thread tells the worker thread to die
- The worker thread tells the object thread that it has died

This is handled using two Win32 objects. The object thread creates an unsignaled event object and passes it to the worker thread. The worker thread can check this event object periodically to see if it has been set. (Remember the **m_dwInterval**? This is the interval between checks on this event object.) When the object thread is told to die (in other words, the **EventWatcher** is being destroyed), it can set this event object to initiate the death of the worker thread. However, the object itself must not die at this point because the worker thread is still alive, and so there are resources that still need to be freed.

The object thread must wait until the worker thread has died, and it can do this by waiting on the worker thread handle. Once the thread has died its handle becomes signaled (which means that it changes from the unsignaled to the signaled state), and the object thread can continue in its death throes.

Before we add the code, there is just a little more information about threads that you need to know. A thread is a unit of execution and, like a process needs to have a **main()** function to operate, a thread needs a thread function. This function must have the signature:

```
unsigned __stdcall ThreadFunction(LPVOID);
```

The parameter is a **void** pointer that can be used to pass information to the thread when it is initialized. The return value is the handle of the thread, which can be used when waiting for a thread to die.

Our thread function should be a private method of the **CEvents** class, since logically only the object can call it. However, to allow a method to access object data, C++ passes an implicit first parameter — the **this** pointer. If you did this, the thread function would not match the compulsory signature of a thread function. To prevent this from happening, you should make the function a class method, by declaring it as **static**. As a class method, however, it will not have access to any object's data (because it doesn't have a **this** pointer). To solve the problem, you should pass the **this** pointer via the **LPVOID** parameter of the method.

So, change the **CEvents** class to add the thread function and associated data members:

```
private:
    static unsigned __stdcall Watch(LPVOID pThis);
    LPWSTR m_strEventName;
    DWORD  m_dwInterval;
    HANDLE m_hThread;
    HANDLE m_hDie;
    HANDLE m_hEvent;
    BOOL m_bEventState;
};
```

Initialize these values in the constructor:

```
public:
    CEvents() : m_dwInterval(500),
                m_strEventName(NULL),
                m_hThread(NULL),
                m_hDie(NULL),
                m_hEvent(NULL),
                m_bEventState(false)
    {
    }
```

m_strEventName is the name of the event for which the object should watch, and **m_hEvent** will hold the handle of the event that is being watched. Now we are ready to write the **WatchEvent()** method:

```
#include <process.h>

////////////////////////////////////////////////////////////////////////
// CEvents


STDMETHODIMP CEvents::WatchEvent(wchar_t * strEventName)
{
    // Check that the requested event actually exists
    HANDLE hEvent;
#ifdef WINNT
    hEvent = OpenEventW(EVENT_ALL_ACCESS, false, strEventName);
#else
    USES_CONVERSION;
    hEvent = OpenEvent(EVENT_ALL_ACCESS, false, W2A(strEventName));
#endif

    if (hEvent == NULL)
        return E_POINTER;
```

```
    m_bEventState = (WAIT_OBJECT_0 == WaitForSingleObject(hEvent, 0));

if (m_hThread != NULL)
{
    // Thread is already active, so suspend it and change the values
    SuspendThread(m_hThread);

    delete [] m_strEventName;
    m_strEventName = new  WCHAR[wcslen(strEventName)+1];
    wcscpy(m_strEventName, strEventName);
    CloseHandle(m_hEvent);
    m_hEvent = hEvent;
    ResumeThread(m_hThread);

    return S_OK;
}

// Set up the values
m_hEvent = hEvent;
m_hDie = CreateEvent(NULL, true, false, NULL);
m_strEventName = new WCHAR[wcslen(strEventName)+1];
wcscpy(m_strEventName, strEventName);

// Start thread to watch this event
unsigned threadID;
m_hThread = (HANDLE)_beginthreadex( NULL, 0, Watch,
                                    reinterpret_cast<void*>(this),
                                    0, &threadID );
return S_OK;
}
```

Let's go through this code line by line. First, we check to see if the named event exists — if it doesn't, there is no point in waiting for its state to change! I'm use conditional compilation here: if you are compiling under NT, then you will have all of the Unicode Win32 functions, and so you can use the **BSTR** passed to the method as a **LPCWSTR** for the **OpenEventW()** function. Otherwise, if you are compiling under Windows 95, the Unicode version of this function will not exist, so you need to convert the **LPWSTR** to a **LPCSTR** for the **OpenEvent()** function. If the named event does not exist, either function will return **NULL** and so the method should return immediately with an error.

The next section uses the **WaitForSingleObject()** function to test the state of the event. It does this by waiting with a timeout of 0ms, and testing to see if the return value is **WAIT_OBJECT_0**. If it is, the event is signaled.

Next, the code checks to see if the worker thread has already been created. If it has, then the code suspends it, clears up the previously set values, sets the new values and resumes the thread. There is a slight chance here that the worker thread could be suspended while it is using the **m_strEventName** or the **m_hEvent** values. The code ignores this possibility, but you could use Win32 mutex objects to remove the risk completely.

If the thread has not already been created, this now needs to be done. Firstly, an event object is created that is used later in the program to indicate that the worker thread should die. Secondly, the name of the event object we are watching is cached, and finally the thread is created. The CRT method **_beginthreadex()** is used rather than the Win32 **CreateThread()** because its use ensures that the C runtime library is correctly initialized in the new thread. The address of the thread function is passed as a parameter, as well as the **this** pointer cast to a **void***. The value returned from this function call is the handle of the thread.

Now that the worker thread has been created and started, the **WatchEvent()** method can return. As noted earlier, this is one way of writing an asynchronous COM method. Remember that COM calls are synchronous, so if **WatchEvent()** went into a loop checking for the state of an event object, this would block the client thread until **WatchEvent()** returned. A blocked client thread will freeze out its user interface, which is certainly not what we want.

You can try to compile this file, but you will get the following error:

error C2065: '_beginthreadex' : undeclared identifier

You have added a **#include** for the **process.h** header that declares **_beginthreadex()**, but this declaration is bracketed with the conditional compilation directive **#ifdef _MT**. To get the function declared, you need to get this symbol defined.

In order to do this, you'll have to change the CRT used by the project. Select Project | Settings..., make sure that the project is selected in the left hand pane, and select the C/C++ tab. From the Category box select Code Generation, and finally in the Use run-time library select a multithreaded library appropriate to the build that is being performed. (What I do is select All Configurations from the Settings For box, and then select Multithreaded as the runtime library; then I select Win32 Debug and Debug Multithreaded.) You should be able to compile the project now, although it won't link, of course, because we haven't yet implemented the thread function.

The Worker Thread Function

The worker thread function should go into a loop to check for one of two events:

The thread is told to die

The requested event object changes state

```
unsigned __stdcall CEvents::Watch(LPVOID pThis);
{
   CEvents* pThisObject = static_cast<CEvents*>(pThis);
   CoInitializeEx(NULL, COINIT_MULTITHREADED);

   while(true)
   {
      if (WAIT_OBJECT_0 == WaitForSingleObject(pThisObject->m_hDie, 0))
         break;

      if (WAIT_TIMEOUT == WaitForSingleObject(pThisObject->m_hEvent, 0))
      {
         // Event is not signalled
      }
      else
      {
```

311

```
        // Event is signalled
      }
      Sleep(pThisObject->m_dwInterval);
   }

   CoUninitialize();
   return 0;
}
```

The first thing to notice about this code is that the parameter passed to the thread function is cast to a **CEvents** pointer, so that we can access the data members of the class. We have to do this because the **Watch()** method is **static**, so it has no **this** pointer (which is why it was declared as **static**) and so has no direct access to an object's data.

Next, notice the calls to **CoInitializeEx()** and **CoUninitialize()**. This object is free threaded, and so runs in a Multi Threaded Apartment (MTA). Every thread in the MTA can access the COM object freely and concurrently. It is the developer's responsibility to ensure that this will not cause a problem. To make a thread join an MTA, the thread must call **CoInitializeEx()** with the value **COINIT_MULTITHREADED**.

After that, there is the main loop. This checks to see if the thread should die by waiting on the **m_hDie** event object; again, a timeout of 0ms is used just to get the state of the event object. If this is signaled, then the loop is broken and the thread can clean up and die. If the thread should not die, then it needs to check for the state of the named event object and react according to the value returned. Between each iteration of the loop, the thread sleeps for the amount of time set by **SetInterval()**.

Since this server is going to be free threaded, you will need to change its initialization. By default, the server is initialized with a single threaded apartment (STA) and all requests will come in via that STA. To make the object free threaded, you will need to change the project so that the requests come in on a thread in the MTA. These threading issues were covered in the last chapter.

To do this, open **EventWatcher.cpp** and scroll to the **_tWinMain()** entry point function. Here you will see that the necessary code exists (the Wizard put it there) but it is commented out, so move the commenting to the **CoInitialize()** line:

```
extern "C" int WINAPI _tWinMain(HINSTANCE hInstance,
   HINSTANCE /*hPrevInstance*/, LPTSTR lpCmdLine, int /*nShowCmd*/)
{
   lpCmdLine = GetCommandLine(); //this line necessary for _ATL_MIN_CRT
   // HRESULT hRes = CoInitialize(NULL);
   //  If you are running on NT 4.0 or higher you can use the following
   //   call instead to make the EXE free threaded.
   //  This means that calls come in on a random RPC thread
   HRESULT hRes = CoInitializeEx(NULL, COINIT_MULTITHREADED);
```

Killing the Worker Thread

The worker thread needs to be killed when the **EventWatcher** object is destroyed. The best way to do this is to give the **CEvents** class a **FinalRelease()** method. This is effectively a destructor for the ATL object, and so the C++ object's state will still be valid.

In the declaration for **CEvents**, add this line after the declarations of the **IEvents** methods:

```
// IEvents
public:
   STDMETHOD(SetInterval)(/*[in]*/ LONG lInterval);
   STDMETHOD(WatchEvent)(/*[in, string]*/ wchar_t* strEventName);
   void FinalRelease();
```

Now add the method itself to **Events.cpp**:

```
void CEvents::FinalRelease()
{
   // Tell the thread to die
   SetEvent(m_hDie);

   // Wait for it to die
   WaitForSingleObject(m_hThread, INFINITE);

   if (m_strEventName)
      delete [] m_strEventName;
   CloseHandle(m_hDie);
   CloseHandle(m_hEvent);
   CloseHandle(m_hThread);
}
```

This method sets the **m_hDie** event object and then waits on the thread handle. This wait is infinite, so it won't time out. The **WaitForSingleObject()** function will return when the thread it is waiting on has died. At this point the object can safely clean up the data members of the class. (Note that using **CloseHandle()** on a **NULL** parameter is perfectly safe.)

This is just about all you can do to the object for now. You have defined the object's interface, which is required by the client, and implemented most of the worker thread code. However, you cannot fully write the connection point code because you do not yet know what the sink interface on the client object looks like. So that is the next thing to do.

EventCtrl Client Object

The client will be an ActiveX control. It need not be, but we will need some visual feedback to show any events fired from **EventWatcher**. ATL does practically all that is required to implement a control, so it makes the coding simple. You will see more about the details of controls in the next couple of chapters.

Close the **EventWatcher** project and then start a new project. Again, select the ATL COM AppWizard, this time using **EventCtrl** as the name of the project. In the Wizard dialog, make sure that Dynamic Link Library is selected as the Server Type — controls are *always* inproc. We now need to perform two steps:

▶ Create the ActiveX control

▶ Create the sink interface

ActiveX Control

To create the ActiveX control, select New ATL Object... from the Insert menu. From this dialog, select Controls from the left-hand pane, and then Full Control in the right-hand pane:

Click Next >, and in the next dialog type EventControl in the Short Name box, and change the Interface name to be IEventSink. Move to the Attributes tab and ensure that the interface type is Custom before clicking on OK.

Open the **EventControl.h** file by double-clicking on CEventControl in the ClassView, and add a private data member and these two methods to the bottom of the class:

```
public:
    HRESULT OnDraw(ATL_DRAWINFO& di);
    HRESULT FinalConstruct();
    void FinalRelease();

private:
    LPTSTR m_strEventStatus;
};
```

The variable will hold the textual description of the event object state, that is, whether the named event object that we will be checking is signaled or not; we need to initialize this, so the **FinalConstruct()** method is declared. This string must be freed when the control is destroyed, so **FinalRelease()** is declared to do this. Finally, we need the control to tell us what the event object state is, so **OnDraw()** is changed to write the **m_strEventStatus** value. All these changes are:

```
HRESULT CEventControl::OnDraw(ATL_DRAWINFO& di)
{
    RECT& rc = *(RECT*)di.prcBounds;
    Rectangle(di.hdcDraw, rc.left,  rc.top, rc.right, rc.bottom);
    DrawText(di.hdcDraw, m_strEventStatus, -1, &rc,
        DT_CENTER | DT_VCENTER | DT_SINGLELINE);
```

```
      return S_OK;
   }
```

```
   HRESULT CEventControl::FinalConstruct()
   {
      m_strEventStatus = new TCHAR[14 * sizeof(TCHAR)];
      lstrcpy(m_strEventStatus, _T("Uninitialized"));
      return S_OK;
   }
```

```
   void CEventControl::FinalRelease()
   {
      delete [] m_strEventStatus;
   }
```

We will change **m_strEventStatus** when the control discovers from **EventWatcher** that the named event object's state has changed.

Sink Interface

Next, we need to add the methods to the sink interface that the server will call when it fires events. Right click on **IEventSink** and select Add Method... twice, to add two methods called **OnEventSet()** and **OnEventReset()**, both with the same parameter:

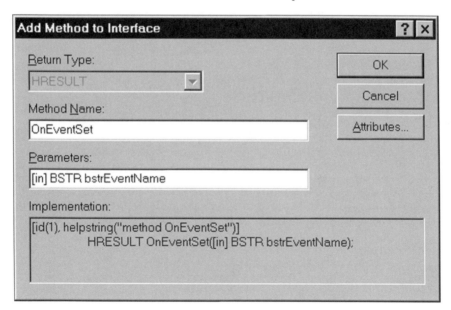

These two methods are the actual events that the server will generate: the event object has been set (signaled) or reset (unsignaled). Now add the bodies of these methods:

```
   STDMETHODIMP CEventControl::OnEventSet(BSTR bstrEventName)
   {
      USES_CONVERSION;
      LPTSTR strEvt = OLE2T(bstrEventName);
```

```
        delete [] m_strEventStatus;

        // Save space for name and message
        m_strEventStatus = new TCHAR[lstrlen(strEvt) + 8];
        wsprintf(m_strEventStatus, _T("%s is SET"), strEvt);
        FireViewChange();
        return S_OK;
    }

    STDMETHODIMP CEventControl::OnEventReset(BSTR bstrEventName)
    {
        USES_CONVERSION;
        LPTSTR strEvt = OLE2T(bstrEventName);
        delete [] m_strEventStatus;

        // Save space for name and message
        m_strEventStatus = new TCHAR[lstrlen(strEvt) + 10];
        wsprintf(m_strEventStatus, _T("%s is RESET"), strEvt);
        FireViewChange();
        return S_OK;
    }
```

The code copies the name of the event and the current state into the **m_strEventStatus** data member, and the **FireViewChange()** function is called to tell the control to redraw itself. Compile this code at this point to convince yourself that you have typed in everything correctly! The control now has all the code that it needs to update itself when the event object state changes.

Connecting the Two Together

Let's consider where we're up to:

▶ The server has a connection point to which the client can connect

▶ The client has a sink interface and code to change the display of the control when the sink interface is called.

Now we need to add code that actually makes the connection to the server, and gets the server to callback on the client.

Calling the Server

The first thing we need to do is create the **EventWatcher** object. To make life easier, we can use the COM native support classes to generate a smart pointer to the server object — this way, you don't have to worry about **#include**ing the server object's header and constants file. To do this, we use the **#import** directive, which generates both the 'header' (**.tlh**) and 'implementation' (**.tli**) for this smart pointer class.

Typically, you will need to add the directive into the CPP file, which was the approach used in earlier chapters of the book. However, in this example we will add the smart pointer as a data member of the control class. This means that when the C++ class implementing the control is destroyed, the smart pointer will be destroyed too, and it will release the server object. In this case, the declaration of the smart pointer class must be made before **EventControl.h** is included.

The **#import** directive has a feature allowing it to be used to generate the header or implementation portion independently, and this is what we will do now. Open **EventControl.h** and add the following line:

```
#include "resource.h"          // main symbols
#import "..\EventWatcher\EventWatcher.tlb" no_namespace, no_implementation

///////////////////////////////////////////////////////////////////////////
// CEventControl
```

The TLB file was generated when you compiled the **EventWatcher** project. **no_implementation** specifies that *only* the header portion of the smart pointer class will be included, so further down in the class add the data members:

```
private:
    LPTSTR m_strEventStatus;
    IEventsPtr m_ptr;
    DWORD m_dwCookie;
    void DisconnectServer();
};
```

The **m_dwCookie** is used to hold the unique ID that identifies the connection to the server, and **DisconnectServer()** is a helper function to break the connection to the server. The cookie value should be initialized in the constructor:

```
public:
    CEventControl() : m_dwCookie(0)
    {
    }
```

To use the smart pointer class, you will need to use **#import** in **EventControl.cpp** as well:

```
// EventControl.cpp : Implementation of CEventControl
#include "stdafx.h"
#include "EventCtrl.h"
#include "EventControl.h"
#import "..\EventWatcher\EventWatcher.tlb" no_namespace, implementation_only
```

Now you need to create the **EventWatcher** object. **FinalConstruct()** may appear to be the best place to do this, but the control object will not have been completely constructed at this stage. Making a connection to the server object here will break the ATL object construction, since it will involve the control object's reference count being increased (the connection point object **QI()**s the client control object, which results in the increase). The control's class factory will not expect this; indeed, it **ASSERT()**s that the reference count is zero.

To get the server object created when the control is created, you need to put the code in a method that will only be called at this time. The **CComControlBase** class has a method called **InPlaceActivate()** which is called when the control is activated. The implementation of this method initializes the control's data members, connecting it to the container. Note that **InPlaceActivate()** will be called in several circumstances, but we only want to apply our special handling when the control is first created; when this happens, it is passed a value of **OLEIVERB_SHOW**.

We will need to override this method, so add the declaration:

```
public:
   HRESULT InPlaceActivate(LONG iVerb, const RECT* prcPosRect);
```

Implement it like this:

```
HRESULT CEventControl::InPlaceActivate(LONG iVerb,
                                                 const RECT* prcPosRect)
{
   HRESULT hr;
   hr = CComControlBase::InPlaceActivate(iVerb, prcPosRect);

   if (FAILED(hr) || iVerb != OLEIVERB_SHOW)
      return hr;

   // _com_ptr_t does not use CoCreateInstanceEx(), so we need
   // to do it and attach
   MULTI_QI qi[1] = {&__uuidof(IEventsPtr), NULL, S_OK};
   hr = CoCreateInstanceEx(__uuidof(Events), NULL, CLSCTX_ALL,
                                          NULL, 1, qi);

   if (SUCCEEDED(hr))
   {
      if (m_dwCookie)
         DisconnectServer();

      try
      {
         m_ptr.Attach(reinterpret_cast<IEvents*>(qi[0].pItf));

         // The event name
         LPWSTR strEventName = L"Test";

         // Make connection
         hr = AtlAdvise(m_ptr, this->GetUnknown(), IID_IEventSink,
                                          &m_dwCookie);
         if (FAILED(hr))
            _com_issue_error(hr);
         m_ptr->WatchEvent(strEventName);
      }
      catch (_com_error e)
      {
         ATLTRACE(_T("Cannot create server, %x"), e.Error());
```

```
            return e.Error();
        }
    }
    return 0;
}
```

The COM native support class **_com_ptr_t** can be used to create instances of inproc and local objects using the **CreateInstance()** method. This ultimately calls **CoCreateInstance()**, so there is no way that you can specify the name of a remote server. (You could use **DCOMCnfg** to set a **RemoteServerName** in the registry, but this is inflexible.) In this example, we will call **CoCreateInstanceEx()** and attach the returned interface pointer to the smart pointer. This means that, if you choose, you can have the control and **EventWatcher** object on two different machines.

This code uses C++ exception handling, so you may need to enable this in the project settings (Project | Settings...; select All Configurations; then on the C/C++ tab choose C++ Language and check Enable exception handling).

> Note that if you use C++ exception handling, then the C runtime library must be initialized and so the CRT start up code must be called. This adds about 25k to the size of the control.

By default, the release builds exclude this code by defining the symbol **_ATL_MIN_CRT**. To use exception handling, you need to remove the definition of this symbol from the project: on the C/C++ tab, select Preprocessor and remove the symbol from the Preprocessor definitions.
The code first calls the base class **InPlaceActivate()** to ensure that the control is properly activated, then it calls **CoCreateInstanceEx()**; notice how we use **__uuidof()** to get the CLSID and the IID that are required. In this case, the **COSERVERINFO** parameter is set to **NULL**, meaning that the local machine will be used. The interface obtained from this function call is then attached to the smart pointer.

Next, the connection is made by calling **AtlAdvise()**. As we saw earlier, the first parameter is the **IUnknown** on the server object, while the second one is the **IUnknown** on this control, which will be used to obtain the sink interface. The IID of this sink interface is passed as the next parameter, followed by a pointer to a **DWORD** that gets passed as the last parameter. This **[out]** parameter returns a 'cookie' value that is used to disconnect from the server at a later stage.

After that, the server is called and told to watch a particular event. The event name is hard coded as '**Test**', but note that even though **WatchEvent()** takes a **BSTR,** a **LPWSTR** is passed. C++ does the automatic conversion from an **LPWSTR** to the **_bstr_t** parameter that the smart pointer takes, and then this will be converted to a **BSTR** when the actual object method is called.

When the control is destroyed, the connection needs to be broken; this is done in the **DisconnectServer()** method:

```
void CEventControl::DisconnectServer()
{
    if (m_dwCookie)
        AtlUnadvise(m_ptr, IID_IEventSink, m_dwCookie);
```

```
        m_dwCookie = 0;
    }
```

This uses the cookie obtained during the **AtlAdvise()** function call to disconnect from the connection point. This has to be called when the control is being destroyed, so you may think it should be called in **FinalRelease()**. However, the latter is only called when the reference count falls to zero, which it won't because the **EventWatcher** object will still have a reference to the control's sink interface.

The control implements the **IOleObject** interface, which has a method called **Close()** that's called when the control is being destroyed by the container. ATL implements this in **IOleObjectImpl**, which is a base class of the control, so you need override this method. In the header add:

```
public:
    HRESULT InPlaceActivate(LONG iVerb, const RECT* prcPosRect);
    STDMETHOD(Close)(DWORD dwSaveOption);
```

And in the CPP file:

```
STDMETHODIMP CEventControl::Close(DWORD dwSaveOption)
{
    HRESULT hr;

    hr = IOleObjectImpl<CEventControl>::Close(dwSaveOption);

    if (m_dwCookie)
        DisconnectServer();

    return hr;
}
```

You now have a working version of the control that, barring any errors, you should be able to compile.

Proxy Generator

You are on the home straight now. The final action that needs to be performed is to get the server object to callback on the control when the event object changes state. As we saw earlier in the chapter, you should use the ATL proxy generator to create the event firing code. Open the **EventWatcher** project. You will need to add the proxy into the project, so run the generator by selecting Project | Add to Project | Components and Controls. Insert the ATL Proxy Generator as you did before.

In the TypeLibrary name field in the dialog, type (or browse for) the type library of the **EventCtrl**. This should be in the control's project directory, and was created by MIDL from the IDL file when the project was built. Make sure that Connection Point is selected, and then click on IEventSink, and then on >, followed by Insert. This will produce a dialog suggesting a name for the proxy file (**CPEventCtrl.h**), and that it should be saved in the project directory. Click Save. You can then close the proxy generator and the Component Gallery.

To use this proxy, you need to add the generated proxy class to the **CEvents** class, so add the following lines to the header:

```
#include "..\EventCtrl\EventCtrl.h"
#include "CPEventCtrl.h"

/////////////////////////////////////////////////////////////////////
// CEvents
class ATL_NO_VTABLE CEvents :
    public CComObjectRootEx<CComMultiThreadModel>,
    public CComCoClass<CEvents, &CLSID_Events>,
    public CProxyIEventSink<CEvents>,
    public IConnectionPointContainerImpl<CEvents>,
    public IEvents
```

The **CProxyIEventSink<>** class is generated by the proxy generator, and has methods to obtain the sink interface on the connected client and then call the appropriate method. You will also need to add the following to the **Events.cpp** file, so that the GUIDs of the client control are declared (I could have used **__declspec(uuid())**, but this is simpler.):

```
// Events.cpp : Implementation of CEvents
#include "stdafx.h"
#include "EventWatcher.h"
#include "Events.h"
#include "..\EventCtrl\EventCtrl_i.c"
```

At present, in the worker thread function, the state of the event is checked but not acted upon. In implementing actions, we must keep in mind that if the client is informed of the state every time it is obtained, this could have a serious impact on the performance of the client, since it would be informed of the event state every **m_lInterval** milliseconds. Instead, the *server* should check that the state has changed.

This is the point of the **m_bEventState** data member: it holds the state of the object from one call to the next, so that a test can be made to see if the state has changed:

```
DWORD WINAPI CEvents::Watch(LPVOID pThis)
{
    CEvents* pThisObject = static_cast<CEvents*>(pThis);
    CoInitializeEx(NULL, COINIT_MULTITHREADED);

    while(true)
    {
        if (WAIT_OBJECT_0 == WaitForSingleObject(pThisObject->m_hDie, 0))
            break;

        if (WAIT_TIMEOUT == WaitForSingleObject(pThisObject->m_hEvent, 0))
        {
            // Event is not signaled
            if (pThisObject->m_bEventState)
            {
                // Previously signaled, state changed
                pThisObject->m_bEventState = false;
```

321

```
                    pThisObject->Fire_OnEventReset(
                        CComBSTR(pThisObject->m_strEventName));
                }
            }
            else
            {
                // Event is signaled
                if (!pThisObject->m_bEventState)
                {
                    // Previously not signaled, state changed
                    pThisObject->m_bEventState = true;
                    pThisObject->Fire_OnEventSet(
                        CComBSTR(pThisObject->m_strEventName));
                }
            }
            Sleep(pThisObject->m_dwInterval);
        }

    CoUninitialize();
    return 0;
}
```

Now the code checks **m_bEventState**, and if it indicates that the state has changed, then the appropriate proxy method is called. Again, the method requires a **BSTR**, but now you must explicitly create one using the ATL class **CComBSTR**.

Before you can compile the project, remember that the client and server will talk to each other via the server's interface, **IEvents**, and the control's sink interface, **IEventSink**. Marshaling information must be generated for this, so add the control's interface as a **[source]** interface to the coclass of the server object:

```
library EVENTWATCHERLib
{
    importlib("stdole32.tlb");
    importlib("stdole2.tlb");
    importlib("..\EventCtrl\EventCtrl.tlb");

    [
    uuid(1CA6C311-3EEF-11D1-9C18-0060973044A8),
    helpstring("Events Class")
    ]
    coclass Events
    {
        [default] interface IEvents;
        [default, source] interface IEventSink;
    };
};
```

Finally, you need to add the sink interface to the server's connection point map, otherwise the server will reject any calls when the client calls **IConnectionPointContainer::FindConnectionPoint()**. (Note that the **HRESULT** from such a rejection is **0x80040200** (**CONNECT_E_NOCONNECTION**); you will not find this in **winerror.h**, as it is defined in **olectl.h**.)

```
BEGIN_CONNECTION_POINT_MAP(CEvents)
    CONNECTION_POINT_ENTRY(IID_IEventSink)
END_CONNECTION_POINT_MAP()
```

You can now compile the server project. Note that since the IDL file has changed, it will be recompiled when you build the project. This will recompile the type library, and so the control project will need recompiling as well; you should do that now.

SetEvent

To be able to test this example, you need to be able to create, and change the state of, a Win32 kernel object. To do this, you need to create and compile the **SetEvent** project. This project is MFC based, because it is mainly a UI project. Here are the steps.

Create a new project called **SetEvent** with MFC AppWizard(exe). On step 1 of the Wizard, select Dialog based; on the next page deselect About box and ActiveX Controls, and then click on Finish.

Resources

Open the dialog resource and amend it so that it features the following controls (with the indicated IDs):

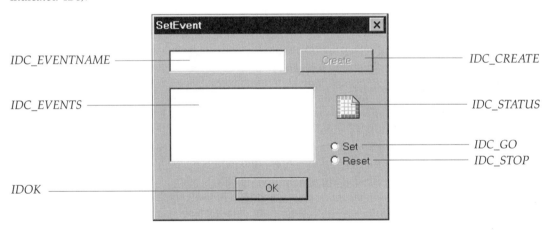

IDC_STATUS is a picture control of type Icon. You should arrange the controls so that the tab order is:

- ▶ **IDC_EVENTNAME**
- ▶ **IDC_CREATE**
- ▶ **IDC_EVENTS**
- ▶ **IDC_STATUS**
- ▶ **IDC_GO**
- ▶ **IDC_STOP**
- ▶ **IDOK**

Then, group the radio buttons by making sure that **IDC_GO** and **IDOK** have G̲roup and Ta̲b stop checked. Disable the C̲reate button by selecting the Disa̲bled check box in its properties.

The picture box holds icons that show the state of the selected event. To implement this, copy the 'traffic signals' icons from Visual Basic (they're in the CD's **tools\graphics\icons\traffic** folder) into the **Res** directory of the project, and then in the ResourceView right-click on Icon and select I̲mport.... Once you have imported an icon, rename the symbol by right clicking on it and selecting Properties. Here are the names to use:

File	Symbol
Trffc10a.ico	IDI_GO
Trffc10b.ico	IDI_READY
Trffc10c.ico	IDI_STOP

Now go back to the dialog and change the **IDC_STATUS** control to have the Image of **IDI_READY**.

Handling Windows Events

The majority of the code in this project is to handle various Windows events as the user navigates through the controls on the dialog. The user uses the dialog in this way:

▶ Create an event by typing a name in the top edit box and then clicking the Create button. This adds the event name to the list box.

▶ The user can then select the name of an event in the list box, and the state of the event will be shown using the radio buttons and the picture box.

▶ The user changes an event's state by clicking on the radio buttons.

The handles of the created kernel event objects will be held as data members of the list box, and this simplifies the code so that you do not need to maintain a separate map. When the dialog is dismissed, the code will go through all these handles and release them.

The first event we need to handle is to enable the C̲reate button if the edit box has a value. Right-click on the edit box in the dialog resource, select ClassW̲izard... and add a handler method for the **EN_CHANGE** message called **OnChangeEventname()**. In this method, you need to enable or disable the button depending on whether there is text in the edit box:

```
void CSetEventDlg::OnChangeEventname()
{
    CButton* pButton = (CButton*)GetDlgItem(IDC_CREATE);
    ASSERT(pButton);
    CWnd* pEdit = GetDlgItem(IDC_EVENTNAME);
    ASSERT(pEdit);
    CString strEvent;
    pEdit->GetWindowText(strEvent);
    pButton->EnableWindow(!strEvent.IsEmpty());
}
```

Now we need to handle the user clicking on the <u>C</u>reate button. Double click on the button control in the dialog resource while holding down the *Ctrl* key. This will create a handler function for you; fill it with the following code:

```
void CSetEventDlg::OnCreate()
{
    CListBox* pList = (CListBox*)GetDlgItem(IDC_EVENTS);
    ASSERT(pList);
    CWnd* pEdit = GetDlgItem(IDC_EVENTNAME);
    ASSERT(pEdit);

    CString strEvent;
    pEdit->GetWindowText(strEvent);

    if (LB_ERR == pList->FindString(0, strEvent))
    {
        // Does not exist so we can add it
        HANDLE hEvent = CreateEvent(NULL, true, false, strEvent);

        if (hEvent)
        {
            int pos = pList->AddString(strEvent);
            pList->SetItemData(pos, (DWORD)hEvent);
            pList->SetCurSel(pos);
            OnSelchangeEvents();
        }
    }
}
```

This checks to see if the list box already has an entry for this event. If not, it creates an event and adds the event name into the list box, and the handle as the associated item data. Note that if the event object already exists, the handle for that event object is returned. The code then calls **OnSelChangeEvents()** to update the icon and radio buttons.

This handler is called when a selection changes in the list box, so select it and open the ClassWizard. Add a handler for the **LBN_SELCHANGE** message called **OnSelchangeEvents()**:

```
void CSetEventDlg::OnSelchangeEvents()
{
    CListBox* pList = (CListBox*)GetDlgItem(IDC_EVENTS);
    ASSERT(pList);

    CStatic* pIcon = (CStatic*)GetDlgItem(IDC_STATUS);
    ASSERT(pIcon);

    HANDLE hEvent = (HANDLE)pList->GetItemData(pList->GetCurSel());
    HICON hIcon;

    // Get the status of the event
    if (WAIT_OBJECT_0 == WaitForSingleObject(hEvent,0))
    {
```

```
        // Event is set
        hIcon = AfxGetApp()->LoadIcon(IDI_GO);
        CButton* pButton = (CButton*)GetDlgItem(IDC_GO);
        ASSERT(pButton);
        pButton->SetCheck(1);
        pButton = (CButton*)GetDlgItem(IDC_STOP);
        ASSERT(pButton);
        pButton->SetCheck(0);
    }
    else
    {
        // Event is not set
        hIcon = AfxGetApp()->LoadIcon(IDI_STOP);
        CButton* pButton = (CButton*)GetDlgItem(IDC_STOP);
        ASSERT(pButton);
        pButton->SetCheck(1);
        pButton = (CButton*)GetDlgItem(IDC_GO);
        ASSERT(pButton);
        pButton->SetCheck(0);
    }

    pIcon->SetIcon(hIcon);
}
```

This gets the data associated with the selected list box item and casts it to an event handle. It then checks for the state of the event with **WaitForSingleObject()** and sets the radio buttons and the icon in the picture control.

The process can now add events and view their states. There are two more tasks to do: change the event state, and handle the shutdown of the process. The first is done by handling the 'click' events on the radio buttons, so in ClassWizard add handlers for the **BN_CLICKED** messages, calling them **OnGo()** and **OnStop()**:

```
void CSetEventDlg::OnGo()
{
    CListBox* pList = (CListBox*)GetDlgItem(IDC_EVENTS);
    ASSERT(pList);

    CStatic* pIcon = (CStatic*)GetDlgItem(IDC_STATUS);
    ASSERT(pIcon);

    HANDLE hEvent = (HANDLE)pList->GetItemData(pList->GetCurSel());
    SetEvent(hEvent);

    HICON hIcon = AfxGetApp()->LoadIcon(IDI_GO);
    pIcon->SetIcon(hIcon);
}

void CSetEventDlg::OnStop()
{
    CListBox* pList = (CListBox*)GetDlgItem(IDC_EVENTS);
    ASSERT(pList);
```

```
    CStatic* pIcon = (CStatic*)GetDlgItem(IDC_STATUS);
    ASSERT(pIcon);

    HANDLE hEvent = (HANDLE)pList->GetItemData(pList->GetCurSel());
    ResetEvent(hEvent);

    HICON hIcon = AfxGetApp()->LoadIcon(IDI_STOP);
    pIcon->SetIcon(hIcon);
}
```

Finally, when the process closes, it needs to go through all the items in the listbox and close all the handles held as item data. Note that if another process has opened one of these events, the event will not be destroyed. It is only when the last reference on an event handle has been closed with **CloseHandle()** that the object will be destroyed.

Open ClassWizard once more, select CSetEventDlg in the Object IDs list box, and double click on WM_CLOSE in the Messages box. Then click on Edit Code and enter the following:

```
void CSetEventDlg::OnClose()
{
    // Release all the event objects
    CListBox* pList = (CListBox*)GetDlgItem(IDC_EVENTS);
    ASSERT(pList);

    int count = pList->GetCount();
    count--;

    while (count>=0)
    {
        HANDLE hEvent = (HANDLE)pList->GetItemData(count--);
        CloseHandle(hEvent);
    }
    CDialog::OnClose();
}
```

Testing

Finally, you should be able to compile the project and test it out. The first test is to run the process and type a name in the edit box — the Create button should become enabled. Click on this to create a new event. You should be able to use the radio buttons to change the state, which should show up by the lights on the traffic lights changing. Try and add several events to check that they can have different states.

In the second test, run two instances of the process and use it to create the same named event in both instances. In one instance, change the state (say, from Set to Reset) and then tab to the other instance and select the event name from the list box. You should see the event state change to reflect the change caused in the other instance.

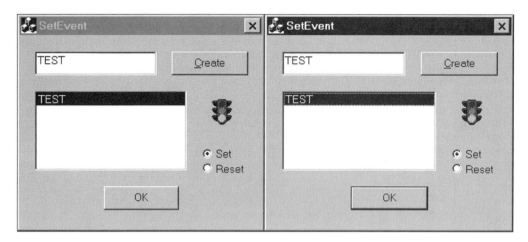

These checks should prove to you that the process is able to create and change the states of kernel event objects.

Testing the Whole Example

Remember that the client and server will be in different processes, and that since they will be using connection points, both the client and server are behaving as COM servers and clients. Thus you will need to build and register proxy-stub objects for both. To do this for **EventWatcher**, open a command prompt and move to the **EventWatcher** directory. If you did not tell the Developer Studio setup program to set environment variables when you first installed Visual C++, you will need to set them now so that you can compile from a command line. Go to your installation's **bin** directory and type:

```
vcvars32
```

This will run a batch file. Next, return to the project directory and enter:

```
nmake EventWatcherps.mk
regsvr32 EventWatcherps.dll
```

Do the same thing for **EventCtrlps.mk**.

If there are problems, you will need to debug the projects; the three projects are debugged in different ways. The technique for **SetEvent** will be the most familiar to you: you should set breakpoints in the code and then run the project under the debugger. You can test how various Windows messages are handled by clicking on various controls on the dialog and checking that the code is handling them correctly.

For the **EventWatcher** project, you can still set breakpoints and run the server, but for any of the breakpoints to be reached, you will need to create an object using a client: the **EventControl** object. Since this is a DLL, you will need to use a container. The two options here are to use Internet Explorer (the ATL Wizard will have created an HTML file for you) or the ActiveX Control Test Container. The easiest option here is to use the Test Container. To specify that this should be used, select Settings... from the Project menu and on the Debug tab, click on the arrow button next to the Executable for debug session. From this menu, select ActiveX Control Test Container. Now when you press *F5* to debug the object server, the Test Container will be started (ignore any warnings that it does not contain any debug information) and from this you can select Insert OLE Control... from the Edit menu and add the **EventControl** class.

One area to pay particular attention to is the registration of the object servers and their proxy-stub DLLs. The complication here is that the **EventControl** project depends on the type library for the **EventWatcher**, while the IDL file of **EventWatcher** depends on the type library of **EventControl**. You have to make sure that all these files are kept up to date.

Assuming you have got these projects to compile correctly, you can test them by running **SetEvent** and creating an event called Test. Then, start the ActiveX Control Test Container (do this from the Tools menu in Developer Studio) and select the **EventControl**:

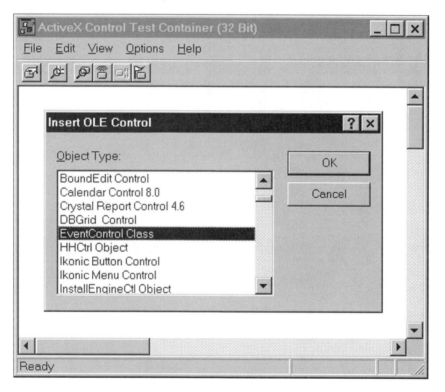

If the object is not created, the most likely reason for failure is security. COM on NT4 maintains a list of the user accounts (and groups) that can create and access an object. If you are logged on as a user other than one of those expressly allowed to launch and access the **EventWatcher** object, the **EventControl** control will not be able to create or access it. You should thus use **DCOMCnfg** to add your user account in the lists of accounts allowed to launch and access this class (Chapter 5 has details of how to do this). The **EventWatcher** object will need to callback on the **EventControl** control to fire an event, and so the account that the **EventWatcher** object is running under will need to have access to the **EventControl**.

Initially, the control will not have had a callback from the server object, so you will get the Uninitialized caption:

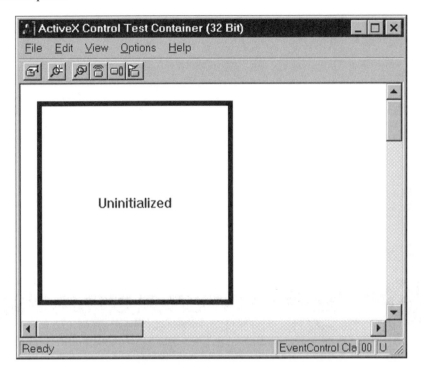

However, when you change the event state with **SetEvent**, the control will be updated with the value:

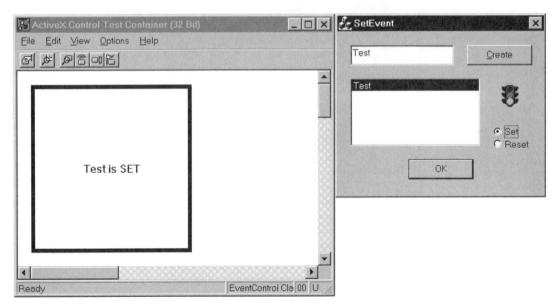

Improvements

There are several ways you could improve this project; here are some suggestions for you to play with.

Using the Control with Remote Objects

The first improvement concerns the fact that the server object is created on the local machine. The code has been written to use **CoCreateInstanceEx()**, and so it could just as well create the object on a remote machine. You could change the code so that it gets the name of the remote host machine from somewhere (the registry, a property, or via a dialog) and use this in the **COSERVERINFO** parameter. An example of how to do this is provided on the Wrox web site (http://www.wrox.com).

Another improvement would be to change the code so that you can look for events other than Test. Once again, the value could be set through a property or via a dialog.

Summary

This chapter has explained what connection points are, and why you need to implement them. The two examples have shown how to write a server that implements a connection point, and how to call a sink interface using the connection point proxy generator.

The chapter has also demonstrated how to write a connection point client and implement a sink interface in Visual Basic and Visual C++. Along the way, we had the chance to experiment with some issues about events and threading.

Properties, Persistence and Collections

An ActiveX control will usually hold some internal **state**, which in many cases will need to be initialized when the control is first created, and saved (made **persistent**) when the control is destroyed. Further, if the control is part of a document (for example, a Word document, or an Excel spreadsheet), then when the document is made persistent, so should any objects within the document. To do this, the container should ask all its objects to save their state.

There are other situations where property persistence is important. When you put a control on a VB form, you use the VB property box to change the control's properties to affect its display and behavior. When you save the VB project, these properties must be persisted to a file, and further, when you compile a VB application the properties must be persisted in way that can be saved in the compiled code.

This chapter covers three main subject areas:

> ▶ Properties. The data items that controls expose.
>
> ▶ Persistence. I will explain the general method of making a control persistent.
>
> ▶ Collections. How to create and access collections of properties.

Control Properties

An ActiveX control can have an internal state, and the object may expose this state using **properties**. Properties come in several forms. They can be simple, single items of data, or they can be arrays of data. As you have seen in previous chapters, although a property is viewed from the client as a data item, they are actually exposed from the object using methods: a readable property has a **get_** method, and a writeable property has a **put_** method. Further, since by nature properties are designed for use with scripting languages, the **put_** method should have the **[out]** parameter marked as **[retval]** so that the scripting language treats it as the return value.

Single item properties can be exposed by single-parameter **put_** and **get_** methods, but array properties are rather more complicated. We looked at how to do this in Chapter 4: Automation defines an array type called a **SAFEARRAY** that describes the type, size and bounds of the array.

ActiveX controls that expose properties are intimately involved with Automation. You can expose properties without using Automation, but such an object will be excluded from use with containers that use late binding, and this means you will not be able to use the object with Internet Explorer or an Active Server Page. To make an ActiveX control useful for all common containers, it should be an Automation object, and so expose a dispinterface or a dual interface. When I talk about properties in this chapter, you can assume that I mean Automation properties.

Arrays are fine, but iterating through an array is tedious, and there are other ways of working with them. Arrays of data can be exposed as **enumerators** or **collections**. Enumerator objects expose an interface that has methods allowing you to read arrays of values. You saw an enumerator briefly in the last chapter when we looked at the connection point interfaces, but that is far from the extent of their usefulness. Enumerations are used extensively in COM.

A collection is an extended array of data that gives access to its members using a map-like syntax by using a keyword, or by using an array-like syntax with an index. Furthermore, iterating through collections really shines with VBA, because it has the **foreach** keyword that allows iteration without requiring an index. Collections are not exposed from an object through a single method (like **SAFEARRAY**s) or a single interface (like enumerators), but instead are exposed through several methods.

The properties of an ActiveX control can be used to affect how a control displays itself. A control can implement two sorts of properties: **custom properties**, which are specific to a particular control and are described by its type library, and **stock properties**, which have standard DISPIDs and so are known to all control containers. Note that containers can also have **ambient properties**, which an ActiveX control can read and use to take on the look and feel of the container.

This first section will concentrate on single item properties. Array properties, enumerators and collections will be covered later in the chapter.

Custom Properties

Custom properties are simply properties on the control's interface, so adding and maintaining properties on a control uses the same techniques as for the properties on any interface.

This is straightforward. When you want to add a property, you can either do it the hard way — editing the IDL by hand — or the easy way, by using the Developer Studio ClassView. We will take the easy route. Usually, you can give the property a DISPID by allowing the Wizard to assign an **[id()]** attribute for you. However, if you want to, you can use the ClassView to specify a value, as you saw in Chapter 4. Giving a property a specific DISPID is necessary when you want to expose the required properties of a collection (explained later), or a stock property.

Stock Properties

When you add a property to an interface, you give it a DISPID. However, a container does not normally know what, for example, a DISPID of 2 means, since different interfaces will use it for different properties (if at all). On the other hand, controls of all types will have certain properties in common: background color, foreground color and text font, for example. It makes sense that these **stock properties** should have well known values, so that when a container sees that a control supports a property with a particular DISPID, it knows exactly what the property is. To distinguish between custom properties and system-defined stock properties, the DISPIDs of custom properties are positive and those of stock properties are negative.

The following table lists standard stock properties:

Name	DISPID	Description
Appearance	DISPID_APPEARANCE	Appearance, for example, 3D or flat
AutoSize	DISPID_AUTOSIZE	Determines if a control can be resized
BackColor	DISPID_BACKCOLOR	The control's background color
BackStyle	DISPID_BACKSTYLE	Background style, usually opaque or transparent
BorderColor	DISPID_BORDERCOLOR	The color of the control's border
BorderStyle	DISPID_BORDERSTYLE	Determines how the border is drawn
BorderVisible	DISPID_BORDERVISIBLE	Determines if the control's border is visible
BorderWidth	DISPID_BORDERWIDTH	Width of the border
Caption	DISPID_CAPTION	Caption displayed on the control
DrawMode	DISPID_DRAWMODE	The paint style used to draw the control
DrawStyle	DISPID_DRAWSTYLE	Line style used to draw the control
DrawWidth	DISPID_DRAWWIDTH	Line width used to draw the control
Enabled	DISPID_ENABLED	Determines if the control is enabled
FillColor	DISPID_FILLCOLOR	The color used to fill the control
FillStyle	DISPID_FILLSTYLE	Determines how a control is filled in; for example, solid or hatched
Font	DISPID_FONT	The font used to draw text
ForeColor	DISPID_FORECOLOR	The color used for text in the control
HWND	DISPID_HWND	**HWND** of the control's window
MouseIcon	DISPID_MOUSEICON	The graphic to be used by the mouse pointer
MousePointer	DISPID_MOUSEPOINTER	The cursor to be used when over the control
Picture	DISPID_PICTURE	A graphic to be used as part of the control
ReadyState	DISPID_READYSTATE	Determines if the control is ready, or still loading
TabStop	DISPID_TABSTOP	Indicates if the control is a tab stop
Text	DISPID_TEXT	Text displayed by the control
Valid	DISPID_VALID	Determines if the control is valid

Clearly, you would not want to have all of these stock properties on your control. Some stock properties are only required when other properties are set, while others are mutually exclusive.

ATL makes adding a stock property to a new Internet Explorer or full control very easy: the Object Wizard allows you to specify which stock properties the control should support, and it will add a data member for this property in the generated C++ class. It will also derive your class from **CStockPropImpl<>**, which implements the **put** and **get** methods for the property that notify the container.

However, if you want to add a new property *after* you have created an object, life is a little harder. The Attributes tab of the Add Property dialog does not allow you to type in a negative number, or a symbol, and the only workaround is to edit the IDL by hand. Further, you will need to edit the class header by hand to derive from **CStockPropImpl<>** and trawl through the ATL header files to determine what class data members you should add. Clearly, you should think carefully before you create a control about the stock properties that it will support!

Ambient Properties

Ambient properties are not properties on your control; they are properties on the container that will house the control. However, your control will depend on the container's ambient properties, and so it is important to understand what they are used for, and how to access them.

Ambient properties are read-only properties like **Font** and **BackColor** that a control container exposes to a control. The control can read ambient properties and use them to set its own properties. This allows a control to blend in well with the container and the other controls it shows. If you can imagine how unprofessional a VB form would look if it had two buttons with captions written in completely different fonts, you can understand the need for ambient properties.

For ambient properties to be useful, the container must be able to inform the control when a property changes. It does this by passing the DISPID of the property to the control. However, so that the control knows what the DISPID means, it must have a value known to both the container and control. Unless your control container will only pass ambient properties to controls that you've written, ambient properties should have Microsoft-defined values (which are negative). When a control is informed that a property has changed, it can handle this by obtaining the property value. The control specification (OCX '96) says that although ambient properties have names, the control should only access them using the standard DISPIDs assigned to them. (In other words, you should use early binding, where the DISPID is compiled into the control's code — this obviously reduces the need to call **GetIDsOfNames()**). The following table lists the standard ambient properties:

Name	DISPID	Description
BackColor	-701	The interior color of the control
DisplayName	-702	The name used in error messages
Font	-703	The font used by the control
ForeColor	-704	The color used to display text and graphics
LocaleID	-705	The locale ID
MessageReflect	-706	Determines if the container reflects Windows messages back to the control

Name	DISPID	Description
ScaleUnits	-707	Specifies the coordinate unit name being used by the container
TextAlign	-708	Text alignment
UserMode	-709	Determines if the control is in a design container or running in an application
UIDead	-710	If true, the control should not respond to the UI
ShowGrabHandles	-711	Determines if grab handles should be displayed when the control is active
ShowHatching	-712	Determines if the control should use UI active hatching feedback when UI active
DisplayAsDefaultButton	-713	Determines if the button should display itself as the default button
SupportsMnemonics	-714	Determines if the container supports mnemonics
AutoClip	-715	Determines if the container will automatically clip the control

Controls that need to communicate with their container must implement the **IOleControl** interface, which has a method called **OnAmbientPropertyChange()** that gets called by the container when an ambient property has changed. The method is passed the DISPID of the changed property.

With the **IOleControlImpl<>** template, ATL does most of the work of implementing this interface for you, but the implementation for **OnAmbientPropertyChange()** does no more than return **S_OK**. If your control needs to react to changing ambient properties, it must override this method, obtain the value of the ambient property, and then use the value.

Adding Properties to a Control

As mentioned earlier, a control that is to support stock properties should have them added at creation time using the Object Wizard. Handling stock properties requires adding a data member into the control class and managing the **put** and **get** methods for the property, as well as container notification.

To add properties later in the development process, you first have to edit the IDL by hand. To add the **Caption** property, for example, you would need to add these lines into your interface's IDL:

```
[propput, id(DISPID_CAPTION)]
    HRESULT Caption([in] BSTR strCaption);
[propget, id(DISPID_CAPTION)]
    HRESULT Caption([out, retval] BSTR* strCaption);
```

Next, you need to derive your ATL class from **CStockPropImpl<>**, using your ATL class, the interface and its IID, and the coclass TypeID as parameters:

```
class ATL_NO_VTABLE CMyStockProp :
    public CComObjectRootEx<CComSingleThreadModel>,
    public CComCoClass<CMyStockProp, &CLSID_MyStockProp>,
    public CComControl<CMyStockProp>,
    public CStockPropImpl<CMyStockProp, IMyInterface,
                                   &IID_IMyInterface, &LIBID_MYLib>,
```

This template provides **get** and **put** methods and notification for *all* stock properties. These stock properties are defined in **atlctrl.h**, and most have their **put_** and **get_** methods defined using one of **IMPLEMENT_STOCKPROP()**, **IMPLEMENT_BOOL_STOCKPROP()** or **IMPLEMENT_BSTR_STOCKPROP()**. The other properties (**Font**, **HWND**, **MouseIcon** and **Picture**) have their **put_** and **get_** methods defined explicitly. However they are defined, the template class assumes the following data members in your ATL control class:

Name	ATL Class Data Member
Appearance	LONG m_nAppearance
AutoSize	BOOL m_bAutoSize
BackColor	OLE_COLOR m_clrBackColor
BackStyle	LONG m_nBackStyle
BorderColor	OLE_COLOR m_clrBorderColor
BorderStyle	LONG m_nBorderStyle
BorderVisible	BOOL m_bBorderVisible
BorderWidth	LONG m_nBorderWidth
Caption	CComBSTR m_bstrCaption
DrawMode	LONG m_nDrawMode
DrawStyle	LONG m_nDrawStyle
DrawWidth	LONG m_nDrawWidth
Enabled	BOOL m_bEnabled
FillColor	OLE_COLOR m_clrFillColor
FillStyle	LONG m_nFillStyle
Font	CComPtr<IFontDisp> m_pFont
ForeColor	OLE_COLOR m_clrForeColor
MouseIcon	CComPtr<IPictureDisp> m_pMouseIcon
MousePointer	LONG m_nMousePointer
Picture	CComPtr<IPictureDisp> m_pPicture
ReadState	LONG m_nReadyState
TabStop	BOOL m_bTabStop
Text	CComBSTR m_bstrText
Valid	BOOL m_bValid

Note that the **DISPID_HWND** stock property is not listed here because **CStockPropImpl<>** implements it using a property called **Window** (**put_Window()** and **get_Window()**) that use the ATL class's **m_hWnd** data member. The **Font**, **MouseIcon** and **Picture** stock properties are objects, and hence are accessed through **IDispatch**-derived interfaces.

When you add a new stock property to your control, you need to add the appropriate data member from the table to your ATL class. I know your next question already: what about all the other data members given in the table that you have *not* added to your ATL class? The stock property macros will still be used and attempt to access these non-existent data members, so how does the code compile? The answer is that your control is derived from **CComControl**, and its base class, **CComControlBase**, has a union with members that have the names of these stock properties. If you do not specify a stock property in the Object Wizard, then the **CStockPropImpl<>** code accesses the member inherited from the union in **CComControlBase**.

If you want to add a custom property to the control, you need to add it from the ClassView. To show how to use properties on a control, we will develop a simple example. This example will be used later in the chapter to demonstrate how to make properties persistent, so to allow it to be used in a container like Word, we will create a Full Control. The difference between a Full Control and an Internet Explorer Control will be covered in the next chapter.

Here are the steps:

1. In Developer Studio, create a new project with the ATL COM AppWizard. Give it a name like Properties and then click on OK.

2. When the ATL COM AppWizard dialog appears, ensure that the Server Type is Dynamic Link Library (DLL) and click on Finish. Finally, accept the project information by clicking on OK in the next dialog.

3. Add a new control to the project using the Object Wizard: select Insert | New ATL Object…, and choose Controls from the left hand pane and Full Control in the right hand pane. Click on Next >.

4. On the Names tab of the property dialog, give the control a Short Name of Prop.

5. At this point, switch to the Miscellaneous tab. Select the Insertable check box; this will allow the control to appear in the Insert Object dialog, so that you can test it later with MS Word.

6. Next, select the Stock Properties tab and add support for Background Color, Caption and Foreground Color by selecting them in the left-hand pane and clicking on >.

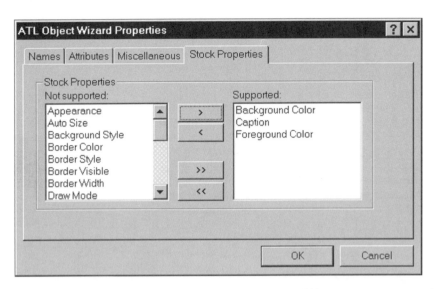

7. If you add the control to the project by clicking on OK, you can now use the ClassView to look at the code that the Object Wizard has added for you:

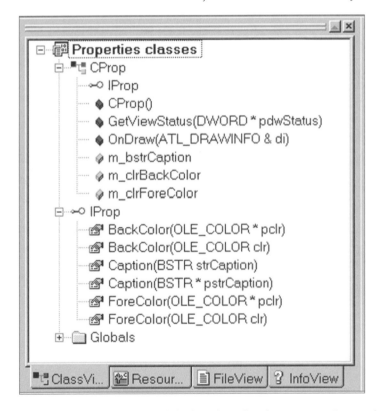

8. The ObjectWizard will not give default values for these properties — the constructor for the **CComBSTR** will initialize the **Caption** property to an empty string, but the color variables will not be initialized, so do this in the constructor:

```
public:
    CProp() : m_clrForeColor(0), m_clrBackColor(0xffffff)
    {
    }
```

Notice how the **IProp** interface has **get** and **put** methods for each of the stock properties that you selected, but that these methods are not implemented as part of the **CProp** class. The reason for this is that they are implemented by the **CStockPropImpl<>** base class. Object Wizard has, however, added two **OLE_COLOR**s and a **BSTR** member for these properties to the class, so you can manipulate them directly in your code (in the control initialization code, for example).

Next, we'll add some custom properties to our control:

1. Right click on the IProp interface in the ClassView, and select Add Property... from the menu. In the next dialog, select a Property Type of BSTR and give it a Property Name of String. Click on OK.

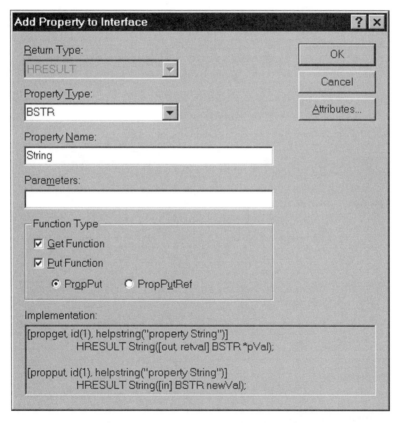

2. Add another property called Number that has a type of long.

3. The Wizard will add the **get** and **put** methods for you, but will not add data members. For this example you will need data members, so open the **Prop.h** header and add the following at the bottom of the class:

```
    OLE_COLOR m_clrBackColor;
    OLE_COLOR m_clrForeColor;
    CComBSTR m_bstrCaption;
    CComBSTR m_bstrString;
    long m_lNumber;
};
```

4. Initialize the **m_lNumber** value in the constructor near the top of the class declaration:

```
public:
    CProp() : m_clrForeColor(0), m_clrBackColor(0xffffff), m_lNumber(0)
    {
    }
```

5. Add the following code to the stub **get**/**put** methods in **Prop.cpp** that the Wizard has added for you:

```
STDMETHODIMP CProp::get_String(BSTR * pVal)
{
    ATLTRACE(_T("String returning: %ls\n"), m_bstrString);
    *pVal = SysAllocString(m_bstrString.m_str);
    return S_OK;
}

STDMETHODIMP CProp::put_String(BSTR newVal)
{
    ATLTRACE(_T("String assigned to: %ls\n"), newVal);
    m_bstrString = newVal;
    SysFreeString(newVal);
    FireViewChange();
    return S_OK;
}

STDMETHODIMP CProp::get_Number(long * pVal)
{
    ATLTRACE(_T("Number returning: %ld\n"), m_lNumber);
    *pVal = m_lNumber;
    return S_OK;
}

STDMETHODIMP CProp::put_Number(long newVal)
{
    ATLTRACE(_T("Number assigned to: %ld\n"), m_lNumber);
    m_lNumber = newVal;
    FireViewChange();
    return S_OK;
}
```

Using a **CComBSTR** here ensures that the data member is initialized when the control is created, and that the enclosed **BSTR** is released when the control is destroyed.

6. Notice the use of the **FireViewChange()** function in the **put** methods. This ensures that whenever a property is changed, the visual representation also changes. This representation is drawn in the **OnDraw()** method, so add the following code to **Prop.cpp**, and compile.

```cpp
HRESULT CProp::OnDraw(ATL_DRAWINFO& di)
{
    USES_CONVERSION;
    int iMode = SetMapMode(di.hdcDraw, MM_TEXT);
    RECT& rc = *(RECT*)di.prcBounds;

    COLORREF clrFront, clrBack;
    HBRUSH hOldBrush, hBrush;
    HPEN hOldPen, hPen;

    OleTranslateColor(m_clrBackColor, NULL, &clrBack);
    OleTranslateColor(m_clrForeColor, NULL, &clrFront);

    hBrush = CreateSolidBrush(clrBack);
    hOldBrush = (HBRUSH)SelectObject(di.hdcDraw, hBrush);
    hPen = CreatePen(PS_SOLID, 1, clrFront);
    hOldPen = (HPEN)SelectObject(di.hdcDraw, hPen);

    Rectangle(di.hdcDraw, rc.left, rc.top, rc.right, rc.bottom);

    SetTextColor(di.hdcDraw, clrFront);
    SetBkColor(di.hdcDraw, clrBack);

    CComBSTR bstrText;
    bstrText = _T("Caption: ");
    bstrText += m_bstrCaption;
    ExtTextOut(di.hdcDraw, rc.left + 2, 2 + rc.top, ETO_CLIPPED,
        &rc, OLE2T(bstrText.m_str), bstrText.Length(), NULL);

    bstrText = _T("String: ");
    bstrText += m_bstrString;
    ExtTextOut(di.hdcDraw, rc.left + 2, 2 + rc.top + 25, ETO_CLIPPED,
        &rc, OLE2T(bstrText.m_str), bstrText.Length(), NULL);

    bstrText = _T("Number: ");
    TCHAR szNum[12];
    wsprintf(szNum, _T("%ld"), m_lNumber);
    bstrText += szNum;
    ExtTextOut(di.hdcDraw, rc.left + 2, 2 + rc.top + 50, ETO_CLIPPED,
        &rc, OLE2T(bstrText.m_str), bstrText.Length(), NULL);

    SelectObject(di.hdcDraw, hOldBrush);
    DeleteObject(hBrush);
    SelectObject(di.hdcDraw, hOldPen);
    DeleteObject(hPen);
    SetMapMode(di.hdcDraw, iMode);
    return S_OK;
}
```

Most of this is straightforward Win32 GDI code. The color properties are of the **OLE_COLOR** type, and so the **OleTranslateColor()** function is called to convert them to the **COLORREF** values used by GDI. I create a brush and a pen using the stock background and foreground colors, and select them into the device context before the call to **Rectangle()**.

Next, I draw the text on the screen. To do this, I need to put the values into a string, and in this code I use the ATL **CComBSTR** to add strings together. This is probably not the most efficient code for doing so, but it is quite compact. I use the **ForeColor** stock property to set the text foreground color, and the **BackColor** stock property to set the text background color before drawing the text on the screen.

The actual drawing is done with the **ExtTextOut()** function. This is used because it can be placed into a metafile, whereas **DrawText()** cannot. You will come across metafiles later in this chapter and in the next chapter, but basically they are recorded GDI commands. The name is something of a misnomer, because a metafile does not have to be a disk file — it can be an application resource, or an in-memory resource. Because of this feature, metafiles can be placed in OLE streams, as explained later. By default, the ATL Object Wizard uses **DrawText()**.

Notice how careful I am about using the bounding rectangle given in **di.prcBounds**. This is because you cannot assume that the top left corner will always be (0,0) — the container may pass you a bounding rectangle that is part of another window. The full details of this are investigated in the next chapter.

Testing the Control

The simplest way to test the control is to use the ActiveX Control Test Container, which you can run from the Tools menu in Developer Studio. To test the control, select Insert OLE Control... from the Edit menu. From this dialog select Prop Class and click on OK. From the Edit menu, select Invoke Methods... so that you can access the properties directly through their **get** and **put** methods.

The Name combo has all the methods that the control implements. When you select a method name, the DISPID of that method, and whether it is a **get** or **put** method, is shown. The dialog also lists all the parameters that the method takes, so that you can enter values before clicking on the Invoke button to call the method.

Select Caption (-518 Put) and type a value into the BSTR (Prop value) box, and then click on Invoke. You should notice that the control is immediately updated. Try the same with the String and Number properties.

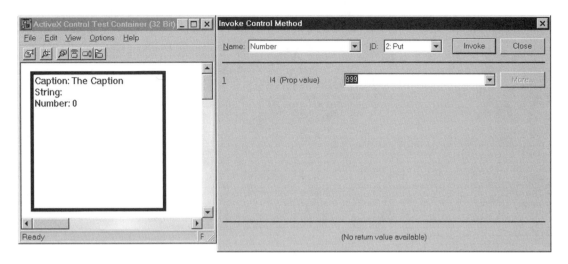

In this dialog, select the BackColor or ForeColor **put** properties. You will find that the edit box used to change the property is grayed out. The reason for this is that the Object Wizard has added a **property page** for these stock properties, and so you need to use this to change the color values. Property Pages will be covered in detail in the next chapter.

To test the color stock properties, close the Invoke Control Method dialog and select Edit | Embedded Object Functions | Properties.

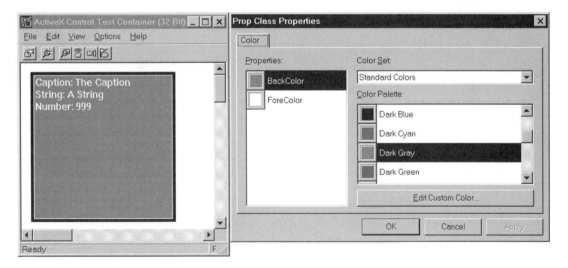

You can select colors from the Color Palette and click on the Apply button to change the control's stock color properties.

Changing Properties via Scripting

The Object Wizard will create a minimal HTML page to place the control on a web page. The properties that you have added can be accessed through scripting, as demonstrated by the following example (add the highlighted code):

```
<HTML>
<HEAD>
<TITLE>ATL 2.0 test page for object Prop</TITLE>
</HEAD>
<BODY>
<OBJECT ID="Prop" <
 NAME="Obj"
 CLASSID="CLSID:7B33B4FD-59B3-11D1-9A48-0060973044A8">
>
</OBJECT>
<P>
<INPUT TYPE="BUTTON"
 NAME="bn"
 VALUE="Click me"
 LANGUAGE=VBS
 onclick="bnclick">
<INPUT TYPE="TEXT"
 NAME="txtString"
 VALUE="">
<SCRIPT LANGUAGE=VBS>
Sub bnclick()
    Obj.Number = Obj.Number + 1
    Obj.String = txtString.Value
End Sub
</SCRIPT>
</BODY>
</HTML>
```

Here, I give the object a name and add two HTML controls. The button click event is handled using the VBScript procedure called **bnclick**, which merely increments the control's **Number** property and copies the data from the text box into the control's **String** property.

> *Note: so that this script will work in Internet Explorer, you may need to change its security settings. The reason is that the scripting code comes from a source external to the control, and to prevent the control from being accessed from a malicious script, IE disables scripting by default. The next chapter will show you how to change your control so that it can tell IE that the control allows scripting.*

In this screen shot, I have clicked on the button a couple of times:

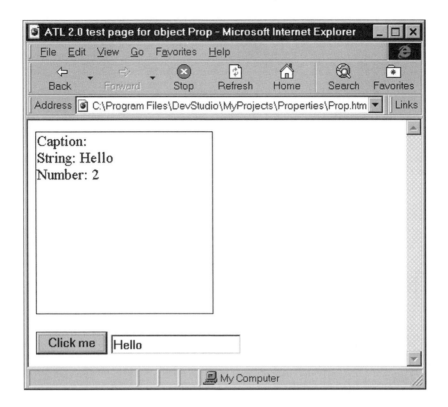

Persistence

Persistence involves initializing a control from some persistent values when it is created, and saving the control's state to some persistent store when the control stops running. ATL adds persistence for you automatically when your object class is derived from the correct class, as we'll discover later. The code that ATL provides for persistence steps through the properties supported by the control, loading or saving the values. This is adequate for most property types, but if you have a complex property (like a **SAFEARRAY**), or you want to make a value persistent that is not described by a property, you will need to write the persistence code yourself.

It will surely come as no surprise to you that this functionality is implemented using interfaces; what then are the interfaces required for persistence?

Persistence Interfaces

The COM interfaces for persistence all start with the name **IPersist...**. If you peruse the documentation, the first such interface you will come across is **IPersistFile**. However, although it sounds a likely candidate, this interface is not used by controls. The reason for this is that controls are loaded into containers, and generally are one of many components that the container uses to maintain state. It is the responsibility of the container — not the control — to open a file and maintain the connection to the file object.

When writing to the file, the container asks its controls to serialize their states into a byte stream that can be written to the file. When reading from a file, the container obtains this byte stream and passes it to the control. Since the control created the byte stream, it should be able to read and interpret the data, and hence initialize itself. So how does this work?

COM defines two interfaces called **IStream** and **IStorage** that allow servers to implement **structured storage**. The **IStream** interface allows an object to read and write a byte stream. Simple data can be written to a stream, but more complicated data should be structured, and this is the reason for **storages**. The usual way of explaining storages and streams is to compare them with a file operating system; I will use that here too, but with a warning not to take the analogy too far: structured storage does not have to use a file.

Think of a storage as being a bit like a folder in Explorer. The folder has a name, and it can contain other folders, but it cannot hold raw data. To put data into a folder, you need to put the data into a file and then put the file into the folder. You should think of a stream as being like a file: it is there to hold raw data. A file cannot hold other files or have folders, and likewise a stream cannot have other streams or storages.

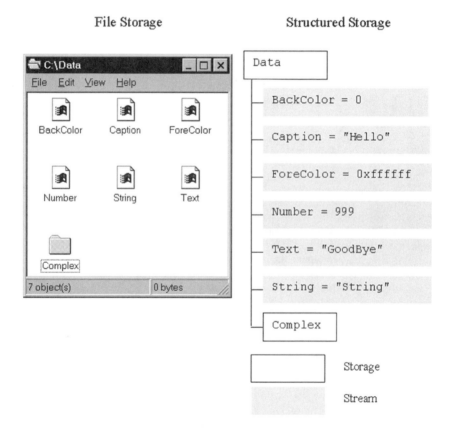

You can put storages and streams into a file called a **compound document**. Such a document can contain many storages, so to be able to identify a particular storage (or a stream within a storage), storages and streams have names, just as folders and files do. One obvious application for storages is a container that has many controls: when it wants to save its state, it can create a storage for each control, and ask the controls to save their states to the storages. Within the storage assigned to it, the control is free to create as many storages and streams as it wants, because it has the responsibility of reading the data back from the storage in the future, when the control is initialized.

As I have said, the container has the responsibility of creating the structured storage file (also known, for historical reasons, as a **DocFile**). If a control can persist itself, then it should implement one of the persistence interfaces. When the container wants to persist its document, it will query each control for an appropriate persistence interface and, if the control supports it, call the persistence methods to let the control save its data. The appropriate interfaces for streams and storages are **IPersistStreamInit** and **IPersistStorage**.

Why both? Streams are where the actual data is saved, and are the leaves at the end of the storage tree — that is, streams cannot contain storages or other streams. Since a stream is a single object, it does not require any other objects to be created, and so can be efficient for making simple data persistent. When using a stream to persist a control, the container will create the stream and then call **IPersistStream::Save()**, passing this stream.

However, since the persisting object only has one stream to write to, it must handle structuring itself. If it has several data items, each must be serialized into a byte stream before they can all be written to the same stream. For objects that contain complicated data, this can be a real inconvenience. If the control is passed a storage instead, it can structure the data accordingly, adding as many storages and streams as it needs. Since there are two ways to persist data, a container could use either, and so controls should support both. This does not necessarily mean that the persistence code is doubled, as demonstrated by the ATL code for **IPersistStorageImpl<>**: the **Save()** method creates a stream called "**Contents**" and passes this to the control's implementation of **IPersistStreamInit::Save()**.

> *Incidentally, there is also an interface called simply* **IPersistStream**, *which has all the methods necessary to read data from and write data to a stream. However, what it does not do is provide a method to get the object to an initialized state — that is, a state not initialized from an external source.* **IPersistStreamInit** *has a method called* **InitNew()** *that the container can call when it creates a new object. This method should initialize the object's internal state to some default value (note that* **IPersistStorage** *has a method of the same name).*

All the interfaces that have names of the form **IPersist**xxx derive from **IPersist**. This interface has just one method called **GetClassID()**, which returns the CLSID of the object that knows how to handle the persistent object. Usually this is the CLSID of the control, but it could be a proxy or a handler class. The container can call this method if it needs to save an ID in its persistence store, so that when it loads from the storage at a later stage, it can tell what type of object is persisted.

ATL provides default implementations of these two interfaces called **IPersistStreamInitImpl<>** and **IPersistStorageImpl<>**. These implementations use the same basic stream methods to save and load control state. The **Load()** and **Save()** methods of the stream interface call **IPersistStreamInit_Load()** and **IPersistStreamInit_Save()**, whereas the storage implementation first creates a "**Contents**" stream (as explained above) to hold the data, and then **QI()**s itself for the **IPersistStreamInit** interface to actually save the data.

These two methods need to know what data the control maintains, and the ATL class supplies this information through a **property map**.

Property Maps

Property maps are multi-functional (as you'll see in the next chapter), but in this context they are used to list all the control's properties that can be persistent. This implies that only those properties that appear in the property maps are made persistent. If you need to persist other data that cannot be put into the property map, then you will need to override the **Load()** and **Save()** methods of the persistence classes. An example of this is shown in the next chapter, where we will persist a **SAFEARRAY**.

Open the **Prop.h** file and look beneath the COM map. There you will find the property map:

```
BEGIN_PROPERTY_MAP(CProp)
    // Example entries
    // PROP_ENTRY("Property Description", dispid, clsid)
    PROP_PAGE(CLSID_StockColorPage)
END_PROPERTY_MAP()
```

The Wizard has already added an entry for you: the **PROP_PAGE()** macro specifies the property page to be used for the stock color properties. Design tools like Visual Basic allow a developer to view and change control properties; VB does this by reading the control's type information and presenting it in the Property window. Other design tools may not do this, so instead the control can implement a window — a **property page** — to give access to the control's properties. Property pages will be covered in more detail in the next chapter, where you will develop your own.

The property map also lists all the properties that can be made persistent; this is done with the **PROP_ENTRY()** macro. The Wizard supplies a sample entry that you can use as a guideline for your own entries.

```
    // PROP_ENTRY("Property Description", dispid, clsid)
```

The first item is the name of the property, which is used to identify the property in a **property bag**. A property bag is a mechanism whereby properties can be persisted as named items. The control is handed an **IPropertyBag** pointer, on which it can call the **Read()** method, passing the name of the property it needs to get, or the **Write()** method, passing the name and value of the property it wants to persist. Property bags are used to implement the **<PARAM>** tag in HTML, and by VB to initialize controls from (or write them to) the **frm** file.

The second item in **PROP_ENTRY()** is the DISPID of the property, and the final item is the CLSID of the property page used to initialize the property. If you specify a property page in **PROP_ENTRY()**, you do not need to use the **PROP_PAGE()** macro. If you do not have a property page for the property, then you can use **CLSID_NULL**.

In the following tests, we'll add all the properties you previously added to the control, to the property map.

> 1. Open **Prop.h** and add all the properties to the property map. Notice how the stock color properties use the standard color property page and the others use **CLSID_NULL**.

350

```
BEGIN_PROPERTY_MAP(CProp)
   PROP_ENTRY("BackColor", DISPID_BACKCOLOR, CLSID_StockColorPage)
   PROP_ENTRY("ForeColor", DISPID_FORECOLOR, CLSID_StockColorPage)
   PROP_ENTRY("Caption", DISPID_CAPTION, CLSID_NULL)
   PROP_ENTRY("String", 1, CLSID_NULL)
   PROP_ENTRY("Number", 2, CLSID_NULL)
END_PROPERTY_MAP()
```

2. Next, add the following code further down in the class declaration:

```
// IViewObjectEx
   STDMETHOD(GetViewStatus)(DWORD* pdwStatus)
   {
      ATLTRACE(_T("IViewObjectExImpl::GetViewStatus\n"));
      *pdwStatus = VIEWSTATUS_SOLIDBKGND | VIEWSTATUS_OPAQUE;
      return S_OK;
   }

// IPersistStreamInit
   STDMETHOD(InitNew)();
   STDMETHOD(Load)(LPSTREAM pStm);
   bool m_bInitialized;
```

3. Change the constructor to initialize this new variable:

```
CProp() : m_clrForeColor(0), m_clrBackColor(0xffffff), m_lNumber(0),
          m_bInitialized(false)
{
}
```

4. And add this code to the bottom of **Prop.cpp**:

```
STDMETHODIMP CProp::InitNew()
{
   if (m_bInitialized)
      return E_UNEXPECTED;
   m_bstrCaption = "Caption";
   m_bstrString = "String";
   m_lNumber = -99;
   m_bInitialized = true;
   return S_OK;
}

STDMETHODIMP CProp::Load(LPSTREAM pStm)
{
   if (m_bInitialized)
      return E_UNEXPECTED;
   else
   {
      m_bInitialized = true;
```

```
        return IPersistStreamInitImpl<CProp>::Load(pStm);
    }
}
```

5. Compile the code

In the second change, the **IPersistStreamInit::InitNew()** is overridden to give the properties default values. This method is also called by **IPersistStorage::InitNew()**, so you only have to add the code in this one place.

The COM specification says that if the control is initialized with **IPersistStreamInit::InitNew()**, then **IPersistStreamInit::Load()** must return **E_UNEXPECTED**, and vice versa. This is the reason for the new variable, **m_bInitialized**, and for overriding **Load()**.

Persisting as Part of a Compound Document

To test that this control can persist its properties to a compound document, we will insert the control into a Word document (you can also insert this control in WordPad). This is why we made sure when creating the control that the Object Wizard marked it as Insertable. (As a result, the control's CLSID has the **Insertable** key in the registry.) To test the control, run Word, and select Insert | Object.... This brings up the Insert Object dialog, similar to the one you saw in the ActiveX Control Test Container. From the Create New tab, select Prop Class and then click on OK:

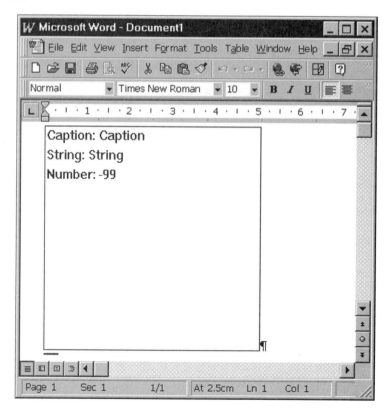

This has the default values you entered in the **InitNew()** method. Now save the document, close it, and then open the document again. When you load the file, you see the control with the values you saw when the control was first inserted into the document — or do you? Actually, you're not looking at the control at all; it's just a visual representation of it. What has happened is this: when you first created the object, Word asked the control to draw itself into a metafile (it did this by calling **IDataObject::GetData()**). Essentially, what this means is that all the GDI commands used in **OnDraw()** are sent to a metafile instead of going to the screen. When you saved the document, Word saved the metafile in its document. When you loaded the document from disk, Word read the metafile and 'played' the GDI commands to the area of the screen where the control should be.

Using metafiles like this is useful, because it means that Word can use them for displaying or printing, and the control does not have to be loaded and asked to draw itself. There could be a hit on performance if the control takes time to load and draw itself.

To activate the control, you should click on it. To edit the control, you should double-click on it, but when you try to do so, you'll get this dialog:

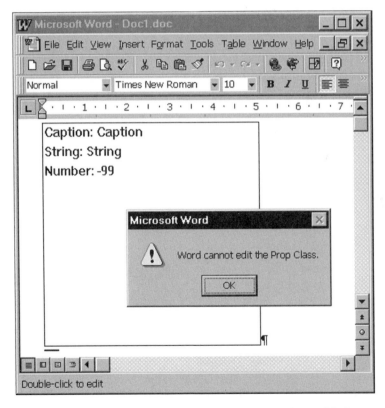

The reason for this is that when the Word document was saved, it told the control to save itself, but the control saved nothing. Now, when the document is loaded, Word passes an empty storage to the control to initialize itself with. **IPersistStorageImpl::Load()** fails, and so the control does not bother to update the view.

To make the control save data, you need to ensure that when a property's value changes, the control knows that its state is different from any state that may have been made persistent. The **CComControlBase** class has a flag specifying whether the state has changed or not. This flag is changed with a call to the **SetDirty()** method, passing **true** to set the flag, and **false** to clear it. You need to add a call to the method whenever a property changes, so open **Prop.cpp**, add the indicated lines, and compile the code:

```
STDMETHODIMP CProp::put_String(BSTR newVal)
{
    ATLTRACE(_T("String assigned to: %ls\n"), newVal);
    m_bstrString = newVal;
    SysFreeString(newVal);
    SetDirty(true);
    FireViewChange();
    return S_OK;
}

STDMETHODIMP CProp::put_Number(long newVal)
{
    ATLTRACE(_T("Number assigned to: %ld\n"), m_lNumber);
    m_lNumber = newVal;
    SetDirty(true);
    FireViewChange();
    return S_OK;
}

STDMETHODIMP CProp::InitNew()
{
    if (m_bInitialized)
        return E_UNEXPECTED;
    m_bstrCaption = "Caption";
    m_bstrString = "String";
    m_lNumber = -99;
    SetDirty(true);
    m_bInitialized = true;
    return S_OK;
}
```

If you find that Developer Studio complains that it cannot write to the control, it is because Word is still running. To remedy this, close Word down. You can't just close the document in this situation, because when you activate the control, COM loads the control's DLL into Word. When the control is deactivated, the DLL is still loaded — this is for efficiency reasons, so that the next time you activate the control, Word won't have to reload the DLL.

Word may periodically call **CoFreeUnusedLibraries()**, *which tells COM to go through each DLL it has loaded into Word and test if the DLL can be unloaded with a call to the exported* **DllCanUnloadNow()** *function. However, there is no way to tell Word to do this explicitly.*

Repeat the test you carried out above: create a new document, insert a new **Prop Class** and save the document. Close the document and then load it again. Finally, activate the control by double-clicking on it, and you should see that the control shows its values. Now when you double-click on the control, you will not get the previous error, the control will be loaded and it will draw itself.

There is one more change required, but the reason for it is not immediately obvious. To understand the problem, try this. Open **Prop.h**, add a message handler to the message map, and declare a handler:

```
BEGIN_MSG_MAP(CProp)
   MESSAGE_HANDLER(WM_PAINT, OnPaint)
   MESSAGE_HANDLER(WM_SETFOCUS, OnSetFocus)
   MESSAGE_HANDLER(WM_KILLFOCUS, OnKillFocus)
   MESSAGE_HANDLER(WM_LBUTTONDOWN, OnClick)
END_MSG_MAP()

   LRESULT OnClick(UINT uMsg, WPARAM wParam, LPARAM lParam,
                                            BOOL& bHandled);
```

In the CPP file, add the message handler:

```
LRESULT CProp::OnClick(UINT uMsg, WPARAM wParam, LPARAM lParam,
                                            BOOL& bHandled)
{
   long lNum;
   get_Number(&lNum);
   lNum++;
   put_Number(lNum);
   return 0;
}
```

When the user clicks on the control, it should increment the **Number** property. Notice that I am using the property methods rather than accessing the property directly; the reason for this is that when I change the property, I want the control to show the new value, which will happen when the **FireViewChange()** function is called.

Compile the code, start Word again, and insert a new **Prop** control. The control will be running, so single click on it a few times. You will find that the **Number** value will increment for every click. Now save the document and reload it. When you load the document, the old image, with a **Number** value of **-99**, will appear. However, when you double-click on the control to activate it, the running control will show the actual value of the **Number** property.

To understand what's happening this time, we need to go back to what I said about the generation of the metafile. It is created when the control is created, but now that the control's properties have changed, Word should be told about this so that it can ask for a new metafile. You do this by calling **SendOnDataChange()**. Close down Word, and change the code like this:

```
STDMETHODIMP CProp::put_String(BSTR newVal)
{
   ATLTRACE(_T("String assigned to: %ls\n"), newVal);
   m_bstrString = newVal;
   SysFreeString(newVal);
   SetDirty(true);
```

```
   SendOnDataChange();
   FireViewChange();
   return S_OK;
}

STDMETHODIMP CProp::put_Number(long newVal)
{
   ATLTRACE(_T("Number assigned to: %ld\n"), m_lNumber);
   m_lNumber = newVal;
   SetDirty(true);
   SendOnDataChange();
   FireViewChange();
   return S_OK;
}
```

Now recompile the code and repeat the test. This time you will find that when you save the document, both the updated metafile *and* the values of its properties will be saved in the document.

Loading Properties from a Web Page

There is another form of persistence that we need to look at. The previous section showed how, when it is initialized, the control is passed a stream containing the values of its properties when the compound document was saved. ATL did all the work here of writing the data to the stream when the control was made persistent, and of reading the data from the stream when the control was initialized. You have also seen that when a control is on a web page, you can use scripting to change the control's properties. There is, however, a third way to initialize a control, and that uses the **<PARAM>** HTML tag.

In this case, the control's initial data is held on the web page. When the browser loads the page, it creates a property bag object with the properties and values named on the page. This property bag object has the **IPropertyBag** interface, while the control itself should implement the **IPersistPropertyBag** interface. Like the other persistence interfaces, this has **Load()** and **Save()** methods — the browser can call the **Load()** method and pass it a pointer to its **IPropertyBag** interface. The control can now iterate through all its properties and call the **IPropertyBag::Read()** method for each of them, passing the name of the property. If the property bag has a value for the property, it is returned.

ATL provides support for property bags through the **IPersistPropertyBagImpl<>** template. To provide support, you should derive your class from this template, and add the properties that you want to initialize using the property bag to the property map. In the **Prop** example, you have already added the properties to the map, so all you need to do is add the new base class to the control.

> 1. Open **Prop.h** and derive **CProp** from **IPersistPropertyBagImpl<>**, adding **IPersistPropertyBag** to the COM map:

```
public IOleInPlaceObjectWindowlessImpl<CProp>,
   public IDataObjectImpl<CProp>,
   public IPersistPropertyBagImpl<CProp>,
```

356

```
      public ISpecifyPropertyPagesImpl<CProp>
{
public:
   CProp() : m_clrForeColor(0),
             m_clrBackColor(0xffffff),
             m_lNumber(0),
             m_bInitialized(false)
   {
   }

DECLARE_REGISTRY_RESOURCEID(IDR_PROP)

BEGIN_COM_MAP(CProp)
   COM_INTERFACE_ENTRY(IProp)
   COM_INTERFACE_ENTRY(IDispatch)
   COM_INTERFACE_ENTRY_IMPL(IPersistPropertyBag)
   COM_INTERFACE_ENTRY_IMPL(IViewObjectEx)
```

2. Compile the project.

3. Copy **Prop.htm** to **Propbag.htm** and change it as follows:

```
<HTML>
<HEAD>
<TITLE>ATL 2.0 test page for object Prop</TITLE>
</HEAD>
<BODY>
<OBJECT ID="Prop" <
 CLASSID="CLSID:7B33B4FD-59B3-11D1-9A48-0060973044A8">
>
<PARAM NAME="Caption" VALUE="Caption #1">
<PARAM NAME="String" VALUE="String #1">
<PARAM NAME="Number" VALUE="100">
<PARAM NAME="BackColor" VALUE="0">
<PARAM NAME="ForeColor" VALUE="16777215">
</OBJECT>
</BODY>
</HTML>
```

The **NAME** in **<PARAM>** is the name of the property — the first parameter of the **PROP_ENTRY()** macro in the property map. The implementation that ATL uses calls **IPropertyBag::Load()**, passing the name of the property and a **VARIANT**. The vt member of this **VARIANT** indicates the type of the expected parameter. The browser will fill the **VARIANT** with the value if it's in the bag; if the value is of a different type, it will coerce it to the required type. The value of 0 passed to **BackColor** represents black, whereas 16777215 is **0xffffff** in hex, and therefore white.

To test this example, double click on the **PropBag.htm** in Explorer, which will start Internet Explorer and load the page. You should see the following:

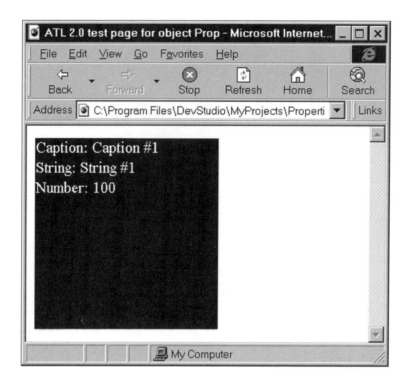

Making Object Properties Persistent

So far, the properties we've made persistent have been basic data types: integers, strings and the like. However, data is not always in this form. You may decide that you want to have an object as a property of your control, and that object will have properties of its own. In this section I will show you how to do this.

Since we are talking about controls that can be used in scripting languages, we can be specific and say that the object we'll create will have an **IDispatch** interface. ActiveX controls with dual interfaces have an **IDispatch** interface, so they fit the bill. Any object with an **IDispatch** interface can be exposed as an Automation property.

In this example, we will create an object that has two properties — a string called **ObjString** and a **long** called **ObjNumber** — and we'll add this object as a property to the **Prop** control.

> 1. Add a new object to the project using Insert | New ATL Object.... In the dialog, select Objects from the left-hand pane, Simple Object from the right, and then click on Next >.
>
> 2. In the next dialog, select the Names page, type **PropObj** as the Short Name and then click on OK.
>
> 3. In the ClassView, right click on the IPropObj interface and select Add Property.... Add a **BSTR** property called **ObjString**.
>
> 4. Repeat the last step, adding a **long** property called **ObjNumber**. ClassView should look like this:

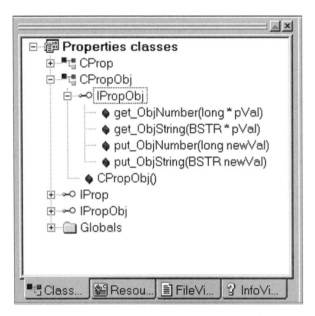

5. Next, add a property to the **Prop** object by right clicking on the IProp interface in ClassView and then selecting Add Property.... In the dialog, add a property of type **LPDISPATCH** and call it **Obj**. ClassView should look like this:

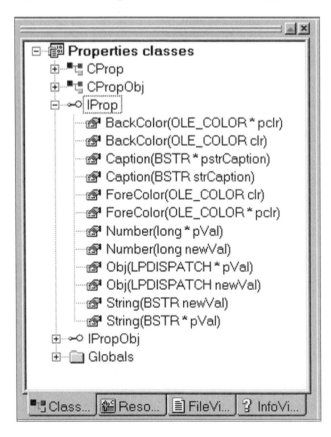

6. Now we need to implement the **PropObj** type. Open **PropObj.h**, add the data members for the properties at the bottom of the class, and initialize the number in the constructor:

```
// IPropObj
public:
   STDMETHOD(get_ObjNumber)(/*[out, retval]*/ long *pVal);
   STDMETHOD(put_ObjNumber)(/*[in]*/ long newVal);
   STDMETHOD(get_ObjString)(/*[out, retval]*/ BSTR *pVal);
   STDMETHOD(put_ObjString)(/*[in]*/ BSTR newVal);

private:
   CComBSTR m_ObjString;
   long m_ObjNumber;
};

public:
   CPropObj() : m_ObjNumber(0)
   {
   }
```

We want to persist the **Obj** property of the **CProp** class, so the **CPropObj** class will need to be derived from a persistence interface. At first sight, it would appear that all you need to do is derive your **CPropObj** from **IPersistStreamInitImpl<>**. However, the latter class relies on the ATL class being also derived from **CComControl<>**, since this implements many of the **IPersistStreamInitImpl<>** methods.

7. Change the **CPropObj** derivation to:

```
class ATL_NO_VTABLE CPropObj :
   public CComObjectRootEx<CComSingleThreadModel>,
   public CComCoClass<CPropObj, &CLSID_PropObj>,
   public CComControl<CPropObj>,
   public IPersistStreamInitImpl<CPropObj>,
   public IDispatchImpl<IPropObj, &IID_IPropObj, &LIBID_PROPERTIESLib>
```

8. Change the COM map to give access to this new interface:

```
BEGIN_COM_MAP(CPropObj)
   COM_INTERFACE_ENTRY(IPropObj)
   COM_INTERFACE_ENTRY(IDispatch)
   COM_INTERFACE_ENTRY_IMPL(IPersistStreamInit)
   COM_INTERFACE_ENTRY_IMPL_IID(IID_IPersistStream, IPersistStreamInit)
END_COM_MAP()
```

The first macro states that the object supports **IPersistStreamInit**, and that the ATL class that implements the interface has the interface name with an **Impl** added, i.e. **IPersistStreamInitImpl**. The second macro states that the interface implementation of the second parameter (**IPersistStreamInitImpl**) also implements interfaces of the first parameter (**IPersistStream**). This is perfectly reasonable, since **IPersistStreamInit** is derived from **IPersistStream**.

9. There are two other changes you need to make to the declaration. First, since this is a simple object, you do not have a property map. Second, the additional derivation from the **CComControl<>** class requires that a message map be added. Add the following code after the COM map:

```
BEGIN_PROPERTY_MAP(CPropObj)
   PROP_ENTRY("ObjString", 1, CLSID_NULL)
   PROP_ENTRY("ObjNumber", 2, CLSID_NULL)
END_PROPERTY_MAP()

BEGIN_MSG_MAP(CPropObj)
END_MSG_MAP()
```

10. Now open **PropObj.cpp** and add handlers for the properties:

```
STDMETHODIMP CPropObj::get_ObjString(BSTR * pVal)
{
    ATLTRACE(_T("ObjString returning: %ls\n"), m_ObjString);
    *pVal = m_ObjString.Copy();
    return S_OK;
}

STDMETHODIMP CPropObj::put_ObjString(BSTR newVal)
{
    ATLTRACE(_T("ObjString assigned to: %ls\n"), newVal);
    m_ObjString = newVal;
    return S_OK;
}

STDMETHODIMP CPropObj::get_ObjNumber(long * pVal)
{
    ATLTRACE(_T("ObjNumber returning: %ld\n"), m_ObjNumber);
    *pVal = m_ObjNumber;
    return S_OK;
}

STDMETHODIMP CPropObj::put_ObjNumber(long newVal)
{
    ATLTRACE(_T("ObjNumber assigned to: %ld\n"), newVal);
    m_ObjNumber = newVal;
    return S_OK;
}
```

11. To add support for the new property into the control, open **Prop.h** and at the top add:

```
#ifndef __PROP_H_
#define __PROP_H_

#include "resource.h"       // main symbols
#include "PropObj.h"
```

12. At the bottom of the class, add a new member for the embedded object, and a helper method to return the values in the object:

```
long m_lNumber;
CComQIPtr<IPropObj, &IID_IPropObj> m_Obj;

private:
   bool GetPropObj(CComBSTR& bstr, long* lVal);
};
```

The **CComQIPtr<>** is used here rather than **CComPtr**, because later in the code we will want to initialize it using an **IDispatch** pointer, and so the smart pointer will need to **QI()** the **IDispatch** pointer for its **IPropObj** interface automatically.

13. The last thing that needs to be done in **Prop.h** is to add the property to the property map:

```
PROP_ENTRY("Number", 2, CLSID_NULL)
PROP_ENTRY("PropObj", 3, CLSID_NULL)
END_PROPERTY_MAP()
```

14. Open **Prop.cpp** and implement the handlers for the new property:

```
STDMETHODIMP CProp::get_Obj(LPDISPATCH * pVal)
{
   CComBSTR str;
   long num;
   GetPropObj(str, &num);
   ATLTRACE(_T("Obj returning: %ls, %ld\n"), str, num);
   *pVal = m_Obj;
   m_Obj->AddRef();
   return S_OK;
}

STDMETHODIMP CProp::put_Obj(LPDISPATCH newVal)
{
   // Will release any held pointer
   m_Obj = newVal;

   CComBSTR str;
   long num;
   GetPropObj(str, &num);
   ATLTRACE(_T("Obj assigned to: %ls, %ld\n"), str, num);

   SetDirty(true);
   SendOnDataChange();
   FireViewChange();
   return S_OK;
}
```

```
bool CProp::GetPropObj(CComBSTR& bstr, long* lVal)
{
   if (!m_Obj)
      return false;

   m_Obj->get_ObjString(&bstr);
   m_Obj->get_ObjNumber(lVal);

   return true;
}
```

In **get_Obj()**, a copy of the **PropObj** object, **m_Obj**, is made to pass to the caller. The caller *must* release this interface pointer when it has finished with it, so **get_Obj()** must call **AddRef()**. This ensures that the method follows the COM rules.

In **put_Obj()**, a new object is passed in through an **IDispatch** pointer. The **m_Obj** is a smart pointer around an **IPropObj** interface, so there must be a **QI()** going on somewhere. In fact, it is hidden. The **CComQIPtr<IPropObj>** has an assignment operator for initializing it from **IPropObj** pointers, and if the right hand argument is not an **IPropObj** pointer, then a more generic assignment operator that takes an **IUnknown** pointer will be used. (Any COM interface pointer created within the process can be cast to an **IUnknown** pointer.) In this situation, it the latter operator that is used, and so to initialize the object through this pointer it will have to be **QI()**'d for **IPropObj**.

The assignment releases any interfaces previously held by the **m_Obj** object, and since it calls **QI()**, this will ensure that **AddRef()** has been called on this pointer. There is a lot of ATL magic going on here, however, but as long as you are aware of the way that the smart pointers work, you should not get in any trouble. The rule is that the smart pointer assignment operator will release any interface in the left hand operand, then assign it to the value in the right hand operand, and then **AddRef()** itself.

The **GetPropObj()** helper function queries the object for its properties and returns them to the caller. This is so that you can print out their values in calls to **ATLTRACE()**.

15. So that you can see the value of the object, change **CProp::OnDraw()**:

```
bstrText = _T("Embedded Object");
ExtTextOut(di.hdcDraw, rc.left + 2, 2 + rc.top + 75, ETO_CLIPPED, &rc,
   OLE2T(bstrText.m_str), bstrText.Length(), NULL);

bstrText = _T("  .ObjString: ");
CComBSTR str;
long num;
GetPropObj(str, &num);
bstrText += str;
ExtTextOut(di.hdcDraw, rc.left + 2, 2 + rc.top + 100, ETO_CLIPPED,
            &rc, OLE2T(bstrText.m_str), bstrText.Length(), NULL);

bstrText = _T("  .ObjNumber: ");
wsprintf(szNum, _T("%ld"), num);
bstrText += szNum;
```

```
      ExtTextOut(di.hdcDraw, rc.left + 2, 2 + rc.top + 125, ETO_CLIPPED,
                 &rc, OLE2T(bstrText.m_str), bstrText.Length(), NULL);
```

```
   SelectObject(di.hdcDraw, hOldBrush);
```

16. The very last change of all is to add code to ensure that the embedded object is initialized properly:

```
STDMETHODIMP CProp::InitNew()
{
   if (m_bInitialized)
      return E_UNEXPECTED;
   m_bstrCaption = "Caption";
   m_bstrString = "String";
   m_lNumber = -99;
   m_Obj = new CComObject<CPropObj>;
   m_Obj->put_ObjString(SysAllocString(L"ObjString"));
   m_Obj->put_ObjNumber(-999);
   SetDirty(true);
   m_bInitialized = true;
   return S_OK;
}
```

If you compile the code and test it with Word, as before, you'll see the new property items:

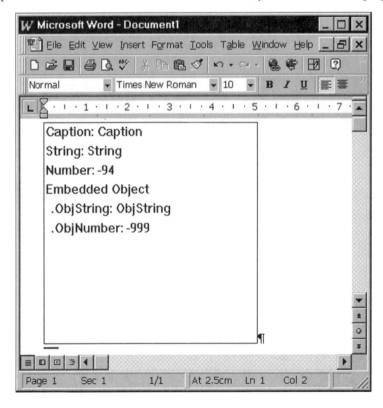

As a further test, you can save this document and then start up the DocFile Viewer (**DFView.exe**), which you can find in the **DevStudio\VC\bin** directory. This allows you to look at all the storages and streams in a structured storage file. For a Word document, the appropriate storage to look in is ObjectPool:

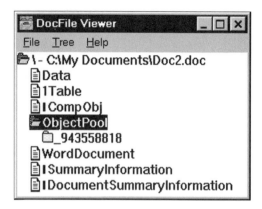

You can expand a node in the tree by double clicking on it. Within the ObjectPool is a single storage called _943558818 (the name in your pool will be different), and within that are streams pertinent to the control. Of particular interest to us is the Contents stream; double clicking on it will show you what it contains:

```
Stream: Contents [0x00000086 bytes]                                    _ □ ×
0x00000000: 02 02 00 00 D8 13 00 00  D8 13 00 00 13 00 FF FF   ........ ........
0x00000010: FF 00 13 00 00 00 00 00  08 00 10 00 00 00 43 00   ........ ......C.
0x00000020: 61 00 70 00 74 00 69 00  6F 00 6E 00 00 00 08 00   a.p.t.i. o.n.....
0x00000030: 0E 00 00 00 53 00 74 00  72 00 69 00 6E 00 67 00   ....S.t. r.i.n.g.
0x00000040: 00 00 03 00 9D FF FF FF  09 00 24 7F DC 8C C4 73   ........ ..$I...s
0x00000050: D1 11 83 B0 D0 8A 06 C1  00 00 02 02 00 00 D8 13   ........ ........
0x00000060: 00 00 D8 13 00 00 08 00  14 00 00 00 4F 00 62 00   ........ ....O.b.
0x00000070: 6A 00 53 00 74 00 72 00  69 00 6E 00 67 00 00 00   j.S.t.r. i.n.g...
0x00000080: 03 00 19 FC FF FF                                   ......
```

This shows that the data saved using the control's **IPersistStreamInitImpl<>** class includes the **ObjString** and **ObjNumber** values from the embedded object. The data at **0x66** is **0x0008**, which is **VT_BSTR**, and this is followed by the number of bytes in the string (**0x00000014 == 20 == 2 * length of string including the terminating NULL**), and then the string itself. At **0x80** is **0x0003**, which is **VT_I4** (**long**), followed by **-999** in hex.

What this example has shown is that objects can be added as properties to a control. All you have to do is make the property type **LPDISPATCH**. You have also seen that as long as the sub-object has simple properties itself (**long**, **BSTR**, **float**, etc.), it can be persisted. To do this, you just have to add the sub-object's properties to its property map, and derive from **IPersistStreamInitImpl<>** and **CComControl<>**. When you have added this new sub-object to the parent object's property map and the parent is made persistent, the code in **IPersistStreamInitImpl<>** will see that the property is an object and call on the sub-object's persistence interfaces. You don't have to do any special processing.

Collections

So far, our example has only used single property types: single strings, single numbers and single objects. Of course, data is rarely structured like that: quite often, there will be a variable number of items, and you'll need to be able to return all those items as one property.

For example, imagine a control that represents a business unit in a software company. Each business unit has a manager and a secretary, but may have any number of developers. You may decide to expose the manager and secretary **Employee** objects as properties, but what about the developers? Properties are defined at design time in the object's IDL, but at design time you do not know how many developers there will be, so you cannot expose them as **Employee** objects.

Instead, you must expose a single property that's an array, or **collection**, of these Employee objects. There are several ways to do this, depending on what client software you intend to support.

Problems with SAFEARRAYs

SAFEARRAYs were introduced in Chapter 4. There, you saw that a **SAFEARRAY** is a self-describing array type that holds the size and type of each element, the number of elements, and the bounds of the array. An Automation object can have a property that is a **SAFEARRAY**, but it must be added as a **VARIANT** property; all you need to do then is copy the **SAFEARRAY** into **VARIANT**'s **parray** member. The Universal Marshaler will read the members of the **SAFEARRAY** and determine how to marshal the data.

Note that since the **SAFEARRAY** has a pointer to the buffer of raw memory for its elements, it means that when you pass a **SAFEARRAY** as an **[out]** parameter of a method, you will need to make a copy first. This means that if the client makes a change, it has to send the new copy in its entirety back to the object, which should then release its **SAFEARRAY** and make a copy of the new one. A lot of data is passed around and lots of processing has to be done. This is compounded if the method access is cross process, when the **SAFEARRAY** will have to be marshaled.

So, **SAFEARRAY**s are fine for arrays of static data — that is, data that the object knows about at one point in time and that the client will not decide to change. They are also fine for relatively small arrays. However, what happens if the property is a parts catalog containing, say, ten thousand parts? The result would be pretty disastrous, because when the client accesses the array, the whole 10,000 items will be copied into an array and marshaled to the client.

If your client is a VB application for browsing through these parts (by placing them in a list box), you will find that the application will hang for a while when the array property is accessed, even if the object is inproc. If the object is out of process, the delay could be so long that the user might think that the application has crashed.

What's required here is a method of asking the object to return, say, the first 100 items and add them to the list box. When the user attempts to scroll down beyond the end of the list, the client could then read the next 100 items, and so on. This way the user interface is update little and often.

You could define your own methods to support obtaining data in this way (perhaps returning the subset of items in a **SAFEARRAY**), but it would be much nicer if a standard mechanism could be used. You won't be surprised to discover that such a mechanism already exists in COM. It's called an **enumerator**, and in the next two sections I will explain what an enumerator is. After that, I will explain how to implement a **collection** that uses an enumerator.

Enumerators

The COM documentation defines an interface called **IEnumXXXX**, which defines the methods for an enumeration interface. In fact this is not a real interface at all, but a template describing how an enumeration interface should look. COM does define some 'real' interfaces as well, and useful ones are:

- **IEnumString**, which enumerates arrays of **LPOLESTR** strings
- **IEnumUnknown**, which enumerates arrays of **IUnknown** pointers
- **IEnumVARIANT**, which enumerates arrays of **VARIANT**s

As well as the **IUnknown** methods, these interfaces have four common methods. Two of these, **Next()** and **Clone()**, respectively return more enumerated items, and a copy of the enumerator. Since these have typed parameters (e.g. **IEnumString::Clone()** returns a double pointer to an **IEnumString**), these interfaces cannot be defined by deriving from some base interface. What is needed is a template interface, but such a thing is not possible in IDL.

> *You may be interested to find out that macros in IDL can be handled by MIDL. You can simulate templates with some clever macro management, but we will not explore that technique here.*

In the absence of templates, the COM designers have provided the **IEnumXXXX** interface and said, "When you design an enumerator, copy this interface and replace **ELT_T** with your enumerated type." Enumerator objects are not created by the system: you have to design your enumerator interface (or use one of the predefined interfaces), and implement it using your data.

```
interface IEnumXXXX : IUnknown
{
    HRESULT Next(
            [in] ULONG celt,
            [out, size_is(celt), length_is(*pceltFetched)] ELT_T[ ] rgelt,
            [out] ULONG* pceltFetched );
    HRESULT Skip([in] ULONG celt);
    HRESULT Reset(void);
    HRESULT Clone([out] IEnumXXXX** ppenum);
};
```

> *As an aside, **Clone()** could return an **IUnknown** pointer, and **Next()** could return an array of **void*** pointers, and in that way a generic interface could be used. This is flawed, though, because the call to **Clone()** would have to be followed with a call to **QueryInterface()** to get the typed enumerator interface. Equally unsatisfactorily, A call to **Next()** that returned an array of **void*** pointers would require an additional parameter to give the size of each member of the array.*

The **Next()** method passes a value that *requests* a number of items (in **celt**), and the client allocates an array large enough to return these items and passes this as the second item, **rgelt**; the **[size_is()]** attribute tells the marshaler the total size of the array. The enumerator object attempts to return the next **celt** items, either from the start or from the position in the array after any previous call to **Next()**. If it succeeds, it returns **S_OK**, along with the items in **rgelt** and the number of items in **pceltFetched**. If the object cannot return all the requested items, but only a few, it will return these items in **rgelt** and the number in of items in **pceltFetched**. This is the reason why **rgelt** has the **[length_is()]** attribute: it is telling the marshaler how many items in the array are valid, so it can optimize the marshaling based on this.

If the client wants to move ahead through the enumerated items without reading them, it can call **Skip()**, passing the number of items to skip. After several calls to **Next()** or **Skip()**, the object-maintained position in the array of items will be somewhere within the array (but there is no way that a client can find out where). To restore it to the beginning of the array, the **Reset()** method should be called. Finally, the **Clone()** method makes a copy of the array of items that the interface is enumerating. Typically, you will implement this as making a deep copy. For example, if you are implementing an enumerator with an **IEnumString** interface, the **Clone()** method should not simply copy the array of string pointers; rather, all the strings are copied and a new array of pointers is created, and the enumerator interface on this array is returned.

How you implement an enumerator object is entirely up to you: you could allocate an array of items and return the values from that array, or you could use one of the STL containers (a popular one to use is **vector**).

Enumerator objects involve a fair amount of code, and to help you ATL provides the **CComEnum<>** template that implements an enumerator as a template. This means that to create an enumerator, you just need to pass the template some information about the type of data that it will hold, and then initialize it with the data. The **CComEnum<>** template has these parameters:

```
CComEnum < class     Base,
          const IID* piid,
          class      T,
          class      Copy,
          class      ThreadModel = CComObjectThreadModel >
```

Here, **Base** is the enumeration interface that you want to support, **piid** is the IID of that interface, and **T** is the type of the items in the enumerator object. **Copy** is a class with three member functions that act on items that will be enumerated: one for initializing those items, another for copying them, and the last one for destroying the items. As you might imagine, the methods of this class are called on each data item when the enumerator object is first called, when items are put into the enumerator object, and finally when the enumerator object is destroyed.

Writing a **Copy** class is straightforward, but ATL provides versions that will suffice for all the common enumeration interfaces:

ATL Class	Used for...?
`template <class T> class _Copy`	shallow copy
`template<> class _Copy<VARIANT>`	uses the **Variant*** API
`template<> class _Copy<LPOLESTR>`	copies strings using memory from the task allocator
`template<> class _Copy<OLEVERB>`	copies **OLEVERB** structures that contain a string member that has to be copied with memory from the task allocator
`template<> class _Copy<CONNECTDATA>`	**CONNECTDATA** contains an **IUnknown** pointer, so COM rules of copying and releasing COM pointers must be applied
`template <class T> class _CopyInterface`	COM rules must be applied when copying and releasing pointers

An example of using the **CComEnum** template is shown here creating an enumerator object for **VARIANT**s.

```
typedef CComObject< CComEnum< IEnumVARIANT,
                              &IID_IEnumVARIANT,
                              VARIANT,
                              _Copy<VARIANT> > > EnumVar;
EnumVar* pVar = new EnumVar;
pVar->Init(…);
```

Notice that there is a space between each `>` in `_Copy<VARIANT> > >`. This is to avoid confusion with the C++ right shift operator `>>`, which will be used if you miss out the spaces. Take a moment to look this over. The actual enumerator code is in **CComEnumImpl<>**, and **CComEnum<>** is derived from this. **CComEnum<>** is abstract, so to get the **IUnknown** methods you need **CComObject<>**. This takes the class for which it is providing the **IUnknown** methods as a parameter, and it then derives from this class. This means that any **public** methods defined in **CComEnum<>** can be called from **CComObject< CComEnum<> >**. As you can see, the parameters passed to the **CComEnum<>** template specify that the object will implement the **IEnumVARIANT** interface.

Before the enumerator object can be used, it has to be initialized by calling the **Init()** method inherited from the **CComEnumImpl<>** base class. This method saves pointers to the first and last items that will be enumerated. You have two choices here: you can indicate that the enumerator object will own the enumerated data, or you can say that it will be owned by another object. In the former case, **Init()** will make a copy of every item that will be used — if the enumerator handles many items, this will take up a lot of resources and time. On the other hand, if you do not make the copy and the enumerator passes out references to objects, this means that the client will have access to the actual objects (not copies), and so be able to change them. It may be that this is what you want, but you need to be aware of what you're doing.

Whoever owns the items, **Init()** is passed pointers to the first item and the last item to use. The function assumes that the items are held in an array — that they are consecutive in memory. This will be the case if the items are held in an STL **vector<>**, but not if they are held in an STL **map**. So, if you pass a **map**, copying the data (or accessing the items) will fail hopelessly. You have to make sure that the data for the enumerator is held in contiguous memory between the two pointers you pass to **Init()**.

Using **CComEnum<>** means that you do not have to worry about implementing the enumerator interface methods, but it is not a solution for every problem. One such situation is where the data is not static — that is, items may be added and removed while you're still giving access to them with the enumerator. In such a case you would have to implement your own object, because **CComEnum<>** is not designed for such data.

You will see an example of implementing an enumerator shortly, when we look at creating collections in C++.

VB Collections

Collections are not specific to VB but, as with **SAFEARRAY**s, access to collections is simpler with VB than with C++, and historically they were aimed at VB programmers. Collections hold objects, and they allow you to iterate through these objects using an enumerator. What you get in addition to the enumerator are methods to add objects, remove objects, access specific objects, and get a count of the objects in the collection.

The idea of collections is to group objects together so that you can build up a hierarchy. All the Microsoft Office applications, for example, expose their objects through collections. The following figure shows some of the objects used in Excel97. The convention is that collections have a name that is the plural of the objects they contain. The **WorkBooks** object, for example, is a collection of individual **WorkBook** objects.

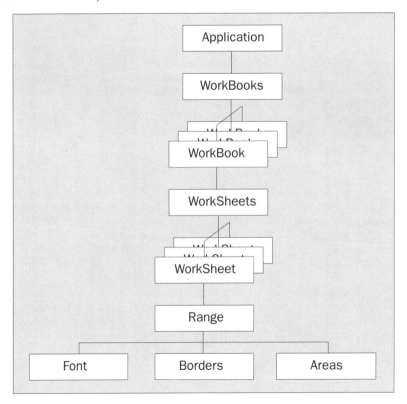

The user must be able to access a particular object within a collection. In the picture, the **WorkBooks** collection contains three individual **WorkBook** objects. The collection must be able to determine which one to use. This is not the case for other, non-collection objects, because there will only ever be one of them. Once you have a **WorkBook**, for example, you can obtain the contained **WorkSheets** collection because each **WorkBook** object has only one **WorkSheets** object.

One thing that is implicit in the picture above is that a collection can contain more than one object. A client using this hierarchy must be able to determine how many items there are in a collection, and then be able to access a particular object. Every collection object must provide a property called **Count** that returns the number of objects in the collection. It must also expose a method called **Item()** that gives access to a particular object in the collection, and a property called **_NewEnum** that returns an enumerator object. You have already seen enumerator objects in the last section; here they are used to iterate through all the objects in the collection.

The **Item()** method is quite interesting. In essence, it is passed the index of the object that the client wants to access, but this index can be anything that the collection author chooses to use as such. If the collection uses a vector (or an array) to hold the objects, the index would be a number that was the offset into that vector. Alternatively, if the collection uses a map, the index would be the key that was used when inserting the object into the map.

In Excel, for example, the **WorkSheet** objects in a **WorkSheets** collection can be accessed using either a number (between 1 and **WorkSheets.Count**) or the name of the **WorkSheet**. So if **MyAccounts** is the second sheet in the **WorkSheets** collection, then these two lines of VB code are the same:

```
WorkSheets(2).Visible = True
WorkSheets("MyAccounts").Visible = True
```

Both of these lines call the **Item()** method, which in order to enable passing both an integer and a string should take a **VARIANT** in this case. This is fine when you know which object in the collection you want to access, but what if you want to access every object in the collection?

One possible method would be to access the **Count** property, and then to access every object in a loop, using a counter. However, we have already seen a better way to access whole collection: enumerators. VBA makes good use of enumerators with the **For Each** keywords, as shown in the following example, which fills the list box **List1** with the names of all the **WorkSheets** in the first **WorkBook** in the file **book1.xls**.

```
Dim ex As New Excel.Application
ex.Workbooks.Open "book1.xls"
Dim shs As Excel.Sheets
Dim sheet As Excel.Worksheet

Set shs = ex.Workbooks(1).Worksheets

For Each sheet In shs
   List1.AddItem sheet.Name
Next
```

To make this clear, the enumerator obtained by **For Each** (which calls **_NewEnum** on the collection) gives access to the objects in the collection. In the above code, I access each sheet in the collection and then get the **Name** property from each **WorkSheet** object.

Finally, collections can be filled by the object that implements them, or they may allow the user to add and remove objects. To do so, the convention is for a collection to expose two methods called — you've guessed it — **Add()** and **Remove()**. Unlike the other three items I have mentioned (the properties **Count** and **_NewEnum**, and the method **Item()**), these two methods are optional.

Writing Collections in C++

We'll write a collection that can be used in VB in a moment, but first we need go through in some depth what you need to implement in order to write a collection object.

Count

This is a read only, **long** property that returns the number of objects in the collection. The property can have whatever DISPID you choose.

Item

This method gives access to a particular item in the collection. The method must be the default method of the collection object. There is a special DISPID for the default method: **DISPID_VALUE**, which has a value of **0**. The feature of default methods is that you can miss out the method name in scripts, so in VB the following two lines of code are the same:

```
Set shs = ex.Workbooks(1).Worksheets
Set shs = ex.Workbooks.Item(1).Worksheets
```

Item() returns an **IDispatch** pointer that gives access to the specified object, but the parameter passed *to* the method can be any type applicable to the collection object. If the collection only gives access to items using a numeric index, **Item()** could take an integer; if the index is a name, then a **BSTR** should be used. Collections that allow both types of access should take a **VARIANT** as a parameter. Remember, VB will attempt to coerce the index used in the script to the type required by **Item()**.

_NewEnum

This read-only property gives access to the enumerator object of the collection. It is usually called **_NewEnum** (note the underscore to prevent object browsers from showing the property), although to some extent this name is not really important, because clients that know about collection enumerators will access it directly through its DISPID, which is the standard value **DISPID_NEWENUM**. This property should also be marked as **[restricted]** in IDL, which is used to mark in the type library that the property should not be accessed directly by scripting code.

The property should return a **IUnknown** pointer to the enumerator object that implements the **IEnumVARIANT** interface; the client can then **QueryInterface()** for this interface. The **IEnumVARIANT** interface is used because in general, collections can contain any type.

Add

This optional method allows a client to add a new item to the collection. The DISPID can be any value, and the method can take any parameters suitable for the collection. Typically, it should take a **IDispatch** pointer used to indicate the object to add, but it could additionally take an index indicating where in the collection to add the object, or a reference (the name perhaps) of an object after which to insert the new object.

Remove

This too is an optional method, and it allows a client to remove objects. The DISPID can be any value, and the method does not return any data. The parameter depends on the type of the objects that the collection contains.

Other Methods and Properties

As a collection object is an Automation object, you can implement any other properties and methods you want on the collection object. However, by convention, Office exposes the following properties: **Application** gives access to the top level **Application** object, through which Office applications provide Automation; **Parent** is the immediate parent of the collection in the object hierarchy; and **Creator** is an identifier of the application that created the object.

Example: The DeveloperCollection Object

I have talked in previous sections about VB collections. In the following example, you will see the steps needed to create a collection object and the objects that it will contain. I will use a collection of **Employee** objects called the **DeveloperCollection**, following the example given in the introduction to this section.

In this example, I am modeling a company business unit that will have a **Manager**, a **Secretary**, and zero or more developers. In the model, each person is an **Employee** object, with a name and an employee ID, and I use a **DeveloperCollection** object to hold the developers:

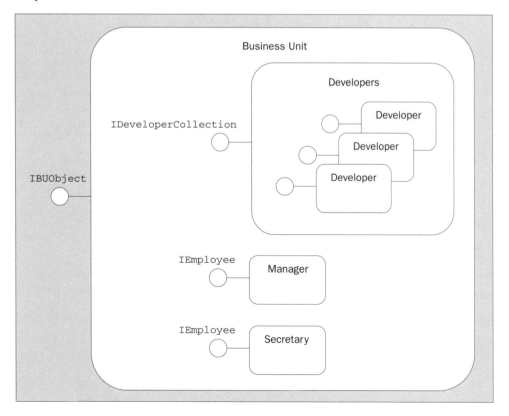

The first task, then, is to create a **DeveloperCollection** object, which is a collection of **Employee** objects.

The Employee and DeveloperCollection Objects

These are the steps used to create the **Employee** and **DeveloperCollection** classes:

1. Create a new ATL COM AppWizard project called BUObject, accepting all the defaults supplied by the Wizard.

2. Once the AppWizard has finished, use the Object Wizard to insert a new Simple Object into the project. In the Properties dialog, give the object a Short Name of Employee. This is the object that will be inserted into the business unit **DeveloperCollection** object later on.

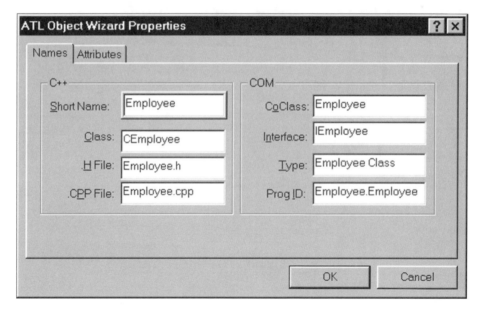

3. This object really will be quite simple. It should have two properties: a string property called **Name**, and a long property called **EmployeeID**. In ClassView, click on the BUObject Classes tree to show the IEmployee branch.

4. Right click on this interface and select Add Property.... In the next dialog, select a Property Type of **BSTR** and a Property Name of **Name**. This property will be read/write, so the Get Function and Put Function check boxes should remain checked. Repeat this procedure for the **long EmployeeID** property.

4. Open **Employee.h** and add the following members to the bottom of the class declaration to hold the property values, and initialize the employee ID in the constructor:

```
    CEmployee() : m_lEmployeeID(0)

private:
    CComBSTR m_bstrName;
    long     m_lEmployeeID;
};
```

6. Next, implement the property handlers to give access to these data members, and then compile the code to make sure you haven't introduced any typing errors.

```
STDMETHODIMP CEmployee::get_Name(BSTR * pVal)
{
    *pVal = m_bstrName.Copy();
    return S_OK;
}


STDMETHODIMP CEmployee::put_Name(BSTR newVal)
{
    m_bstrName = newVal;
    return S_OK;
}


STDMETHODIMP CEmployee::get_EmployeeID(long * pVal)
{
    *pVal = m_lEmployeeID;
    return S_OK;
}


STDMETHODIMP CEmployee::put_EmployeeID(long newVal)
{
    m_lEmployeeID = newVal;
    return S_OK;
}
```

7. Our next task is to create the **DeveloperCollection** class that will hold **Employee** objects. Add another Simple Object, this time with a Short Name of DeveloperCollection.

8. This object will have an **Add()** member in addition to the mandatory members. In ClassView, right click on the IDeveloperCollection interface and select Add Method.... This collection will only hold **Employee** objects, and by default they will be added to a map using the **Employee.Name** as the key. The method should not return any value. In the dialog, type **Add** for the Method Name and **[in] IEmployee* pEmployee** for the Parameters:

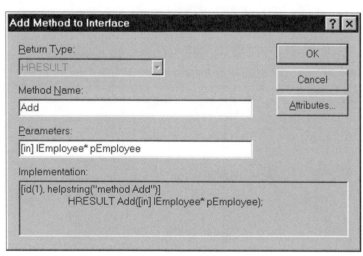

375

9. Next, add the **Count** property as detailed in the following dialog. Take particular care to ensure that the Put Function check box is unchecked (the property is read-only):

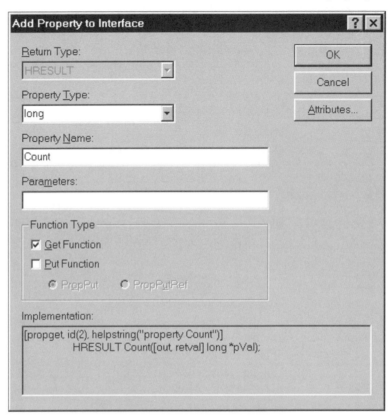

10. Now use the Add Method dialog to add the **Item()** method, whose parameters should be a **VARIANT** and a pointer to a **VARIANT**. You must also click on the Attributes button and change the id to 0 to make this the default method:

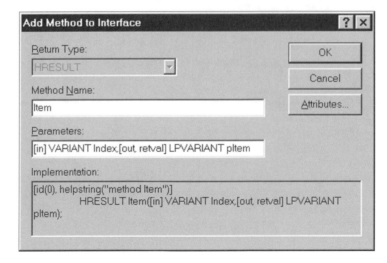

11. The final property to add has a Property Name of **_NewEnum** and a Property Type of **LPUNKNOWN**. Ensure that the property is read only by unchecking Put Function. This property must have a DISPID of **DISPID_NEWENUM** (-4), but if you click on Attributes... and try to type the symbol or the value, you will get an error box saying that the attribute should be a positive 32-bit value. We will have to edit the IDL by hand, which we'll do shortly.

12. Before dismissing the dialog, however, click on Attributes... and add the **[restricted]** attribute to ensure that VB users cannot access this property. Click on the empty item in the Name column and select restricted from the drop-down list. You can then close both dialogs.

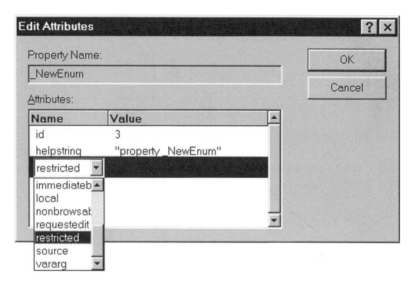

13. Since you could not add a negative ID in the Attributes dialog, you will have to do it by hand. Open the **BUObject.idl** file and change the DISPID of the **_NewEnum** property to -4:

```
[propget, id(-4), helpstring("property _NewEnum"), restricted]
   HRESULT _NewEnum([out, retval] LPUNKNOWN *pVal);
```

14. Now open **DeveloperCollection.h** and add the following headers above the class declaration, so that you can use the STL map template. The pragma is added because when you use STL containers, the symbol names used in debug builds are likely to be very large. If they are longer than 256 characters, you will get warning 4786, which we are therefore suppressing.

```
#include "resource.h"        // main symbols
#include <map>
#include "Employee.h"
#pragma warning(disable : 4786)
```

15. At the bottom of the class, add the following data member (you will change this line later on, but use this declaration for the time being) and two methods. **FinalRelease()** is used for cleanup code when the object is destroyed, the **m_map** holds the actual employees, and **GetEmployee()** is a helper function for debugging:

```
    void FinalRelease();

private:
    std::map<CComBSTR, IEmployee*> m_map;
    void GetEmployee(IEmployee* pEmployee,
                 CComBSTR& bstrName, long& pEmployeeID);
```

16. Open **DeveloperCollection.cpp** and enter empty implementations for the two methods at the bottom of the file:

```
void CDeveloperCollection::FinalRelease()
{
}

void CDeveloperCollection::GetEmployee( IEmployee* pEmployee,
                              CComBSTR&   bstrName,
                              long&       pEmployeeID )

{
}
```

17. Now we need to implement the property handlers and methods. The first one is the easiest to code, since the STL **map** has a method, **size()**, that returns the number of items in the **map**:

```
STDMETHODIMP CDeveloperCollection::get_Count(long * pVal)
{
    *pVal = m_map.size();
    return S_OK;
}
```

18. Next up is the **Add()** method:

```
STDMETHODIMP CDeveloperCollection::Add(IEmployee * pEmployee)
{
    CComBSTR bstrName;
    long ID;
    GetEmployee(pEmployee, bstrName, ID);

    if (bstrName.Length() == 0)
    {
        ATLTRACE(_T("Employee %ld must have ")
            _T("a name\n"), ID);
        return E_INVALIDARG;
    }
```

```
        ATLTRACE(_T("Adding Employee %ls (%ld)\n"), bstrName, ID);
        m_map[bstrName] = pEmployee;
        pEmployee->AddRef();
    return S_OK;
}
```

This code checks that the **Employee** object passed in has a non-empty name; this is because the **Name** property is used as the key for the entry in the STL map. The name and employee ID are obtained with the helper method **GetEmployee()** that we'll implement in a moment. The item is then added into the map with the line:

```
        m_map[bstrName] = pEmployee;
```

This is the wonderful thing about STL containers: you can insert, and access, an item in the map using the **[]** operator. The parameter on the left-hand side is the key to use when inserting an item, while the right-hand side is the item to insert. The map will own the **pEmployee** object put into it, so you have to call **AddRef()** on it.

19. Compile this code, and assuming that you have made no typing mistakes, you will get the following error:

error C2676: binary '<' : 'const class ATL::CComBSTR' does not define this operator or a conversion to a type acceptable to the predefined operator

The reason for this is that the STL map holds data items in a binary tree, so that finding an item in a map is optimized. However, to do this, **map** must compare the key of the new item with the keys of existing items, and by default it does this using the **<** operator. **CComBSTR** does not declare this operator and so the error is generated. To remedy this, you need to write your own predicator.

*The container classes provided by STL are very helpful, but you have to do your bit too,
and provide parameters that have the methods that the STL template requires. The STL
map template is declared like this:*

```
template< class  Key,
                 class  T,
                 class  Pred  =  less<Key>,
                 class  A  =  allocator<T>  >  class  map;
```

The third parameter is called a predicator, *which is a class with an* **operator()()** *that
is used to compare the items passed as parameters. The default value for this parameter is*
less<Key>, *where* **Key** *is the first parameter, and* **less<>** *simply performs a
comparison using the* **<** *operator.*

20. Open **DeveloperCollection.h** and add the following code above the class declaration. The **operator()()** is called to make the comparison, and here I use the CRT **wcscmp()** function to compare two **BSTR**s:

```
struct BSTRless : std::binary_function<CComBSTR, CComBSTR, bool>
{
    bool operator()(const CComBSTR& _X, const CComBSTR& _Y) const
```

```
        {
            return (wcscmp(_X.m_str, _Y.m_str) > 0);
        }
};
```

21. Change the declaration of the data member to use this new predicator, and then compile the project to confirm that the changes fix the previous problem:

```
private:
    std::map<CComBSTR, IEmployee*, BSTRless> m_map;
    void GetEmployee(IEmployee* pEmployee,
                     CComBSTR& bstrName, long& pEmployeeID);
};
```

22. Back in step 18, we increased each object's reference count when it was added to the map, so that the collection owned a reference. When the collection object is released, these objects must be released too, and this should be done in **FinalRelease()**. In the CPP file, implement **FinalRelease()** to iterate through the map and call **Release()** on each item:

```
void CDeveloperCollection::FinalRelease()
{
    std::map<CComBSTR, IEmployee*, BSTRless>::iterator it;
    for (it = m_map.begin(); it != m_map.end(); it++)
    {
        IEmployee* pEmp = (*it).second;
        pEmp->Release();
    }
}
```

This code uses an STL iterator to move through all the items in the map. Note that although we are releasing the objects in the map, we do not release the keys. The reason for this is that the keys are **CComBSTR**s. When the **DeveloperCollection** object is destroyed, the **m_map** object's destructor will be called. This in turn will result in the destructors of the keys being called, and they will therefore be released. All this magic comes to you courtesy of C++ and STL.

23. Now implement the **GetEmployee()** method. This is used to get the **Name** and **EmployeeID** from an **Employee** for debugging purposes. Since it is used for debugging, I have enclosed the code between #ifdef **_DEBUG** conditional compilation directives:

```
void CDeveloperCollection::GetEmployee( IEmployee* pEmployee,
                                        CComBSTR&  bstrName,
                                        long&      pEmployeeID )
{
#ifdef _DEBUG
    pEmployee->get_Name(&bstrName);
    pEmployee->get_EmployeeID(&pEmployeeID);
#endif
}
```

24. The two remaining methods are the big ones, which is why I have left them until
last! The `Item()` method will support accessing items in two ways: by passing in an
index, and by passing in a key. Enter the following implementation for `Item()`:

```
STDMETHODIMP CDeveloperCollection::Item(VARIANT Index, LPVARIANT pItem)
{
    VariantInit(pItem);

    // Check to see if a number has been passed
    if (Index.vt == VT_I4)
    {
        // 1 based index
        if (Index.lVal <= m_map.size() && Index.lVal > 0)
        {
            int i = 1;
            std::map<CComBSTR, IEmployee*, BSTRless>::iterator it;

            // Find the item by index
            for (it = m_map.begin(); it != m_map.end(); it++, i++)
            {
                if (i == Index.lVal)
                {
                    // Found it! Copy the object into pItem
                    pItem->vt = VT_DISPATCH;
                    IEmployee* pEmp;

                    // Get the item
                    pEmp = (*it).second;

                    // Put the IDispatch into pItem (also implicit AddRef())
                    return pEmp->QueryInterface(IID_IDispatch,
                                            (void**) &(pItem->pdispVal));
                }
            }

            // Didn't find it; should never get here
            return E_INVALIDARG;
        }

        // Index out of range
        else
            return E_INVALIDARG;
    }

    // Check to see if a string has been passed
    else if (Index.vt == VT_BSTR)
    {
        // Indexed by name
        std::map<CComBSTR, IEmployee*, BSTRless>::iterator it;
```

```
      // Look for an item with this key
      it = m_map.find(Index.bstrVal);
      VariantClear(&Index);
      if (it == m_map.end())
      {
         // Can't find it
         return E_INVALIDARG;
      }
      pItem->vt = VT_DISPATCH;
      IEmployee* pEmp;
      pEmp = (*it).second;

      // Copy the item's IDispatch into pItem (also implicit AddRef())
      return pEmp->QueryInterface(IID_IDispatch,
                                 (void**) &(pItem->pdispVal));
   }

   // Unrecognised index type
   else
      return E_INVALIDARG;
}
```

Access via the key is obviously the most efficient here, since maps are designed for such access. However, the index method is provided to show you that it is possible. Notice that a **QI()** is made to get the **IDispatch** pointer when an item is found. This involves an implicit **AddRef()** on the interface, because when you **QI()** you are making a copy of the pointer. The client is required to call **Release()** on the pointer when it has finished with it (and VB will do this for you).

25. Finally, implement the **_NewEnum** property, and then compile the project:

```
STDMETHODIMP CDeveloperCollection::get__NewEnum(LPUNKNOWN * pVal)
{
   long lCount = m_map.size();

   // Temporary array to hold the objects
   VARIANT* var = new VARIANT[lCount];
   std::map<CComBSTR, IEmployee*, BSTRless>::iterator it;
   int i = 0;

   // Fill the temporary array with the objects
   for (it = m_map.begin(); it != m_map.end(); it++, i++)
   {
      IEmployee* pEmp = (*it).second;
      VariantInit(&var[i]);
      var[i].vt = VT_DISPATCH;

      // VARIANT holds IDispatch pointers, also QI AddRef()s the objects
      pEmp->QueryInterface(IID_IDispatch, (void**)&(var[i].pdispVal));
   }
```

```
   // Do this typedef to make the following code readable!
   // We need a VARIANT enumerator
   typedef CComObject< CComEnum< IEnumVARIANT,
                                 &IID_IEnumVARIANT,
                                 VARIANT,
                                 _Copy<VARIANT> > > EnumVar;

   // Create a new instance of the object
   EnumVar* pVar = new EnumVar;

   // Initialize it with the objects, a copy will be made
   pVar->Init(&var[0], &var[i], NULL, AtlFlagCopy);

   // Now release the objects put in the temporary array
   lCount--;
   while(lCount >= 0)
   {
      VariantClear(&var[lCount]);
      lCount--;
   }
   delete [] var;

   // Return the IUnknown for the enumerator
   pVar->QueryInterface(IID_IUnknown, (void**)pVal);

   // We do not delete pVar, this is not a leak!
   return S_OK;
}
```

If you look at the code for **get_NewEnum()**, you can see how the enumerator is initialized. First, an array is created, and all the items from the map are entered into it. To understand the reason for this, you have to go back to the explanation for **Init()**. This method gets two pointers, and it assumes that all the items are in the memory between these pointers, arranged consecutively. STL **map**s do not hold their data in arrays, so we need to create our own array. **vector**s guarantee to hold their data in contiguous memory, but do not allow access to their elements using keys; only by index.

The enumerator object is created with the line:

```
   EnumVar* pVar = new EnumVar;
```

This creates a new object on the heap. The **CComObject<>** does have a method called **CreateInstance()** that we could use, which calls **FinalConstruct()** on the **CComEnum<>** class. Since that method does nothing in this example, it is simpler just to use **new**.

You'll surely have noticed that there is no accompanying call to **delete**, so isn't this a memory leak? Well, no, it isn't. Remember that the enumerator object will be used by the client (so you can't delete it in the **get_NewEnum()** method), and anyway, objects handle their own lifetime: they will delete themselves when their reference count falls to zero. Calling **new** does not increase the reference count, but at the end of the method we call **QueryInterface()** on the enumerator, causing an implicit **AddRef()** (as the COM rules require) and hence the reference count will be non-zero.

383

When the client releases the object and the reference count falls to zero, the object will delete itself, and so there will be no memory leak.

The enumerator is initialized with a call to **Init()**, to which information is supplied by passing pointers to the first and last items in the array. Using an array guarantees that the members are contiguous. Ownership of the data is given to the enumerator, so **Init()** will do a **VariantCopy()** on every item in the array, which results in an **AddRef()** being called on each item. Once the enumerator is initialized, you have to go through every item in the array and call **VariantClear()** to release that extra reference count (remember that the call to **QI()** when you put the objects in the array increased the each object's reference count).

Finally, the array is deleted (since it is no longer used), and the enumerator is **QI()**'d for the **IUnknown** interface that is returned to the client.

Testing the DeveloperCollection Class

Now we need to test this collection. To do that, we will use a simple VB test application.

1. Start VB5 and create a new Standard EXE project.

2. Add the following controls with the names indicated:

3. In the Project menu, select References..., find the BUObject 1.0 Type Library entry, and check it.

4. Double click on the form and move the cursor above **Form_Load** (you will have to enter a new line) and add the following:

```
Dim Devs As DeveloperCollection
Dim id As Long
```

This defines an object called **Devs** that should be created when the form loads. The other variable is the ID that we will use to initialize the new **Employee**s that we add to the collection.

    5. You need to create the collection when the form loads, so add the following code:

```
Private Sub Form_Load()
    Set Devs = New DeveloperCollection
    id = 0
End Sub
```

This code does a **CoCreateInstance()** to create a new **DeveloperCollection** object. The **Devs** object has the default interface of the new object, which is **IDeveloperCollection**.

    6. Now double click on the Add button and add the following code:

```
Private Sub cmdAdd_Click()
    If txtItem = "" Then Exit Sub
    Dim Emp As New Employee
    id = id + 1
    Emp.Name = txtItem
    Emp.EmployeeID = id
    Devs.Add Emp
    LblCount = Str$(Devs.Count)
    txtItem = ""
End Sub
```

If there is a value in the text box this code will add a new **Employee** to the collection using the text as the name of the **Employee**. To do this, we create a new **Employee** object (using **New**) and initialize its properties with the text in **txtItem** and the number in the global **id** variable. (This variable is incremented so that the next time Add is clicked, a different value is used.) This new **Employee** object is put into the collection by calling **Add**, and then the label is updated with the number of items in the collection.

    7. Finally, double click on the Show button and add this code:

```
Dim Emp As Employee
    lstItems.Clear
    For Each Emp In Devs
        lstItems.AddItem Emp.Name & ", " & Str$(Emp.EmployeeID)
    Next
End Sub
```

This code uses **For Each** to iterate through the collection. VB gets the collection's **_NewEnum** property and uses the enumerator to iterate through all the items in the collection. In this code, I just read the name and ID of each item and add them into the list box.

You can now run this test application and add several names to the collection by typing each one into the edit box and then clicking on Add. To get the contents of the collection, click on Show.

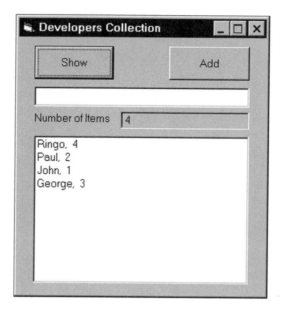

This screenshot shows the results of adding the names John, Paul, George and Ringo in that order. These are held in the map in a sorted order, so the enumerator returns the names in reverse alphabetical order.

The BUObject Object

The original specification had the **DeveloperCollection** as a property of a **BusinessUnit** object, so let's do that.

> 1. Close VB, so that it releases the **BUObject.dll**, and then return to Developer Studio. Reopen the **BUObject** project, and use Insert | New ATL Object... to add a Simple Object. Give it a Short Name of BusinessUnit.
>
> 2. Add two properties called Manager and Secretary that are of type **LPDISPATCH**, and which have both put and get functions.
>
> 3. Add another **LPDISPATCH** property called Developers that is read only — in other words, it has only a get function.
>
> 4. Now we need to add variables to hold these properties. Open **BusinessUnit.h** and add the following **private** data members:

```
private:
    CComQIPtr<IEmployee, &IID_IEmployee> m_pManager;
    CComQIPtr<IEmployee, &IID_IEmployee> m_pSecretary;
    CComPtr<IDeveloperCollection> m_pDevelopers;
```

The first two of these use the **CComQIPtr** smart pointer, because they will be initialized with an **IDispatch** pointer in their **put_** methods. The **m_pDevelopers** member is read-only, so we do not need the automatic **QueryInterface()** supplied by **CComQIPtr**.

5. The property methods are straightforward. Open **BusinessUnit.cpp**, and add this code:

```
STDMETHODIMP CBusinessUnit::get_Manager(LPDISPATCH * pVal)
{
    *pVal = m_pManager;
    m_pManager->AddRef();
    return S_OK;
}


STDMETHODIMP CBusinessUnit::put_Manager(LPDISPATCH newVal)
{
    m_pManager = newVal;
    return S_OK;
}


STDMETHODIMP CBusinessUnit::get_Secretary(LPDISPATCH * pVal)
{
    *pVal = m_pSecretary;
    m_pSecretary->AddRef();
    return S_OK;
}


STDMETHODIMP CBusinessUnit::put_Secretary(LPDISPATCH newVal)
{
    m_pSecretary = newVal;
    return S_OK;
}


STDMETHODIMP CBusinessUnit::get_Developers(LPDISPATCH * pVal)
{
    *pVal = m_pDevelopers;
    m_pDevelopers->AddRef();
    return S_OK;
}
```

The **get_** methods use C++ upcasting to get the **IDispatch** on the object required; since a copy is being made of an interface pointer, it has to be **AddRef()**'d to comply with the COM rules. The **put_** methods use the overloaded **operator=()** of **CComQIPtr** to automatically **QueryInterface()** the passed-in **IDispatch** pointer for the **IEmployee** interface.

6. The code has not created any of these properties, so we need to do that when the **BusinessUnit** object is created. The best place to do this is in **FinalConstruct()**. In **BusinessUnit.h**, add this declaration after the COM map:

```
HRESULT FinalConstruct();
```

7. Add this code to the top of the CPP file so that we can access the **CEmployee** and **CDeveloperCollection** classes:

```
#include "BusinessUnit.h"
#include "Employee.h"
#include "DeveloperCollection.h"
```

8. Add this code and then compile:

```
HRESULT CBusinessUnit::FinalConstruct()
{
   HRESULT hr;
   CComObject<CDeveloperCollection>* pDevs;
   hr = CComObject<CDeveloperCollection>::CreateInstance(&pDevs);
   if (FAILED(hr))
      return hr;
   m_pDevelopers = pDevs;

   CComObject<CEmployee>* pEmp;
   hr = CComObject<CEmployee>::CreateInstance(&pEmp);
   if (FAILED(hr))
      return hr;
   pEmp->put_Name(CComBSTR(_T("<vacant>")));
   m_pManager = pEmp;

   hr = CComObject<CEmployee>::CreateInstance(&pEmp);
   if (FAILED(hr))
      return hr;
   pEmp->put_Name(CComBSTR(_T("<vacant>")));
   m_pSecretary = pEmp;

   return hr;
}
```

As mentioned before, the ATL classes we are creating cannot be created directly, because they are abstract classes. To create objects from these classes, we need to use the **CComObject<>** template. Since the classes we are creating may have **FinalConstruct()** methods (although they do not in this example), this code uses the **static** method **CreateInstance()** to create instances of the objects.

```
      CComObject<CDeveloperCollection>* pDevs;
      hr = CComObject<CDeveloperCollection>::CreateInstance(&pDevs);
```

The lines above create a new **DeveloperCollection** COM object, and put a reference to it in **pDevs**. At this point, the reference count on this object is zero, but the line

```
      m_pDevelopers = pDevs;
```

uses the **CComPtr**'s overloaded **operator=()**, which copies the pointer and calls **AddRef()** on it.

The **Manager** and **Secretary** objects are created in a similar way, except that to indicate that they have no **Employee**, the **Name** is initialized to "**<vacant>**", and the **EmployeeID** is left with its default value of **0**.

Testing the BusinessUnit Class

Finally, we need to test **BusinessUnit**, and we will do this with a VB project.

1. Start VB5 and create a new Standard EXE project.

2. Add the following controls with the names indicated:

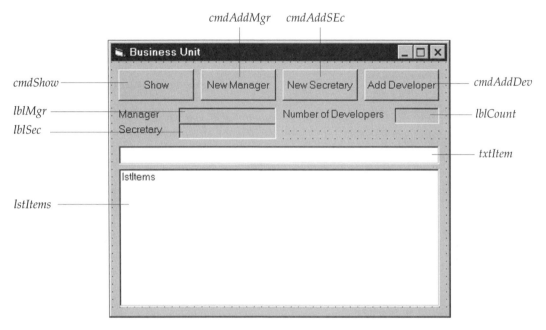

3. Through the Project | References... dialog, add the BUObject 1.0 Type Library. Next, double click on the form, and as before add two variables above **Form_Load**:

```
Dim bu As BusinessUnit
Dim id As Long
```

4. In **Form_Load**, add these lines:

```
Private Sub Form_Load()
    Set bu = New BusinessUnit
    id = 0
    lblCount = Str$(bu.Developers.Count)
    lblMgr = bu.Manager.Name
    lblSec = bu.Secretary.Name
End Sub
```

This creates a new, uninitialized **BusinessUnit** object. It also fills the labels with the values of the properties of this object. The next thing you need to do is add handlers for adding new developers to the collection, and changing the **Manager** and **Secretary**.

5. Double-click on the **cmdAddMgr** button, and add these lines to change the **Manager** property:

```
Private Sub cmdAddMgr_Click()
    If txtItem = "" Then Exit Sub
    Dim emp As New Employee
    id = id + 1
    emp.Name = txtItem
    emp.EmployeeID = id
    bu.Manager = emp
    lblMgr = bu.Manager.Name
    txtItem = ""
End Sub
```

First, we check the text box to see if it has data, and if it is empty, we do no more processing. Then we create a new **Employee** object and initialize its properties with the value in the text box and the **id** variable. The **Manager** member of the **BusinessUnit** object is assigned to this new object, and finally we update the display.

6. The **Secretary** property is handled in a similar way. Double-click on the **cmdAddSec** button, and add these lines to change the **Secretary** property:

```
Private Sub cmdAddSec_Click()
    If txtItem = "" Then Exit Sub
    Dim emp As New Employee
    id = id + 1
    emp.Name = txtItem
    emp.EmployeeID = id
    bu.Secretary = emp
    lblSec = bu.Secretary.Name
    txtItem = ""
End Sub
```

7. Adding a new developer is similar as well, except that the new **Employee** must be added to the **Developers** collection. Double-click on the **cmdAddDev** button and add these lines to add a new developer:

```
Private Sub cmdAddDev_Click()
    If txtItem = "" Then Exit Sub
    Dim emp As New Employee
    id = id + 1
    emp.Name = txtItem
    emp.EmployeeID = id
    bu.Developers.Add emp
    lblCount = Str$(bu.Developers.Count)
    txtItem = ""
End Sub
```

8. Finally, add a handler to read the values from the **BusinessUnit** object. Double-click on the **cmdShow** button and add these lines:

```
Private Sub cmdShow_Click()
    lblCount = Str$(bu.Developers.Count)
    lblMgr = bu.Manager.Name
    lblSec = bu.Secretary.Name

    lstItems.Clear
    lstItems.AddItem "Manager: " + bu.Manager.Name _
        + ", " + Str$(bu.Manager.EmployeeID)
    lstItems.AddItem "Secretary: " + bu.Secretary.Name _
        + ", " + Str$(bu.Secretary.EmployeeID)
    lstItems.AddItem "Developers:"
    If bu.Developers.Count = 0 Then
        lstItems.AddItem "  No developers"
        Exit Sub
    End If

    Dim emp As Employee
    For Each emp In bu.Developers
      lstItems.AddItem "  " + emp.Name + ", " + Str$(emp.EmployeeID)
    Next
End Sub
```

This code updates the labels and then adds the names and IDs of the **Manager** and **Secretary** to the list box. It then checks how many developers are in the collection, and if it is zero, adds a message saying that there are no developers. If there *are* developers, it adds details of each using the enumerator accessed through the VB **For Each** statement.

To test the **BusinessUnit** object, run this application. You will see something like this:

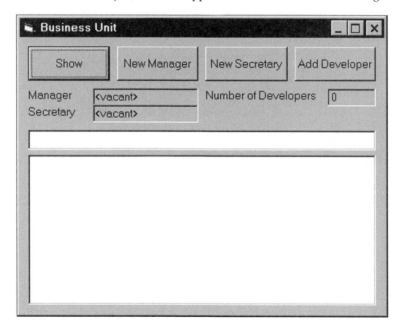

Notice that the Manager and Secretary positions are both **<vacant>**, and the number of developers is zero. Type a name in the text box and click on New Manager, and the Manager label is updated with the new name. Do the same to add a secretary and a developer. When you click on Add Developer, you will find that the Number of Developers should increase by one.

Finally, click on Show, and you should find all the data entered in the list box:

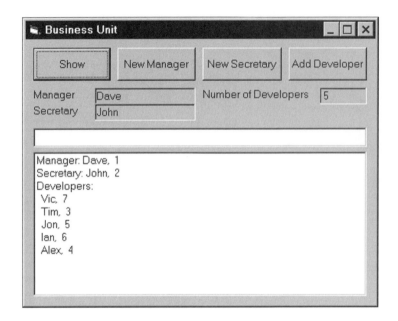

Summary

This chapter has introduced you to using properties, persisting properties, and using collections in ActiveX controls. In the first section, properties were introduced. The distinction was made between custom properties, stock properties and ambient properties, and how each can be used by a control.

After that, we discussed persistence, talking about the COM interfaces used to apply persistence and the templates that ATL provides to do most of the work for you. These templates use a property map, and the example showed how to use simple property types and objects with a property map, providing persistence with very little extra code.

Finally, the last part of the chapter introduced the methods to provide arrays or collections of data. In these last few sections I explained (and gave examples of) enumerators and VB collections.

A Full Control

The purpose of this final chapter is to wrap up all the techniques that you have seen so far. In it, I'll show you the support that the ATL Wizards provide for writing controls, and how to utilize this support. The example that forms a large part of the chapter illustrates most of the techniques you will use when implementing controls: message handling, drawing, property pages, and property persistence. The example also shows you how to superclass an existing Windows class.

Controls

A control is generally a visible object. Controls are *contained* by an application. The container and the control must be able to communicate with each other, so both sides expose interfaces. The container will want to tell the control to do things, notify it of events, and may also implement the control's window; while the control will want to notify the container of events so that the container can act upon them.

A visible control will need to render itself in a window, which may be created by either the control or the container. If the container creates the window, the container will use the control's interfaces to give it access to this window. When the state of the control changes, it will need to redraw itself, and hence its visual representation will change. The control will inform the container to let it know that if the container has any cached representation of the control, then that too should be updated.

Internet Explorer and Full Controls

The ATL Object Wizard gives you the option of creating two types of control: Internet Explorer Control and Full Control.

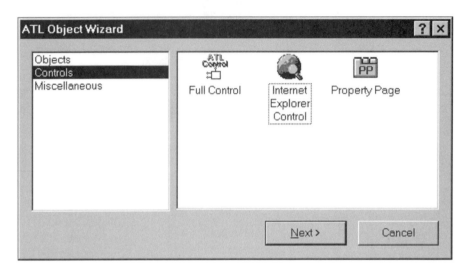

The difference between the two is the number of interfaces that the Wizard will add to the control. The Internet Explorer control is designed to support the minimal set of interfaces that a visual control needs to communicate effectively with Internet Explorer. The Full Control is designed to work with most containers and provides richer functionality to the generated control.

The table below shows the interfaces provided by the Wizard-generated controls and which ATL class provides the implementation of that interface.

Interface	ATL Implementation Class	Supported by IE Controls	Supported by Full Controls
`IViewObject`	`IViewObjectExImpl<>`	✓	✓
`IViewObject2`	`IViewObjectExImpl<>`	✓	✓
`IViewObjectEx`	`IViewObjectExImpl<>`	✓	✓
`IOleWindow`	`IOleInPlaceObjectWindowlessImpl<>`	✓	✓
`IOleInPlaceObject`	`IOleInPlaceObjectWindowlessImpl<>`	✓	✓
`IOleInPlaceObject Windowless`	`IOleInPlaceObjectWindowlessImpl<>`	✓	✓
`IOleInPlaceActive Object`	`IOleInPlaceActiveObjectImpl<>`	✓	✓
`IOleControl`	`IOleControlImpl<>`	✓	✓

Interface	ATL Implementation Class	Supported by IE Controls	Supported by Full Controls
IOleObject	IOleObjectImpl<>	✓	✓
IPersistStreamInit	IPersistStreamInitImpl<>	✓	✓
IQuickActivate	IQuickActivateImpl<>	✗	✓
IPersistStorage	IPersistStorageImpl<>	✗	✓
ISpecifyPropertyPages	ISpecifyPropertyPagesImpl<>	✗	✓
IDataObject	IDataObjectImpl<>	✗	✓
IProvideClassInfo	IProvideClassInfo2Impl<>	✗	✓
IProvideClassInfo2	IProvideClassInfo2Impl<>	✗	✓

You can see that a single implementation class can support a number of interfaces when those interfaces are derived from each other. You can also see that a full control *is* an Internet Explorer control, since it supports all the interfaces required by IE — you can put a full control on a web page. Both control types can draw themselves and can interact with their containers. The full control provides additional persistence interfaces and support for property pages.

There are a lot of interfaces here, because the interactions between a control and its container can be pretty complicated, but ATL hides most of this complexity with its implementation classes.

Control Implementation

ATL controls derive from **CComObjectRootEx<>** and **CComCoClass<>**, just like any other ATL COM class, but they also derive from **CComControl<>**. This class, and more importantly its base class **CComControlBase**, actually provides a lot of the power that you might think is wrapped up in the implementation classes. The following implementation classes rely on **CComControlBase**:

- IDataObjectImpl<>
- IOleInPlaceObjectWindowlessImpl<>
- IOleObjectImpl<>
- IPersistPropertyBagImpl<>
- IPersistStreamInitImpl<>
- IQuickActivateImpl<>
- ISpecifyPropertyPagesImpl<>
- IViewObjectExImpl<>

CComControlBase is a non-templated class, and implements those methods that do not depend on the type of the control. Wrapping the code for all these interface implementations into a non-template base class, leads to smaller code when there are multiple controls in a module.

In addition to providing much of the implementation of a control's interfaces, **CComControlBase** also has some data members. These members hold:

>   Pointers to interfaces exposed by the container
>
>   The size and position of the control
>
>   The control's (non-implemented) stock properties

The class also provides methods used to communicate with the container, such as retrieving the ambient properties or sending notifications.

CComControl<> is a template class derived from **CComControlBase** that implements methods that require access to the control's ATL class (which is the template parameter). In particular, this class implements **FireOnRequestEdit()** and **FireOnChanged()** which require access to your control's **IUnknown** interface. The control can call these methods for properties marked with the **[requestedit]** and **[bindable]** IDL attributes to let the container know when the properties are about to change, and when they have changed. These methods are used when the container has passed **IPropertyNotifySink** interfaces to the control in order to be informed when properties change.

Drawing a Control

Drawing a control is typically one of the hardest parts of its implementation, particularly since your control may need to draw itself in response to a number of different method calls or messages. For example, you need to draw the control in response to a **WM_PAINT** message, a call to **IViewObject::Draw()**, or even a call to **IDataObject::GetData()** when the container asks for a metafile representation of the control.

ATL handles one part of this for you by funneling all the drawing requests into a single method in your class called **OnDraw()**. Whenever your control needs to be drawn, ATL will make sure that **OnDraw()** is called.

OnDraw() is passed a reference to an **ATL_DRAWINFO** structure. This structure is not documented in the ATL help files, but you can find the definition in **AtlCtrl.h**:

```
struct ATL_DRAWINFO
{
    UINT cbSize;
    DWORD dwDrawAspect;
    LONG lindex;
    DVTARGETDEVICE* ptd;
    HDC hicTargetDev;
    HDC hdcDraw;
    LPCRECTL prcBounds;
    LPCRECTL prcWBounds;
    BOOL bOptimize;
    BOOL bZoomed;
    BOOL bRectInHimetric;
    SIZEL ZoomNum;
    SIZEL ZoomDen;
};
```

The first member is the size of the structure. The rest are equivalent to their namesake parameters for **IViewObject::Draw()**. **dwDrawAspect** determines what sort of drawing will be done and will be typically **DVASPECT_CONTENT**, in other words the visual representation of the control. If the control is being asked to draw itself for a window in a container, **ptd** will be **NULL**.

If another device is used, the **ptd** and **hicTargetDev** parameters may be used to pass information about the device. A **DVTARGETDEVICE** structure is used to pass the device and driver name (for information) but also a **DEVMODE** that can be used to get information about the printer device which is being used. The **hicTargetDev** device context can be used in this case to test for the device capabilities and is provided for information purposes only.

The actual drawing should be done to the device context in **hdcDraw**. The dimensions of the window are given in the **RECTL** structure pointed to by **prcBounds**. If the drawing will be in a metafile, then **prcWBounds** will be non-**NULL** and indicate the bounding rectangle of the metafile; **prcBounds** will be within this rectangle.

The **bOptimized** flag is used to indicate whether the device context has been normalized (it's true if the DC has been normalized). If **bZoomed** is **true** then **ZoomNum** and **ZoomDen** give the x and y zoom ratios of the DC bounding rectangle to the natural size of the object.

Typically you will use **hdcDraw** as the device context to draw to and **prcBounds** to get the bounding rectangle. If the container uses zooming (for example changing the zoom in Word) and zooms to anything other than 100%, the control must be zoomed too. You can get this zoom information in the **ZoomNum** and **ZoomDen** members.

OnDrawAdvanced()

By default, ATL also makes your drawing code simpler by setting the mapping mode of the device context to **MM_TEXT** (i.e. pixel units) and the origin of the window and viewport to (0,0). This happens in the **CComControlBase::OnDrawAdvanced()** function, which is called before **OnDraw()**.

You can override **OnDrawAdvanced()** in your own class if you want unfettered access to the device context. The easiest way to do that is to uncheck the Normalize DC box on the Miscellaneous tab of the Object Wizard when you create your control. When the box is checked, the Wizard adds an **OnDraw()** function to the generated class; when it's unchecked, the Wizard adds **OnDrawAdvanced()** instead, and you can add your drawing code to that function.

Metafiles

CComControlBase::OnDrawAdvanced() does not make any changes to device contexts that represent metafiles. These device contexts will be passed directly to **OnDraw()**. Typically, you'll be asked to draw into a metafile when a container calls **IDataObject::GetData()**, asking for the control to cache a metafile representation. The **CComControlBase** implementation of **IDataObject_GetData()** sets up the metafile before calling **OnDrawAdvanced()**. Some containers may also ask you to draw into a metafile device context with a call to **IViewObject::Draw()**. This is the approach taken by Internet Explorer when it requires a visual representation of a control in order to print a web page containing the control. Once again, all these requests for drawing will be passed through **OnDrawAdvanced()** to your control's **OnDraw()** function.

Windows metafiles are essentially scripts made up of GDI (Graphic Device Interface) calls. You can create a device context (DC) based on a metafile, and draw into this DC just as you would with any other. However, a metafile DC is not attached to any device, and so to see the effect of these drawing commands, you need to 'play' the metafile into the DC of an actual device. The advantage is that you can save a metafile in a disk file to play later; once loaded in memory you can play it any number of times, and you can scale the metafile according to the mapping mode and viewport coordinates when you play it back.

There are restrictions as to which GDI commands you can use to draw in a metafile DC. The commands are stored as tokens, so you can see what commands are possible by looking for the token definitions in **WinGDI.h** (search for the line **#ifndef NOMETAFILE**).

This means that if your drawing should be different for a metafile and a screen DC, you'll need to detect this. You can do that with the following code (**bMetafile** will be **TRUE** if the device context represents a metafile).

```
BOOL bMetafile = GetDeviceCaps(di.hdcDraw, TECHNOLOGY) == DT_METAFILE;
```

> *Note that the Wizard-generated* **OnDraw()** *code uses* **DrawText()**, *which is one GDI function that can not be used in metafiles. If you want to output text to a metafile device context, you'll need to use* **TextOut()** *instead.*

Sizing & Positioning Controls

There are two approaches to sizing controls: either the control will do it (autosizing) or the container will. If the container sizes the control, there are two options: content sizing and integral sizing. For integral sizing, the container passes a preferred size to the control, and the control should then resize itself. In content sizing, the container passes the control a suggested size and the control can adjust this size according to the space it thinks it should take. This communication happens when the container calls **IViewObjectEx::GetNaturalExtent()**.

ATL controls can set the data member **m_bAutoSize** to **true** to indicate that the control will autosize (and hence the control cannot be resized by the container). The default setting is **false**. ATL controls use content sizing, so when told to resize by the container they will return to the container their *natural size*.

An ATL control handles sizing through the methods and data members inherited through **CComControlBase**. The **m_sizeNatural** member is the size that the object thinks it is, and by default the constructor sets this to 2 by 2 inches. This is the size returned via **GetNaturalExtent()**. The container may not be able to show this size in its view, so the actual window size is passed to the control with **IOleObject::SetExtent()**. In ATL this size, the visible portion of the control, is held in **CComControlBase::m_sizeExtent**. Thus if you resize a control within a container, you will find that **m_sizeExtent** will change but **m_sizeNatural** will remain constant. Both of these values are held in **HIMETRIC** units (1 unit = 0.01mm), but they can be converted to pixels with **AtlHiMetricToPixel()**.

In many cases, you can forget about the natural size of the control and just use the extent provided by the container. Whatever happens, the **ATL_DRAWINFO::prcBounds** passed to **OnDraw()** will always reflect the extent rather than the natural size. The natural size is only used in two cases (both when the normally false **m_bDrawFromNatural** is set to true). The first

case is when the container has asked the object to render itself in a metafile using
IDataObject::GetData(), and the second is when calculating zoom information.

The control will have some size and position within the document of the container, and the control is told of this when the container calls **IOleInPlaceObject::SetObjectRects()**. ATL stores this value in **m_rcPos**, but note that it is in the screen coordinate units of the container. You'll rarely need to use this, but it could be used if, for example, you want to create a floating modeless dialog associated with the control and position this dialog so that you can see the control.

Sizing Example

To show you how these values change, let's develop a simple control. Use Developer Studio to create a new ATL COM AppWizard project called Extents. Ensure that the Server Type is set to Dynamic Link Library (DLL).

Now insert a new Full Control into the project using the ATL Object Wizard. Give the control a short name of Sizes and click on OK.

Open **Sizes.cpp** and replace the implementation of **OnDraw()** with the code shown below:

```
HRESULT CSizes::OnDraw(ATL_DRAWINFO& di)
{
    RECT& rc = *(RECT*)di.prcBounds;
    TCHAR str[1024];
    wsprintf(str, _T("Natural: (%ld,%ld)"),
             m_sizeNatural.cx, m_sizeNatural.cy);
    TextOut(di.hdcDraw, rc.left, rc.top, str, lstrlen(str));
    wsprintf(str, _T("Extent: (%ld,%ld)"), m_sizeExtent.cx,
                                           m_sizeExtent.cy);
    TextOut(di.hdcDraw, rc.left, rc.top + 20, str, lstrlen(str));
    wsprintf(str, _T("Position: (%ld,%ld)-(%ld,%ld)"),
       m_rcPos.left, m_rcPos.top, m_rcPos.right, m_rcPos.bottom);
    TextOut(di.hdcDraw, rc.left, rc.top + 40, str, lstrlen(str));
    wsprintf(str, _T("rcBounds: (%ld,%ld)-(%ld,%ld)"),
       di.prcBounds->left, di.prcBounds->top, di.prcBounds->right,
       di.prcBounds->bottom);
    TextOut(di.hdcDraw, rc.left, rc.top + 60, str, lstrlen(str));
    wsprintf(str, _T("Zoomed: (%ld,%ld):(%ld,%ld)"),
       di.ZoomNum.cx, di.ZoomNum.cy, di.ZoomDen.cx, di.ZoomDen.cy);
    TextOut(di.hdcDraw, rc.left, rc.top + 80, str, lstrlen(str));
    int caps = ::GetDeviceCaps(di.hdcDraw, TECHNOLOGY);
    if (caps == DT_METAFILE)
       wsprintf(str, _T("MetaFile"));
    else
       wsprintf(str, _T("Other %ld"), caps);
    TextOut(di.hdcDraw, rc.left, rc.top + 100, str, lstrlen(str));
    MoveToEx(di.hdcDraw, rc.left, rc.top, NULL);
    LineTo(di.hdcDraw, rc.right, rc.bottom);
    MoveToEx(di.hdcDraw, rc.right, rc.top, NULL);
    LineTo(di.hdcDraw, rc.left, rc.bottom);
    return S_OK;
}
```

This simply prints out the various sizes on the control. Note I have made no attempt to ensure that the data stays within the control. If the control is smaller than 100 pixels high then some of the lower values will be clipped.

So that you can see that the control is being drawn in the values given by **prcBounds**, I draw a line across each diagonal.

Compile the code. Now run the ActiveX Control Test Container (from the Tools menu) and from the Edit menu select Insert OLE Control. In the dialog, select Sizes Class and click OK. Drag the control around the container; when you drop the control, you should find that the value given by Position will change.

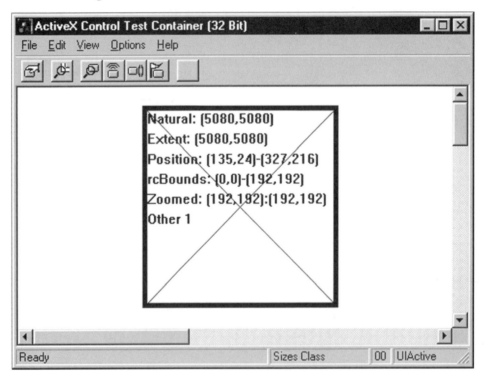

Now resize the control and watch the values.

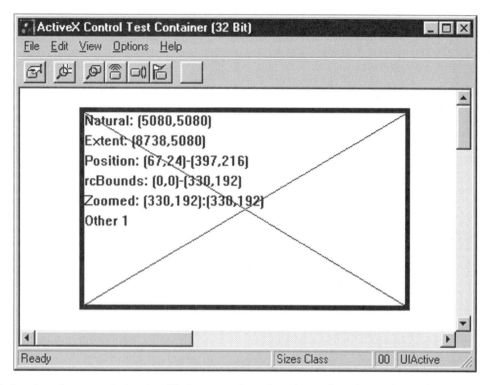

Notice that the natural size is still the same, but the other values have changed. The value of Other 1 is the constant **DT_RASDISPLAY**, and indicates that the drawing is being done to the screen.

From the Edit menu select Draw Metafile. You should see the same values, except at the bottom of the picture will be MetaFile.

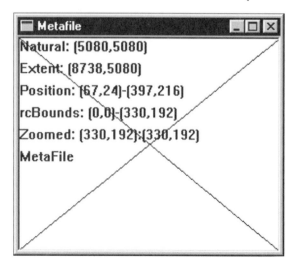

If you resize this window, you'll find that the values do not change. When you selected Draw Metafile the container called **IViewObject::Draw()** with a metafile device context. When you carry out GDI calls, these will be saved in the metafile, which the container can play back later in the new window. When you resize the window, the same GDI commands will be played again, so the text does not change.

Interaction with the Container

As I said earlier, controls are embedded within a container. To do this they should implement the **IOleInPlaceObject** and **IOleInPlaceActiveObject** interfaces (both of these are derived from **IOleWindow**), so that they can receive information about their site in the container.

The first interface is used by the container to activate and deactivate the control, in particular it is used to tell the control the size and position of the control in the container's window, as we have already seen, with **SetObjectRects()**. This interface is implemented by **CComControlBase**, and exposed through **IOleInPlaceObjectWindowlessImpl<>**.

The second interface is quite interesting in that the container uses it to inform the control of changes in its frame and document windows. So when the container's document activates, it should call the control's **OnDocWindowActivate(TRUE)**, which the control should use if it wants to add menus or toolbars to the container. Likewise when the document window deactivates, the container calls **OnDocWindowActivate(FALSE)** so that these additional features can be removed. The ATL implementation, **IOleInPlaceActiveObjectImpl<>**, however, does nothing.

Windowless Controls

A control does not need to create a window of its own, instead it may allow the container to create and maintain its window. This way, if there are many controls, the container can conserve Windows resources by giving each control access to part of its document window. This also means that a control does not need to be rectangular, since the container document will be responsible for painting the background behind the control.

These 'windowless' controls need special support from the container, which has to implement the **IOleInPlaceSiteWindowless** interface. If the container does not provide this support, the control can simply create its own window. An ATL control has a data member, **m_bWindowOnly** that can be set to **true** to force the control to create its own window.

> *Windowless controls are a relatively recent COM standard so some containers may not support them. In that case, the ATL control will create a window for itself.*

The term 'windowless' is a bit misleading since these controls have still have a window, it is just that they are not responsible for creating the window. Since the 'windowless' control's window is managed by the container, a control relies on the container to forward Windows messages to it. The control must implement **IOleInPlaceObjectWindowless**, which derives from **IOleInPlaceObject**. The container can call **IOleInPlaceObjectWindowless::OnWindowMessage()** passing the message applicable to the control. ATL implements this method using **ProcessWindowMessage()** which is provided when you add a message map to the class. Message maps are explained later in this chapter.

Advise Interfaces

The container typically holds much information about the control. As the user interacts with the control, its state will change, and this may mean that the information that the container has about the control will be out of date. The container can decide to ask the control to notify it of changes in the control. There are two ways that this can be done, through a connection point, or through an advise interface. Both mechanisms are used for standard communications with the container.

Connection Points

The advise interface mechanism can be seen as a lightweight version of connection points. Remember, with a connection point, a client implements a sink interface on a sink object, and connects to the control passing an interface pointer to this object for notifications from the control. This connection is made through a separate object called a connection point, specific to the control source interface with which the client is trying to connect. The connection point maintains an array of sink interface pointers connected to the connection point.

When the client wants to make the connection, it asks the control if it has a connection point for the source interface. If so, the connection point container in the control gives the client access to the connection point object. The client can then pass the **IUnknown** pointer of its sink object to the connection point object, in a method called **Advise()**. The connection point object holds this sink interface pointer in an internally held array. In ATL, **Advise()** will do a **QI()** on the passed in sink interface, to get the sink interface it expects.

When the control wants to notify the connected clients: it obtains the connection point object for the source interface and it can then enumerate the sink interfaces held in the connection point. The control can then call the appropriate notification method on each of these sink interfaces. As you saw in Chapter 6, you have to write this enumeration code or get the Proxy Generator to do it for you.

The advantage of this approach is that multiple clients can connect to a single control, and it means that a single control can have multiple connectable interfaces. The client can call **IConnectionPointContainer::FindConnectionPoint()** to determine if the control supports the connectable interface. However, the sink interface and connectable interfaces are not Microsoft defined and of course the client and control need to know about both. This means that the control will need to define the outgoing interface in its IDL (and mark it as **[source]**) so that the marshaling code and interface header files are generated.

IAdviseSink

An advise interface is a sink interface that the client (the container) implements. This is a Microsoft defined interface called **IAdviseSink**, and when compiling applications that use (or implement) this interface, you only need to have access to the interface C++ header as part of the standard SDK files. Further, every machine will have a marshaling proxy in the **ole32.dll** already installed and registered, so it means you do not have to change your object's IDL to support advise interfaces. However, it does mean that the client is restricted in the notifications it can receive; and these are defined by the methods of **IAdviseSink**.

A control can accept advise sinks from many clients and so to maintain these interfaces it should create a separate object, called an advise holder. This object is like a connection point object, but it differs in two important respects. Firstly, advise holders are created and implemented by COM. Client notification is carried out by calling on a single method of the advise holder, rather than having to enumerate all the sink interfaces, as is necessary with connection points. The second difference is that advise holders can only manage one interface type: **IAdviseSink**.

COM defines two advise holders created with **CreateDataAdviseHolder()** and
CreateOleAdviseHolder() and accessed through the **IDataAdviseHolder** and
IOleAdviseHolder interfaces. The first, the data advise holder, notifies clients when data
(properties) changes in the control. The second, the OLE advise holder, informs connected clients
when the control is saved, closed, or if the control has a new moniker.

Compare the following diagram with the equivalent in Chapter 6.

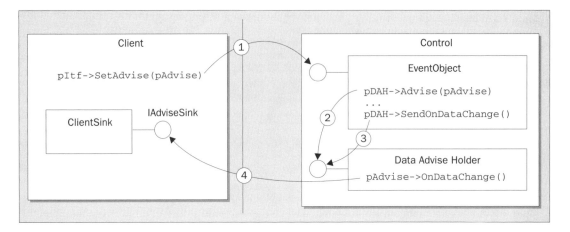

1 The client informs the control of its advise sink

2 The control adds this to its list by calling on its advise holder object (here it is a data
advise holder) to save the interface pointer.

3 At some later point in time, an event occurs and the control notifies all the connected
clients. To do this it calls on the data advise holder's **SendOnDataChange()** method

4 This goes through all the interface pointers that it holds and on each it calls
OnDataChange(). The client sink object can then handle this event.

Notice the advantages of this approach. Firstly, you do not have to implement these advise
holders, COM implements two for you, and when you release a holder, it will automatically
release all the interfaces it holds. To notify connected clients, you do not have to enumerate all
the sink interfaces, instead the holder will do this for you.

But there are problems. The main one is that only one interface is supported — **IAdviseSink**
— and this restricts the events that are handled. These events are evident from the names of
these methods: **OnClose()**, **OnDataChange()**, **OnRename()**, **OnSave()** and **OnViewChange()**.
These methods take parameters pertinent to the event they handle, so you cannot readily use
them for other events (if you implement a container for example).

ATL holds these advise holder objects using the smart pointers **m_spDataAdviseHolder** and
m_spOleAdviseHolder in **CComControlBase**. The advise sink interfaces are registered with
the control by the container calling either of the **IOleObject::Advise()** or
IDataObject::DAdvise() methods. In addition to these holders, the control may be informed
of an OLE advisory connection by the container calling **IViewObject::SetAdvise()**. Only a
single advisory connection can be registered in this way and ATL saves this in

m_spAdviseSink. This interface is used to notify the container of the one event not covered by the two previously mentioned advise holders: **OnViewChange()**, which is called when the view of the control has changed.

So when are these interfaces used?

The data advise holder is used by **CComControl<>::SendOnDataChange()** when properties change in the control. Note that you call this method in the **put_** method of a property, but if the control uses a stock property its **put_** method will be implemented for you by the stock property implementation macro **IMPLEMENT_STOCKPROP()**. This implementation does not call **SendOnDataChange()**, so you will have to provide the code yourself. **SendOnDataChange()** is used to make sure that the container knows that the data in the object has changed, and to pass the container the interface pointer to the control's **IDataObject** interface. Containers like Word handle the advisory call by calling upon the control to provide a metafile representation through the **IDataObject** interface.

The OLE advise holder is used by the **SendOnRename()**, **SendOnSave()**, and **SendOnClose()** methods which your control code should call at appropriate times — when the moniker changes, or if the control is saved. The **m_spAdviseSink** interface is called by **SendOnViewChange()**, this is called by **FireViewChange()** when the control is inactive so that the container knows that any cached representations are invalid. If the control is active, it is merely told to redraw itself.

Site Interfaces

In addition to these **IAdviseSink** interfaces, the container can also implement other interfaces that the client can call. The control should implement the **IOleObject**, and the container can call the **SetClientSite()** method to pass a pointer to its **IOleClientSite** interface; ATL holds this interface in the smart pointer **m_spClientSite**. The control can use this interface to get information about the display site in the container.

The final data member of interest for controls is **m_spInPlaceSite**. This smart pointer is valid if **m_bNegotiatedWnd** is set to true (which it is once the control is activated) and is the container's **IOleInPlaceSiteWindowless** interface pointer (or one of the base interfaces). The control can use this interface to specify how activation is handled by the container and also to handle mouse capture and route windows messages.

Properties Support

Properties have been covered in the last chapter. However, there is one interface that I didn't mention that is pertinent here, especially with the discussion about connection points above. A control may have stock properties that the container may have a particular interest in. If these properties are marked as **[bindable]** or **[requestedit]** in the control's IDL then the control must inform the container when the property is about to change, or has changed.

The mechanism used here is connection points. The control must be derived from **IPropertyNotifySinkCP**, and the container can connect to this like any other connection point container. When a bindable property is about to be changed, you can call **CComControl<>::FireOnRequestEdit()**. This informs the container, passing the DISPID of the property. The container can then decide if the property can change or not. You can see an example of this with the stock property implementation macro **IMPLEMENT_STOCKPROP()**. In a similar way when a bindable property has changed, you can call **CComControl<>::FireOnChanged()** and pass its DISPID. The container can then update itself according to the value of this stock property.

Object Wizard Options

Most of the options in Object Wizard have already been discussed in the other chapters, so let's look at the options that were missed out.

The Miscellaneous tab of the Object Wizard looks like this:

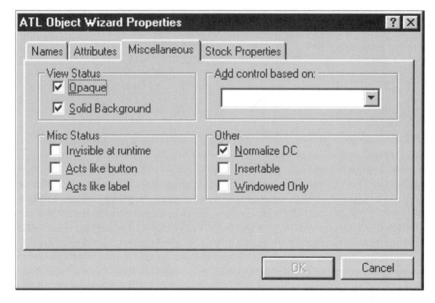

The two options in the View Status frame are inter-related. Solid Background is only enabled if Opaque is selected and indicates that the control has a solid background rather than a patterned background. Opaque means that the control draws to the entire control rectangle and will erase the background that it does not draw to. If it is not selected, it means that the control can have some transparent parts through which the container's background can be seen.

The three items in Misc Status affect the control's **MiscStatus** entry in the registry. The container calls **IOleObject::GetMiscStatus()** on the control when it is created and ATL implements this by calling the standard **OleRegGetMiscStatus()** function that obtains this value from the registry. Each of these check boxes sets an appropriate bit in this value.

Invisible at runtime indicates that the control is invisible when run — the control will not show in the container's window. Acts like button, means that the control's window behaves as a button, so that it can be drawn with a thick border if it is selected as the default button. Finally Acts like label, makes the control behave like a label, that is, selecting the mnemonic for the control will activate the control after it in the tab order. The container decides how to interpret this bit.

Add control based on allows you to base your control on an existing Windows class. There is an example of how to use this later in this chapter. Note that the drop down list box is single selection so you can base the control on just one Windows control. However, using more than one control is trivial and the example shows you how.

Normalized DC means that the device context is normalized so that the origin starts at (0,0). This makes the drawing code simpler. When selected, your control must implement the drawing code in **OnDraw()**; the normalization is carried out in **OnDrawAdvanced()** which calls **OnDraw()**. If you do not select this box, normalization will not happen and you have to implement the drawing code in **OnDrawAdvanced()**. Depending on your drawing code, you may get slightly better performance if you don't check this box.

Windowed Only means that the control *must* create its own window if checked. The Wizard just adds **m_bWindowOnly = TRUE** to the constructor. Normally you will leave this unchecked so that the container will handle control windows if possible.

Finally, Insertable allows the object to appear in the standard Insert Object dialog – it does this by adding the **Insertable** key in the control's CLSID registration code in the RGS file.

Property Pages

Control properties can usually be set and obtained using **put_** and **get_** methods. Tools like VB use these methods to implement property windows where a user (programmer) can view or change an object's properties at design time. These property windows are extremely useful as they provide the user with a way of changing a control's properties without requiring any effort by the control's designer.

However, some controls may have interdependent properties, properties of some complex data type, or the control's creator may simply wish to provide a more intuitive way of setting a property than is possible via the dialogs provided by the container. In any of these situations, a property page can be used to provide an alternative (or the only) means of setting the property.

If you have any experience of using controls, you've probably seen property pages in action. Let's look at a couple of examples of the property pages used by some well known commercial controls to get an idea of the kind of things that you can do with property pages and when you'd want to make use of them for your own properties.

First, we'll take a look at the property page used by most controls that expose color properties.

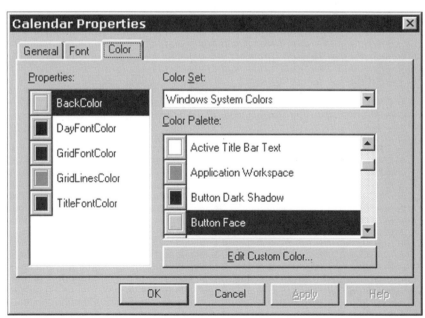

You can see that this property page provides a nice, intuitive way of setting the color value for all the different color properties supported by a control (in this case, the Microsoft Calendar control). Although colors are simple hex values that can easily be supported by any container, the property page provides a better means of setting the property. You might know that **0x000000** is black and **0xffffff** is white, but most people find it pretty hard to work out the color corresponding to **0x0080ff** (it's a dull orange). By providing a visual means of setting the property, and by offering choices from the standard colors and Windows system colors, the color property page is clearly an improvement on a simple hex value.

Another possible use for property pages is to provide a way of setting the properties for subobjects of your control. You can see an example of this in the Column Headers page for Microsoft's List View control, shown below:

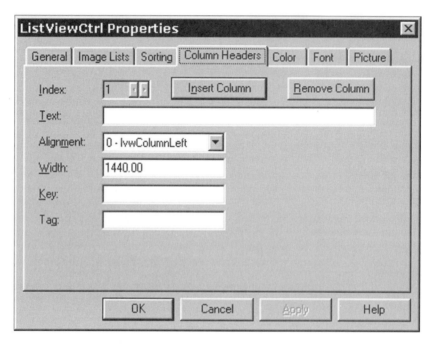

This page provides a way of creating and deleting column headers and setting each column header's properties. Each column header is a COM object provided by the List View control. Clearly property pages can be used for more than just setting top level properties on a control.

Finally, we can see how property pages can be used to group together related sets of properties. In the case of the Common Dialog control property pages shown here, all the properties are simple enough to be supported by a container's properties window. The property pages simply provide a way of separating the properties related to each of the dialogs (file, color, font, print, and help) supported by the control.

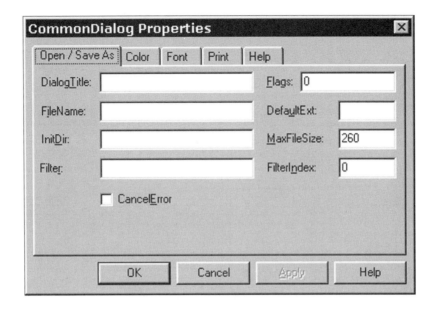

What Are Property Pages?

A property page is a COM object that implements the **IPropertyPage** interface. The property page is responsible for creating all the controls within the page, and for updating the properties in the control when asked to. The property page is *not* responsible for creating the dialog or even the tab that it appears in, nor is it responsible for the state of the buttons at the bottom of the dialog. Those things are the responsibility of a container and its **property page site**.

The property page site is a COM object that implements the **IPropertyPageSite** interface. The property page site is provided by the container and takes responsibility for the property dialog as a whole. This enables property pages that appear in the same dialog to be written independently of each other.

These controls are provided by the property page

The remainder of the dialog is provided by the container and its property page site

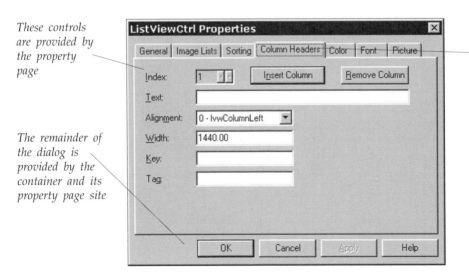

The title on the tab is obtained from the property page

Creating a Property Page

The easiest way to create a property page is to use the ATL Object Wizard to add one to your project. Since property pages are closely associated with controls, you can find the Property Page item in the Controls group of the Object Wizard.

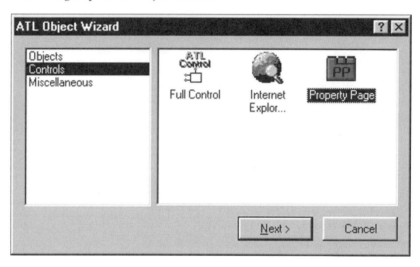

The Wizard presents you with the familiar Names and Attributes pages to provide the standard COM settings for the property page that you're about to create, and it also provides a Strings page that is specific to property pages.

Yes, the pages used by the ATL Object Wizard itself are also COM property pages!

This information will be stored as string resources in your project and automatically returned to the container when it asks. The most important string here is the <u>T</u>itle, which is used by the container to label the tab that it creates for your page. The <u>D</u>oc String can be used to describe your page, but is rarely used by containers. The <u>H</u>elpfile is just the name of a Windows help file for use with your page. This is only used if the page does not fully implement **IPropertyPage::Help()**. ATL-generated property pages implement **IPropertyPage::Help()** automatically.

The property page class that gets added to your project by the Wizard, derives from **CDialogImpl<>** and **IPropertyPageImpl<>**. Together these classes provide 90% of the implementation that a property page needs. There are only four things that you need to do for yourself:

- Add controls to the dialog
- Initialize the page
- Tell the property page site about any changes
- Update the control

Add Controls to the Dialog

Your property pages will look pretty bare without any controls on them. Use Developer Studio's dialog editor to add controls to the dialog resource generated by the Wizard, or add some code to your class to create the controls at runtime. The types of control that you add to the page will depend entirely on the use to which you're putting your page and the types of property that you'll be adjusting.

Initialize the Page

When the property page is displayed, you'll need to initialize the page with the data from the control that it's being displayed for. You can handle the **WM_INITDIALOG** message to find out when the dialog has been created, and you can get the **IUnknown** pointer for the control whose properties the page should be setting from the **m_ppUnk** member of **IPropertyPageImpl<>**.

m_ppUnk is an array of **IUnknown** pointers that were passed to the property page by a call to **IPropertyPage::SetObjects()** (the implementation of this method is provided by **IPropertyPageImpl<>**). The size of this array is held in **m_nObjects**. The container calls **SetObjects()** with the **IUnknown** pointer of the control. You can use this pointer to query for the desired interface pointer, then use that to read the property values from the control.

Tell the Page Site About Changes

When the user changes the properties of the control via your property page, you need to tell the property page site so that it can enable the Apply button. You should call **IPropertyPageImpl<>::SetDirty()** with an argument of **TRUE** to indicate that something has changed. The implementation of this function handles the call to the property page site, which it does by calling **m_pPageSite->OnStatusChange()**.

*There is a bug in Visual Basic 5 such that it requires **two** calls to the page site's* **OnStatusChange()** *method to update the status of the* **Apply** *button. You'll need to add the second call manually (it can't be another call to* **SetDirty()**). *This second call won't have any adverse effect on correctly operating containers.*

Update the Control

Finally, your page will need to update the properties of the control when told to do so by the container. The container will call **IPropertyPage::Apply()** when this should happen. The Object Wizard adds the following skeleton implementation of the **Apply()** method to your property page's class definition.

```
STDMETHOD(Apply)(void)
{
    ATLTRACE(_T("CTestPage::Apply\n"));
    for (UINT i = 0; i < m_nObjects; i++)
    {
        // Do something interesting here
        // ICircCtl* pCirc;
        // m_ppUnk[i]->QueryInterface(
        //    IID_ICircCtl,(void**)&pCirc);
        // pCirc->put_Caption(
        //    CComBSTR("something special"));
        // pCirc->Release();
    }
    m_bDirty = FALSE;
    return S_OK;
}
```

To take advantage of ATL smart pointers, this sample code should really be:

```
for (UINT i = 0; i < m_nObjects; i++)
{
    // Do something interesting here
    // CComPtr<ICircCtl> pCirc;
    // m_ppUnk[i]->QueryInterface(
    //    IID_ICircCtl,(void**)&pCirc);
    // pCirc->put_Caption(
    //    CComBSTR("something special"));
}
```

But we'll ignore that oversight! The point is clear: you need to query the pointer(s) in the **m_ppUnk** array to get an interface that gives access to the control's properties, then copy the data from your page's controls to these properties.

This generated **Apply()** method is implemented inline, I prefer to copy it into the source file, because typically I have to change it several times. Wherever the code lies, you'll need to make sure that the header for the control's interface is included.

Relating the Page to the Control

We've seen how to code up a property page with the four simple steps outlined above, but how does the container find out from a control which property pages to display? The simple answer is that it asks it. The container will call the **GetPages()** method of the control's **ISpecifyPropertyPages** interface to get an array of GUIDs containing the property pages for that control.

ATL provides an implementation of **ISpecifyPropertyPages** in the form of the **ISpecifyPropertyPagesImpl<>** class, which is used as a base class for full controls. This class uses the information in the property map for the control to decide what GUIDs to return in response to a call to **ISpecifyPropertyPages::GetPages()**.

This code will look through all the entries in the property map and build up an array of property page GUIDs. The property page GUIDs can appear in the map in one of three ways:

- As part of a **PROP_ENTRY()** macro
- As part of a **PROP_ENTRY_EX()** macro
- As part of a **PROP_PAGE()** macro

The **PROP_ENTRY()** and the **PROP_ENTRY_EX()** macros are used to provide full descriptions of a property. These descriptions can be used by a number of ATL classes including the **IPersist**xxx implementations we saw in the last chapter, **IPerPropertyBrowsingImpl<>**, and **ISpecifyPropertyPagesImpl<>** itself. The **PROP_PAGE()** macro is used solely to provide an entry in the map to be used by **ISpecifyPropertyPagesImpl<>**.

The array will contain a single GUID for each property page specified in the map, even if it appears many times. The array will contain these GUIDs in the order that they appear in the map. Typically, this is the order that they will appear in the property dialog displayed by the container.

Message Maps

As you know from your experience of Windows programming, windows receive Windows messages (**WM_PAINT**, etc.) — the windows used by controls are no different in this respect. These messages are as important to a control as the method calls on its COM interfaces. The control must intercept the messages and handle them.

In ATL, messages are handled using **message maps**. If you have any experience with MFC, you'll see that ATL's message maps look very similar to the maps provided by MFC (one crucial difference, however, is that there's no ClassWizard support for ATL message maps).

You can see message maps declared in the Wizard-generated classes for Full Controls, Internet Explorer Controls, Property Pages and Dialogs. All of these types use windows, so they need to handle messages. Here's an example of the default message map from a Full Control:

```
BEGIN_MSG_MAP(CMyCtrl)
    MESSAGE_HANDLER(WM_PAINT, OnPaint)
    MESSAGE_HANDLER(WM_SETFOCUS, OnSetFocus)
    MESSAGE_HANDLER(WM_KILLFOCUS, OnKillFocus)
END_MSG_MAP()
```

Essentially, **BEGIN_MSG_MAP()** declares an inline function in the class called **ProcessWindowMessage()**. This function takes a Windows message as a parameter, and uses the information in the message map to pass the message to a handler function in an appropriate form.

> *Classes that provide message maps should derive from* **CMessageMap**, *an abstract class that just declares the* **ProcessWindowMessage()** *function. This allows ATL to provide type safe ways of using the message maps.* **CDialogImpl<>** *and* **CWindowImpl<>** *derive from* **CMessageMap**.

Each handler entry in the message map associates a message (or range of messages) with a function. Each entry adds an **if** statement to see if the message passed to the function should be handled by that entry. If so, the code calls the function specified, passing the arguments in a form appropriate to that message type.

MESSAGE_HANDLER() is the basic way to handle messages, however, there are other macros you can use, and these are given in the following table.

Macro	Parameters	Handler Type
MESSAGE_HANDLER()	**msg, func**	message
MESSAGE_RANGE_HANDLER()	**msgFirst, msgLast, func**	message
COMMAND_HANDLER()	**id, code, func**	command
COMMAND_ID_HANDLER()	**id, func**	command
COMMAND_CODE_HANDLER()	**code, func**	command
COMMAND_RANGE_HANDLER()	**idFirst, idLast, func**	command
NOTIFY_HANDLER()	**id, code, func**	notify
NOTIFY_ID_HANDLER()	**id, func**	notify
NOTIFY_CODE_HANDLER()	**code, func**	notify
NOTIFY_RANGE_HANDLER()	**idFirst, idLast, func**	notify

Where:
func	The handler function
msg	Message to handle
msgFirst, msgLast	Range of messages to handle
id	The identifier of the menu item, control, or accelerator
code	The notification code
idFirst, idLast	Range of IDs

The different handler types (message, command, and notify) require different signatures for the handler functions. These are shown in the following table:

Handler Type	Function Signature
message	`LRESULT MessageHandler(UINT uMsg, WPARAM wParam, LPARAM lParam, BOOL& bHandled);`
command	`LRESULT CommandHandler(WORD wNotifyCode, WORD wID, HWND hWndCtl, BOOL& bHandled);`
notify	`LRESULT NotifyHandler(int idCtrl, LPNMHDR pnmh, BOOL& bHandled);`

All three types of handler function take a reference to a **BOOL** as the final parameter; this is set to **TRUE** before ATL calls the handler function. You should set this parameter to **FALSE** if the handler does not handle the message, or wants other handlers to also handle the message. If you set the **bHandled** parameter to **FALSE**, the message will be passed on to the other entries in the message map to see if it matches the message that they handle. Ultimately, if a message is not handled after all the message map entries have been checked, it will be sent to a default message handler, as is standard in Windows programming.

The return value of the handler depends on the message handled. You'll need to look into the Win32 SDK documentation to see what this return value should be. For most messages the return value is **0** for a successfully handled message.

The macros starting with **MESSAGE_** handle Windows messages, either a single message or a range of messages. The function that handles the message is passed the actual message ID so if you want to handle a range of messages with one function you can tell which message was sent. The command and notify handlers are specifically for **WM_COMMAND** and **WM_NOTIFY** messages. These messages could be handled using a **MESSAGE_** macro, but the command and notify message contain a lot of information that is best split out using the macros designed specifically for the task. Command and notify messages are typically sent from child windows to their parent. The example at the end of the chapter shows how to use these handlers.

Alternative Message Maps

ATL provides a couple of ways of handling messages sent by different windows in a single message map: **alternative message maps** and **chained message maps**. We'll consider alternative message maps first.

The idea behind alternative message maps is that a window object is initialized to send all its messages to a particular message map in another class. That message map can be subdivided, so that messages from one source are treated differently to messages from another.

Typically this is used by a main window class (such as one that represents a dialog), which contains other Windows controls represented by ATL classes. The controls on the dialog are created as members of ATL's **CContainedWindow** class, and are initialized with a pointer to their parent (so that they can get access to its message map) and the number of the alternative message map. The main window subdivides its message map (using numeric IDs) so that it can have handlers for its own messages and for the messages sent by the contained windows.

Here is a message map from a main window with an alternative map shown highlighted:

```
BEGIN_MSG_MAP(CMainCtrl)
    MESSAGE_HANDLER(WM_PAINT, OnPaint)
    MESSAGE_HANDLER(WM_SETFOCUS, OnSetFocus)
    MESSAGE_HANDLER(WM_KILLFOCUS, OnKillFocus)
    MESSAGE_HANDLER(WM_CREATE, OnCreate)
ALT_MSG_MAP(1)
    MESSAGE_HANDLER(WM_LBUTTONDBLCLK, OnLButtonDblClk)
END_MSG_MAP()
```

As we mentioned earlier, **BEGIN_MSG_MAP()** declares the **ProcessWindowMessage()** function. This function has a parameter for the message map to use: the default value for this parameter is **0**. After the function declaration there is a **switch** statement starting with a **case 0:**. In other words, the handlers that appear immediately after **BEGIN_MSG_MAP()** are in message map **0**. The **ALT_MSG_MAP()** expands to a **case** statement with the identifier from the macro, so the alternative message map declared above expands to **case 1:**.

When the contained windows receive a message, they just call **ProcessWindowMessage()** in their parent, passing all the information for the message itself, in addition to the message map ID that the contained window was initialized with in its constructor.

The main window can use as many **ALT_MSG_MAP()** macros as it needs and it can initialize the contained window members to use whichever of the alternative message maps is most appropriate. Multiple contained windows can use the same alternative message map in the parent if they need to.

> *If you call* **Create()** *on a contained window in response to the* **WM_CREATE** *message of its parent, make sure that you don't set the contained window to use the same part of the message map. The creation of the contained window would trigger another* **WM_CREATE** *message, which would result in another attempt to create the contained window, and so on.*

Example

Let's take a look at a simple example that shows how to use alternative message maps, and message handlers. We'll create a full control with a contained window. The control window and its contained window will use different message maps in the control class.

Start Developer Studio, and create a new ATL COM AppWizard project called MsgMaps. Make sure that the Server Type is set to Dynamic Link Library (DLL). Add a new Full Control to the project using the Object Wizard. Give the control the Short Name of Click and on the Miscellaneous page select Insertable. From the Add control based on select Edit, then click on OK.

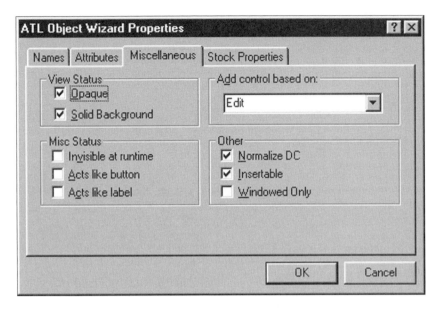

Open **Click.h** and take a look at the class definition, and particularly the constructor:

```
public:
   CContainedWindow m_ctlEdit;

   CClick() :
      m_ctlEdit(_T("Edit"), this, 1)
   {
      m_bWindowOnly = TRUE;
   }
```

You can see that our control class has a **CContainedWindow** member to represent the edit control and that this has been initialized in the control's initializer list with three parameters:

▶ The class of the window (**"Edit"**)

▶ A pointer to the object containing the message map (**this**)

▶ The ID of the message map (**1**).

> *Note that **m_bWindowOnly** is set to **TRUE** to ensure that the control always gets its own window. This allows it to handle **WM_CREATE** for the Click control itself and create the edit control in response to that.*

If you look at the message map itself, further down the class definition, you'll see that the Wizard adds the alternative message map to be used by the edit control :

```
BEGIN_MSG_MAP(CClick)
   MESSAGE_HANDLER(WM_PAINT, OnPaint)
   MESSAGE_HANDLER(WM_SETFOCUS, OnSetFocus)
   MESSAGE_HANDLER(WM_KILLFOCUS, OnKillFocus)
```

```
    MESSAGE_HANDLER(WM_CREATE, OnCreate)
ALT_MSG_MAP(1)
    // Replace this with message map entries for subclassed Edit
END_MSG_MAP()
```

> *Although the comment talks about subclassing, the Wizard-generated*
> **CContainedWindow** *member actually* **superclasses** *the Edit window class. Have a*
> *look at the documentation for* **CContainedWindow** *for further information on*
> *superclassing and subclassing.*

Now let's start adding some code. By default, the Wizard-generated code positions the edit control so that it covers the whole of the control. We want to position it so that it only covers the top half of the area that the control takes up. In this way, we'll be able to receive **WM_LBUTTONDOWN** messages from our control and from the edit box.

Edit the code in **OnCreate()** so that it matches that shown below:

```
    LRESULT OnCreate(UINT uMsg, WPARAM wParam, LPARAM lParam, BOOL&
bHandled)
    {
        RECT rc;
        GetWindowRect(&rc);
        rc.right -= rc.left;
        rc.bottom -= rc.top;
        rc.top = rc.left = 0;
        // Divide the height by 2
        rc.bottom /= 2;
        // Create the edit control in the top half of our
        // control and give it a border
        m_ctlEdit.Create(m_hWnd, rc, NULL,
            WS_CHILD | WS_VISIBLE | WS_BORDER);

        return 0;
    }
```

Here we've got the rectangle of our window by calling **GetWindowRect()**, set it so that the top left is at (0,0) then divided the height of the rectangle by 2. Then we call **m_ctlEdit.Create()** to create the edit box using the rectangle and ensuring that the edit box has a border so that we can see it.

We also need to ensure that the edit box always takes up half of the control even when the control is resized. We can do this by editing **SetObjectRects()** as shown:

```
    STDMETHOD(SetObjectRects)(LPCRECT prcPos,LPCRECT prcClip)
    {
        IOleInPlaceObjectWindowlessImpl<CClick>::SetObjectRects(prcPos,
                                                        prcClip);
        int cx, cy;
        cx = prcPos->right - prcPos->left;
        cy = prcPos->bottom - prcPos->top;
```

```
            // Give the edit control the top half of our control to live in
            ::SetWindowPos(m_ctlEdit.m_hWnd, NULL, 0,
                0, cx, cy/2, SWP_NOZORDER | SWP_NOACTIVATE);
        return S_OK;
    }
```

Now we can add a data member and some drawing code to the control. The data member will be a simple string that we can set to indicate whether the control has been clicked. Add the new data member just below the data member for the edit box and initialize it in the constructor as shown:

```
    CContainedWindow m_ctlEdit;
    TCHAR m_str[80];


    CClick() :
        m_ctlEdit(_T("Edit"), this, 1)
    {
        m_str[0] = 0;
        m_bWindowOnly = TRUE;
    }
```

Add the drawing code to **CClick::OnDraw()**. This code just draws a rectangle around the lower half of the control and outputs the text from **m_str**.

```
    HRESULT CClick::OnDraw(ATL_DRAWINFO& di)
    {
    RECT& rc = *(RECT*)di.prcBounds;
    Rectangle(di.hdcDraw, rc.left,
            rc.top + (rc.bottom - rc.top)/2,
            rc.right, rc.bottom);
    TextOut(di.hdcDraw, 0,
            rc.top + (rc.bottom - rc.top)/2,
            m_str, lstrlen(m_str));
    return S_OK;
    }
```

Now we just need to add the entries to the message map and a couple of handler functions, then our work is done. Add the entries to the message map shown below:

```
BEGIN_MSG_MAP(CClick)
    MESSAGE_HANDLER(WM_PAINT, OnPaint)
    MESSAGE_HANDLER(WM_SETFOCUS, OnSetFocus)
    MESSAGE_HANDLER(WM_KILLFOCUS, OnKillFocus)
    MESSAGE_HANDLER(WM_CREATE, OnCreate)
    MESSAGE_HANDLER(WM_LBUTTONDOWN, OnCtrlLButton)
ALT_MSG_MAP(1)
    MESSAGE_HANDLER(WM_LBUTTONDOWN, OnEditLButton)
END_MSG_MAP()
```

You can see that we are going to handle mouse button down messages sent to the control in a function called **OnCtrlLButton()**, and messages sent to the edit box will go to **OnEditLButton()**.

Now add these handlers just below the message map:

```
LRESULT OnCtrlLButton(UINT uMsg, WPARAM wParam, LPARAM lParam,
                      BOOL& bHandled)
{
   lstrcpy(m_str, _T("Clicked the control"));
   m_ctlEdit.SetWindowText(_T(""));
   FireViewChange();
   return 0;
}

LRESULT OnEditLButton(UINT uMsg, WPARAM wParam, LPARAM lParam,
                      BOOL& bHandled)
{
   m_str[0] = 0;
   m_ctlEdit.SetWindowText(_T("Clicked the edit box"));
   FireViewChange();
   return 0;
}
```

When the control is clicked (in other words you click in the bottom half of the area of the control), we set the text in the control to say that it has been clicked and we set the text in the edit box to nothing. When the edit box is clicked, we do the reverse. In both cases, the call to **FireViewChange()** ensures that the view gets updated.

Now you can compile the project and test it using the ActiveX Control Test Container. Insert a Click Class into the container and click in the top half, then the bottom half of the control to see it in action.

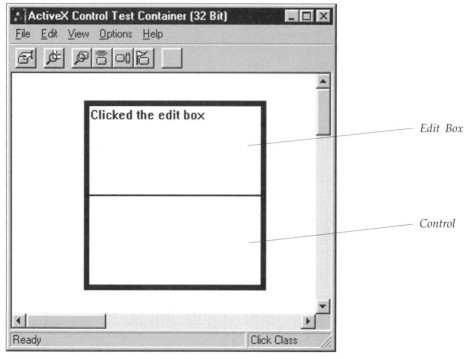

Once you've tested the control, go back to **OnEditLButton()** and add the following line of code:

```
LRESULT OnEditLButton(UINT uMsg, WPARAM wParam, LPARAM lParam,
                      BOOL& bHandled)
{
    m_str[0] = 0;
    m_ctlEdit.SetWindowText(_T("Clicked the edit box"));
    FireViewChange();
    bHandled = FALSE;
    return 0;
}
```

Now test the control again. By setting **bHandled** to **FALSE**, we're allowing the **WM_LBUTTONDOWN** message to propagate back to the default window procedure. This will allow you to edit the text in the edit box, as you'd expect to be able to.

Chaining Message Maps

ATL also provides a mechanism for chaining message maps. This routes the message through to the message map in another class or object. If a handler in that class handles the message then no other handler will get a chance, otherwise the rest of the original message map is checked for a handler.

There are three types of **CHAIN_MSG_MAP**xxx**()** macro (with two variants of each):

Macro	Parameters	Description
CHAIN_MSG_MAP()	theChainClass	Routes the message to the default message map in a base class
CHAIN_MSG_MAP_ALT()	theChainClass, msgMapID	Routes the message to the default message map of a member
CHAIN_MSG_MAP_MEMBER()	theChainMember	Routes the message to an alternative message map in a base class
CHAIN_MSG_MAP_ALT_MEMBER()	theChainMember, msgMapID	Routes the message to an alternative message map of a member
CHAIN_MSG_MAP_DYNAMIC()	dynaChainID	Routes the message to the default message map of a member which is determined at runtime
CHAIN_MSG_MAP_ALT_DYNAMIC()	dynaChainID, msgMapID	Routes the message to an alternative message map of a member which is determined at runtime

Where:

theChainClass	Base class containing the message map
theChainMember	A data member that has a message map
dynaChainID	Identifies an object with a message map
msgMapID	Message map identifier

So, the message can be routed to a base class, to a data member in the class, or to another object that is determined at runtime. The two variants allow you to route the message to the default message map or to an alternative message map.

The first four macros are straightforward. The dynamic chaining macros are more interesting in that they allow you to build up a routing at runtime. Any class that uses the **CHAIN_MSG_MAP_DYNAMIC()** macro must derive from **CDynamicChain**. At runtime, you can call **CDynamicChain::SetChainEntry()** to associate another object with an ID that matches an ID in the **CHAIN_MSG_MAP_DYNAMIC()** macro. You can add as many dynamic maps as you like as long as each has a unique ID.

You can see chained message maps in action just by taking a look at the message map that the Object Wizard generates for a property page:

```
BEGIN_MSG_MAP(CPropPage)
    CHAIN_MSG_MAP(IPropertyPageImpl<CPropPage>)
END_MSG_MAP()
```

Property pages derive from **IPropertyPageImpl<>** which provides a default handler for the **WM_STYLECHANGING** message. The **CHAIN_MSG_MAP()** entry allows the handler in the base class to continue working.

Windowless Controls and Message Maps

It's relatively easy to see how the messages get to the message map when the window is owned by the object containing the message map (because it has total control over the window procedure), but what about windows that are owned by the container? In other words, how does a windowless control receive messages?

The answer is in the **IOleInPlaceObjectWindowless** interface, which must be implemented by all windowless controls. This interface has a method called **OnWindowsMessage()**, which the container must call to provide the control with Windows messages. The ATL implementation of this interface, **IOleInPlaceObjectWindowlessImpl<>**, implements this method so that it calls the **ProcessWindowMessage()** function — that is, it passes all the messages received by **OnWindowsMessage()** directly to the message map, where they can be routed to handler functions.

Full Control Example

Now that you've seen the basics of ATL controls, let's develop a control that uses most of these concepts. This example is a full control that wraps the Windows tree view and edit box common controls. The tree view will display a hierarchical view of URLs using simple names. The edit box will show the full URL for the currently selected item. Double-clicking on an item in the tree view will launch a new instance of Internet Explorer and load the URL specified by that item.

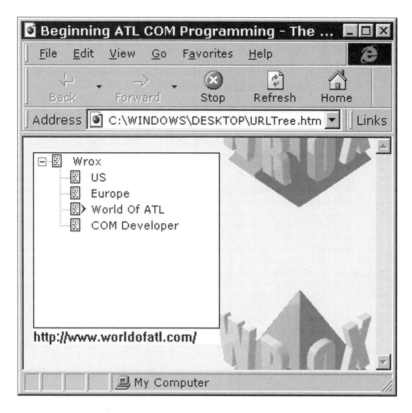

The URLs displayed in the control will be obtained from a **URLs** property. This property will be a **SAFEARRAY** of **BSTR**s wrapped up in a **VARIANT** (like the **SAFEARRAY** example from Chapter 4). Each string in the array will have the following form:

```
branch,url
```

branch is the branch of the tree, with sub-branches separated with forward slashes (**/**). The final item in the branch corresponds to the URL specified by **url** (which can be any URL that Internet Explorer can handle). For example, the **World Of ATL** sub-branch of the **Wrox** branch that points to **http://www.worldofatl.com/** will have an entry like this:

```
Wrox/World Of ATL,http://www.worldofatl.com/
```

Notice that there is no white space around the comma.

Since we want this control to be usable from different containers including Visual Basic, we'll provide a property page, shown here, that allows the developer to add the values used to initialize the control:

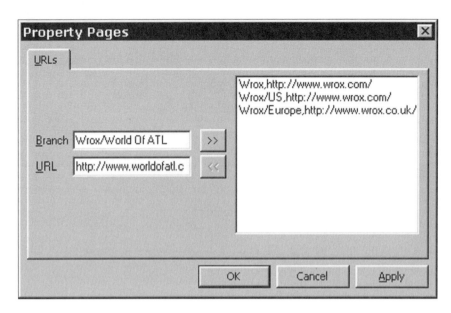

Here, I have entered the branches US and Europe on the Wrox branch, and I am about to add a new branch off the Wrox branch called World Of ATL. When I click on the >> button, the string Wrox/World Of ATL,http://www.worldofatl.com/ will be added to the list box.

We'll also need to provide persistence code for our control. The persistence code will allow the control to be used in Visual Basic and also allow us to provide values using the **<PARAM>** tags when the control is embedded in a web page.

Tree View Common Controls

Because we're going to be using a tree view in our control, we need to understand a little about how they work. There are several articles on MSDN that explain this in detail, but here is a potted explanation to get you started.

The tree view that you are most familiar with is the left-hand pane of the Windows Explorer, shown next.

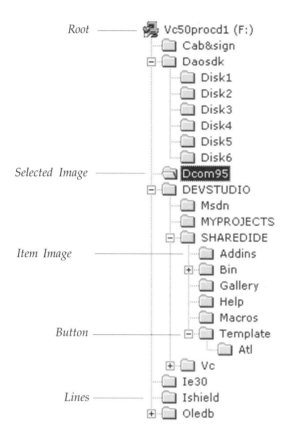

Root ——— Vc50procd1 (F:)

Selected Image ——— Dcom95

Item Image ——— Addins

Button ——— Template

Lines ——— Ishield

In the picture, you can see that the tree view has many branches coming off a root; in this case the root has an image of the icon for the VC++ installation program. Each item is joined to the root using lines, and each item that contains child items has a button to allow you to expand or contract it. The presence of these lines and buttons isn't mandatory; the tree view control lets you set these using the window styles of the control.

Each item in the tree view is shown with a folder image. Two images are used: one when an item is selected, and another when it is not. These images are supplied by an associated image list control. When you add an item to the tree, you can specify which images in the image list to use when the item's selected and which image to use when it's not. Note that each item can have completely distinct images if you want, or no image at all.

The **URLTree** control should look similar to the Explorer tree, each item should have selected and non-selected images, and they should be connected with lines and buttons. Compare the picture of Explorer with **URLTree**, and you should be able to identify the corresponding parts:

http://www.worldofatl.com/

Creating a Tree View Control

The declarations for the common controls (including the tree view control) are in **CommCtrl.h** and the import library is in **ComCt132.lib**. The ATL wizards won't add either to your project, so you need to **#include** the header in every file that uses the common control macros and functions, and add the library to the link options yourself.

> *Before you can use a common control you need to call **InitCommonControls()** to ensure that the common control library is loaded. However, calling this function is the responsibility of the container, so this requirement won't affect our code at all. Internet Explorer and Visual Basic call this function automatically, but if you want to write your own container, using MFC for example, you will need to call this function in your code.*

To create a tree view in ATL, you call the **CWindow::Create()** method passing "**SysTreeView32**" as the Windows class name, you may also specify styles for the control. In this example, we will use a combination of these three styles:

TVS_HASLINES	Lines connecting the items
TVS_LINESATROOT	Root child items have lines to connect them to the root
TVS_HASBUTTONS	Parent items have buttons

The tree view control is designed for use by C programmers; it requires you to send a lot of messages to the control. Every time that you add, delete, and access items in a tree view, you have to send it a Windows message. Sending messages to controls means using **SendMessage()** and may involve some horrible casts, which leads to ugly, unreadable code. MFC wraps up this up nicely in its **CTreeCtrl** class, but we can't use that directly from an ATL project. Fortunately, Microsoft has also declared some macros that wrap up **SendMessage()** and the necessary casts, which we *can* use from ATL. The tree view macros have names that start with **TreeView_**. I will describe the most useful macros after describing the tree view data structures.

TVITEM Structure

To add, delete or query an item in a tree view, you need to pass data to the control via data structures. The **TVITEM** structure represents an item in the tree. It has these members:

```
typedef struct tagTVITEM{
    UINT       mask;
    HTREEITEM  hItem;
    UINT       state;
    UINT       stateMask;
    LPTSTR     pszText;
    int        cchTextMax;
    int        iImage;
    int        iSelectedImage;
    int        cChildren;
    LPARAM     lParam;
} TVITEM, FAR *LPTVITEM;
```

The **mask** determines which of the other members is valid (when passing data to the tree view) or required (when asking for information about an item). The **hItem** member is a handle for the item and is used in a similar way to how **HWND**s are used to manage windows. **stateMask** determines which bits of **state** are valid, and the lower eight bits of **state** determine what state the item is in (selected, expanded, etc).

pszText is the text that is shown in the tree view control for the item (for example, the folder name in Explorer). If you are setting the item text, use a null-terminated string and the control will make a copy of it. If you have the **UNICODE** symbol defined then you should pass a Unicode string, otherwise you should pass an ANSI string. This copy of the string is maintained by the control and is freed automatically when the control is destroyed. If you are querying for the item's name then you should pass a caller-allocated buffer in **pszText** which the control will fill with the text. You should pass the size of this buffer in the **cchTextMax** member.

A tree view can have an associated image list and the **iImage** and **iSelectedImage** members are indices of images in this list, which will be used for selected and non-selected items respectively.

The final member is **lParam**, which is a 32-bit value associated with the item. This can be any value you like, but if the value corresponds to a caller-allocated memory buffer, you have the responsibility to free the memory when the item is deleted. You can do this when the parent control gets the delete item notification message, which it will whenever an item is deleted (including when the control is destroyed). In the case of our control, we'll use the **lParam** to point to the string holding the URL for that item.

Adding Items

When you add an item you need to use a **TVINSERTSTRUCT** structure:

```
typedef struct tagTVINSERTSTRUCT {
   HTREEITEM hParent;
   HTREEITEM hInsertAfter;
   TVITEM item;
} TVINSERTSTRUCT, FAR *LPTVINSERTSTRUCT;
```

This has a **TVITEM** member for the item that you are adding, and it also has the handles for the parent of this item and the sibling item after which it is added. If the item is to be added as a child of the root, then **NULL** can be used for **hParent**. The **hInsertAfter** member can be a handle to an existing item or one of the following 'magic' values:

TVI_FIRST	Inserts the item at the beginning of the list
TVI_LAST	Inserts the item at the end of the list
TVI_SORT	Inserts the item into the list in alphabetical order

You add an item using the **TreeView_InsertItem()** macro passing the **HWND** of the tree view control and a pointer to a filled **TVINSERTSTRUCT** structure. If the insertion is successful, the macro returns the handle to the new item. For example:

```
TVITEM tvi;
tvi.mask = TVIF_TEXT;
tvi.pszText = _T("New Item");
TVINSERTSTRUCT tvins;
tvins.item = tvi;
```

```
tvins.hInsertAfter = TVI_LAST;
tvins.hParent = NULL;
HTREEITEM hItem;
hItem = TreeView_InsertItem(hWnd, &tvins);
```

This adds a new item with the name New Item as a child to the root of the control.

Image List Controls

As I mentioned above, items can have images. To do this you have to create an image list control and add bitmaps into it. The image list is then associated with the tree view. When you insert a new item, you can use the index of the bitmap in the image list as the **iImage** or **iSelectedImage** members of **TVITEM**. To create an image list control you use the **ImageList_Create()** function, and you add bitmaps to the image list with **ImageList_Add()**, this returns the index which should be used in **iImage** or **iSelectedImage**. The image list is associated with the tree view with the **TreeView_SetImageList()** macro, and when the image list is no longer needed it should be released with **ImageList_Destroy()**. For example:

```
HBITMAP hBitmap;
HIMAGELIST hImageList;
hImageList = ImageList_Create(16, 16, ILC_COLOR, 2, 10);
hBitmap = LoadBitmap(...);
int iImage = ImageList_Add(hImageList, hBitmap,(HBITMAP)0);
DeleteObject(hBitmap);
hBitmap = LoadBitmap(...);
int iSelectedImage = ImageList_Add(hImageList, hBitmap,(HBITMAP)0);
DeleteObject(hBitmap);
TreeView_SetImageList(hWnd, hImageList, TVSIL_NORMAL);
```

This indicates that the images are 16 x 16 color bitmaps, initially holding two bitmaps, but the image list can grow by 10 bitmaps at a time. Bitmaps are then added into the image list. Finally the image list is passed to the tree view control with **TreeView_SetImageList()**, and the last parameter of this macro in this case indicates that the image list is used for unselected items, rather than selected ones.

Querying Values

There are many macros to query the tree view for values, here are a few that are used in this example.

TreeView_GetItem() obtains information about a particular item. You use this by passing in a **TVITEM** structure with the **hItem** member set to the handle of the item you are interested in, and the **mask** member set to indicate the properties of the item you are interested in. If you want the text of the item you use the **pszText** to point to a caller allocated buffer and **cchTextMax** to indicate how big the buffer is.

TreeView_GetSelection() returns the **HTREEITEM** of the currently selected item or **NULL** if there is not a selection. **TreeView_GetChild()** retrieves the **HTREEITEM** of the first child of an item and you can then call **TreeView_GetNextSibling()** to get the next sibling of that child item.

Notifications

When something happens to a tree view control, it will tell its container by posting a notification message to the container's window. The notification is passed as a **WM_NOTIFY** message and ATL handles this in a control's message map with the **NOTIFY_CODE_HANDLER()**, **NOTIFY_HANDLER()** and **NOTIFY_ID_HANDLER()** macros, as explained earlier in the chapter. The two notification messages pertinent to this example are **TVN_SELCHANGED** and **TVN_DELETEITEM**.

The first message is sent by the tree view control to its parent window when the selection moves from one item to another item, and is used to indicate the item from which the selection is moved and the item to which the selection has moved. The message also indicates how the selection changed (by a mouse click or by the keyboard). **URLTree** uses this message to get the URL associated with the new item and put the text in the edit box.

Since the **lParam** of the tree view items is used to hold a string, it means that the memory allocated for this string will have to be freed at some point when the control is destroyed, or reinitialized. This is why the **URLTree** handles the **TVN_DELETEITEM** notification. When the control is destroyed it will go through all the items and post this notification before deleting them and it gives us a chance to test for the **lParam** of the item and, if necessary, free the associated buffer.

Creating the Control

We want this control to be used both in Internet Explorer and in VB, so it will have to be a full control rather than just an IE control. Here are the steps for creating the initial files:

Start Developer Studio and create a new ATL COM AppWizard project called URLTree. Ensure the Server Type is Dynamic Link Library (DLL).

Once the project has been generated, add a new Full Control to the project using the ATL Object Wizard. On the Names tab, give the control the Short Name of URLTreeView. Select the Miscellaneous tab and check the Insertable check box and from the Add control based on drop down list box, select SysTreeView32.

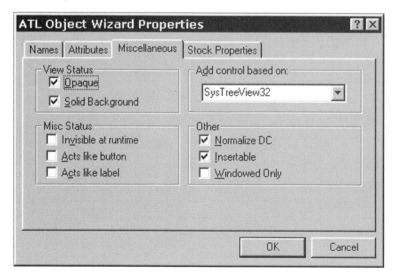

These are all the changes that you need to make, so click on OK.

The URLs used in the tree control will be passed around as a **VARIANT** holding a **SAFEARRAY** of **BSTR**s, so you will need to add a property to hold this data. In ClassView right-click on IURLTreeView and select Add Property.... In the next dialog, select a Property Type of VARIANT and give it a Property Name of URLs. Once you've okayed the dialog, ClassView should look like this:

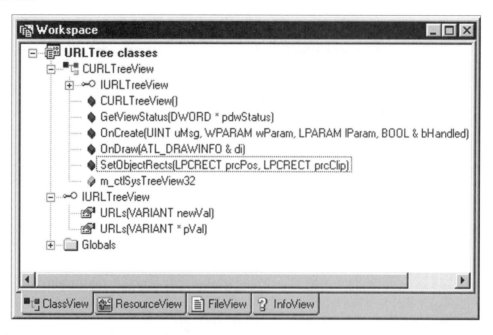

Before writing any code, let's tidy up the generated code a little. The idea is to move code out of the header and into the implementation file. This is not strictly necessary, but it does mean that if you want to change code in the affected methods, only one source file is recompiled and not *all* the source files that include the header.

Open **URLTreeView.h** and **URLTreeView.cpp** and copy the code for **OnCreate()**, **SetObjectRects()** and the constructor from the header file and paste it into the source file.

Edit the methods that you've just added to the source file so that their header lines are as shown:

```
CURLTreeView::CURLTreeView() :
   m_ctlSysTreeView32(_T("SysTreeView32"), this, 1)
{
...
}
```

```
LRESULT CURLTreeView::OnCreate(UINT uMsg, WPARAM wParam, LPARAM lParam,
                               BOOL& bHandled)
{
...
}
```

```
STDMETHODIMP CURLTreeView::SetObjectRects(LPCRECT prcPos,
                                          LPCRECT prcClip)
{
...
}
```

Now edit the header file to remove the C++ code for these methods (leave the declaration and remember to add the semicolon):

```
CURLViewTree();

LRESULT OnCreate(UINT uMsg, WPARAM wParam, LPARAM lParam,
                                           BOOL& bHandled);
STDMETHOD(SetObjectRects)(LPCRECT prcPos, LPCRECT prcClip);
```

While you're tidying up the code, edit the property map in **URLTreeView.h** to remove the support for the stock color page (since the example will not use any color properties). The property map should look like this:

```
BEGIN_PROPERTY_MAP(CURLTreeView)
END_PROPERTY_MAP()
```

The Contained Controls

If you look near the top of the **CURLTreeView** class declaration, you will see the tree view control that we requested from the Object Wizard in the form of a **CContainedWindow** member:

```
CContainedWindow m_ctlSysTreeView32;
```

This member is initialized in the constructor to use alternative message map 1, and is created in response to the **WM_CREATE** message sent to our control's window (which is the reason that our control is windowed only, even though we didn't set that option in the Object Wizard):

```
CURLTreeView::CURLTreeView() :
  m_ctlSysTreeView32(_T("SysTreeView32"), this, 1)
{
  m_bWindowOnly = TRUE;
}
```

Our control also needs an edit control, so we need to add a **CContainedWindow** member for it, create the control in response to **WM_CREATE**, and resize it and the tree control so that they don't overlap.

At the top of the class definition, add the following declaration for the edit control:

```
public:
  CContainedWindow m_ctlSysTreeView32;
  CContainedWindow m_ctlEdit;
```

In the source file, add the line to initialize the contained window as an edit control and set it up to use the message map with an index of 2. (Don't forget to include the comma after the initialization of the tree view object):

433

```
CURLTreeView::CURLTreeView()  :
   m_ctlSysTreeView32(_T("SysTreeView32"), this, 1),
   m_ctlEdit(_T("EDIT"), this, 2)
{
   m_bWindowOnly = TRUE;
}
```

Now add the second alternative message map to the definition for **CURLTreeView**:

```
ALT_MSG_MAP(1)
   // Replace this with message map entries for subclassed SysTreeView32
ALT_MSG_MAP(2)
   // Message map for edit box
END_MSG_MAP()
```

Sizing the Contained Controls

Our next task is to ensure that the controls are positioned where we want them. We want the edit control to be at the bottom of the area of the control. It should take up the whole width, but only needs to be tall enough to display a single line of text. The tree control needs to fill the remaining area of the control.

First we'll declare a member to hold the height of a line of text. We'll use this whenever we need to resize the contained windows. We'll see how to initialize it to a useful value in a while.

Add a **private** data member at the bottom of the class:

```
private:
   int m_tmHeight;
};
```

And initialize it to zero in the constructor:

```
   m_tmHeight = 0;
   m_bWindowOnly = TRUE;
```

Now edit **OnCreate()** so that both the tree view and the edit control will be created with the right size:

```
LRESULT CURLTreeView::OnCreate(UINT uMsg, WPARAM wParam, LPARAM lParam,
                               BOOL& bHandled)
{
   RECT rc;
   GetWindowRect(&rc);
   rc.right -= rc.left;
   rc.bottom -= rc.top;
   rc.top = rc.left = 0;
   rc.bottom -= m_tmHeight;
   m_ctlSysTreeView32.Create(m_hWnd, rc);
   rc.top = rc.bottom;
   rc.bottom = m_tmHeight;
```

```
    m_ctlEdit.Create(m_hWnd, rc, NULL,
                     WS_CHILD | WS_VISIBLE | ES_AUTOHSCROLL);
    return 0;
}
```

The **RECT** passed to **Create()** has the position of the child control as the (**left**, **top**) members (relative to the parent) and its size in the (**right**, **bottom**) members. The added line makes the tree view control smaller in height by **m_tmheight**. The line for the edit control positions it directly below the tree view control and makes it **m_tmHeight** pixels high.

Note that we've specified the window styles for the edit control explicitly, to enable the **ES_AUTOHSCROLL** style. This will allow the users of the control to see all the text if it doesn't fit within the area of the control, without having to make room for scroll bars.

The control will be shown in a window in the container. When this window is resized, the container will call **IOleInPlaceObject::SetObjectRects()** to tell the control how big the window is so that it has a chance to change how it shows itself. The Wizard-generated code resizes the tree view to fill the entire area of the control. Now that there's an edit control, we need to resize both of them to fit.

Add the following lines to **SetObjectRects()** (which is now in **URLtreeView.cpp**):

```
STDMETHODIMP CURLTreeView::SetObjectRects(LPCRECT prcPos,LPCRECT prcClip)
{
    IOleInPlaceObjectWindowlessImpl<CURLTreeView>::SetObjectRects(prcPos,
                                                                prcClip);
    int cx, cy;
    cx = prcPos->right - prcPos->left;
    cy = prcPos->bottom - prcPos->top;
    cy -= m_tmHeight;
    ::SetWindowPos(m_ctlSysTreeView32.m_hWnd, NULL, 0,
        0, cx, cy, SWP_NOZORDER | SWP_NOACTIVATE);
    ::SetWindowPos(m_ctlEdit.m_hWnd, NULL, 0,
        cy, cx, m_tmHeight, SWP_NOZORDER | SWP_NOACTIVATE);
    return S_OK;
}
```

So far we've resized our contained windows according to the height of a line of text that will be stored in the **m_tmHeight** member. However, we haven't initialized this to a useful value yet. We need to set this member so that it represents the height of the text used in the edit control, which will be the system font. The best place to get the size of the font is when the control is sent a **WM_SIZE** message, since you will need to resize the child controls.

In the header add a handler for the message into the message map and a declaration in the class definition:

```
    MESSAGE_HANDLER(WM_CREATE, OnCreate)
    MESSAGE_HANDLER(WM_SIZE, OnSize)
ALT_MSG_MAP(1)
    // Replace this with message map entries for subclassed SysTreeView32
ALT_MSG_MAP(2)
```

```
    // Message map for edit box
END_MSG_MAP()

    LRESULT OnCreate(UINT uMsg, WPARAM wParam, LPARAM lParam,
                                            BOOL& bHandled);
    STDMETHOD(SetObjectRects)(LPCRECT prcPos,LPCRECT prcClip);
    LRESULT OnSize(UINT uMsg, WPARAM wParam, LPARAM lParam,
                                            BOOL& bHandled);
```

Add the following code to the bottom of the CPP file:

```
    LRESULT CURLTreeView::OnSize(UINT uMsg, WPARAM wParam, LPARAM lParam,
                            BOOL& bHandled)
    {
        if (m_tmHeight == 0)
        {
            HDC hdc = m_ctlEdit.GetDC();
            TEXTMETRIC tm;
            ::GetTextMetrics(hdc, &tm);
            ReleaseDC(hdc);
            m_tmHeight = tm.tmHeight;
        }
        WORD nWidth = LOWORD(lParam);
        WORD nHeight = HIWORD(lParam);
        nHeight -= m_tmHeight;
        ::SetWindowPos(m_ctlSysTreeView32.m_hWnd,
            NULL, 0, 0, nWidth, nHeight,
            SWP_NOZORDER | SWP_NOACTIVATE);
        ::SetWindowPos(m_ctlEdit.m_hWnd, NULL, 0,
            nHeight, nWidth, m_tmHeight,
            SWP_NOZORDER | SWP_NOACTIVATE);
        return 0;
    }
```

This code gets hold of the device context and through this gets information about the system font by calling **GetTextMetrics()**. The **WM_SIZE** message has the new size of the parent window and this is used to resize and reposition the child controls: the edit control's height is always the height of the system font.

Testing the Code

Now we can compile the code and test it with the ActiveX Control Test Container. Since the control will need constant testing, we'll make the test container the executable to use to debug the control. To do this, select Settings... from the Project menu, select the Debug tab, and click on the arrow next to the Executable for debug session box. From the menu, select ActiveX Control Test Container.

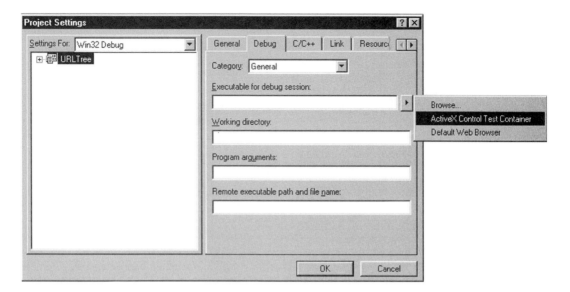

Now when you press the Go or Execute Program buttons in Developer Studio, the test container will be launched and you can use it to insert a URLTreeView Class.

There's not much to see if you test the container at this stage, but you can type into the edit box at the bottom of the control.

The URLs Property

Now let's go back to the code and fix up the **URLs** property so that it actually stores and returns the array of strings that represents the items in the tree. We're going to store the strings in a vector internally. We'll use the **vector<>** class provided by the C++ standard library for this purpose.

First, open **URLTreeView.h** and include the **vector** header at the top, as well as the **pragma** shown below:

```
#include "resource.h"        // main symbols
#include <vector>
#pragma warning(disable : 4530)
```

The **pragma** turns off any warnings that the compiler will give about exception handling not being enabled. The standard library's **vector<>** class uses exception handling code, but by default, the ATL projects don't have exception handling enabled. This means that when you compile the code, a warning will be issued. To prevent this, you could include support for exceptions as we've discussed before, but this will increase the control size. So here we've chosen to use a **pragma** to ignore the warning.

At the bottom of the class, add this data member:

```
private:
    int m_tmHeight;
    std::vector<CComBSTR> m_URLs;
};
```

This is the data member that will be used to store the **BSTRs**. You can see that we're actually storing them as **CComBSTRs** so that we don't have to worry about manually freeing these strings.

Now open **URLTreeView.cpp** and add the following for **get_URLs()**:

```
STDMETHODIMP CURLTreeView::get_URLs(VARIANT * pVal)
{
    VariantInit(pVal);
    pVal->vt = VT_ARRAY | VT_BSTR;
    SAFEARRAY* psa;
    SAFEARRAYBOUND bounds = {m_URLs.size(), 0};
    psa = SafeArrayCreate(VT_BSTR, 1, &bounds);

    BSTR* bstrArray;
    SafeArrayAccessData(psa, (void**)&bstrArray);
    std::vector<CComBSTR>::iterator it;
    int i = 0;
    for (it = m_URLs.begin(); it != m_URLs.end(); it++, i++)
    {
        bstrArray[i] = (*it).Copy();
    }
    SafeArrayUnaccessData(psa);
    pVal->parray = psa;
    return S_OK;
}
```

The code is conceptually straightforward, we just create a **SAFEARRAY** of the same size as our stored vector and loop through, copying each **BSTR** from our vector into the safe array before returning it to the client.

We can do a similar thing in **put_URLs()**, except we do it in the reverse direction:

```
STDMETHODIMP CURLTreeView::put_URLs(VARIANT newVal)
{
    if (newVal.vt != (VT_BSTR | VT_ARRAY))
        return E_INVALIDARG;

    m_URLs.clear();
    BSTR* bstrArray;
    SafeArrayAccessData(newVal.parray, (void**)&bstrArray);

    for (int x = 0;
        x < newVal.parray->rgsabound->cElements;
        x++)
```

```
    {
        m_URLs.push_back(CComBSTR(bstrArray[x]));
    }

    SafeArrayUnaccessData(newVal.parray);
    FillTree();
    SetDirty(TRUE);
    return S_OK;
}
```

First we check the type of the **VARIANT** passed in. If it's of the right type, we clear our vector of any existing strings, then populate it with the new strings. We call **FillTree()** to fill the tree control with the new array of strings. We'll implement the **FillTree()** function shortly. Finally, we call **SetDirty()** so that when it comes to implementing persistence code, everything will work as expected.

URLTree Tree View Code

Now we'll turn our attention to the tree view code. First **#include CommCtrl.h** at the top of **URLTreeView.h**, so that we can use the **TreeView_** macros:

```
#include "resource.h"        // main symbols
#include <vector>
#pragma warning(disable : 4530)
#include <CommCtrl.h>
```

While you are thinking about the common controls, you might as well add the static link library to the libraries that the project links with. From the Project menu select Settings... and on the Link tab select General from the Category box and All Configurations from the Settings For box. Add **ComCtl32.lib** to the end of the files in the Object/library modules box. Now click OK.

The tree view control should have lines and buttons, but the Wizard-generated code does not create the tree view with the right styles, so edit **OnCreate()** so that the right styles are specified, as shown below:

```
    m_ctlSysTreeView32.Create(m_hWnd, rc, NULL,
                    WS_CHILD | WS_VISIBLE | WS_BORDER |
                    TVS_HASLINES | TVS_LINESATROOT | TVS_HASBUTTONS);
```

Open the class header file and add the following **public** and **private** methods and data members:

```
    void FinalRelease();
private:
    void FillTree();
    HIMAGELIST m_hImageList;
    int m_iImage;
    int m_iSelect;
    int m_tmHeight;
    std::vector<CComBSTR> m_URLs;
};
```

Initialize the data members in the constructor:

```
    m_hImageList = NULL;
    m_iImage = -1;
    m_iSelect = -1;
    m_tmHeight = 0;
    m_bWindowOnly = TRUE;
```

The **m_hImageList** member will hold the handle for the image list associated with the tree control. **m_iImage** and **m_iSelect** will be used to hold the index of the images within the list for the normal and selected items.

Add the following code for **FinalRelease()** to the source file to ensure that the image list is released when the control is destroyed:

```
void CURLTreeView::FinalRelease()
{
    ImageList_Destroy(m_hImageList);
}
```

We'll create the image list in **OnCreate()**, so change the code as shown below:

```
LRESULT CURLTreeView::OnCreate(UINT uMsg, WPARAM wParam, LPARAM lParam,
                               BOOL& bHandled)
{
    ...
    m_ctlEdit.Create(m_hWnd, rc, NULL,
                     WS_CHILD | WS_VISIBLE | ES_AUTOHSCROLL);

    HBITMAP hBitmap;
    m_hImageList = ImageList_Create(16, 16, ILC_COLOR, 2, 10);
    hBitmap = LoadBitmap(_Module.GetResourceInstance(),
                         MAKEINTRESOURCE(IDB_IMAGE));
    m_iImage = ImageList_Add(m_hImageList, hBitmap,(HBITMAP)0);
    DeleteObject(hBitmap);
    hBitmap = LoadBitmap(_Module.GetResourceInstance(),
                         MAKEINTRESOURCE(IDB_SELECT));
    m_iSelect = ImageList_Add(m_hImageList, hBitmap,(HBITMAP)0);
    DeleteObject(hBitmap);
    TreeView_SetImageList(m_ctlSysTreeView32.m_hWnd,
                          m_hImageList, TVSIL_NORMAL);

    FillTree();
    return 0;
}
```

Here, we create the image list, load two bitmaps from the resources, and add them to the list. Then we set the tree view to use the newly created image list. We'll see how to add the bitmap resources shortly. Finally we call **FillTree()** to ensure that the tree is loaded as soon as the control is created.

Add the implementation of **FillTree()** as shown below:

```
void CURLTreeView::FillTree()
{
   TreeView_DeleteAllItems(m_ctlSysTreeView32.m_hWnd);

   std::vector<CComBSTR>::iterator it;
   HTREEITEM hRoot = TreeView_GetRoot(m_ctlSysTreeView32.m_hWnd);
   for (it = m_URLs.begin(); it < m_URLs.end(); it++)
   {
      LPWSTR strBranch =  new WCHAR[(*it).Length() + 1];
      LPWSTR strURL;

      wcscpy(strBranch, (*it).m_str);

      if ((strURL = wcschr(strBranch, L',')) != NULL)
      {
         *strURL = 0;
         strURL++;
         TVAddItem(hRoot, strBranch, strURL, m_iImage, m_iSelect);
      }
      delete [] strBranch;
   }
   m_ctlEdit.SetWindowText((LPCTSTR)_T(""));
}
```

FillTree() empties the tree view if it has items, and then it iterates through the items in the vector and adds them to the tree with a call to **TVAddItem()**, a method that you'll add in a moment. Finally, it clears the text in the edit box.

Because we are using the wide character C runtime library (CRT) functions here (**wcscpy()** and **wcschr()**), you will need to add **wchar.h** to the list of headers at the top of the source file:

```
#include "stdafx.h"
#include "URLTree.h"
#include "URLTreeView.h"
#include <wchar.h>
```

We also need to remove the **_ATL_MIN_CRT** symbol from the project settings for the release builds. When this symbol is defined, it prevents the linker from linking the CRT start up code, which saves about 25Kb, but will cause link errors if you use any functions that need the start up code. To use the CRT you need to undefine this symbol.

From the Project menu, select Settings... to bring up the Project Settings dialog. In the Settings For dropdown, select either Win32 Release MinSize or Win32 Release MinDependency (whichever you intend to use), and then click on the C/C++ tab. From the Category box select Preprocessor, and in the Preprocessor definitions box remove the reference to **_ATL_MIN_CRT**.

Bitmap Resources

The image list uses bitmap images, so the next thing to do is use Developer Studio's resource editor to add these images.

Click on the ResourceView tab, right-click on URLTree Resources and select Insert.... In the dialog select Bitmap and click on New. This will add a new bitmap resource to your project.

You need to resize this image so that it's 16 pixels square, so from the View menu select Properties... and set both the Width and Height to 16. Also change the ID to IDB_IMAGE:

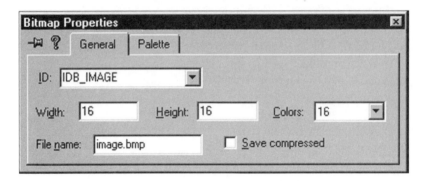

Now draw the image for a non-selected item. Here's my attempt.

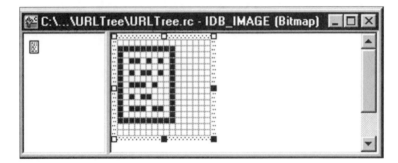

Notice that I've drawn it off-center so that when the image changes from non-selected to selected, I can make it look like an arrow has been added.

Now add another 16x16 bitmap, this time for the selected item. Give it an ID of IDB_SELECT:

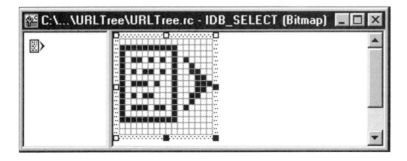

Finally, since this is a component that can be used in VB, we want a bitmap that can be used to represent the control in the toolbox. The Wizard-generated registration code for the control indicates that the resource with an ID of 1 will be the image for this toolbar button, so you need to create a bitmap with this resource ID.

Create another 16 x 16 image and give it an ID of IDB_TOOL=1. By using =1 you are giving the resource editor the actual value to use rather than allowing it to generate a value. When you move the focus from the ID box you will notice that the =1 disappears, but the resource editor will have remembered it. Here's my image, notice that it is centered horizontally, and that the background is Windows background gray:

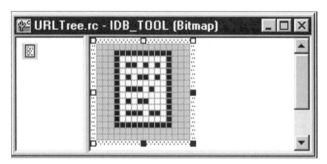

TVAddItem

Now add the following to the header:

```
private:
    void TVAddItem(HTREEITEM hParent, LPWSTR strBranch, LPWSTR strURL,
        int iImage = -1, int iSelect = -1);
    void FillTree();
```

And this stub function to the source file:

```
void CURLTreeView::TVAddItem(HTREEITEM hParent, LPWSTR strBranch,
                             LPWSTR strURL, int iImage, int iSelect)
{
}
```

You can compile the project at this stage to ensure that there are no typing mistakes.

The next task is to implement **TVAddItem()**. First, add a new data member:

```
    std::vector<CComBSTR> m_URLs;
    int m_cbMaxSize;
};
```

m_cbMaxSize is the maximum size of the text string that has been added into the tree view control for an item. This will be used to ensure that we can dynamically create strings that are large enough to hold the text from any item in the tree. The member will be updated as we add new items to the tree. Initialize the member in the constructor:

```
    m_cbMaxSize = 256; // Default URL size
```

Here is the code for **TVAddItem()**:

```
void CURLTreeView::TVAddItem(HTREEITEM hParent, LPWSTR strBranch,
                             LPWSTR strURL, int iImage, int iSelect)
{
    USES_CONVERSION;

    // Get a pointer to the first forward slash in the branch string
    LPWSTR ptr = wcschr(strBranch, L'/');

    // If the ptr is NULL, there are no forward slashes, so the contents
    // of strBranch must be the final item to add.
    // Once that's done, we can return from the function
    if (ptr == NULL)
    {
        // End of the string, add the item!
        TVAddItemCore(hParent, strBranch, strURL, iImage, iSelect);
        return;
    }

    // Create a string with the first part of the branch
    // and ensure that it's null-terminated
    LPWSTR strParent = new WCHAR[1 + ptr - strBranch];
    wcsncpy(strParent, strBranch, ptr - strBranch);
    strParent[ptr - strBranch] = 0;

    // Find child with the name contained in strParent
    HTREEITEM hItem;
    hItem = TreeView_GetChild(m_ctlSysTreeView32.m_hWnd, hParent);

    if (hItem == NULL)
    {
        // If there are no children, add the new item here
        hItem = TVAddItemCore(hParent, strParent, NULL, iImage, iSelect);
    }

    // Now loop through all the children and see
    // if we can find the item already in the tree
    LPTSTR strCmp = new TCHAR[m_cbMaxSize];
    while (hItem)
    {
        TVITEM thisItem;
        thisItem.mask = TVIF_HANDLE | TVIF_TEXT;
        thisItem.pszText = strCmp;
        thisItem.cchTextMax = m_cbMaxSize;
        thisItem.hItem = hItem;

        TreeView_GetItem(m_ctlSysTreeView32.m_hWnd, &thisItem);
        if (lstrcmp(W2T(strParent), strCmp) == 0)
```

```
            {
                // Here we've found the item, so we call TVAddItem() recursively
                // with the handle of the item and the latest position in the
                // branch
                TVAddItem(hItem, ptr + 1, strURL, iImage, iSelect);
                break;
            }
            else
            {
                HTREEITEM nextItem =
                        TreeView_GetNextSibling(m_ctlSysTreeView32.m_hWnd,
                                                                  hItem);
                if (nextItem == NULL)
                {
                    // If we get here, the item isn't there so we need to add it,
                    // then we can call TVAddItem() recursively
                    HTREEITEM hNewItem =
                            TVAddItemCore(hParent, strParent, NULL, iImage,
                                                                   iSelect);
                    TVAddItem(hNewItem, ptr + 1, strURL, iImage, iSelect);
                    break;
                }
                else
                {
                    hItem = nextItem;
                }
            }
        } // while (hItem)

        delete [] strParent;
        delete [] strCmp;
    }
```

Let's go through this code and see what it does.

This routine is recursive. Basically the idea is that **strBranch** has the name of the item,
similar to a fully qualified path name in DOS, except the items are separated by forward rather
than back slashes.

The first part of the code checks for a forward slash. If there is not one present, **strBranch** is
just the name of an item. The item can be added into the tree view under the parent given by
hParent.

If there is a slash in **strBranch**, the code must extract the first item in the string and check to
see if **hParent** has a child with the same name. If it doesn't then a new item is created. The
method can then be called recursively with the rest of **strBranch** to add the item.

The **while** loop checks to see if **hParent** has a child with the name held in **strParent**
(which is the string in **strBranch** up to the first slash); this is done by first calling
TreeView_GetChild() to get the first child of **hParent** and then calling
TreeView_GetItem() to get the item text to compare with **strParent**. If the comparison

fails then it calls **TreeView_GetNextSibling()** to get the next child. This loop continues until either a child is found or there are no more children. In the second case, a new item is created. In both cases, **TVAddItem()** is called recursively.

The tree item is actually created by the function **TVAddItemCore()**. Declare this function in **URLTreeView.h**:

```
private:
    HTREEITEM TVAddItemCore(HTREEITEM hParent, LPWSTR strItem,
        LPWSTR strURL, int iImage = -1, int iSelect = -1);
    void TVAddItem(HTREEITEM hParent, LPWSTR strBranch, LPWSTR strURL,
        int iImage = -1, int iSelect = -1);
```

Add the implementation to **URLTreeView.cpp**:

```
HTREEITEM CURLTreeView::TVAddItemCore(HTREEITEM hParent, LPWSTR strItem,
                            LPWSTR strURL, int iImage, int iSelect)
{
   USES_CONVERSION;
   TVITEM tvi;
   tvi.mask = TVIF_TEXT;
   tvi.pszText = W2T(strItem);

   // Update the max size member
   // This member is used to create strings large
   // enough to hold the text for any of the items
   int cbSize = wcslen(strItem) + 1;
   if (cbSize > m_cbMaxSize)
      m_cbMaxSize = cbSize;

   if (strURL)
   {
      tvi.mask |= TVIF_PARAM;
      cbSize = wcslen(strURL) + 1;
      LPTSTR newStr = new TCHAR[cbSize];
      lstrcpy(newStr, W2T(strURL));
      tvi.lParam = (LPARAM)newStr;
   }

   if (iImage != -1)
   {
      tvi.mask |= TVIF_IMAGE;
      tvi.iImage = iImage;
   }

   if (iSelect != -1)
   {
      tvi.mask |= TVIF_SELECTEDIMAGE;
      tvi.iSelectedImage = iSelect;
   }
```

```
    TVINSERTSTRUCT tvins;
    tvins.item = tvi;
    tvins.hInsertAfter = TVI_LAST;
    tvins.hParent = hParent;

    return TreeView_InsertItem(m_ctlSysTreeView32.m_hWnd, &tvins);
}
```

The code is quite straightforward. Note that we update the size of **m_cbMaxSize** as necessary to ensure that the code in **TVAddItem()** that retrieves strings from the tree control can always allocate a big enough string.

Testing the Control

Now you can compile and test the project once more. If you use the test container, you won't see any changes since the last time (except the tree control now has a border), because the control has no data, so it will show an empty window. There is no way to send data in the correct form to the control using the test container, so we'll have to use something else. In this case, we'll create a tiny Visual Basic application to send an array of strings to the control.

Start VB and select Standard EXE as the project type. From the Project menu select Components... and check the box next to URLTree 1.0 Type Library. Note that the image for the control will be added to the toolbox:

Add an instance of our URLTreeView control to the form. Then add the following code to the form load handler to test the control:

```
Private Sub Form_Load()
    Dim str(4) As String
    str(1) = "First Level,url1"
    str(2) = "First Level/Two,url2"
    str(3) = "First Level/Second/Three,url3"
    str(4) = "First Level/Second/Third/Four,url4"
    URLTreeView1.URLs = str
End Sub
```

447

Now run the project and you should see this (after expanding the branches):

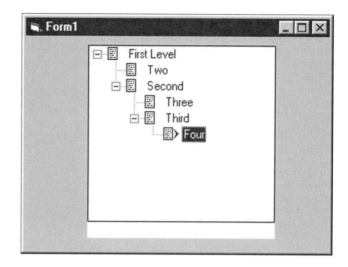

Note that the selection image automatically moves to the selected item (because that's handled by the tree control), but the URL for the item doesn't appear in the edit box. We need to add some message handlers to rectify that.

Notification Code

There are three messages that we need to handle. Two of them (**TVN_DELETEITEM** and **TVN_SELCHANGED**) are notification messages sent from the tree view to our control's main window. The third is the **WM_LBUTTONDBLCLK** message sent to the tree view.

The first message handler will allow us to delete the string that we're storing a pointer to in the **LPARAM** of each item. As the code stands at the moment, it will leak memory because we have no code to delete these strings. The **TVN_DELETEITEM** message will let us know when these strings are no longer needed and give us a perfect opportunity to delete them.

The second message handler will be called when the selected tree item changes. This will allow us to update the edit box with the URL for the currently selected item.

The third message will enable us to open the URL for the currently selected item in a new Internet Explorer window, when the user double-clicks on the tree view.

First we'll edit the message map to hook up the handlers for all three messages:

```
    MESSAGE_HANDLER(WM_SIZE, OnSize)
    NOTIFY_CODE_HANDLER(TVN_DELETEITEM, OnDeleteItem)
    NOTIFY_CODE_HANDLER(TVN_SELCHANGED, OnSelChanged)
ALT_MSG_MAP(1)
    MESSAGE_HANDLER(WM_LBUTTONDBLCLK, OnLButtonDblClk)
ALT_MSG_MAP(2)
    // Message map for edit box
END_MSG_MAP()
```

Note that the notify handlers are in the main message map and that the double-click handler is in alternative message map 1. This is because the first two messages are sent to the control's main window, whereas the double-click message is sent to the tree view.

Now add the declarations of these handlers to the class definition.

```
LRESULT OnCreate(UINT uMsg, WPARAM wParam, LPARAM lParam,
                                     BOOL& bHandled);
STDMETHOD(SetObjectRects)(LPCRECT prcPos,LPCRECT prcClip);
LRESULT OnSize(UINT uMsg, WPARAM wParam, LPARAM lParam,
                                     BOOL& bHandled);
LRESULT OnDeleteItem(int idCtrl, LPNMHDR pnmh, BOOL& bHandled);
LRESULT OnSelChanged(int idCtrl, LPNMHDR pnmh, BOOL& bHandled);
LRESULT OnLButtonDblClk(UINT uMsg, WPARAM wParam, LPARAM lParam,
                        BOOL& bHandled);
```

The signatures of the handlers match those we gave for each type earlier in the chapter.

The implementations need to be added to the source file as shown (we'll leave the implementation of the double-click handler aside for a while):

```
LRESULT CURLTreeView::OnDeleteItem(int idCtrl, LPNMHDR pnmh,
                                     BOOL& bHandled)
{
    NMTREEVIEW* pnmtv = (NMTREEVIEW*) pnmh;
    if (pnmtv->itemOld.lParam != NULL)
        delete [] (LPTSTR)pnmtv->itemOld.lParam;
    return 0;
}


LRESULT CURLTreeView::OnSelChanged(int idCtrl, LPNMHDR pnmh,
                                     BOOL& bHandled)
{
    NMTREEVIEW* pnmtv = (NMTREEVIEW*) pnmh;
    TVITEM tvi = pnmtv->itemNew;
    tvi.mask = TVIF_HANDLE | TVIF_PARAM;

    if (!TreeView_GetItem(m_ctlSysTreeView32.m_hWnd, &tvi))
        return 0;

    m_ctlEdit.SetWindowText((LPCTSTR)tvi.lParam);

    return 0;
}

LRESULT CURLTreeView::OnLButtonDblClk(
    UINT uMsg, WPARAM wParam, LPARAM lParam, BOOL& bHandled)
{
    return 0;
}
```

In both of the notify handlers, the **pnmh** parameter is cast to a pointer to a **NMTREEVIEW** structure. This is then used to find out the item that is being deleted, or being selected, and hence to get access to its associated data.

Once again, you can compile the code. This time you can use the VB test program to verify that as you select an item, the associated URL is shown in the edit box.

Internet Explorer

The final message for which we need to write a handler is the **WM_LBUTTONDBLCLICK**. Add the following code to **CURLTreeView::OnLButtonDblClk()**:

```
LRESULT CURLTreeView::OnLButtonDblClk(
    UINT uMsg, WPARAM wParam, LPARAM lParam, BOOL& bHandled)
{
    TVITEM tvi;
    tvi.hItem = TreeView_GetSelection(m_ctlSysTreeView32.m_hWnd);
    LPTSTR str = new TCHAR[m_cbMaxSize];
    tvi.mask = TVIF_TEXT | TVIF_HANDLE | TVIF_PARAM;
    tvi.pszText = str;
    tvi.cchTextMax = m_cbMaxSize;

    if (!TreeView_GetItem(m_ctlSysTreeView32.m_hWnd, &tvi))
    {
        delete [] str;
        return 0;
    }

    m_ctlEdit.SetWindowText((LPCTSTR)tvi.lParam);

    if (lstrlen((LPTSTR)tvi.lParam) > 0)
    {
        // Create browser object
        HRESULT hr;
        CComPtr<IWebBrowserApp> pNav;
        hr = CoCreateInstance(
            CLSID_InternetExplorer, NULL,
            CLSCTX_ALL, IID_IWebBrowserApp,
            reinterpret_cast<void**>(&pNav));
        if (SUCCEEDED(hr))
        {
            CComVariant varZero(0);
            CComVariant varNull("");
            hr = pNav->put_Visible(true);
            hr = pNav->Navigate(
                CComBSTR((LPCTSTR)tvi.lParam),
                &varZero, &varNull, &varNull,
                &varNull);
        }
    }
```

```
        delete [] str;
    return 0;
}
```

The code just gets the currently selected tree item and if there's a URL associated with it, launches Internet Explorer, makes it visible and navigates to the URL specified. The **Navigate()** method takes the URL as the first parameter. The second parameter states that a new window should be created, and the other parameters are for the target frame name, data sent with HTTP POST and HTTP headers, which we're not interested in.

So that the compiler knows about Internet Explorer, add these includes to the top of the source file:

```
#include "URLTreeView.h"
#include <wchar.h>
#include <initguid.h>
#include <exDisp.h>
```

Now compile the project. To test it, you need to change the VB code to have real URLs. The easiest thing to do (if you haven't got a permanent connection to the Internet) is create a series of files called **Url1.html**, **Url2.html**, **Url1.htm3** and **Url4.html** with the minimal HTML shown below (change the title accordingly, so you know which is which):

```
<HTML>
<TITLE>
URL1
</TITLE>
</HTML>
```

Save these in the Visual Basic project's directory and change the VB code to this:

```
Private Sub Form_Load()
    Dim str(4) As String
    str(1) = "First Level," & App.Path & "\url1.html"
    str(2) = "First Level/Two," & App.Path & "\url2.html"
    str(3) = "First Level/Second/Three," & App.Path & "\url3.html"
    str(4) = "First Level/Second/Third/Four," & App.Path & "\url4.html"
    URLTreeView1.URLs = str
End Sub
```

Notice that IE is clever enough to know that these are files on the local file system and so you do not need to give the **file:** protocol. Now when you run this code and double-click on an item, IE will pop up with the associated HTML file.

Persistence Code for IE

So far the control can show a hierarchy of URLs, it will show an item's URL when the item is selected, and it will launch Internet Explorer when the item is double-clicked. The control can be manipulated at runtime using the **URLs** property. However, it doesn't provide any way of initializing itself using design-time mechanisms such as the **<PARAM>** tags on a web page. This requires that the control support the **IPersistPropertyBag** interface, so this section will show you how to add that support.

At first sight you may think that all you need to do is derive the control class from
IPersistPropertyBagImpl<> and add **URLs** to the property map. However, this does not
work because the **IPropertyBag** implemented by IE does not know about arrays, so instead
you will need to override the default implementation of
IPersistPropertyBagImpl<>::Load() to read in the data in a custom format.

The format we shall use is to read in each item as a property called **Item**N (where N is a
number). The total number of items will be in a property called **noItems**. Strictly speaking
this should not be necessary — the code could just read in the **Item**N property incrementing N
until the container cannot find the property — but it does give a good check.

Using this scheme, you will be able to implement a web page like this:

```
<HTML>
<BODY>
<OBJECT CLSID="...">
<PARAM NAME="noItems" VALUE=4>
<PARAM NAME="Item1"
 VALUE="First Level,c:\temp\url1.html">
<PARAM NAME="Item2"
 VALUE="First Level/Two,c:\temp\url2.html">
<PARAM NAME="Item3"
 VALUE="First Level/Three,c:\temp\url3.html">
<PARAM NAME="Item4"
 VALUE="First Level/Four,c:\temp\url4.html">
</OBJECT>
</BODY>
</HTML>
```

Here are the steps:

Open the **CURLTreeView** class header file and add **IPersistPropertyBagImpl<>** to the list
of base classes:

```
    public IPersistStorageImpl<CURLTreeView>,
    public IPersistPropertyBagImpl<CURLTreeView>,
    public IQuickActivateImpl<CURLTreeView>,
```

Add the interface to the COM map:

```
    COM_INTERFACE_ENTRY_IMPL(IPersistStreamInit)
    COM_INTERFACE_ENTRY_IMPL(IPersistPropertyBag)
    COM_INTERFACE_ENTRY_IMPL(ISpecifyPropertyPages)
```

Add the following declaration to the class definition, to override
IPersistPropertyBagImpl<>::Load():

```
    // IPersistPropertyBag
    STDMETHOD(Load)(LPPROPERTYBAG pPropBag, LPERRORLOG pErrorLog);
```

In the source file, add this implementation:

```
STDMETHODIMP  CURLTreeView::Load(LPPROPERTYBAG pPropBag,
                                               LPERRORLOG pErrorLog)
{
   CComVariant var;
   HRESULT hr;
   var.vt = VT_I4;
   hr = pPropBag->Read(L"noItems", &var, pErrorLog);
   if (FAILED(hr))
      return hr;
   if (var.vt != VT_I4)
      return E_INVALIDARG;

   long items = var.iVal;
   var.Clear();

   OLECHAR strParam[8];
   for (long idx = 1; idx <= items; idx++)
   {
      swprintf(strParam, L"Item%d", idx);
      hr = pPropBag->Read(strParam, &var, pErrorLog);
      if (FAILED(hr))
         return hr;
      if (var.vt == VT_BSTR)
         m_URLs.push_back(CComBSTR(var.bstrVal));
      var.Clear();
   }
    return IPersistPropertyBagImpl<CURLTreeView>::Load(pPropBag,
                                               pErrorLog);
}
```

The first few lines of this method obtain the **noItems** parameter. Notice how the type of the **VARIANT** is set to **VT_I4** before getting the parameter; this indicates to the container that it ought to try to coerce the parameter to a **long** type. If this coercion fails, and another type is returned, the method returns with an error.

We store the value returned in the **items** variable. After that, the **VARIANT** is cleared and a loop is entered to read all the other parameters. Notice that I haven't set the type of the **VARIANT** to **BSTR** before calling **Read()**; Internet Explorer's implementation of **IPropertyBag::Read()**, is clever enough to realize that the parameters are strings without any hints.

Once we've looped through all the items, we call ATL's default implementation of the **Load()** method so that any properties we add to the property map in the future will still be loaded.

Now compile the code. Open the **URLTreeView.htm** that the AppWizard generated for you in the project directory and edit it according to the following highlighted lines:

```
<HTML>
<HEAD>
<TITLE>ATL 2.0 test page for object URLTreeView</TITLE>
</HEAD>
```

```
<BODY>
<OBJECT ID="URLTreeView" <
 CLASSID="CLSID:36C563C1-634C-11D1-9A5A-0060973044A8">
>
   <PARAM NAME="noItems" VALUE=4>
   <PARAM NAME="Item1" VALUE="First Level,c:\temp\url1.html">
   <PARAM NAME="Item2" VALUE="First Level/Two,c:\temp\url2.html">
   <PARAM NAME="Item3" VALUE="First Level/Three,c:\temp\url3.html">
   <PARAM NAME="Item4" VALUE="First Level/Four,c:\temp\url4.html">
</OBJECT>
</BODY>
</HTML>
```

You can now test the control by double-clicking on **URLTreeView.htm** in Explorer to get Internet Explorer to start up.

Security Code

You may find that you get this dialog from Internet Explorer 4.0 when it starts:

If you're using an older version of Internet Explorer, you may even find that you are unable to initialize the control if your IE options are set to a high security setting which tells IE to ignore parameters. This is designed to protect the control (and ultimately your computer) from possibly bogus values.

You have two options here. The first is to change the security settings, and the second is to mark the control safe for scripting and initialization. We'll go for the second option.

We can implement our control so that it can tell IE that it is OK to read the parameters and pass them onto the control. This is achieved by implementing the **IObjectSafety** interface. The interface has a method, **SetInterfaceSafetyOptions()**, that IE will call to specify the options it is expecting the control to support.

This method has three parameters: the first is the IID of the control interface that the container is interested in, the second specifies safety options that should be supported, and of these options the ones that should be enabled are given in the last parameter. These options are currently:

INTERFACESAFE_FOR_UNTRUSTED_CALLER
INTERFACESAFE_FOR_UNTRUSTED_DATA

The first means that the control will accept scripting, and the second means that the control will accept parameters.

In ATL, we can support this interface by deriving our control from the **IObjectSafetyImpl<>** class. However, the implementation of **IObjectSafetyImpl<>** only checks if the container is setting scripting options for **IDispatch**. If the requested interface is not **IDispatch** (which is the case here because IE will ask if it is safe to send data to **IPersistPropertyBag**), the ATL implementation will return **E_NOINTERFACE**, and Internet Explorer will think that it cannot send data to the control. To get round this, you will need to write your own version of **SetInterfaceSafetyOptions()**.

In the class header, derive the control class from **IObjectSafetyImpl<>**:

```
public IObjectSafetyImpl<CURLTreeView>,
```

Add the interface to the COM map:

```
COM_INTERFACE_ENTRY_IMPL(IObjectSafety)
```

Declare the method you want to override:

```
// IObjectSafety
  STDMETHOD(SetInterfaceSafetyOptions)(REFIID riid,
          DWORD dwSupportedOptions, DWORD dwEnabledOptions);
```

Finally, in the source file enter this code:

```
STDMETHODIMP CURLTreeView::SetInterfaceSafetyOptions(
   REFIID riid, DWORD dwSupportedOptions, DWORD dwEnabledOptions)
{
   if (riid == IID_IPersistPropertyBag)
   {
      if (dwEnabledOptions != INTERFACESAFE_FOR_UNTRUSTED_DATA)
         return E_FAIL;
      return S_OK;
   }
   return IObjectSafetyImpl<CURLTreeView>::SetInterfaceSafetyOptions(
                         riid, dwSupportedOptions, dwEnabledOptions);
}
```

Compile the code and try the HTML page again. This time you won't get any warning dialogs.

Property Page

In this section, we'll add a property page for the control to allow you to change the URLs held by the control at design-time. Since the **URLs** property is a complex one, Visual Basic's Properties window can't handle it, so a property page will be a valuable addition to our control.

It would be possible to define a string property on the control that in its **get_** method concatenates the strings in the **m_URLs** vector (using some deliminator like '|'). This would mean that VB could show this long string and the user could then edit it. The **put_** method of the property could then parse through this string and enter the item strings into the vector.

However, such a scheme is cumbersome and it requires the VB developer to type long strings into the property box and ensure that the correct syntax is used. It would be much better if the VB developer is given a dialog to enter the data, and have the dialog code make sure that the text is correctly formatted. Such a dialog, of course, is a property page.

In Developer Studio, select New ATL Object... from the Insert menu. In the left-hand pane select Controls and in the right-hand pane select Property Page and then Next >. In the next dialog, give the page a Short Name of URLPage and then click on the Strings tab. Enter &URLs as the Title and clear the other edit boxes. Then click on OK.

This will change the IDL file to include a reference to the **coclass** for the property page, and it will add the page to the object map. In addition to this, the Wizard will add a new header and source file to the project. You will need to edit the control to use the property page, but first you need to write the property page code.

The first task is to edit the resources for the page. Open the IDD_URLPAGE dialog resource in the editor and add two edit boxes, two buttons and a list box, as shown on the next page.

IDC_NAME   IDC_ADD

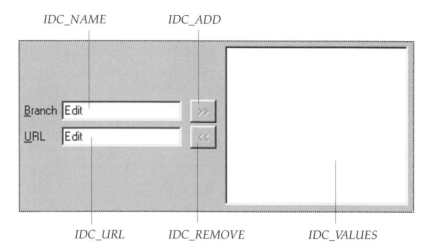

IDC_URL   IDC_REMOVE   IDC_VALUES

The buttons are disabled and the list box has the 'sort' attribute turned off. The property page should work like this: the **IDC_ADD** button should be enabled if there is a string in the **IDC_NAME** edit box. When the user clicks on the **IDC_ADD** button, the two strings in the edit boxes should be added together separated by a comma and then this new string should be added to the list box.

When the user clicks on an item in the list box, the **IDC_REMOVE** button should be enabled. If the user clicks on this button, the string should be removed from the edit box, split into its constituent parts, and these new strings added to the edit boxes. There is a lot of control handling code needed here (at this point you may wish that you were writing the control with MFC!).

Before we get into the control manipulation, we can write the relatively simple functions to initialize the page with the URLs from the control when the dialog is created, and to update the control with the values from the dialog when the **Apply()** method is called.

Open **URLPage.h**, remove the **Apply()** method and paste it into the **URLPage.cpp** file. Edit the first line so that it looks like this:

```
STDMETHODIMP CURLPage::Apply(void)
{
...
}
```

Add a declaration for this method in the header:

```
STDMETHOD(Apply)(void);
```

In the page's message map, add the following:

```
MESSAGE_HANDLER(WM_INITDIALOG, OnInitDialog)
```

And add this declaration to the **CURLPage** class definition:

```
LRESULT OnInitDialog(UINT uMsg, WPARAM wParam, LPARAM lParam,
                     BOOL& bHandled);
```

In **URLPage.cpp**, add this include at the top:

```
#include "stdafx.h"
#include "URLPage.h"
#include "URLTree.h"
```

And add this method:

```
LRESULT CURLPage::OnInitDialog(UINT uMsg, WPARAM wParam, LPARAM lParam,
                               BOOL& bHandled)
{
   USES_CONVERSION;
   CComPtr<IURLTreeView> pURL;
   m_ppUnk[0]->QueryInterface(IID_IURLTreeView,
                               reinterpret_cast<void**>(&pURL));

   CWindow wndValues(GetDlgItem(IDC_VALUES));
   CComVariant var;

   if (SUCCEEDED(pURL->get_URLs(&var)))
   {
      if (var.vt != (VT_BSTR | VT_ARRAY))
         return 0;

      BSTR* bstrArray;
      SafeArrayAccessData(var.parray, (void**)&bstrArray);

      for (UINT x = 0;
         x < var.parray->rgsabound->cElements;
         x++)
      {
         wndValues.SendMessage(LB_ADDSTRING, 0,
                               (LPARAM)(LPCTSTR)OLE2T(bstrArray[x]));
      }

      SafeArrayUnaccessData(var.parray);
   }

   return 0;
}
```

You've seen code like this before. All it does is use the **get_** method of the **URLs** property to obtain a **SAFEARRAY** of strings, then loops through the array adding each string to the list box. To add these strings you must send the **LB_ADDSTRING** message, as there is no equivalent of MFC's **CListBox** class in ATL. The **m_ppUnk** array has the **IUnknown** pointers for the objects currently using the property page. For this page, we'll only support one object.

Now edit the **Apply()** method to add these lines:

```
STDMETHODIMP CURLPage::Apply(void)
{
    USES_CONVERSION;
    CWindow wndValues(GetDlgItem(IDC_VALUES));
    int count = 0;
    int idx = wndValues.SendMessage(LB_GETCOUNT, 0, 0);

    CComVariant var;
    var.vt = VT_ARRAY | VT_BSTR;
    SAFEARRAY* psa;
    SAFEARRAYBOUND bounds = {idx, 0};
    psa = SafeArrayCreate(VT_BSTR, 1, &bounds);
    BSTR* bstrArray;
    SafeArrayAccessData(psa, (void**)&bstrArray);

    while (count < idx)
    {
        int textSize = wndValues.SendMessage(LB_GETTEXTLEN,
                                             (WPARAM)count, 0);
        LPTSTR str = new TCHAR[textSize + 1];
        wndValues.SendMessage(LB_GETTEXT, (WPARAM)count,
                                          (LPARAM)(LPCTSTR)str);
        bstrArray[count] = SysAllocString(T2OLE(str));
        delete [] str;
        count++;
    }

    SafeArrayUnaccessData(psa);
    var.parray = psa;

    CComPtr<IURLTreeView> pURL;
    m_ppUnk[0]->QueryInterface(IID_IURLTreeView, (void**)&pURL);
    pURL->put_URLs(var);

    m_bDirty = FALSE;
    return S_OK;
}
```

This code asks the list box for how many items it has (**LB_GETCOUNT**) and then creates a **SAFEARRAY** of the correct size. Next it asks for each of the items using **LB_GETTEXTLEN** first to get the length of the string, and then **LB_GETTEXT** to get the string. Once the **SAFEARRAY** has been filled, the code then uses the control's **put_** method to write the data to the control.

Of course, this code is not much use at this point because you cannot add values into the list box, so we'll add code to do that now. First you need to test when data changes in the **IDC_NAME** box and use this to decide whether the **IDC_ADD** button is enabled.

Add the following in the message map

```
COMMAND_HANDLER(IDC_NAME, EN_CHANGE, OnNameChange)
COMMAND_ID_HANDLER(IDC_ADD, OnAddItem)
```

And add these declarations to the page's class definition:

```
LRESULT OnNameChange(WORD wNotify, WORD wID, HWND hWnd, BOOL& bHandled);
LRESULT OnAddItem(WORD wNotify, WORD wID, HWND hWnd, BOOL& bHandled);
```

Copy this code into the **URLPage.cpp** file for **OnNameChange()**:

```
LRESULT CURLPage::OnNameChange(WORD wNotify, WORD wID, HWND hWnd,
                               BOOL& bHandled)
{
  CWindow wndName(GetDlgItem(IDC_NAME));
  CWindow bnAdd(GetDlgItem(IDC_ADD));

  bnAdd.EnableWindow(wndName.GetWindowTextLength() > 0);

  CWindow bnRemove(GetDlgItem(IDC_REMOVE));
  bnRemove.EnableWindow(FALSE);
  return 0;
}
```

Finally, add this for **OnAddItem()**:

```
LRESULT CURLPage::OnAddItem(WORD wNotify, WORD wID, HWND hWnd,
                            BOOL& bHandled)
{
  CWindow wndName(GetDlgItem(IDC_NAME));
  CWindow wndURL(GetDlgItem(IDC_URL));
  CWindow wndValues(GetDlgItem(IDC_VALUES));

  int nameSize = wndName.GetWindowTextLength() + 1;
  int urlSize = wndURL.GetWindowTextLength() + 1;
  LPTSTR strName = new TCHAR[nameSize + urlSize];
  wndName.GetWindowText(strName, nameSize);
  wndName.SetWindowText("");
  lstrcat(strName, _T(","));
  LPTSTR strURL = new TCHAR[urlSize];
  wndURL.GetWindowText(strURL, urlSize);
  wndURL.SetWindowText("");
  lstrcat(strName, strURL);

  wndValues.SendMessage(LB_ADDSTRING, 0, (LPARAM)(LPCTSTR)strName);
  SetDirty(TRUE);
  // Need to do the next line for VB
  m_pPageSite->OnStatusChange(
                    PROPPAGESTATUS_DIRTY | PROPPAGESTATUS_VALIDATE);
```

```
      delete [] strName;
      delete [] strURL;
      return 0;
}
```

This code is mostly self-explanatory. The only odd bit comes near the end. After adding the string to the list box, the Apply button must be enabled on the property page so that the data can be sent to the control (if required). This is done by calling **IPropertyPageImpl<>::SetDirty()**, which calls **OnStatusChange()** on the container's **IPropertyPageSite** interface. However, as mentioned before, there is a bug in VB5 which requires the extra call to **OnStatusChange()**.

Now we'll set up the code for removing items from the list. In the property page header, add the following to the message map:

```
    COMMAND_HANDLER(IDC_VALUES, LBN_SELCHANGE, OnSelChange)
    COMMAND_ID_HANDLER(IDC_REMOVE, OnRemoveItem)
```

Add these method declarations:

```
    LRESULT OnSelChange(WORD wNotify, WORD wID, HWND hWnd, BOOL& bHandled);
    LRESULT OnRemoveItem(WORD wNotify, WORD wID, HWND hWnd, BOOL& bHandled);
```

The handler for the **LBN_SELCHANGE** sent to the list box should enable the **IDC_REMOVE** button:

```
    LRESULT CURLPage::OnSelChange(WORD wNotify, WORD wID, HWND hWnd,
                                  BOOL& bHandled)
    {
       CWindow(GetDlgItem(IDC_REMOVE)).EnableWindow(TRUE);
       return 0;
    }
```

The handler for clicking on the **IDC_REMOVE** button should extract the strings from the selected item and put them in the edit boxes and, of course, remove the item:

```
    LRESULT CURLPage::OnRemoveItem(WORD wNotify, WORD wID, HWND hWnd,
                                   BOOL& bHandled)
    {
       CWindow wndName(GetDlgItem(IDC_NAME));
       CWindow wndURL(GetDlgItem(IDC_URL));
       CWindow wndValues(GetDlgItem(IDC_VALUES));

       int idx = wndValues.SendMessage(LB_GETCURSEL, 0, 0);
       if (idx == -1)
          return 0;

       int textSize = wndValues.SendMessage(LB_GETTEXTLEN, (WPARAM)idx, 0);
       LPTSTR str = new TCHAR[textSize + 1];
       wndValues.SendMessage(LB_GETTEXT, (WPARAM)idx, (LPARAM)(LPCTSTR)str);
       wndValues.SendMessage(LB_DELETESTRING, (WPARAM)idx, 0);
```

```
        LPTSTR ptr;
        ptr = _tcsstr(str, _T(","));
        if (ptr)
        {
            *ptr = 0;
            ptr++;
        }

        wndName.SetWindowText(str);
        if (ptr)
            wndURL.SetWindowText(ptr);

        SetDirty(TRUE);
        // Need to do this line for VB
        m_pPageSite->OnStatusChange(
                            PROPPAGESTATUS_DIRTY | PROPPAGESTATUS_VALIDATE);

        delete [] str;
        return 0;
    }
```

You will need to add the following header to **URLPage.cpp** so that you can use the CRT functions

```
#include "stdafx.h"
#include "URLPage.h"
#include "URLTree.h"
#include <tchar.h>
```

Now open **URLTreeView.h** and add this to the property map

```
PROP_PAGE(CLSID_URLPage)
```

> *Note that we don't add a description for the* **URLs** *property, because ATL's persistence implementations would try to persist the property using the container's* **IPropertyBag** *interface. Many containers can't handle arrays, so we'll add our own code to persist the property later.*

Now you can compile the code and test it in Visual Basic or using the ActiveX Control Test Container. You can use the property page to add and remove items from the control.

Persistence Code for VB

Now you should be able to load the control in VB and alter its properties. Try these steps:

- Start VB and select Standard EXE as the project type.
- Use the Components... item in the Project menu and add the URLTree component
- Add a URLTreeView control to the form and in the Properties box click on the ellipsis next to the Custom item.

▶ Use the property page to add some items and then click on OK. The items should be added to the control.

▶ Now save the project, close VB and then start it again, loading the project you saved. You'll find that VB issues an error saying that it can't load the control. This is because the code we provided for `IPersistPropertyBag::Load()` expects to find `noItems` in the property bag, and we haven't yet written to the code to save this information. We'll do that now.

Add the declaration for `IPersistPropertyBag::Save()` to the `CURLTreeView` class:

```
// IPersistPropertyBag
   STDMETHOD(Load)(LPPROPERTYBAG pPropBag, LPERRORLOG pErrorLog);
   STDMETHOD(Save)(LPPROPERTYBAG pPropBag, BOOL fClearDirty,
                   BOOL fSaveAllProperties);
```

In `URLTreeView.cpp,` add the code for the `Save()` method like this:

```
STDMETHODIMP CURLTreeView::Save(LPPROPERTYBAG pPropBag, BOOL fClearDirty,
                                BOOL fSaveAllProperties)
{
   // First say how many items
   CComVariant var = (long)m_URLs.size();
   HRESULT hr = pPropBag->Write(L"noItems", &var);
   if (FAILED(hr))
      return hr;

   short item = 0;
   OLECHAR strParam[8];
   std::vector<CComBSTR>::iterator it;
   for (it = m_URLs.begin(); it < m_URLs.end(); it++)
   {
      item++;
      swprintf(strParam, L"Item%d", item);
```

463

```
        var = (*it);
        hr = pPropBag->Write(strParam, &var);
        if (FAILED(hr))
            return hr;
    }
    return IPersistPropertyBagImpl<CURLTreeView>::Save(
                            pPropBag, fClearDirty, fSaveAllProperties);
}
```

Now compile the project, start up VB, select a Standard EXE as the project type and add the control as a component as you have done before. Add a new control to the form and use the property page to add items for the URLTreeView control. Close the property page and save the project.

Using a text editor, open the file for the form. Here's the result from one of my tests. I have shown only the text pertinent to the control:

```
Begin URLTREELibCtl.URLTreeView URLTreeView1
    Height      =   2895
    Left        =   960
    TabIndex    =   0
    Top         =   120
    Width       =   2895
    noItems     =   3
    Item1       =   "One/Two,url1"
    Item2       =   "One/Three,url2"
    Item3       =   "Two,url3"
End
```

Notice that the custom 'properties' have been added to the end.

Now with VB open, run the application, what do you see? The control is empty, the values you entered on the property page are not shown, and further, when you stop the application and look at the control on the form in the VB IDE, you will see that the values have completely disappeared. Why is this?

The reason is that although **IPersistPropertyBag** is used to persist the data to a file, the VB IDE uses **IPersistStreamInit** to initialize the control when you run the VB application. VB calls **Save()** to get the state of the design time control and passes the initialized stream to the **Load()** of the runtime control. When the application stops, VB reverses the process, calling **Save()** on the runtime control and then passing the stream to the design time control with **Load()**.

VB also uses this interface to serialize the state of the control when you compile a VB project. The stream that **Save()** should fill is stored in the compiled EXE, and when the application is run, the VB runtime will load this serialized data as a stream and call the control's **Load()** method.

The ATL implementation of **IPersistStreamInit** does not handle **SAFEARRAY**s, so once again you need to implement the **Load()** and **Save()** methods of this interface. This time the data is saved to a stream, so we need to concatenate all the strings together.

In the control header, add these declarations:

```
//IPersistStreamInit
   STDMETHOD(Load)(LPSTREAM pStm);
   STDMETHOD(Save)(LPSTREAM pStm, BOOL fClearDirty);
```

Implement the **Save()** method in the source file:

```
STDMETHODIMP CURLTreeView::Save(LPSTREAM pStm, BOOL fClearDirty)
{
    // Add all strings together and serialize
    CComBSTR bstr = "";
    std::vector<CComBSTR>::iterator it;
    for (it = m_URLs.begin(); it < m_URLs.end(); it++)
    {
        if (it != m_URLs.begin())
            bstr.Append(L"|");
        bstr += (*it);
    }

    bstr.WriteToStream(pStm);
    m_bRequiresSave = FALSE;
    return IPersistStreamInitImpl<CURLTreeView>::Save(pStm, fClearDirty);
}
```

This iterates through all the strings in the vector and adds them together, separating each with a pipe character (|). The serialization is done right at the end where the code calls the **WriteToStream()** method of **CComBSTR**. As usual, we call the base class implementation to ensure that any properties we decide to add to the property map at a later date also get persisted.

The reverse process is just as simple. Add the following as the implementation for the **Load()** method:

```
STDMETHODIMP CURLTreeView::Load(LPSTREAM pStm)
{
    m_URLs.clear();
    CComBSTR bstr;
    bstr.ReadFromStream(pStm);
    LPOLESTR ptr = bstr;
    LPOLESTR str = ptr;
    while (ptr)
    {
        ptr = wcschr(str, L'|');
        if (ptr)
        {
            *ptr = 0;
            ptr++;
        }
```

```
        CComBSTR newStr;
        newStr = str;
        m_URLs.push_back(str);
        str = ptr;
    }

    return IPersistStreamInitImpl<CURLTreeView>::Load(pStm);
}
```

Now when you compile the project, you should be able to run the VB application in the VB IDE and get the state passed correctly to the control at runtime. Further, you should also be able to compile the VB application and when you run this EXE outside of the VB IDE, you will get the items you added with the property page.

Final Notes: Printing

If you use this control on a web page and then print the page, you'll find that the control will not show. The reason for this, as explained earlier in this chapter, is that when the control is printed, IE uses the **IViewObject::Draw()** method passing the device context of the printer. This results in the control's **OnDraw()** method being called. This control, however, does nothing in **OnDraw()** since the tree view and edit controls take up the entire control window.

If you want to print out the control you'll have to add code to **OnDraw()** to show the data of the control. Note that if you put the code directly into **OnDraw()** it will not be seen in IE since the tree view control is drawn on top of the DC that you'll be drawing to. However, there is a chance that you'll briefly see the drawing code when the control updates. To get round this you should only do drawing in **OnDraw()** when the device context is for a printer. There are several ways to do this; and here is one of them:

```
HRESULT CURLTreeView::OnDraw(ATL_DRAWINFO& di)
{
    int caps = GetDeviceCaps(di.hdcDraw, TECHNOLOGY);
    if (caps != DT_RASDISPLAY)
    {
        RECT& rc = *(RECT*)di.prcBounds;
        Rectangle(di.hdcDraw, rc.left, rc.top, rc.right, rc.bottom);
        int len = m_ctlEdit.GetWindowTextLength();
        LPTSTR str = new TCHAR[len + 1];
        m_ctlEdit.GetWindowText(str, len);

        SIZE size;
        ::GetTextExtentPoint32(di.hdcDraw, str, len, &size);
        if (size.cx > (rc.right - rc.left))
            size.cx = rc.left;
        else
            size.cx = (rc.left + rc.right - size.cx) / 2;

        if (size.cy > (rc.bottom - rc.top))
            size.cy = rc.top;
        else
            size.cy = (rc.top + rc.bottom - size.cy) / 2;
```

```
        ExtTextOut(di.hdcDraw, size.cx, size.cy, ETO_CLIPPED, &rc,
            str, lstrlen(str), NULL);

        delete [] str;
    }
    return S_OK;
}
```

This checks the device context and if it is *not* a screen DC, the code centers the edit box's text inside a rectangle the size of the control.

Summary

In this chapter, we've created a detailed and realistic ATL control. You've seen how to draw a control, how to base it on an existing control and how to handle messages. I have also shown you how to add property pages to your control and how to make these work with VB.

These techniques were illustrated with the **URLTreeView** example. This control is based upon a Win32 tree view common control and an edit control. **URLTreeView** implements persistence interfaces to allow it to be initialized from parameters on a web page, or within Visual Basic I have also shown you how to write a property page which has interdependent controls.

Much of the code for the control was concerned with making it work with VB. You have seen how VB uses **IPersistPropertyBag** to write the data from the control to the form's file, and how it uses **IPersistStreamInit** when the actual VB application is run.

Finally, I have addressed the issue of providing drawing code that will be used when the control is printed.

HRESULT Facility Codes

In Chapter 1, we briefly mentioned facility **codes**, which occupy bits 16 to 26 of **HRESULT**s, and are used to define groups of related return codes. The table below lists the predefined facility codes and describes what they mean:

Facility Name	Value	Description
FACILITY_NULL	0	For broadly applicable common status codes such as **S_OK**.
FACILITY_RPC	1	For status codes returned from remote procedure calls.
FACILITY_DISPATCH	2	For late-binding **IDispatch** interface status codes.
FACILITY_STORAGE	3	For status codes returned from **IStorage** and **IStream** method calls.
FACILITY_ITF	4	For most status codes returned from interface errors. The error is defined by the interface itself. The same status code returned from two different interfaces could have very different meanings.
FACILITY_WIN32	7	Used to provide a means of handling error codes in the Win32 API as an **HRESULT**.
FACILITY_WINDOWS	8	Used for additional error codes from Microsoft-defined interfaces.
FACILITY_SSPI	9	Security-related status codes.
FACILITY_CONTROL	10	ActiveX controls-related status codes.
FACILITY_CERT	11	Security certificate-related status codes.
FACILITY_INTERNET	12	Internet-related status codes.

The return codes that occupy bits 0 to 15 of an **HRESULT** are facility-specific. You can make up your own **HRESULT**s with the **MAKE_HRESULT()** macro from **<winerror.h>**, or break an **HRESULT** into its constituent parts with the **HRESULT_CODE()**, **HRESULT_FACILITY()**, and **HRESULT_SEVERITY()** macros.

Generally, you should only make custom **HRESULT**s with **FACILITY_ITF**, as the other facilities belong to development groups at Microsoft. It would be very unusual to need to have your own custom facility. You should use return codes in the range 0x0200–0xFFFF when constructing **FACILITY_ITF HRESULT**s.

Standard **HRESULT**s usually have a three-part symbolic name: *facility_severity_reason*, such as **STG_E_FILENOTFOUND** or **MK_S_MONIKERALREADYREGISTERED**. However, the **FACILITY_NULL HRESULT**s omit the **NULL** from their name; e.g., **S_OK** and **E_OUTOFMEMORY**.

.

Beginning
ATL COM
Programming

Symbols

O

The World of ATL

World of ATL is a website devoted to all things ATL.
Created and run by Alex Stockton, author and technical editor at
Wrox Press, World Of ATL features a wide range of ATL-related goodies.
You'll find everything from descriptions of undocumented features,
through new ATL Object Wizard templates, to ATL-based extension
classes. There's plenty of code for you to download and an up-to-date
list of other resources of interest to ATL programmers.

- Resources
- Downloads
- Productivity

- Bugs & Fixes
- FAQ
- Source Code

PROFESSIONAL VISUAL C++5 ActiveX/COM CONTROL PROGRAMMING

Authors: Sing Li and
Panos Economopolous
ISBN: 1861000375
Price: $40.00 C$56.00 £36.99

"We believe that we can show you how to crack open COM and produce robust ActiveX controls to use now. It's our aim to show you the efficient route past all the pitfalls and dead-ends we've encountered and to help you succeed with the best methods. We've grappled with this technology since its inception and we know we can help you put solutions into practice. For some, it'll be the first time you've seen these new programming tools in action, but by the end of the book, you'll be using them to relieve some of your major development headaches"
Sing and Panos

This book is for anyone taking up the challenge of programming in the COM environment, using Visual C++, to produce industrial-strength ActiveX controls. You should be familiar with fundamental Windows development and using MFC. You will get the full benefit of learning how to develop professional controls for Win32 with the Active Template Library (ATL) included in Visual C++ 5

PROFESSIONAL DCOM PROGRAMMING

Author: Dr. Richard Grimes
ISBN: 186100060X
Price: $49.95 C$69.95 £46.99

This book is for Win32 programmers taking up the challenge of building applications using the distributed component object model. There is a strong emphasis on the practicalities of distributed object design and use, and the text is also a complete examination of COM programming. The code is described and developed using Visual C++ 5, MFC and ATL.

Professional MFC with Visual C++ 5

Author: Mike Blaszczak
ISBN: 1861000146
Price: $59.95 C$83.95 £56.49

Written by one of Microsoft's leading MFC developers, this is the book for professionals who want to get under the covers of the library. This is the 3rd revision of the best selling title formerly known as 'Revolutionary Guide to MFC 4' and covers the new Visual C++ 5.0 development environment.

This book will give a detailed discussion of the majority of classes present in Microsoft's application framework library. While it will point out what parameters are required for the member functions of those classes, it will concentrate more on describing what utility the classes really provide. You will learn how to write a few utilities, some DLLs, an ActiveX control and even an OLE document server, as well as examining Microsoft's Open Database Connectivity (ODBC) and Data Access Objects (DAO) strategies. At the very end of the book, you'll take a look at what the Microsoft Foundation Classes provide to make programming for the Internet easier.

There's a CD_ROM included which has the complete book in HTML format - now you can use any browser to read your book on the road.

Clouds to Code

Author: Jesse Liberty ISBN: 1861000952
Price: $40.00 C$55.95 £36.99

Clouds to Code is about the design and implementation of a real project, from start to finish, hiding nothing. Books on theory are all well and good, but there is nothing like living through the process. You'll watch as we struggle to understand the requirements, as we conceive a design, implement that design in C++, then ready it for testing and rollout. You'll see the complete iterative development process as it happens. This is not an example or a thought experiment, it's a real life case study written in real time.

Along the way you'll learn about object-oriented analysis and design with UML, as well as C++, design patterns, computer telephony, and COM. You'll also learn about professional software development and what it takes to ship a product on time and on budget. This is programming in the trenches.

'Ever thought about writing a book'

Have you ever thought to yourself "I could do better than that"? Well, here's your chance to prove it! Wrox Press are continually looking for new authors and contributors and it doesn't matter if you've never been published before.

Interested?

contact John Franklin at Wrox Press, 30 Lincoln Road, Birmingham, B27 6PA, UK.

e-mail johnf@wrox.com

WROX

Register Beginning ATL COM Programming
and sign up for a free subscription
to The Developer's Journal.

A bi-monthly magazine for software developers, The Wrox Press Developer's Journal features in-depth articles, news and help for everyone in the software development industry. Each issue includes extracts from our latest titles and is crammed full of practical insights into coding techniques, tricks, and research.

Fill in and return the card below to receive a free subscription to the Wrox Press Developer's Journal.

Beginning ATL COM Programming Registration Card

Name _____

Address _____

_____

_____

City _____ State/Region _____

Country _____ Postcode/Zip _____

E-mail _____

Occupation _____

How did you hear about this book? _____

☐ Book review (name) _____

☐ Advertisement (name) _____

☐ Recommendation _____

☐ Catalog _____

☐ Other _____

Where did you buy this book? _____

☐ Bookstore (name) _____ City _____

☐ Computer Store (name) _____

☐ Mail Order _____

☐ Other _____

What influenced you in the purchase of this book?

☐ Cover Design
☐ Contents
☐ Other (please specify) _____

How did you rate the overall contents of this book?

☐ Excellent   ☐ Good
☐ Average   ☐ Poor

What did you find most useful about this book? _____

What did you find least useful about this book? _____

Please add any additional comments. _____

What other subjects will you buy a computer book on soon? _____

What is the best computer book you have used this year?

_____

Note: This information will only be used to keep you updated about new Wrox Press titles and will not be used for any other purpose or passed to any other third party.

WROX

WROX PRESS INC.

Wrox writes books for you. Any suggestions, or
ideas about how you want information given in
your ideal book will be studied by our team.
Your comments are always valued at Wrox.

Free phone in USA 800-USE-WROX
Fax (312) 397 8990

UK Tel. (0121) 706 6826   Fax   (0121) 706 2967

—— *Computer Book Publishers* ——

NB. If you post the bounce back card below in the UK, please send it to:
Wrox Press Ltd. 30 Lincoln Road, Birmingham, B27 6PA